DESIGNING
ELECTRONIC
HARDWARE

G. C. LOVEDAY

Longman
Scientific &
Technical

Longman Scientific & Technical
Longman Group UK Limited
Longman House, Burnt Mill, Harlow
Essex CM20 2JE, England
and Associated Companies throughout the world

First published 1992

British Library Cataloguing in Publication Data
is available for this title

ISBN 0-582-08612-4

Set by 4 in Compugraphic Times 9½/11½

Printed in Hong Kong
WC/01

CONTENTS

1 THE DESIGN PROBLEM

1.1 INTRODUCTION

Anyone working or interested in electronics may, at some time, wish, or be required to design and build their own working circuit or system. Unfortunately this can prove to be a frustrating experience, since electronic circuit design requires a combination of several skills, and the links between these skills are not always obvious. It is possible to have a sound theory background but insufficient practical knowledge to know exactly where to begin a design; or to have a good practical technique, but to lack some of the theory required for a particular task. In addition, there are plenty of traps and twists in the design process. The simple 400 Hz sawtooth oscillator shown in Fig. 1.1 can illustrate just a few of the problems. But before we look at these problems it is worth pointing out that in presenting this trial circuit we have already jumped at least two steps in the design sequence. These first two steps are:

(a) to prepare a *design specification*,

(b) to choose (usually from several options) a suitable circuit method.

These two points are covered in detail later in the book.

Here we shall assume that a suitable specification has already been prepared:

Frequency : 400 Hz ± 20 Hz (preset)
Amplitude : +6 V ± 1 V
Linearity of ramp : better than ± 5%
Flyback time : not greater than 100 μs
Power supply : ±9 V regulated

and you can see that I have chosen a simple unijunction oscillator to produce the required waveform. In order to get a linear sawtooth the timing capacitor C_1 is supplied from a constant current source formed around Tr_1, and an op-amp, wired as a unity gain follower, is used to act as a buffer between the waveform produced at the UJT emitter and the output load. In this way the linearity of the

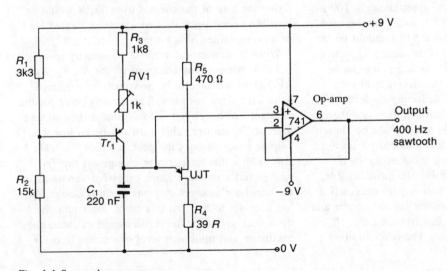

Fig. 1.1 Sawtooth generator

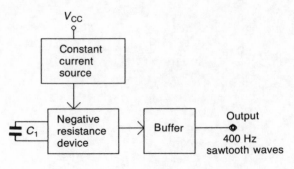

Fig. 1.2 Block diagram of oscillator

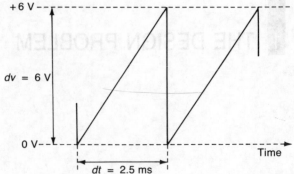

Fig. 1.3 Required output

sawtooth is not reduced by the external load because very little of the current from Tr_1 collector is diverted away from its job of charging C_1.

In the circuit there are five resistors, a trimpot, a capacitor, a p-n-p transistor, a unijunction and an op-amp. The types and the values for all these components must be decided by the designer. Where does he start? The theory behind the operation of the active devices must be known (or available) and data sheets will enable suitable types to be selected. Luckily, since they are specialised devices, there are only a few unijunction transistors to choose from, the 2N2646 ($\eta = 0.567 \rightarrow 0.75$) is ideal. Most small-signal, general purpose p-n-p transistors will function adequately as the current source, therefore a BCY70, BC177, BC477 or similar can be used.

The op-amp can be any general purpose type, the only restriction on it being that it must have a slew-rate capable of following the flyback of the waveform. Assuming a flyback of approximately 100 μs, a basic 741 (slew-rate = 0.5 V μs^{-1}) can be used.

Following this, the component that should be the first to have its value fixed is the timing capacitor C_1. The reasons behind this starting point can be appreciated by considering the circuit in block form, shown in Fig. 1.2. The timing capacitor is the key element in the oscillator section and therefore in the whole circuit. Its value could be chosen to be anywhere between a few hundred pF up to as high as 10 μF, but neither of these extremes is desirable. A 220 nF is probably the most suitable, since this size of capacitor will require only half a milliamp or so from the constant current source and will also give a reasonably fast flyback time. (R_4 value will finally decide this.) The other limiting

factor on the capacitor's size is the minimum value of valley current (I_v) specified for the 2N2646 unijunction. This is given as 4 mA. If the constant current is set near or above this value there is the possibility of the unijunction being forced into a latched-up state and consequently the oscillator will fail.

When $C_1 = 200$ nF the value of current required from Tr_1 can be calculated:

$$I = \frac{CV}{T}$$

where $T = 1/f = 2.5$ ms (T = ramptime, see Fig. 1.3 for output waveform) and $V = 6$ V (this depends on η, the intrinsic standoff ratio of the UJT).

Thus $I \approx 0.5$ mA.

Note that if we had decided to start the design by fixing the size of the current from Tr_1 it would be possible to end up with a non-preferred value for C_1 or an unsuitable flyback time.

With Tr_1 collector current set nominally to 0.5 mA, what values are required for R_1, R_2, R_3 and RV_1? Here we have to be aware of the preferred values for fixed resistors. The starting point for the constant current circuit is to assume a d.c. voltage level at Tr_1 emitter. This must not be so low that C_1 voltage never reaches the peak point of the UJT, nor so high that temperature changes at the Tr_1 base−emitter junction cause excessive variations in the transistor's output current. For this design V_E has been set to 8 V. At this point you could check the values given for the resistors and calculate the maximum and minimum level of current from Tr_1

with RV_1 as a 1 kΩ variable as given (answer at foot of page).*

No doubt you can see from this example what are meant by traps and twists in design. Even in such a simple circuit, several choices have to be made and items of theory need to be understood. The aim in this book is to show how most of the traps can be avoided, and how the various skills can be sharpened up, or acquired if necessary, and then combined so that useful circuit designs can be created. By starting off with relatively simple problems such as amplifiers or timers, and using standard solutions modified to suit the particular requirement, it is possible to build up a sound design technique. This is the method we shall use. Hopefully you have noticed that we are considering design, not research; in other words, using approaches and methods that have already been tried and tested. We are not intending to push back the frontiers of electronics with completely novel solutions. These breakthrough developments can be left to inventors and engineers in the research department.

However, this doesn't mean that there isn't some element of innovation in the sort of design work envisaged here. Consider the following definition:

Design — to plan and make (something) artistically and skilfully.

Note the accent on planning: design is not a haphazard process. It consists of a series of well defined steps, and some hard thinking is required, together with a dash of art and imagination. Perhaps it is easy to see that more art than science may be needed in the design of a watch or a garden than in an electronic circuit, but this doesn't mean that there isn't room for some flair in designing electronic circuits and systems. The work should not be dull.

1.2 REQUIREMENTS

Apart from a sharp pencil, a calculator and some clean sheets of A4 paper, what else is necessary to start a design task? The answer could be 'nothing!' provided one had a perfect memory and a complete knowledge of all electrical and electronic theory.

Naturally, this isn't the case and something more is going to be needed. A list of the basic requirements include:

(*a*) a reasonable understanding of electrical and electronic theory (i.e. circuit theorems, transistor and FET operation, linear and digital IC theory),

(*b*) access to reference texts on theory and circuits (see list at end of chapter),

(*c*) access to data and characteristics on electronic components (both passive and active devices),

(*d*) an ability to interpret these data sheets.

The depth of knowledge and understanding of electronic theory determines the type of design problem that can be tackled. For example, you might have a sufficient information and skill level to attempt a successful design of a d.c. regulated power supply but not enough to design a microprocessor-based controller. It is important to restrict yourself to tasks that are manageable and consistent with the skills you have, before moving on to more complex designs. Nor should one 'work blind' and ignore the need to consult useful reference books. If you reach a point in a design where your understanding seems hazy (not everybody knows about UJT intrinsic standoff ratio, for example), avoid the temptation to fudge it. Turn to a book on theory to assist you in sorting out the problem. Most main libraries have a good Engineering reference section and a short list of recommended books is included at the end of this chapter.

Having the correct data on components is vital in design work since it is only by knowing the parameter values, characteristics and limits of a device that we can use it correctly in an application. If possible, build up a data bank on commonly used devices, but restrict the choice to a limited set. For example, under the heading *general purpose transistors*, have data on only two or three types for the power ratings as illustrated in Fig. 1.4. In the same way, a small library of data can be built up on thyristors, small signal FETs, powerFETs, op-amps, logic ICs and so on. The use and interpretation of component data sheets is covered in Chapter 2.

So far we have considered the requirements for a *paper only* design, but this will normally be translated into actual hardware to enable the design to be tested and the performance compared with the

* Answer: I_{min} = 0.36 mA, I_{max} = 0.56 mA

Power rating P_{tot}	Type	n-p-n	p-n-p complement
360 mW	Small signal	BC107	BC177
Up to 1 W	Low power	BC441	BC461
Up to 15 W	Medium power	BD131	BD132
15 W to 120 W	High power	2N4915	2N4905

Example of BC441 short-form data:

Case	P_{tot}	I_c	V_{CEO}	V_{CBO}	h_{FE}	f_T
T039	1 W	2 A pk	60 V	75 V	40–250	50 MHz

Fig. 1.4

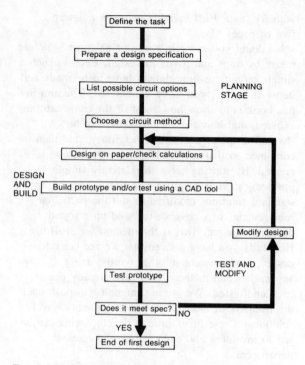

Fig. 1.5 The design sequence

design specification. The amount and type of test equipment required naturally depends upon the application. For many projects, for example, a power switch interfaced to a microcomputer, the operation can be checked without the need for complicated and expensive test gear. Often, a good analog multimeter is all that is necessary. Many of the designs and examples we shall be working on are of this type. Otherwise the main items of test gear are a dual-beam oscilloscope, a signal generator and a digital multimeter.

1.3 THE DESIGN SEQUENCE

The sequence of actions necessary for successful design is shown in Fig. 1.5 and consists of three main stages:

1 **A planning stage:** where the feasibility of the project is examined. The initial target or design specification will be drawn up and the design approach decided. This design approach involves a choice, usually from a number of competing options, of a standard type of circuit, and therefore the type of IC or ICs that will be most suitable for the task. At this stage, it may be necessary to examine more than one of the options in greater detail, listing the advantages to be gained from each, and often constraints such as cost, availability and preference will affect the designer's final choice. In any large system design the *preference* constraint often operates, forcing the designer of any

sub-unit to use similar ICs to those contained in the rest of the system.

Ideally, the type of circuit approach chosen should be the one that can be used by the designer to meet the specification in the most effective manner. Here, *effective* means reasonable cost with minimum space use, coupled with high reliability and close conformity to the specification.

2 **Design and calculations:** The circuit choice is now examined in detail and *bent* to meet the application. The key components and devices are selected, values are calculated and performance predictions made. These predictions will be closely checked against the design figures. All design calculations should be double checked at this stage.

3 **Prototype construction, testing and modification:** A prototype of the circuit should be constructed, using if possible a similar layout to the final model. Then by using a suitable test strategy all performance parameters will be checked against the target specification. If possible, some form of

analysis and/or simulation of the circuit should also be made using a CAD software package. A typical professional package for this is PSPICE, a software tool that allows a user to carry out d.c., a.c. or transient analysis and simulation of an analog circuit. Another smaller, but still very useful CAD package, that can be run on IBM PC or BBC computers, is ANALYSER II. The latter is more modestly priced and, although more limited in its scope, can nevertheless be most helpful in analysing a design.

These software tools are being increasingly used but a good understanding of the models employed within the software for the circuit devices is important if one is to gain the maximum benefit from the package. A description of ANALYSER II with a brief illustration of its use is given later in this chapter.

Apart from the simplest circuits, it is probable that the first prototype will fail to work correctly. Either some important parameter will not be within the specification limits, oscillations will be set up, or excessive current may be taken from the supply. The first step is to check the construction carefully. When this is proved to be satisfactory it may then become apparent that some piece of data or condition has been overlooked at the design stage. For example, the effect of a circuit on the power supply is often ignored when designing pulse or square wave generators and then excessive noise or ringing can appear on the supply rail. In other cases, the design calculations may be in error, or the combination of component tolerances has not been taken into account. At the worst, the circuit fails totally to operate as expected; sinewave oscillators give out square waves (at the wrong frequency!) and amplifiers oscillate. Modifications are often necessary.

The design process is therefore contained within a feedback loop and it is important, when the need for modifications is found, to return to the initial design stage. It may even be necessary to discard the chosen circuit option and return to square one. This iterative approach will ultimately produce the required result, i.e. a completed design that meets the specification in all respects.

Let us now consider the various stages of the design cycle for the sawtooth circuit discussed previously in Section 1.1.

1 PLANNING

Defining the task

A simple fixed frequency (400 Hz) sawtooth oscillator is required that outputs approximately 6 V positive going ramps to a 5 kΩ load.

Design specification

Frequency : 400 Hz ± 20 Hz (preset)
Amplitude : 6 V ± 1 V (see Fig. 1.6(a))
Linearity of ramp : better than ±5% (see Fig. 1.6(b))
Flyback time : not greater than 100 μs
Power supply : ±9 V regulated

(The design specification adds more detail to the straightforward definition of the task.)

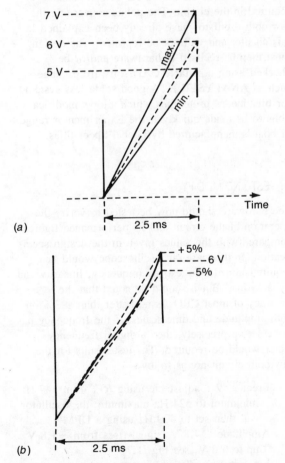

Fig. 1.6 (a) Amplitude limits; (b) Linearity limits

Possible options

Modified 555 astable
Standard IC such as the 8038BC
Unijunction oscillator with constant current
supply
Miller ramp generator

Circuit choice

UJT oscillator, picked as being suitable for the
demonstration of a design task (see Section 1.1).

2 DESIGN AND BUILD

This is the core of the design sequence, which
requires the designer to decide on a starting point
and then to calculate the values of components
required in the circuit. The points concerning the
sawtooth oscillator have already been explained in
this chapter and will not be repeated. The design
must then be realised in hardware and/or be
checked using a suitable CAD software package
such as ANALYSER II. A good solderless system
for breadboard prototypes which allows modifications to be made quickly is the Experimentor range
of boards manufactured by Global Specialities.

3 TEST AND MODIFY

The hardware should now be tested to verify the
operation of the circuit and its performance figures
compared with the values given in the design specification. In this case, an oscilloscope would be
required in order to test the frequency, linearity and
flyback time. But it should be noted that the
accuracy of most CROs is no better than ±3% on
both amplitude and time scales. If the frequency has
to be set up precisely, then a digital frequency
meter would be required. The test results for the
sawtooth circuit are as follows:

Frequency : adjustable using RV_1 from 347 Hz
minimum to 524 Hz maximum; the oscillator
was then set to 400 Hz using a DFM
Amplitude : 4.8 V (signal rises from +1.8 V
up to 6.6 V, see Fig. 1.7)
Linearity : well within spec.
Flyback time : 75 μs

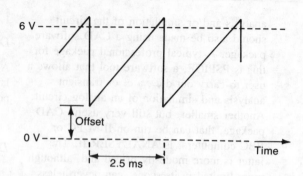

Fig. 1.7 Actual output of prototype

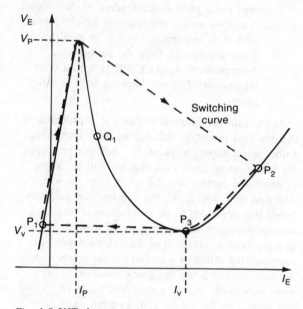

Fig. 1.8 UJT characteristics

Any modifications that become apparent during the
prototype testing can then be carried out and, as
you can see from the above results, there is a
problem in this design prototype with the output
amplitude. An offset of nearly 2 V has been introduced and the amplitude is low. This mistake, like
many in design work, has occurred because of a
false assumption made early in the design. Here it
was assumed that the unijunction would fully
discharge C_1 by the end of the flyback period. It
doesn't; and a study of the UJT characteristics given
in Fig. 1.8 will show why. The operating point for
astable operation must lie on the negative resistance
portion of the characteristics, at say Q_1. As the
capacitor is charged, the *curve* (the ideal *switching*

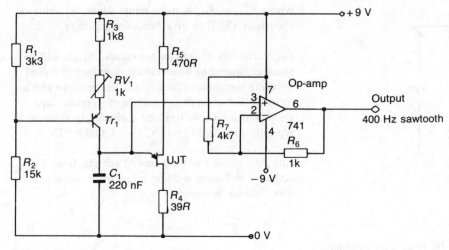

Fig. 1.9 Modification to eliminate offset

curve is shown dotted) moves from P_1 in the cut-off region until V_P is reached. C_1 then discharges rapidly from V_P towards V_v, i.e. the valley point $(I_v V_v)$, the negative resistance region is again entered and the unijunction returns to its high resistance state, allowing C_1 to be again charged towards V_P. Thus, at the end of the flyback period, the voltage across C_1 is equal to V_v, the valley voltage, which is typically about 2 V for a 2N2646. Hence the offset. A simple modification to eliminate this offset is to introduce an equal but opposite d.c. level into the op-amp buffer. The modification is shown in Fig. 1.9, where the buffer op-amp is converted from unity gain to a non-inverting amplifier with a voltage gain of approximately 1.2. The resistor R_7 is returned to the +9 V rail so that the d.c. level at the output is made nearly zero volts. R_6 and R_7 act in the inverting mode to produce an effective d.c. at the op-amp output (without the UJT signal) of:

$$V_{out} = \frac{-R_6}{R_7} V + \approx -1.9 \text{ V}$$

This -1.9 V cancels the positive offset contained in the UJT waveform. In addition, R_6 and R_7 provide non-inverting gain

$$A_{vcl} = \frac{R_6 + R_7}{R_7}$$

to increase the amplitude of the output from 4.8 V to nearly 6 V. The amplitude is now within specification and the frequency remains unchanged at 400 Hz.

Up to this point, I have avoided any mention of stability, that is, drift of circuit parameters (frequency, amplitude, etc.) from their initial values. The main causes of drift in any circuit can be listed as:

(a) changes in ambient temperature,
(b) changes in power supply voltage,
(c) variations in the load, and
(d) time.

Of these, it is temperature variation that is often the prime source of drift. In our oscillator, for example, we can ensure that the power supply is well regulated, the load is buffered by the op-amp and short term (i.e. 24 hour) changes in component characteristics would be very small, leaving changes in ambient temperature as the main cause of drift. This would mostly affect the frequency of the circuit, since any changes in amplitude will be small compared with the specification figures.

Recalling the earlier design work, the frequency is given by:

$$f \approx \frac{I}{CV_P} \text{ Hz.}$$

Thus, a change in V_P, I or C will directly alter the frequency. The main effects of temperature on the circuit can be described as:

(i) The peak point (V_P) of the unijunction falls with increasing temperature. This causes the frequency to increase.
(ii) Changes in temperature will alter the capacitor's value.

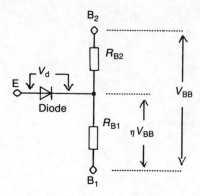

Fig. 1.10

(iii) The current from Tr_1 rises with increasing temperature. This causes the frequency to increase.

Unfortunately, (i) and (ii) are acting together to increase frequency as the temperature rises, and are not effects that cancel out.

The effects should be investigated in turn.

(i) Changes of V_P with temperature. A simplified equivalent circuit of the UJT, given in Fig. 1.10, shows that it consists of a p-n junction, i.e. a diode, connected to the middle of a resistance R_{BB}. Thus:

$$V_P = \eta V_{BB} + V_D$$

where V_P = peak point, η = intrinsic standoff ratio — a value set by the geometry of the device, V_{BB} = interbase voltage, and V_D = forward volt drop across the diode (0.6 V approximately).

The interbase resistance (R_{BB}) is split into two parts R_{B2} and R_{B1}, where $\eta \approx R_{B1}/R_{BB}$.

V_P drops with temperature because of the p-n junction. All semiconductor junctions exhibit a fall in forward volt drop with temperature, and this change is typically in the range -2 mV to -2.4 mV per °C. If left uncompensated, the change in V_D with temperature will cause V_P to fall also. However, the bulk resistance R_{BB} of the device rises with temperature by about 0.8%/°C. An external resistor R_5 can therefore be used to force V_{BB} to rise as the temperature increases and thus compensate for the fall in diode volt drop.

$$R_5 \approx \frac{0.3 R_{BBO}}{\eta V_{BB}}$$

where R_{BBO} is R_{BB} at room temperature. R_5 value is chosen as 180 Ω to give best compensation.

(ii) Variations of component values, which will be small compared to other effects, can be minimised by using components with small temperature characteristics. For example, a multilayer ceramic capacitor used for C_1 will exhibit a change in value of typically only ± 30 ppm/°C (i.e. 0.003%/°C).

(iii) Any change in the value of current from Tr_1 collector will have a direct effect on frequency. This follows because:

$$t = \frac{CV}{I}$$

where t = ramp time.

Tr_1 current changes with temperature because of the 2.2 mV/°C fall in V_{BE} of Tr_1. As the temperature rises, a higher voltage will appear across R_3 and RV_1 causing a consequent increase in Tr_1 current. Assuming RV_1 and R_3 combined have a value of 2 kΩ, then the change in Tr_1 collector current is approximately 1 μA/°C.

$$\Delta I_C = \frac{\Delta V_{BE}}{R_3 + RV_1} \text{ per °C}$$

Suppose the ambient temperature changes by $+10$ °C, then the current charging C_1 will also change by 10 μA, causing an 8 Hz increase in frequency. Thus the frequency stability of the circuit will be about $+0.2$%/°C. Note that in practice the drift from this source might be either slightly better or worse than this figure.

Methods of improving the stability of the current source could be:

(a) to use a constant current device such as the J503 in place of Tr_1 and its components. A J503 has excellent temperature stability but is relatively expensive, or

(b) to include a small signal silicon diode (IN914) in series with R_1. This diode should be located very near Tr_1 (see Fig. 1.11) so that it experiences the same temperature effects. Then, as the temperature rises or falls, the base voltage (V_B) of Tr_1 will change by the same amount as V_{BE}, thus allowing the voltage across R_3 and RV_1 to remain almost constant. As indicated in Fig. 1.11, the value of R_1

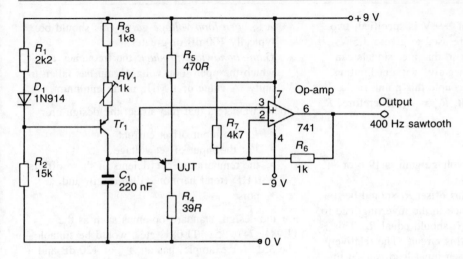

Fig. 1.11 Temperature compensated circuit

must be changed to 2.2 kΩ (2k2) to allow for the additional diode volt drop. A modification such as this would improve the frequency stability with temperature to about +0.05%/°C.

As a further example of the design cycle, we shall consider the following target specification for an audio preamplifier.

1 PLANNING

Target specification

Voltage gain : 26 dB ± 0.5 dB
Frequency response : 10 Hz to 30 kHz
Input impedance : 50 kΩ at 1 kHz
Output impedance : not greater than 2 Ω at 1 kHz
Maximum output : 5 V pk−pk
THD at max. output : less than 0.2%
Supply voltage : +9 V
Supply current : not greater than 10 mA

Circuit options

The requirement is for an a.c. coupled amplifier to give a voltage gain of 20. The possible circuit choices are:

(i) an inverting amplifier using a standard op-amp such as the 351 or 741,

(ii) a non-inverting amplifier using a standard op-amp, or

(iii) an amplifier using a transistor array wired with external passive components to give the required gain.

For this application the last option is overcomplicated, so let us concentrate on the merits of options (i) and (ii). Both circuits are shown in Fig. 1.12.

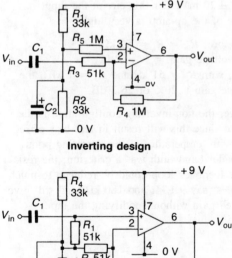

Inverting design

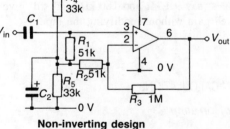

Non-inverting design

Fig. 1.12 Possible design solutions

Since a single supply of +9 V is specified, two resistors of 33 kΩ each are used to give a 4.5 V bias to the op-amp inputs so that a.c. signals can swing both positive and negative without limiting. A capacitor is used to decouple this point.

For the inverting circuit, $R_{in} = R_3$. Therefore, R_3 must be at least 50 kΩ.

$$Av = -R_4/R_3$$

With R_4 made 1 MΩ the voltage gain is 19.6 or 25.8 dB.

In order to minimise bias offset R_5 should be the same value as the resistance in the inverting lead to ground. In other words, R_5 should equal R_4. This is one of the drawbacks of this circuit. The relatively large resistance seen in each input lead can set up bias offset voltages and drifts of the bias level with temperature.

Also, for bandwidth purpose, it is advisable to keep feedback resistors to reasonably low values, i.e. a few kΩ if possible. With this inverting design R_3 has to be 50 kΩ to meet the specification requirement on input impedance, and therefore R_4 cannot be lower than 1 MΩ.

The non-inverting circuit will certainly have less bias offset and better d.c. stability, since the resistors placed in the input leads will be approximately 50 kΩ. The offset in bias at the amplifier's output is then only ±20 mV. For this circuit the input impedance of the op-amp is very high.

Therefore, $R_{in} = R_1 = 51$ kΩ.
The voltage gain = $1 + R_3/R_2$.
Thus, with $R_2 = 51$ kΩ and $R_3 = 1$ MΩ, the voltage gain is 20.6 or 26.3 dB.

On balance, the non-inverting configuration is the best choice since this will result in less bias offset and drift with temperature of the operating point. Also, if wider bandwidth was a criterion, the resistors in the feedback loop could be reduced to much lower values, say 9.1 kΩ and 180 kΩ, and still give the required gain without modifying the input impedance.

2 DESIGN CALCULATIONS

Choice of op-amp

The two main parameters of interest are:

A_{vol}, *open loop voltage gain*. This should be typically 100 dB or greater.
Gain—bandwidth product: the frequency at which the open loop voltage gain has fallen to unity. A value of 1 MHz is the minimum.

Other parameters that may affect the design are:

- I_{io}: the input offset current
- V_{io}: the input offset voltage
- the temperature coefficients of these offsets
- THD (total harmonic distortion), and
- noise.

For the design, standard op-amps such as the TL084, 741, 351, TL081, etc., would be suitable. The 351, for example, has an A_{vol} of 120 dB and a unity gain frequency of 3 MHz.

Passive components

We have already determined the value of the resistors in the circuit:

$R_1 = 51$ kΩ, $R_2 = 51$ kΩ, $R_3 = 1$ MΩ,
$R_4 = 33$ kΩ, $R_5 = 33$ kΩ.

The tolerance of each resistor should be ±2% in order that the specification limit on the gain is maintained and also to minimise any variation of the bias point.

The two capacitors C_1 and C_2 set the low frequency cut-off point, i.e. the frequency at which the voltage gain is 3 dB (0.7071) down from its mid-band value. Here, mid-band can be assumed to be 1 kHz. Only one of the capacitors, C_1, should be allowed to dominate the low frequency response, otherwise the combined effect of both could cause a too rapid fall off in gain with reducing frequency and additional phase shifts at low frequencies. C_2 must be made a value that would result in a cut-off frequency of at least one tenth of that set by C_1.

C_1 forms a high pass filter circuit with R_1, and when the reactance of C_1 equals R_1, the signal at the amplifier's non-inverting input will be reduced by 3 dB, hence the gain of the circuit will be 3 dB down.

Since $f_L = \dfrac{1}{2\pi C_1 R_1}$,

$$C_1 = \frac{1}{2\pi f_L R_1} \qquad \text{where } f_L = 10 \text{ Hz}$$

Therefore, $C_1 = 312$ nF.

This is the minimum value for C_1. To allow a safety margin, we shall specify C_1 as a 500 nF polyester film or polycarbonate capacitor.

The value of C_2 must be such that at 1 Hz ($f_L/10$) its reactance is equal to the parallel resistance of R_4 and R_5.

Therefore $C_2 = 10/2\pi f_L R'$
where $R' = R_4//R_5$.
Therefore $C_2 = 10\ \mu F$ (16 V wkg tantalum).

The high frequency cut-off, i.e. the frequency at which the voltage gain will again be 3 dB down, is determined primarily by the op-amp gain bandwidth.

3 DESIGN TESTING

Before the prototype was constructed the design was evaluated using the CAD software tool ANALYSER II previously mentioned. A brief description of the package now follows.

ANALYSER II, a Linear Circuit Analysis Program developed and produced by Number One Systems Ltd, is an interactive, menu-driven software tool that allows the user to analyse analog circuits of up to 60 nodes and 180 components. Components can be resistors, capacitors, inductors and active devices such as transistors (BJTs and FETs) and op-amps.

Initially, after loading the program into the PC, the main menu is presented on the screen to allow the user to select one of ten options.

    <1>   START NEW CIRCUIT
    <2>   MODIFY CIRCUIT
    <3>   ANALYSE CIRCUIT
    <4>   SELECT DATA DISC DRIVE
    <5>   LOAD CIRCUIT OFF DISC
    <6>   SAVE CIRCUIT ON DISC
    <7>   LIST CIRCUIT VALUES
    <8>   CHANGE CIRCUIT NAME
    <9>   CATALOGUE DISC
    <0>   RETURN TO DOS

Before making a selection it is important to have the circuit diagram to hand, with the components numbered and values given, and with the nodes all marked clearly, since there is no circuit diagram presented on the screen. The program models the

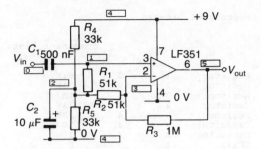

Fig. 1.13 Circuit model ready for CAD analysis

circuit out of view. The marked-up circuit being analysed is given in Fig. 1.13. Note that one node must be 0 (zero) and that a power supply lead has the same a.c. node number as ground. Thus, the +9 V supply lead and 0 V are both labelled 4 in this circuit.

Having selected option 1 from the main menu and responded to the program by naming the circuit (LINI), component references, positions and values are entered:

    C_1(space) 0(space) 1(space)   500nD (CR)
    R_1(space) 1(space) 2(space)   51K   (CR)
    R_2(space) 2(space) 3(space)   51K   (CR)

and so on, until all components have been correctly listed. The list is then completed by entering the node numbers of the input, output and ground ports — in this case

    P   0   5   4

A full print of the list is given in Fig. 1.14 which is a copy of the screen output. Unless the user wishes to make modifications to correct mistakes or add components, the model is stored on disc and the main menu again generated.

Option 3 is selected to enable the circuit to be analysed and the program responds by outputting prompts for:

    'number of steps?'
    'start frequency?'
and 'end frequency?'

A maximum of 45 steps is allowed and these can be logarithmic or linear. In this case the number of steps selected is -12 (minus sign indicates logarithmic which would normally be required for amplifier analysis), the start frequency is 2 Hz and the end frequency 200 kHz.

```
gain response of pre-amp


                                      Component list:


R1      Resistor       1       2       51K
R2      Resistor       3       2       51K
R3      Resistor       3       5       1M
R4      Resistor       2       4       33K
R5      Resistor       2       4       33K
C1      Capacitor      0       1       500n
C2      Capacitor      2       4       10u
AA      LF351          1       3       5
P       Ports          0       5       4
```

Fig. 1.14 Print of list

```
                  Analysed Results

Frequency           Gain            Phase
   (Hz)             (abs)           (deg)

    2.00            5.83            70.90
    5.70           13.09            49.44
   16.22           18.94            22.77
   46.20           20.38            8.39
  131.59           20.58            2.92
  374.76           20.60            879.55m
    1.07K          20.61           -103.94m
    3.04K          20.60           -1.21
    8.66K          20.57           -3.77
   24.66K          20.29           -10.76
   70.22K          18.39           -28.88
  200.00K          11.65           -61.37
```

Fig. 1.15 Calculated response

A second menu requests the user to select the parameter to be analysed:

<1>   VOLTAGE GAIN

<2>   INPUT IMPEDANCE

<3>   OUTPUT IMPEDANCE

If <1> is selected, as in this case, the final menu is presented to allow choice of gain in dB [dB = 20 log Av] or as a ratio:

<1>   GAIN (dB absolute)

<2>   GAIN (dB relative)

<3>   GAIN (linear absolute)

<4>   GAIN (linear % error)

<5>   GAIN (real and imaginary)

For all the following examples option <3> was selected.

After the input of <3> the program then calculates the voltage gain and phase shift of the circuit over the selected frequency range previously input by the user. A printout of the results is given in Fig. 1.15.

Even more useful is the program's ability to graph the frequency and phase response. The result for the preamplifier, using a 351 op-amp, is shown in Fig. 1.16. This was produced on a general purpose n.l.q. printer. Thus, in the space of a few minutes we have a frequency response plot of the circuit, which can be seen to have 3 dB points of 8 Hz and 120 kHz approximately, and a mid-band gain of just over 20. In the same way, Z_{in} was determined to be 50 kΩ and Z_{out} less than 1 Ω over the bandwidth of the circuit. All these values were verified later by constructing and testing the circuit.

The real value of ANALYSER II can be illustrated by the following diagrams where various modifications have been introduced to the circuit model and the results observed over the selected frequency range. Figure 1.17 shows the effect on response of using a standard 741 op-amp (gain—bandwidth product of 1 MHz) in place of the 351. The low frequency response and mid-band gain remain at the previous values as expected, but the upper cut-off frequency is reduced to just over 40 kHz. This is, however, still within the target specification, indicating that a 741 would be suitable for this design.

In Fig. 1.18 the value of C_2 has been reduced to 1 μF. Note how the low frequency response has deteriorated, giving a low frequency cut-off of about 20 Hz.

The effect of stray capacitance across the relatively high value of feedback resistor (1 MΩ) is shown when a 15 pF capacitor is placed between nodes 3 and 5, see Fig. 1.19. Here, the high frequency cut-off is reduced to about 8.5 kHz. The earlier comment about keeping feedback resistors to low values if wide bandwidth is required is clearly demonstrated.

What is the expected result of placing a small capacitor across R_2? In Fig. 1.20, a 33 pF capacitor is assumed to be in circuit between nodes 2 and 3 and the graph shows the resulting peak in the amplifier's high frequency response.

By now you have probably begun to appreciate the usefulness of a software tool such as this. At the least it can serve as a double check of a design, but in a more complex circuit it may reveal performance peculiarities or failures well before any prototype has to be constructed and therefore save valuable design time.

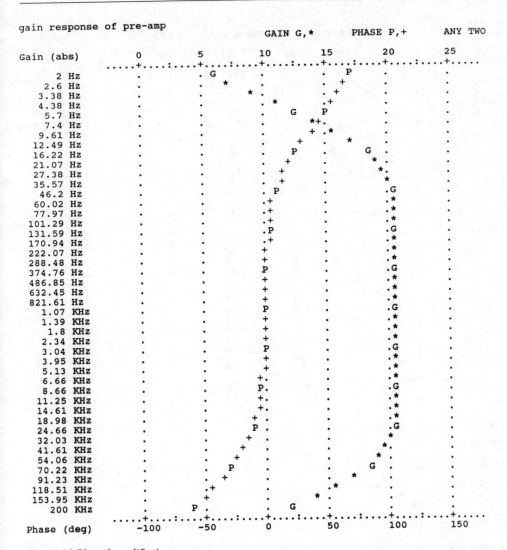

Fig. 1.16 Plot of amplifier's response

1.4 TESTABILITY

The task of design is not complete when suitable component values have been selected, a prototype built and modifications incorporated. Attention now has to be focused on the *layout* and *testability* of the circuit. These two features are closely linked and a good ground return and separation of sensitive inputs from output leads to prevent oscillations, etc., will also allow simple and effective tests to be made. Being confronted with a faulty circuit or system and not being able to get at some important point to check operation is very frustrating; made worse if the design is one's own. Whether the unit is a one-off or is to be put into production, the ease with which it can be tested is a vital feature. For large-scale production automatic testing (ATE) is very cost effective, and then testability becomes even more necessary.

Testable design can be defined as:

A circuit or system design that has built-in facilities that allow simple and effective testing to be carried out.

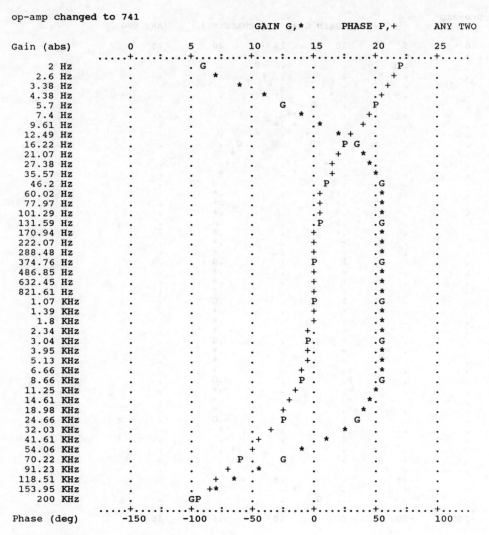

```
op-amp changed to 741
                                  GAIN G,*       PHASE P,+      ANY TWO
Gain (abs)      0         5        10        15        20        25
            ....+....:....+....:....+....:....+....:....+....:....+....
     2 Hz        .        . G      .         .         . . P       .
   2.6 Hz        .        .  *     .         .         . +         .
  3.38 Hz        .        .     *. .         .         . +         .
  4.38 Hz        .        .        .*        .         .+          .
   5.7 Hz        .        .        . G       .         . P         .
   7.4 Hz        .        .        .     *   .         .+.         .
  9.61 Hz        .        .        .         .*        +  .        .
 12.49 Hz        .        .        .         .    * +  .           .
 16.22 Hz        .        .        .         .   P G   .           .
 21.07 Hz        .        .        .         .    +   *.           .
 27.38 Hz        .        .        .         .   +     *.          .
 35.57 Hz        .        .        .         .   +     *           .
  46.2 Hz        .        .        .         . P       .G          .
 60.02 Hz        .        .        .         .+        .*          .
 77.97 Hz        .        .        .         .+        .*          .
101.29 Hz        .        .        .         .+        .*          .
131.59 Hz        .        .        .         .P        .G          .
170.94 Hz        .        .        .         +         .*          .
222.07 Hz        .        .        .         +         .*          .
288.48 Hz        .        .        .         +         .*          .
374.76 Hz        .        .        .         P         .G          .
486.85 Hz        .        .        .         +         .*          .
632.45 Hz        .        .        .         +         .*          .
821.61 Hz        .        .        .         +         .*          .
  1.07 KHz       .        .        .         P         .G          .
  1.39 KHz       .        .        .         +         .*          .
   1.8 KHz       .        .        .         +         .*          .
  2.34 KHz       .        .        .        +.         .*          .
  3.04 KHz       .        .        .        P.         .G          .
  3.95 KHz       .        .        .        +.         .*          .
  5.13 KHz       .        .        .        +.         .*          .
  6.66 KHz       .        .        .       + .         .*          .
  8.66 KHz       .        .        .       P .         .G          .
 11.25 KHz       .        .        .      +  .         .*          .
 14.61 KHz       .        .        .     +   .         .*.         .
 18.98 KHz       .        .        .    +    .         .*          .
 24.66 KHz       .        .        .    P    .         G .         .
 32.03 KHz       .        .        .  +      .         *           .
 41.61 KHz       .        .        . +       .      *              .
 54.06 KHz       .        .        . +       .    *                .
 70.22 KHz       .        .      P  . .      G                     .
 91.23 KHz       .        .      +  . .*     .                     .
118.51 KHz       .        .    +  * .        .                     .
153.95 KHz       .        .    +* .          .                     .
   200 KHz       .        GP       .         .                     .
            ....+....:....+....:....+....:....+....:....+....:....+....
Phase (deg)    -150      -100      -50        0        50       100
```

Fig. 1.17 Response using a 741

Take the example given in Fig. 1.21 for a circuit board of a data acquisition system. The unit consists of a sample-and-hold, an 8-bit analog-to-digital converter and a clock generator. The operation is intended to be controlled by software from a microprocessor system as follows:

(a) The sample/hold line is taken high for 10 μs to force the circuit to acquire a new value of analog data.

(b) A *start conversion* command pulse is applied to the ADC.

(c) The output enable signal from the ADC goes low to start the clock, which then delivers nine pulses to the ADC (one for reset, the other eight required for the 8-bit successive approximation routine).

(d) At the end of the conversion the output enable line goes high to stop the clock and to signal to the microprocessor system that data is ready for collection.

To correctly verify operation it may be necessary to test the three main parts of the circuit separately. Test points must be provided at appropriate input and output nodes for each section as indicated in Fig. 1.21. By providing these test points it is then possible to inject a suitable signal to, say, the clock

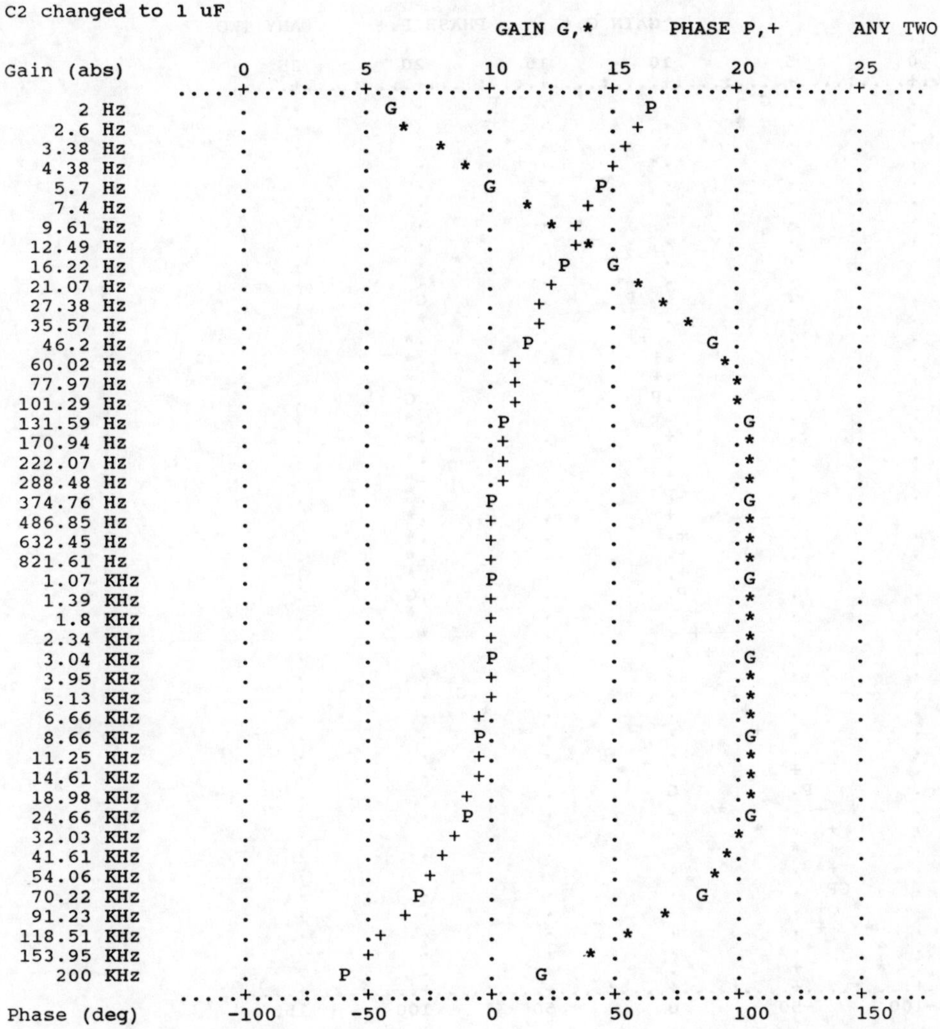

C2 changed to 1 uF

	GAIN G,*	PHASE P,+	ANY TWO

```
                                GAIN G,*        PHASE P,+      ANY TWO

Gain (abs)      0      5       10      15      20      25
           ....+....:....+....:....+....:....+....:....+....:....+.....
     2 Hz       .      . G     .      . P     .       .
   2.6 Hz       .      . *     .      . +     .       .
   3.38 Hz      .      .       *  .      .+     .       .
   4.38 Hz      .      .       *  .      +      .       .
   5.7 Hz       .      .       G      P.     .       .
   7.4 Hz       .      .       *     +      .       .
   9.61 Hz      .      .       .     * + .      .       .
  12.49 Hz      .      .       .     +* .      .       .
  16.22 Hz      .      .       .   P   G     .       .
  21.07 Hz      .      .       .  +      .*      .       .
  27.38 Hz      .      .       .   +     .   *    .       .
  35.57 Hz      .      .       .   +     .    *   .       .
  46.2 Hz       .      .       . P     .      G .    .       .
  60.02 Hz      .      .       . +     .       *.      .
  77.97 Hz      .      .       . +     .       *       .
 101.29 Hz      .      .       . +     .       *       .
 131.59 Hz      .      .       .P      .       .G      .
 170.94 Hz      .      .       .+      .       .*      .
 222.07 Hz      .      .       .+      .       .*      .
 288.48 Hz      .      .       .+      .       .*      .
 374.76 Hz      .      .       P       .       .G      .
 486.85 Hz      .      .       +       .       .*      .
 632.45 Hz      .      .       +       .       .*      .
 821.61 Hz      .      .       +       .       .*      .
   1.07 KHz     .      .       P       .       .G      .
   1.39 KHz     .      .       +       .       .*      .
   1.8 KHz      .      .       +       .       .*      .
   2.34 KHz     .      .       +       .       .*      .
   3.04 KHz     .      .       P       .       .G      .
   3.95 KHz     .      .       +       .       .*      .
   5.13 KHz     .      .       +       .       .*      .
   6.66 KHz     .      .       +.      .       .*      .
   8.66 KHz     .      .       P.      .       .G      .
  11.25 KHz     .      .       +.      .       .*      .
  14.61 KHz     .      .       +.      .       .*      .
  18.98 KHz     .      .      +       .       .*      .
  24.66 KHz     .      .      P .     .       .G      .
  32.03 KHz     .      .      +  .    .       .*      .
  41.61 KHz     .      .      +   .   .       *.      .
  54.06 KHz     .      .     +      . .      *       .
  70.22 KHz     .      .   P     .      .       G       .
  91.23 KHz     .      .   +     .      .      *       .
 118.51 KHz     .      .+       .      .*      .       .
 153.95 KHz     .      .  +     .      .*      .       .
 200 KHz        .      P .     .   G   .       .       .
           ....+....:....+....:....+....:....+....:....+....:....+.....
Phase (deg)   -100    -50      0      50     100     150
```

Fig. 1.18 Response with C_2 reduced to 1 μF

circuit and check, using a CRO for correct operation, that the output pulses are present. The other circuits can be tested similarly.

The most important features of good testable designs include the provision of the following:

(a) suitable test points to allow measurement and/or signal injection at critical circuit nodes,
(b) easy disconnection of feedback so that blocks within loops can be individually tested,
(c) external gating or control signals,
(d) clock disable and possible single step operation (for digital systems),
(e) self-checking facilities (as long as these can be kept simple).

1.5 TESTING

The main purpose of testing is to ensure that a design meets the specification in all respects, but another vital reason is to discover hidden problem areas and 'bugs' within the design, the sort that

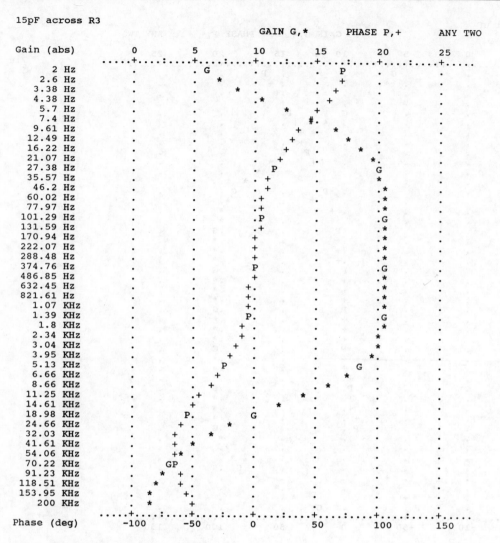

Fig. 1.19 The effect of stray capacitance

won't necessarily show up with a routine test procedure. These problems are often to do with stability. The best way to approach the testing is to plan some form of *test strategy*, in other words a list of actions necessary to cover the required tests and possible problem areas in the most efficient way. This, of course, assumes that the circuit can be tested without inordinate efforts. To make this possible, all designs need to have testability built in. A testability method should be decided and implemented early on in the design cycle; it is often too late to do this once the layout has been fixed. Even the most simple circuit design will benefit from an approach that includes a study of how the circuit is to be tested as an integral part of the design task.

A test strategy normally consists of a fairly predictable sequence of actions:

1 List the parameters to be measured, together with the maximum and minimum allowed values.
2 Decide on the type of test instruments that will be needed for the measurements.
3 Make a sketch of the test set up.
4 Carry out tests as follows:

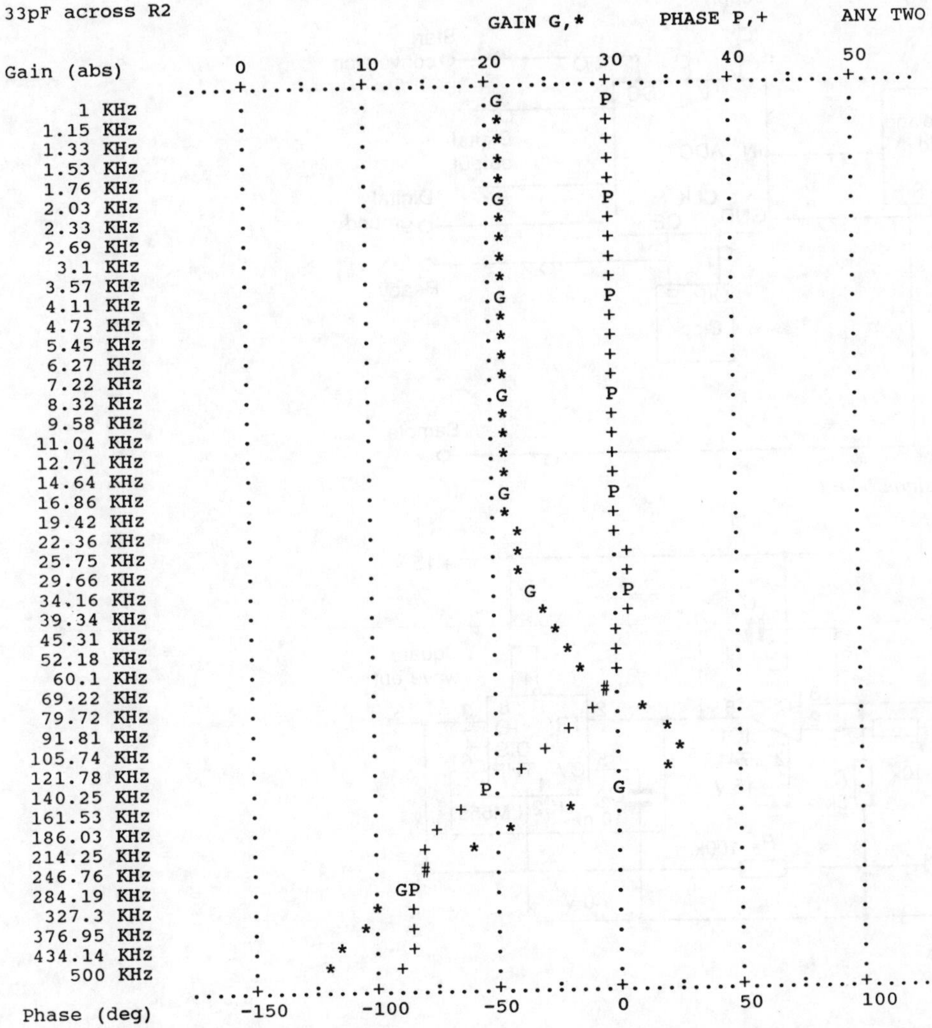

33pF across R2

		GAIN G,*		PHASE P,+	ANY TWO

```
Gain (abs)        0          10          20          30          40          50
             .....+....:....+....:....+....:....+....:....+....:....+.....
     1 KHz       .           .          .G          P           .           .
  1.15 KHz       .           .           .*         +           .           .
  1.33 KHz       .           .           .*         +           .           .
  1.53 KHz       .           .           .*         +           .           .
  1.76 KHz       .           .          .G          P           .           .
  2.03 KHz       .           .           .*         +           .           .
  2.33 KHz       .           .          .*          +           .           .
  2.69 KHz       .           .          .*          +           .           .
   3.1 KHz       .           .          .*          +           .           .
  3.57 KHz       .           .          .*          +           .           .
  4.11 KHz       .           .          .G          P           .           .
  4.73 KHz       .           .          .*          +           .           .
  5.45 KHz       .           .          .*          +           .           .
  6.27 KHz       .           .          .*          +           .           .
  7.22 KHz       .           .          .*          +           .           .
  8.32 KHz       .           .          .G          P           .           .
  9.58 KHz       .           .          .*          +           .           .
 11.04 KHz       .           .          .*          +           .           .
 12.71 KHz       .           .          .*          +           .           .
 14.64 KHz       .           .          .*          +           .           .
 16.86 KHz       .           .          .G          P           .           .
 19.42 KHz       .           .          .*          +           .           .
 22.36 KHz       .           .           *          +           .           .
 25.75 KHz       .           .           *          .+          .           .
 29.66 KHz       .           .          G            .P         .           .
 34.16 KHz       .           .          *            .+         .           .
 39.34 KHz       .           .           .*          .+         .           .
 45.31 KHz       .           .            .*         +          .           .
 52.18 KHz       .           .             .*        +          .           .
  60.1 KHz       .           .             .#        .          .           .
 69.22 KHz       .           .            +  .  *    .          .           .
 79.72 KHz       .           .           +           *          .           .
 91.81 KHz       .           .          +            .*         .           .
105.74 KHz       .           .         +             .  *       .           .
121.78 KHz       .           .     P.                G          .           .
140.25 KHz       .           .    +       .          .          .           .
161.53 KHz       .           .  +      .*             .          .          .
186.03 KHz       .           .+      *              .          .           .
214.25 KHz       .          + .    *                .          .           .
246.76 KHz       .          #       .               .          .           .
284.19 KHz       .        GP                         .          .           .
 327.3 KHz       .       *   +                       .          .           .
376.95 KHz       .     *.    +                       .          .           .
434.14 KHz       .    *   .  +                       .          .           .
   500 KHz       .   *       +                       .          .           .
             .....+....:....+....:....+....:....+....:....+....:....+.....
Phase (deg)    -150       -100        -50          0           50         100
```

Fig. 1.20 Changes to the h.f. response

(i) With no voltage applied, check with an ohmmeter that no d.c. shorts or very low resistances exist between the supply lines or from any supply line to 0 V.

(ii) Apply the specified d.c. voltages (no signals).

(iii) Check that the current taken from the supply is within the expected limits.

(iv) Using a d.c. meter, measure and record all d.c. bias levels.

(v) Apply test signals and measure output levels as required, i.e. carry out a functional test.

(vi) Check power supply lines for signs of instability.

Let's consider the circuit of a voltage controlled oscillator (VCO) as shown in Fig. 1.22. This type of circuit can be required in modulators, measurement applications and convertors where an input voltage is used to give a linear change in oscillator frequency. The design of circuits like this is examined in more detail later in the book, but a brief explanation of operation will be given here. There are three blocks: an integrator, a comparator and a switch.

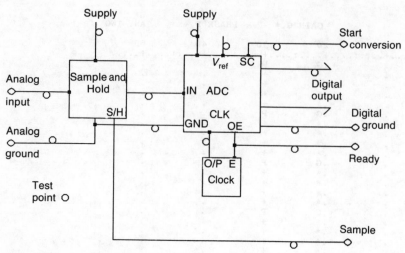

Fig. 1.21 Data acquisition board

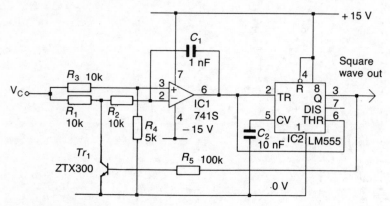

Fig. 1.22 VCO circuit

First assume that the output of the comparator (the 555) is low. The switch (Tr_1) will be off and the output of the integrator (the 741S op-amp) will be linearly moving from a positive voltage towards zero. Since this output is directly connected to the trigger (TR) and threshold (THR) input pins of the 555 when the level falls below $\frac{1}{3}V_{CC}$ the 555 will be triggered on, and its output will switch high. Tr_1 will conduct, causing the integrator's output capacitance to be charged in the opposite direction. The integrator output then moves from $\frac{1}{3}V_{CC}$ linearly towards $+V_{CC}$ until it reaches $\frac{2}{3}V_{CC}$. At this point, the 555 threshold value is exceeded and the timer output switches low. Thus, triangle waves will appear at the output of the 741S and square waves at pin 3 of the 555 with a frequency set by the

charging current of the integrator. This current is itself dependent on the input control voltage V_C. The frequency is typically 3 kHz V^{-1} and V_C can be in the range 50 mV up to 3 V.

The specification is:
 Control voltage V_C : 50 mV to 3 V
 Frequency : 3 kHz at $V_C = 1$ V
 Frequency tolerance : $\pm 10\%$ at $V_C = 1$ V
 Frequency linearity : better than $\pm 10\%$ over the V_C range
 Output amplitude : not less than 12 V
 Rise and fall times : 100 ns

Test instruments required:
 d.c. regulated power supply ± 15 V
 Digital multimeter 4.5 digits

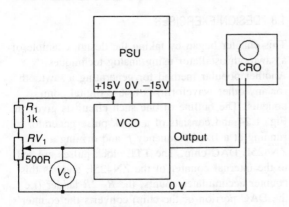

Fig. 1.23 Test layout for VCO

Oscilloscope (bandwidth 10 MHz minimum)
Potentiometer (500 Ω) to set V_C or variable
    voltage source
Frequency counter

The test set up is shown in Fig. 1.23.

Having switched on the power supply and checked that the current taken by the VCO is reasonable — say, less than 30 mA — the potentiometer RV_1 should be adjusted to give $V_C = 1$ V. The frequency of the square wave output is then measured using the oscilloscope and the frequency counter. Note that the accuracy of a CRO on both amplitude and time measurements is normally not better than ±3%, although some modern instruments have built-in digital circuits and can therefore give printouts of time, frequency and amplitude to much closer accuracy than this (i.e. better than ±0.5%).

Suppose at $V_C = 1$ V the frequency is within limits at 3120 Hz. The linearity of the circuit can then be tested by recording the frequency of the output for a number of control input values starting at 50 mV and ending at 3 V. Ten readings would be more than sufficient. A graph can then be plotted to show the change in output frequency with control voltage V_C and the deviation from a straight line characteristic noted to give the linearity of the circuit.

The results for a prototype with the percentage errors in linearity are:

V_C	f	% error
50 mV	146 Hz	−6.4%
500 mV	1520 Hz	−1.3%
1 V	3130 Hz	0% (ref)
1.5 V	4520 Hz	−0.8%
2 V	6118 Hz	−1.96%
3 V	9160 Hz	−2.18%

These indicate that the linearity is within specification.

The CRO could be used to make other checks on circuit performance such as the linearity of the triangle output, the rise and fall times of the square wave output and the noise level induced on the supply leads.

1.6 QUALITY AND RELIABILITY

The term *quality*, as applied to some products, is often taken to mean perfection or excellence in performance. However, in engineering design, quality refers to the degree of match between the actual performance and the specification. Quality control is therefore ensuring that all products of the same type meet the agreed specification. By the correct choice of components, tight control on individual component performance, good mechanical assembly methods and rigorous inspection and testing, a manufacturer can ensure that quality of his output is maintained. These techniques can also be applied to prototypes and one-off designs.

What about creating circuits that last? Here we are discussing *reliability*, i.e. the probability of the circuit or system maintaining its performance without failure for a stated period of time, and under stated operating conditions. Reliability is the maintenance of quality over time.

Accurate prediction of reliability of electronic circuits can be made by using failure rate data on all the individual components that are used in the design, and summing these to obtain an overall circuit or system failure rate. However, accurate analysis is not necessarily of interest to us here. What is important is using the proven techniques that can reduce failure rate and thereby increase the reliability of designs. These techniques can be applied at the design stage and include:

(a) the correct choice of components for each circuit position (see Chapter 2),
(b) derating,
(c) careful components assembly.

Derating is a design technique for improving reliability whereby components are deliberately run at values of current, voltage and power that are well below the maximum ratings quoted for those components. Derating markedly reduces stress-related failure. An example could be to specify 1 W rated resistors when the maximum expected dissipation for any of the resistors is 250 mW. Another is to use capacitors with voltage ratings of twice the expected maximum value in a circuit.

1.7 DOCUMENTATION

Keeping accurate up-to-date records of design work is an important but often neglected area. It is so obviously important that it might seem a waste of space to include a section on the subject. But, unfortunately, many good engineers seem to have a block when it comes to writing down results, comments and short notes concerning modifications on a circuit design. They seem only too keen to complete the circuit and get it into a working state rather than spend a small amount of time and effort in keeping a record of their work. There is, of course, a great temptation to do this; but it is a false economy and the discipline of making up accurate notes is worth it. It will avoid almost certain frustration, at some later date, when an important piece of information is either forgotten or lost.

A file (or notebook) containing the essential information on a design's progress should be made up and retained. Preferably, it should have notes covering each stage of the design:

- design or target specification
- possible circuit options
- circuit choice and components
- design calculations
- test results
- modifications
- final circuit design
- layout details (with test points indicated)
- test procedure.

But the file should not be too large. A bulging file, full of every note and detail, can prove to be a limited asset. The notes should be brief, accurate and date marked.

1.8 DESIGN EXERCISES

This chapter began by taking the design example of a sawtooth oscillator using analog techniques. Another popular method for generating a sawtooth (or any other waveform) is to use digital components. The outline of one such circuit is given in Fig. 1.24 and consists of a clock pulse generator running at a fixed frequency f_c and driving a ZN425E DAC chip. The TTL clock pulses are fed to the internal counter of the ZN425E and, as this counter accumulates counts, the $R-2R$ ladder (i.e. the DAC portion of the chip) converts the counter's state into an analog voltage. In this way, the output of the ZN425E, on pin 14, becomes a *step-like* ramp. When the 8-bit counter overflows, the output returns to zero. The amplitude of the ramp at pin 14 will be given by

$$V_{out} = V_{ref-1LSB}$$

i.e. nearly 2.5 V. A non-inverting amplifier is then used to give the required 6 V amplitude sawtooth.

The design specification is:

> Frequency : 400 Hz ± 20 Hz preset
> Amplitude : 0 to +6 V ±5%
> Linearity : better than ± 5%
> Flyback time : not greater than 100 μs
> Power supply : ±9 V at 150 mA

No independent d.c. supply can be assumed to be available for the nominal ±5 V rail required by the clock pulse generator and the DAC chip, but a 4.7 V ±5% Zener is provided.

Figure 1.25 gives the DAC data sheet.

1 The task is to complete the design showing all connections, component values and component power ratings.

A suggested design approach is as follows:

(a) Choose a suitable clock pulse generator circuit, e.g. a 555 astable or TTL Schmitt oscillator. Design it to free run at the required frequency f_c and ensure that this frequency can be preset.

(b) Check the connections required by the ZN425E for *ramp* output mode, i.e. pins 2 and 3 connected to $+V_{CC}$ via a 1 kΩ resistor, pin 16 connected to pin 15 and decoupled to ground using a 220 nF capa-

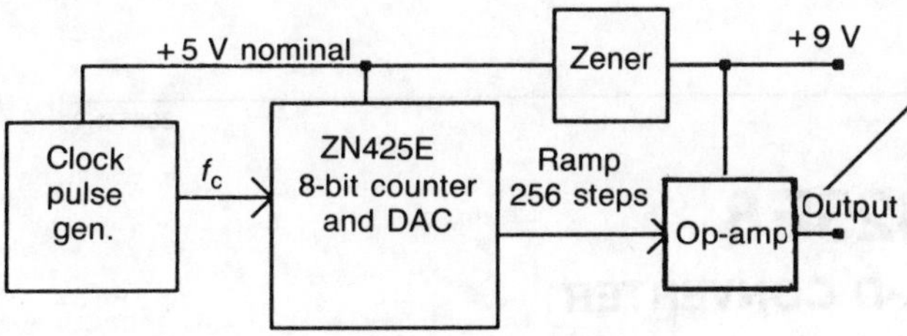

Fig. 1.24 Block diagram for exercise

citor; and don't forget $+V_{CC}$ and ground (0 V) connections.

(c) For your design estimate the maximum current required from the nominal 5 V rail and design a simple voltage regulator. Ensure that the components used for the regulator are capable of dissipating the required power under off load conditions.

(d) Design a non-inverting op-amp circuit using preferred value resistors (no presets are necessary) to increase the 2.5 V ramp to 6 V.

2 Redesign the original UJT sawtooth oscillator using 100 nF in place of the 220 nF value for C_1. The specification remains as given.

3 Modify the UJT sawtooth oscillator so that an additional low impedance negative going ramp (0 V to -6 V) is provided.

4 Using the original target specification as given in the text, design the 400 Hz sawtooth oscillator using a modified 555 timer chip as the circuit choice. The 555 must be connected as an astable and the timing capacitor is to be charged using a constant current source. A value of 100 nF is suggested for C_T.

The timing capacitor (C_T) will be charged from $\frac{1}{3}V_{CC}$ to $\frac{2}{3}V_{CC}$ during the ramp time (dt), therefore use:

$$I = C_T \, dv/dt$$

to find the required value of current.

Include a non-inverting amplifier with offset control so that a 0 V to $+6$ V ramp is provided as a low impedance output.

5 Research other methods for generating the 400 Hz sawtooth waves and design *one* additional circuit.

6 Modify the preamplifier of Fig. 1.13 to meet the following design specification changes:

Voltage gain : 30 dB $\pm$ 0.5 dB
Frequency response : 50 Hz to 50 kHz
Input impedance : 25 kΩ.

7 The input and output signals of an amplifier are measured using

(a) an oscilloscope
(b) a digital multimeter.

The CRO has an accuracy of $\pm 3\%$ on the 1 V cm^{-1} range and $\pm 5\%$ on its 20 mV cm^{-1} range, while the DMM (3.5 digits) has a quoted accuracy of $\pm(0.5\%$ FSD $\pm$ 1 digit) on all a.c. ranges. It reads r.m.s. values. In both cases, calculate the gain as both a ratio and in dB. Estimate the percentage error in the value.

Readings for (a) $V_0 = 3.2$ V pk–pk, $V_i = 80$ mV pk–pk, and for (b) $V_0 = 1.325$ V (2 V range), $V_i = 31.7$ mV (200 mV range).

8 Devise a test strategy for the preamplifier circuit given in Fig. 1.13.

9 For the VCO circuit of Fig. 1.22, prove that the frequency of the output is approximately 3 kHz V^{-1} of V_C.

10 Modify the VCO design as follows:

(a) Provide a low impedance triangle wave output with an amplitude of ± 5 V.
(b) Add a component to allow the frequency to be accurately set.
(c) Change the response to 1 kHz V^{-1}.

Solutions to these design exercises are given in Chapter 8.

GEC PLESSEY
SEMICONDUCTORS

3005-1.0

ZN425E8
8-BIT D-A/A-D CONVERTER

The ZN425 is a monolithic 8-bit D-A converter containing an R-2R ladder network of diffused resistors with precision bipolar switches, and in addition a counter and a 2.5V precision voltage reference. The counter is a powerful addition which allows a precision staircase to be generated very simply by clocking the counter.

FEATURES

■ ±½ LSB Linearity Error

■ 0°C to +70°C

■ TTL and 5V CMOS Compatible

■ Single +5V Supply

■ Settling Time (D-A) 1us Typical

■ Conversion Time (A-D) 1ms Typical, using Ramp and Compare Technique

■ Extra Components Required
D-A:Reference Capacitor (Direct Voltage Output Through 10kohms Typ.)
A-D:Comparator, Gate, Clock and Reference Capacitor

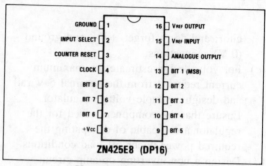

Pin connections - top view

ORDERING INFORMATION

Device type	Operating temperature	Package
ZN425E 8	0°C to +70°C	DP16

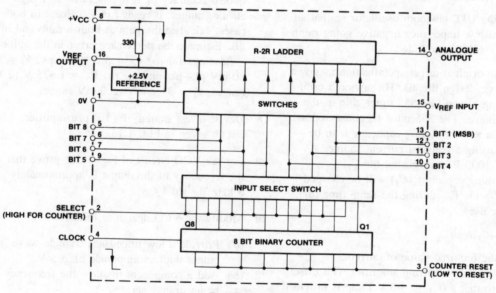

Fig.1 System diagram

(a)

Fig. 1.25 Data sheet for the ZN425E DAC chip

ZN425

INTRODUCTION

The ZN425 is an 8-bit dual mode D-A/A-D converter. It contains an 8-bit D-A converter using an advanced design of R-2R ladder network and an array of precision bipolar switches plus an 8-bit binary counter and a 2.5V precision voltage reference all on a single monolithic chip.

The special design of ladder network results in full 8-bit accuracy using normal diffused resistors.

The use of the on-chip reference voltage is pin optional to retain flexibility. An external fixed or varying reference may therefore be substituted.

By including on the chip an 8-bit binary counter,

A-D conversion can be obtained simply by adding an external comparator (ZN424P) and clock inhibit gating (7400).

By simply clocking the counter the ZN425 can be used as a self-contained precision ramp generator.

A logic input select switch is incorporated which determines whether the precision switches accept the outputs from the binary counter or external digital inputs depending upon whether the control signal is respectively high or low.

The converter is of the voltage switching type and uses an R-2R resistor ladder network as shown in Fig. 2.

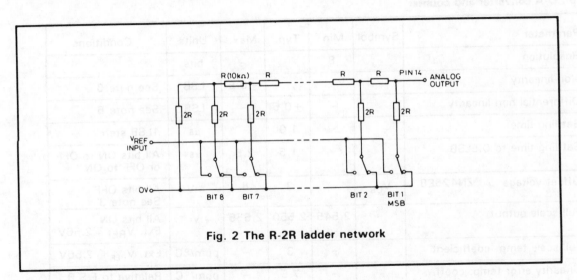

Fig. 2 The R-2R ladder network

Each 2R element is connected either to 0V or V$_{REF}$ by transistor switches specially designed for low offset voltage (typically 1mV).

Binary weighted voltages are produced at the output of the R-2R ladder, the value depending on the digital number applied to the bit inputs.

ABSOLUTE MAXIMUM RATINGS

Supply voltage V$_{CC}$	+7.0V
Max. voltage, logic and V$_{REF}$ inputs	+5.5V See note 3
Operating temperature range	0°C to 70°C
Storage temperature range	−55°C to +125°C

(b)

CHARACTERISTICS (at $T_{amb} = 25°C$ and $V_{CC} = +5V$ unless otherwise specified)

Internal voltage reference

Parameter	Symbol	Min.	Typ.	Max.	Units	Conditions
Output voltage	V_{REF}	2.4	2.55	2.7	V	I = 7.5mA (internal)
Slope resistance	R_S	–	2	4	Ω	I = 7.5mA (internal)
V_{REF} temperature coefficient		–	40	–	ppm/°C	I = 7.5mA (internal)

Note: The internal reference requires a 0.22μF stabilising capacitor between pins 1 and 16.

8-Bit D-A converter and counter

Parameter	Symbol	Min.	Typ.	Max.	Units	Conditions
Resolution		8	–	–	bits	
Non-linearity		–	–	±0.5	LSB	See note 3
Differential non-linearity		–	±0.5	–	LSB	See note 6
Settling time		–	1.0	–	μs	1LSB step
Settling time to 0.5LSB		–	1.5	2.5	μs	All bits ON to OFF or OFF to ON
Offset voltage ZN425E8	V_{OS}	–	3	8	mV	All bits OFF See note 3
Full-scale output		2.545	2.550	2.555	V	All bits ON Ext. V_{REF} = 2.56V
Full-scale temp. coefficient		–	3	–	ppm/°C	Ext. V_{REF} = 2.56V
Linearity error temp. coeff.		–	7.5	–	ppm/°C	Relative to F.S.R.
Analogue output resistance	R_o	–	10	–	kΩ	
External reference voltage		0	–	3.0	V	
Supply voltage	V_{CC}	4.5	–	5.5	V	See note 3
Supply current	I_s	–	25	35	mA	
High level input voltage	V_{IH}	2.0	–	–	V	See notes 1 and 2
Low level input voltage	V_{IL}	–	–	0.7	V	

(c)

Fig. 1.25 (cont.)

ZN425

CHARACTERISTICS (cont.)

Parameter	Symbol	Min.	Typ.	Max.	Units	Conditions
High level input current	I_{IH}	–	–	10	μA	V_{CC} = max. V_I = 2.4V
		–	–	100	μA	V_{CC} = max. V_I = 5.5V
Low level input current bit inputs	I_{IL}	–	–	– 0.68	mA	V_{CC} = max. V_I = 0.3V
Low level input current, clock reset and input select	I_L	–	–	– 0.18	mA	
High level output current	I_{OH}	–	–	– 40	μA	
Low level output current	I_{OL}	–	–	1.6	mA	
High level output voltage	V_{OH}	2.4	–	–	V	V_{CC} = min. Q = 1 I_{load} = – 40μA
Low level output voltage	V_{OL}	–	–	0.4	V	V_{CC} = min., Q = 0 I_{load} = 1.6mA
Maximum counter clock frequency	f_c	3	5	–	MHz	See note 5
Reset pulse width	t_R	200	–	–	ns	See note 4

Notes:
1. The input select pin (2) must be held low when the bit pins (5, 6, 7, 9, 10, 11, 12 and 13) are driven externally.
2. To obtain counter outputs on bit pins the input select pin (2) should be taken to +Vcc via a 1kΩ resistor.
3. (a) Maximum operating voltage. Between 70°C and 125°C the maximum supply voltage is reduced to 5.0V.
   (b) Offset voltage. The difference is due to package lead resistance. This offset will normally be removed by the setting up procedure, and because the offset temperature coefficient is low, the specified accuracy will be maintained.
4. The device may be reset by gating from its own counter.
5. Fmax in A-D mode is 300kHz, see Operating Note 2.
6. Monotonic over full operating temperature range.

(*d*)

1.9 SUGGESTED BOOKS

GENERAL

The Art of Electronics, Horowitz & Hill, Cambridge
    University Press
Electronics Sourcebook for Engineers, Loveday,
    Pitman
Logic Designer's Handbook, Parr, Granada
Operational Amplifiers, Clayton, Butterworths

REFERENCE TEXTS

Electronic Engineer's Handbook, Fink & Christiansen,
    McGraw-Hill
Electronic Engineer's Reference Book, Mazda,
    Butterworths

Modern Electronic Circuits Reference Manual,
    Markus, McGraw-Hill

1.10 SOFTWARE TOOLS FOR USE IN ANALOG CIRCUIT DESIGN

The following is a list of some of the software
packages which allow analysis of analog circuits.
Most run on IBM PCs or compatibles.

- ANALYSER II — Number One Systems Ltd
- ECA-2 — Those Engineers
- Delph 'NODAL — Ankocard Ltd
- MICRO-CAP II — DATECH data Technology
- PACSIM — SIMUCAD
- PSPICE — MicroSim Corporation

2 SELECTING COMPONENTS

2.1 PASSIVES

The term *passive* is used to describe the class of components which are used in a supporting role in electronic circuits, i.e. the resistors, capacitors and inductors. One definition of a passive element is that it is a component that does not contribute to signal energy; it either consumes energy, as is the case for a resistor, or stores it like a capacitor or inductor. For example, two resistors would be used to set the voltage gain of an amplifier to 20 dB (see Fig. 2.1) and a capacitor used to fix the upper cut-off frequency, but it is the active devices (the transistors inside the op-amps) that provide the amplification of the signal.

It might be natural to assume, unless one has looked more closely at the variety of types, that passive component specification is fairly straight-forward. A resistor, for example, is simply just a resistor and nothing more than the value needs to be specified. This is rarely the case and questions such as how much power is it dissipating? what tolerance is required? how will its value change with temperature? can it withstand the voltage? and so on, will usually require an answer before we can proceed to specify the exact type of resistor to be used in a particular application.

For electronic design work to be *sound* we need to be able to select the most suitable and effective devices in terms of performance, stability and cost, and this applies just as much to the basic passive components as it does to the transistors, powerFETs and ICs. What this means in practice is:

(*a*) being aware of the available types of components, their ranges, typical charac-teristics, limiting factors and intended use;
(*b*) having access to up-to-date specifications on these components;
(*c*) being able to interpret these data sheets.

This section addresses these points for passive devices.

As already indicated, within each class of com-ponents there are usually several different types from which to choose. For example, fixed resistor types include:

- carbon composition
- carbon film
- metal film
- metal oxide
- thick film metal glaze (cermet)
- wirewound.

Each type, as we shall see later, has characteristics (either electrical, mechanical or even cost) that suit it to a particular requirement, and from such an array of types we have to choose the one most suit-able for our application allowing, of course, for such constraints as availability of supply, cost, and any preferred standardisations within an organisa-tion. To enable us to make correct choices it is therefore essential to have an understanding of component operation, limitations and intended use. The manufacturer's data sheet is the place to get this essential information.

Component specification sheets will have the following type of layout:

1 device type, part number, title,

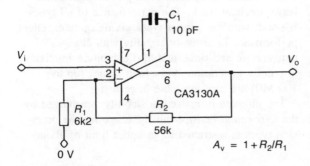

$$A_v = 1 + R_2/R_1$$

Fig. 2.1 Amplifier

2 short description showing features and intended use,

3 mechanical details, i.e. dimensions and usually an outline drawing,

4 absolute maximum electrical ratings,

5 typical characteristics.

These points are illustrated in Fig. 2.2 for a Bourns type 3339 4-turn cermet potentiometer. Here the mechanical details, electrical characteristics and other features are clearly presented by the manufacturer. Let us assume that a 10 kΩ type 3339 is to be used in an oscillator circuit to set the frequency of a 4047B CMOS chip to 10 kHz. This would be a typical situation where a trimpot of this type would be specified, since the cermet element gives infinite resolution, has excellent temperature performance and good adjustability, while the application does not require many rotations to be made. The connections for the 4047B (astable mode), together with other component values, are shown in Fig. 2.3. The periodic time for the 4047B is given by:

$$T_A = 4.4 R_T C_T$$

(this is the typical figure given in the 4047B data. The worst case value for T_A is stated as $4.771 R_T C_T$).

The oscillator is to have a frequency of 10 kHz. Thus, when RV_1 is set to maximum, and ignoring the tolerance of all other component values, we get:

$$\begin{aligned} T_{A(max)} &= 4.4 \times 28 \times 10^3 \times 1 \times 10^{-9} \\ &= 123.2 \ \mu s. \end{aligned}$$

Therefore, $f_{min} = 8.12$ kHz and, when RV_1 is set to minimum,

$$\begin{aligned} T_{A(min)} &= 4.4 \times 18 \times 10^3 \times 1 \times 10^{-9} \\ &= 79.2 \ \mu s. \end{aligned}$$

Therefore, $f_{max} = 12.63$ kHz.

Therefore, a 10 kΩ value for RV_1 will easily allow the desired frequency to be adjusted. At $f = 10$ kHz the *set value* of RV_1 can be calculated as follows:

$$R_T = T_A/4.4 C_T = 22.727 \text{ k}\Omega.$$

Therefore, $RV_1 = R_T - R_1 = 4.728$ kΩ.

In other words, RV_1 must be at almost the mid-point of its four-turn travel. How close can we adjust the frequency to 10 kHz? The specification on the trimpot quotes adjustability as $\pm 0.1\%$, i.e. $\pm 10 \ \Omega$ value. This will result in frequency adjustability of

not worse than ± 5 Hz, which is quite an acceptable figure.

What about stability with temperature? Assuming all other components to be stable with respect to temperature, the contribution of the trimpot can be calculated using its temperature coefficient figure. This is quoted as ± 100 ppm/°C, and results in a drift of frequency of just over 0.5 Hz per °C. In a similar way, other parameter figures for the trimpot could be used to study its performance in the circuit.

2.2 FIXED RESISTORS

The general performance specifications for the resistor types listed previously are given in Table 2.1. Table 2.2 gives the preferred values (to BS2488) in which these resistors can be most easily obtained.

Carbon composition resistors, the general purpose resistors that have been with us for over half a century, are relatively cheap and robust components but do not have high stability. They should only be used in circuits where the changes in resistance value with applied voltage, temperature, loading and time are not critical. Consider the likely effect of a load voltage of 20 V and a 30 °C temperature rise above ambient on a 1000 Ω carbon composition resistor. The change in resistance value could be almost 10%. (See Table 2.1.)

The *carbon film* types have improved stability with voltage and loading but still have a fairly large temperature coefficient. Film resistors are manufactured by depositing an even film of resistive material (nickel chromium for *metal film*; a mixture of a metal and an insulating oxide for *metal oxide*; or a mixture of ceramic and a metal for *cermet*) onto a high grade ceramic base, usually in the shape of a rod. The required resistance value is then obtained by spiralling off part of the film to leave a helical track. The performance of all types is good, with the cermet types giving quite excellent performance in terms of stability with changes of temperature and time, and also exhibiting relatively low noise generation. Very high values (up to 100 MΩ) are also available in cermet.

The ultimate in resistance stability is achieved by the *wirewound resistor* but the range for the precision types is restricted to an upper limit of about

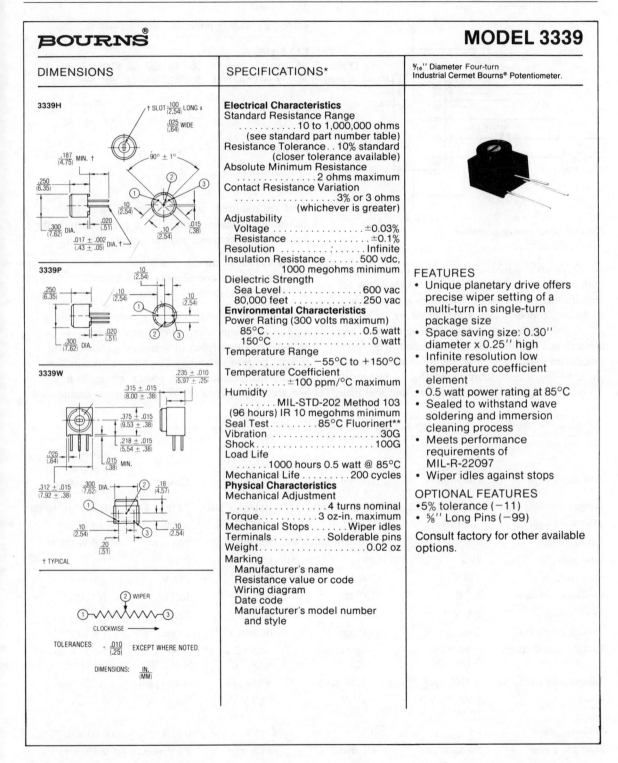

BOURNS®

MODEL 3339

DIMENSIONS

3339H

3339P

3339W

† TYPICAL

TOLERANCES: ± .010/(.25) EXCEPT WHERE NOTED.

DIMENSIONS: IN./(MM)

SPECIFICATIONS*

Electrical Characteristics
Standard Resistance Range
. . . . 10 to 1,000,000 ohms
(see standard part number table)
Resistance Tolerance . . 10% standard
(closer tolerance available)
Absolute Minimum Resistance
. . . . 2 ohms maximum
Contact Resistance Variation
. . . . 3% or 3 ohms
(whichever is greater)
Adjustability
Voltage . . . . ±0.03%
Resistance . . . . ±0.1%
Resolution . . . . : . . . . . Infinite
Insulation Resistance . . . . . . 500 vdc,
1000 megohms minimum
Dielectric Strength
Sea Level . . . . 600 vac
80,000 feet . . . . 250 vac
Environmental Characteristics
Power Rating (300 volts maximum)
85°C . . . . 0.5 watt
150°C . . . . 0 watt
Temperature Range
. . . . −55°C to +150°C
Temperature Coefficient
. . . . ±100 ppm/°C maximum
Humidity
. . . . MIL-STD-202 Method 103
(96 hours) IR 10 megohms minimum
Seal Test . . . . 85°C Fluorinert**
Vibration 30G
Shock 100G
Load Life
. . . . . . 1000 hours 0.5 watt @ 85°C
Mechanical Life . . . . 200 cycles
Physical Characteristics
Mechanical Adjustment
. . . . 4 turns nominal
Torque . . . . 3 oz-in. maximum
Mechanical Stops . . . . . . Wiper idles
Terminals . . . . Solderable pins
Weight . . . . 0.02 oz
Marking
Manufacturer's name
Resistance value or code
Wiring diagram
Date code
Manufacturer's model number
and style

⁹⁄₁₆" Diameter Four-turn
Industrial Cermet Bourns® Potentiometer.

FEATURES
• Unique planetary drive offers precise wiper setting of a multi-turn in single-turn package size
• Space saving size: 0.30" diameter x 0.25" high
• Infinite resolution low temperature coefficient element
• 0.5 watt power rating at 85°C
• Sealed to withstand wave soldering and immersion cleaning process
• Meets performance requirements of MIL-R-22097
• Wiper idles against stops

OPTIONAL FEATURES
•5% tolerance (−11)
• ⅜" Long Pins (−99)

Consult factory for other available options.

Fig. 2.2 Manufacturer's data sheet

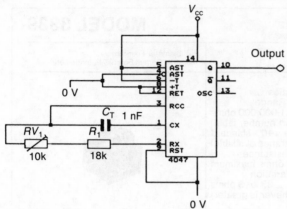

Fig. 2.3 Square wave generator

Table 2.2 BS2428 preferred values (resistors)

E12 Series

10 11 12 13 15 16 18 20 22 24 27 30 33
36 39 43 47 51 56 62 68 75 82 91

E24 Series

10 12 15 18 22 27 33 39 47 56 68 82

E6 Series

10 15 22 33 47 68

10 kΩ. General purpose wirewounds can be obtained with values up to 25 kΩ or more. Wirewounds are manufactured by winding a resistance wire such as nichrome, copper nickel alloys or silver nickel alloys onto an insulating former. End wires or tags are attached and the unit is then sealed. The resistance wire must, of course, be uniform and ductile while having a reasonably high value of resistivity. To get high values the wire must be thin and many

turns are required, hence the restriction to the maximum resistance value. For a precision type the following performance parameters are typical:

Selection tolerance : ±0.1%
Temperature coefficient : ±5 ppm/°C
Full load stability : 35 ppm/year

This gives an indication of why wirewounds are used in situations where the highest stability is necessary. These types of resistors (precision and general purpose) also have high power dissipation and are manufactured with power ratings from a few watts up to over 50 W. Some are available clad

Table 2.1 Comparison of common general purpose resistors

Resistor type	Carbon composition	Carbon film	Metal oxide	Cermet	General purpose wirewound
Range	10 Ω to 22 MΩ	10 Ω to 2 MΩ	10 Ω to 1 MΩ	10 Ω to 1 MΩ	0.25 Ω to 10 kΩ
Selection tolerance	±10%	±5%	±2%	±2%	±5%
Power rating	250 mW/1 W	250 mW/500 mW	500 mW/2 W	500 mW	2.5 W/20 W
Load stability	10%	2%	1%	0.5%	1%
Max. voltage	150 V	200 V	350 V	250 V	200 V
Insulation resistance	10^9 Ω	10^{10} Ω	10^{10} Ω	10^{10} Ω	10^{10} Ω
Proof voltage	500 V	500 V	1 kV	500 V	500 V
Voltage coefficient	2000 ppm V^{-1}	100 ppm V^{-1}	10 ppm V^{-1}	10 ppm V^{-1}	1 ppm V^{-1}
Ambient temp. range	−40 °C to +150 °C	−40 °C to +125 °C	−55 °C to +150 °C	−55 °C to +150 °C	−55 °C to +185 °C
Temperature coeff./°C	±1200 ppm	−1200 ppm	±250 ppm	±100 ppm	±200 ppm
Noise	1 kΩ, 2 $\mu V\ V^{-1}$, 10 MΩ, 6 $\mu V\ V^{-1}$	1 $\mu V\ V^{-1}$	0.1 $\mu V\ V^{-1}$	0.1 $\mu V\ V^{-1}$	0.01 $\mu V\ V^{-1}$
Soldering effect	2%	0.5%	0.15%	0.15%	0.05%
Shelf life 1 year	5% max.	2% max.	0.1% max.	0.1% max.	0.1% max.
Damp heat 95% RH	15% max.	4% max.	1%	1%	0.1%

7-segment LED display (common anode)

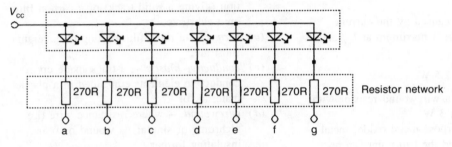

Fig. 2.4 Using a resistor network (SIL) with a display

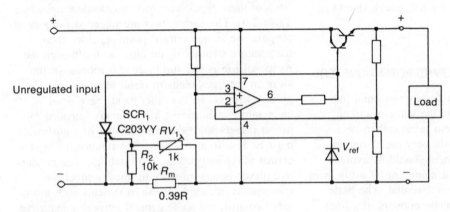

Fig. 2.5 Overcurrent protection circuit

in their own aluminium heatsink to reduce volume, but it is important to site such heat-generating components well away from other sensitive areas of a system. Because wirewound resistors can run at high temperatures without much degradation in stability, they are particularly suited for use in harsh environments.

Resistor networks, where several resistors are fitted onto one encapsulation, are increasing in use. They can be used more efficiently and reliably with integrated circuits since they take up less space on the p.c.b.

Networks are available with the following types of layout:

- a group of isolated resistors (usually 7 or 8)
- bussed resistors
- special function such as an R−2R ladder for

DAC applications or resistors connected as an attenuator.

A typical example is illustrated in Fig. 2.4, showing how seven resistors in a network could be used as the limiting resistors for a seven segment display. Usually resistor networks are specified for use by high volume producers.

Let's consider a simple example of resistor specification for a foldback current trip using a current-monitoring resistor and a thyristor (see Fig. 2.5). For this circuit the trip current is to be set to 2.5 A. If this current passes through R_m the voltage developed across R_2 just exceeds V_{GT} (the gate trigger voltage of the thyristor) and the thyristor conducts to clamp the output of the amplifier at about +1 V.

Assume V_{GT}, the trip voltage of the thyristor, is

0.9 V and that the voltage at I_{trip} across R_m is to be 1 V.

$$R_m = V_{R_m}/I_{trip}$$

Therefore, $R_m = 1/2.5 = 0.4 \, \Omega$ (0.39 Ω is n.p.v. — *nearest preferred value*).

The power loss in R_m, caused by the current flowing through it, will be a maximum at I_{trip} and is:

$$P_{R_m} = V_{R_m} \times I_{trip} = 2.5 \text{ W}.$$

Therefore, R_m should be a wirewound resistor with a power rating of at least 3 W.

R_2 can be a general purpose metal oxide, metal film or cermet resistor and the trip point can be accurately set, to take account of the tolerance on V_{GT} and the two resistors, by RV_1 which should be a 1 kΩ cermet trimpot.

2.3 VARIABLE RESISTORS AND POTENTIOMETERS

These components allow a designer to build into his design some adjustability in the value of circuit resistance to enable a system parameter to be trimmed. They are obviously very useful but any tendency to over-rely on them should be avoided; keep the number down to a minimum by using them only in situations where it is essential. The basic construction of a potentiometer consists of a track of resistive material with which a movable wiper makes contact.

The resistive track can be:

(a) *carbon* — either moulded carbon composition (giving a solid track) or a carbon film on a substrate,

(b) *cermet* — a thick film coating on a ceramic substrate,

(c) *conductive plastic* — a track made up of conductive elements embedded in a plastic material, or

(d) *wirewound* — where resistance wire (i.e. nichrome or similar) is wound onto an insulating former.

Each of these types have their application areas (see Table 2.3). The carbon pots are intended for general purpose use in non-critical positions since their temperature stability is not high, and, although their rotational life is fair (up to 20 000 rotations), the wear on the track tends to result in higher electrical noise. Cermets, on the other hand, have good temperature stability but are normally intended for use as presets since the total number of adjustments must be kept to a low value; the rotational life of a cermet is typically about 200 rotations. The conductive plastic potentiometers are mostly precision components intended for use in systems such as servo control, but some general purpose conductive

Table 2.3

Type	Example of application	Selection tolerance	Linearity	Stability	Life in expected no. of rotations	Suggested component
Preset or trimmer	Fixing a voltage level, pulse width, frequency, etc. (from single to 4-turn)	Up to ±20%	Not important	Required to be high ±0.5%	Less than 50	Cermet
General purpose control	Brilliance and focus control on a VDU (usually single turn)	Up to ±20%	±5%	±5%	10 000	Carbon or wirewound
Precision control	Calibrated dial on an oscillator	±3%	0.5%	±0.5%	50 000	Precision wirewound or conductive plastic

plastic pots are also available. Wirewound potentio-meters have similar stability and performance characteristics to the fixed wirewound resistors, i.e. very low temperature coefficient and excellent long-term stability, and the rotational life is also good, with some manufacturers quoting a life of up to 50 000 rotations. There is, however, a small resolu-tion loss in a wirewound since the track is not continuous; as the wiper moves along the top of the coil the resistance changes in small, but measurable, steps.

In addition to temperature stability and rotational life, other points to check when specifying a potentiometer are:

- tolerance
- power rating
- linearity
- contact resistance — the small value of resis-tance left between the wiper and any end contact when the wiper is moved to an end position
- adjustability
- electrical noise
- maximum wiper current.

An application has been described earlier in this chapter.

2.4 CAPACITORS

If you need to pass an a.c. signal between two circuits without disturbing the d.c. bias level, filter out an unwanted frequency component, store a voltage level for a defined period, shape the frequency response of an op-amp, or remove 100 Hz ripple from a power rail, then a capacitor has to be specified. But what value and which type is right for the application? First let's consider the standard formula for the capacitance of a parallel plate capacitor:

$$C = \frac{\epsilon_0 \epsilon_r A}{d} \text{ farads}$$

where ϵ_0 = permittivity of free space, ϵ_r = relative permittivity of the dielectric, A = area of the plates, d = distance between the plates.

This shows that in addition to the area of the plates and the distance that separates them, the capacitance depends also on the dielectric material.

Table 2.4

Dielectric	ϵ_r
Paper	4
Silver mica	4 to 6
Ceramic: low loss	7
Temperature compensating	90
High K	1000 or more
Polystyrene	2.4
Polypropylene	2.25
Polycarbonate	2.8
Aluminium oxide electrolytics	7 to 9
Tantalum oxide electrolytics	27

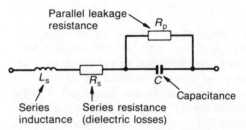

Fig. 2.6 Equivalent circuit for a capacitor

For a given area A and distance d, the higher the value of ϵ_r the greater will be the capacitance value. Capacitors are therefore usually classified by the dielectric material, with the main types being shown in Table 2.4.

The equivalent circuit for a capacitor is shown in Fig. 2.6. The capacitor has a small series resistance (R_s) caused by dielectric losses, in a series induct-ance (L_s), and a parallel leakage resistance (R_p). C, R_s and L_s form a series resonance circuit. At the resonant frequency (f_R) the impedance of the circuit will be a minimum and equal to R_s. Above reson-ance the impedance rises and becomes inductive, causing the capacitor to lose its effectiveness. The value of inductance varies according to the size and construction of the capacitor but *needs to be low* to allow the capacitor to achieve a high resonant frequency. Typical values of resonant frequency are:

Aluminium electrolytics	50 kHz
Tantalum electrolytics	100 kHz
Ceramic polystyrene	10 MHz
Polyester polypropylene	1 MHz

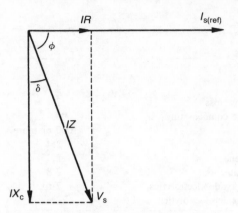

Fig. 2.7 Phasor diagram of capacitor

The low value of resonant frequency for electrolytics shows why these types are only suitable for coupling and decoupling low frequency signals and would not prove effective in removing high frequency switching spikes from a supply rail. Usually the power rail for fast switching circuits (i.e. TTL ICs) is decoupled using a small electrolytic, 4.7 μF, to remove power line ripple (i.e. 100 Hz) in parallel with a ceramic of, say, 10 nF to deal with the switching spikes.

At frequencies below f_R the series resistance, which may only be a few milliohms, causes slight losses. The phasor diagram in Fig. 2.7 illustrates this point. The loss angle is called δ, where tan δ = R_s/X_c.

Tan δ, also called the *dissipation factor* (d.f.), is a measure of the *loss* in the capacitor. Tan δ or d.f. is quoted at 50 Hz for electrolytics and at a frequency of 1 kHz for other types. Typical values are:

Type	*tan δ*
Electrolytics	0.08
Ceramic	0.002
Polystyrene	0.0005

The parallel resistance (R_p) of a capacitor will cause any charge stored on the capacitor's plates to leak slowly away. In certain applications, such as the hold capacitor in a sample-and-hold circuit or the timing capacitor in a long duration monostable, it is important for the leakage resistance to be as high as possible. Electrolytics have the worst leakage (it is usually quoted as a leakage current rather than a

resistance) and for other types the value of R_p ranges from about 10^8 Ω for ceramic up to about 10^{12} Ω for polystyrene.

Electrolytic capacitors, which have a very high CV ratio, are particularly useful as the smoothing element in power supplies and for coupling and decoupling in a.f. amplifiers. When using aluminium electrolytics watch the following points:

1 The capacitor is polarised and the voltage across it must not be reversed.
2 The tolerance on the value can be as high as −20% to +50%.
3 Leakage current can be high, particularly in the physically large high value types. For example, electrolytics designed for use in switch mode and computer power supplies have leakage quoted at 20 °C as:

$$\text{Leakage} = 0.006CV + 4 \ \mu\text{A} \quad (C \text{ is in } \mu\text{F})$$

Thus, a 10 000 μF capacitor operating at 25 V will have a leakage current of:

$$I = 1.504 \text{ mA}.$$

4 The equivalent series resistance (ESR), made up of the resistance of the leads and connectors and the series losses in the dielectric, may have a value of several hundred milliohms. It is this resistance that restricts the ripple current rating of an electrolytic. As alternating current flows, I^2R_s heat losses cause the temperature inside the capacitor to rise. This excess heat must be removed by radiation from the surface area of the capacitor. It is dangerous to exceed the ripple current rating since the internal temperature rise may cause the capacitor to overheat and possibly explode. Some calculations are shown in a later example on power supply design.

APPLICATION EXAMPLES

(a) Decoupling a DIL logic IC *(see Fig. 2.8)*

Most digital ICs demand a brief pulse of supply current on a change of logic state. One standard type TTL gate, for example, takes a 15 mA, 10 ns pulse from its 5 V supply when it switches. Unless the supply is decoupled at the IC pin, a *spike* will

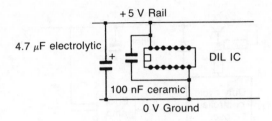

Fig. 2.8 Decoupling capacitors for a logic IC

be generated which could cause false triggering of other gates. In a TTL system the effect is eliminated by decoupling the +5 V rail to 0 V using 100 nF ceramic capacitors, usually one capacitor for every four *gate*-type TTL ICs. A flat ceramic capacitor is available that has low inductance and a very low profile, enabling it to be fitted directly beneath an IC on the p.c.b. Such capacitors are supplied for most standard IC pin configurations. A typical value is 30 nF.

(b) Capacitors used in a 555 monostable design *(see Fig. 2.9)*

The specification for the circuit is:

Power supply : +9 V
Output pulse width : 1 ms ±5%
Trigger input : 2 μs −9 V pulse

Four capacitors are required for the monostable. C_1 is the timing capacitor and its value can be calculated using the formula for pulse width:

$$T = 1.1CR$$

with $T = 1$ ms, $R = 910$ kΩ ±1% metal film, $C_1 = 1000$ pF.

Therefore, a suitable capacitor type would be a polystyrene with a selection tolerance of ±$2\frac{1}{2}$%.

C_2 is a decoupling component to ensure that no pick-up or power line noise gets onto the control input (pin 5). A value of 10 nF is required and a monolithic ceramic type would be appropriate.

C_3 is used to couple the negative going trigger pulse onto pin 2 of the 555. Its value should be such that the time constant it forms with R_2 is not less than the pulse width of the trigger signal. Therefore, C_3 can be calculated from:

$$C_3 = \text{trigger pulse width}/0.7R_2$$

If R_2 is 10 kΩ, $C_3 = 290$ pF.

A 330 pF polystyrene or ceramic capacitor should be used.

C_4 is provided to decouple the +9 V power rail. Its value will depend upon the impedance of the supply at that point and the load current supplied to the 555. Assume the 555 is sourcing a load current of 20 mA and that the impedance at 1 kHz of the supply rail is 0.1 Ω. This would imply that each time the 555 outputs its 1 ms pulse, the power rail drops by 2 mV. C_4 would appear to be an unnecessary addition. However, the impedance of the supply will rise with frequency and may be, say, 5 Ω at 500 kHz. This means that the switching edges of the 1 ms pulse will appear on the supply rail with an amplitude of 200 mV. Using the standard formula for the charge on a capacitor:

$$Q = CV \text{ or } Idt = CdV.$$

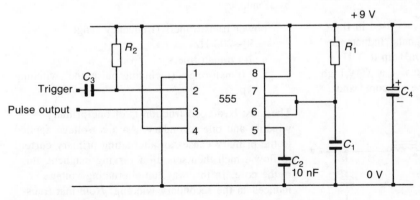

Fig. 2.9 Monostable

We can calculate a value for C_4 to reduce these switching spikes to, say, a 20 mV maximum.

$$C = \frac{I dt}{dV}$$

where $I = 20$ mA, $dt = 5$ μs and $dV = 20$ mV.

Therefore, $C_4 = 5$ μF.

A 4.7 μF polyester or ceramic would be used.

2.5 INDUCTORS AND TRANSFORMERS

An inductor or choke is basically a coil of insulated copper wire wound on a non-conductive former. The value of inductance depends to some extent on the shape of the coil and is proportional to the square of the number of turns. Some coils may be air cored but usually a core of magnetic material is fitted into the former to increase the inductance.

INDUCTORS

Inductors fall into three main categories:

(a) Power chokes — designed to be used in the frequency range 50 Hz to 200 Hz as inductors in power supply smoothing filters (usually referred to as a choke input filter (see Fig. 2.10)). These power chokes will have a core of iron laminations, i.e. several thin strips of iron insulated with varnish from each other. These laminations reduce power losses which would result from the eddy currents set up in a solid core. Inductance values of power chokes can be up to 10 H or higher.

(b) Audio frequency chokes — used in filter circuits to block a.f. signals. Inductance values range from 100 mH up to 1 H.

(c) R.f. inductors and chokes — at very high frequencies these will be air cored and

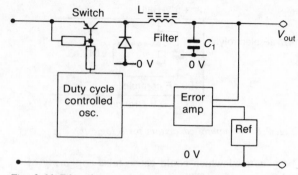

Fig. 2.11 Filter for a switching regulator

consist simply of a few turns of heavy gauge wire, but most other r.f. inductors will be provided with a ferrite core. They are used in tuned circuits, filters and as suppressors. The inductance values range from 1 μH up to 1 mH.

A major use of these inductors, at frequencies in the range 15 kHz to 200 kHz, is in switched mode power supplies as the input element in the filter section directly following the switch (see Fig. 2.11). These must be capable of passing relatively large currents (i.e. several amps) and have inductance values of typically 500 μH. The design of such a choke is discussed in the next chapter.

TRANSFORMERS

Transformers, which consist of separated windings wound on a common core, are used in a variety of impedance matching, voltage level changing and isolating applications. Again, they are categorised by frequency:

> power transformers (frequency range 50–200 Hz)
> audio transformers
> r.f. transformers (including pulse and switching types).

The most basic construction is of one primary winding and one secondary. An a.c. voltage applied to the primary causes an alternating primary current to flow which then sets up a varying magnetic flux in the core. In this way, an alternating voltage is induced in the secondary winding. Note that transformers generate magnetic fields and sensitive components may require shielding from this.

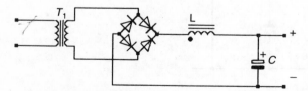

Fig. 2.10 Choke input filter

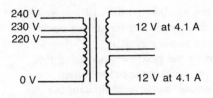

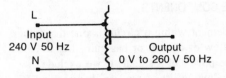

Fig. 2.12 100 VA transformer

Fig. 2.13 Auto transformer

By altering the number of turns in the secondary coil of the transformer with respect to the primary coil, the voltage induced on the secondary can be varied. In this way, step-up (secondary voltage higher than the primary) and step-down transformers can be designed.

Assuming zero losses (most power transformers are very efficient, with efficiencies typically of 95%),

$$P_{in} = P_{out}, \text{ i.e. } I_p V_p = I_s V_s.$$

Suppose a mains transformer designed to give a secondary voltage of 12 V at 2 A is connected to 240 V a.c. on the primary, then we can use the above formula to calculate the primary current. In this case:

$$I_p = \frac{24}{240} \text{ A} = 100 \text{ mA}.$$

In practice, the primary current would be a few milliamps more than this since there will be some losses in the core.

Mains transformers, which may have a tapped primary winding to allow for variations in mains input voltage and more than one secondary, are quoted with the following specifications:

Power rating in VA
Secondary voltage in volts r.m.s. on full load
and regulation (of the secondary voltage)
regulation =

$$\frac{\text{(off-load voltage} - \text{full load voltage)}}{\text{off-load voltage}} \times 100\%$$

(See example in Fig. 2.12.)
100 VA transformer (50 VA per secondary)
Secondary voltages 12 V at 4.1 A and 12 V at
4.1 A
Regulation = 9% (i.e. off-load secondary
voltage = 13.2 V)

Usually, with a transformer such as this, the two secondary windings can be connected either in

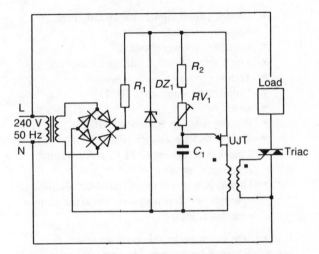

Fig. 2.14 Pulse transformer used in a.c. power control

parallel to give 12 V at 8.2 A (this can only be done when the secondary voltages are equal) or in series to give 24 V at 4.1 A. (However, in this case take care to connect the windings in series addition; if they are connected in series opposing the resulting output is zero volts!)

Apart from auto-transformers all other types of transformer provide isolation between the primary and secondary windings. This is an important feature in any power supply design, especially those that are mains driven. Auto-transformers, which have one winding and various tapping points, should only be used for testing purposes. (See Fig. 2.13 for a diagram of an auto-transformer.)

The cores of mains and a.f. transformers will be laminated, whereas r.f. (pulse and switching regulator) transformers will have coils wound on a ferrite core. A typical application of a pulse transformer is in coupling the trigger signal from a unijunction oscillator to the gate of a triac or thyristor (see Fig. 2.14). The transformer, with a turns ratio of 1:1, provides the required isolation between the firing circuit and the load. The bandwidth is typically 3 kHz to 1 MHz for such transformers and fully encapsulated DIL units are available.

2.6 ACTIVE COMPONENTS

An active element within a circuit is one that either directs the flow of current or has gain, i.e. it increases the power of a signal. If we exclude valves and relays, a list of modern discrete and IC active devices includes:

- Diodes (small signal, backward, PIN, Schottky, tunnel, Zener)
- Rectifiers (power diodes)
- Thyristors (silicon controlled rectifiers)
- Triacs
- Unijunction transistors (UJT)
- Diacs
- Bipolar junction transistors (BJT)
- Field effect transistors (FET)
- Linear ICs (op-amps, PLL, comparators, regulators, etc.)
- Digital ICs (logic gates, bistables, registers, counters, microprocessors, interface chips, memories, etc.).

It is not the intention in this book to cover the operating principles of these devices; in any case, I have probably omitted something from the list. What is important is developing the technique of selecting the correct or 'best' component for an application. This is not always an easy task as there may be tens of competing devices to choose from and/or some compromise between available devices and the design requirements may be necessary. In this section, I shall assume that you have an understanding of the basic principles of the various components, and concentrate on discussing specifications, ratings, important parameters and any useful rules-of-thumb for design work.

2.7 BIPOLAR JUNCTION TRANSISTORS

The choice of the *best fit* component for an application can only be properly made by a careful study of the relevant data sheet and also by following a procedure that consists of a series of logical steps. These are:

1. To define the task the device is required to perform.
2. To calculate the values of important parameters that are expected for the device when it is working at the operating point of the circuit.
3. To list the maximum values of voltage, current and power that the device could experience in the circuit.
4. To estimate the maximum operating frequency or switching speed required.
5. To define any mechanical limitations.

When this information is collected together, an initial list of suitable devices can be made by studying *short-form data*. Short-form data simply give values for all the important parameters and ratings for a component. For example, the short-form data for transistors such as the BC182L and ZTX653 would be presented as shown:

Here, quoted at 25 °C ambient, we have values for:

P_{tot} : the maximum power rating of the transistor

I_c : the maximum collector current

V_{ceo} : the maximum collector to emitter voltage rating with base to emitter open circuit

h_{FE} : the typical value of the large signal common emitter current gain ($h_{FE} = I_c/I_B$)

f_T : the transition frequency — the frequency at which the magnitude of common emitter current gain (h_{FE}) has fallen to unity.

What the short-form data presentation does is to allow users to see at a glance the main features of a device. Then, if the device appears to fit the application, we can move on to study the full component data sheet. Never rely just on the short-form data when specifying a component. It is essential to check out the way in which it will operate in the application by a careful study of the complete data sheet. Parameters of any device will vary as the applied voltages and currents are changed and the short-form presentation may well mask some variation (in the h_{FE} of a transistor, for example) that would disqualify it for the intended use.

The full data sheet should cover all possible operating conditions and will be in a format that gives:

(*a*) a brief description of the device and details of its intended application,

(*b*) the mechanical outline,

(*c*) a list of important parameter values,

(*d*) the absolute maximum ratings,

(both (*c*) and (*d*) are similar to the short-form data presentation)

(*e*) the complete electrical and parameter data

Transistor	n/p	Case	P_{tot}	I_c	V_{ceo}	h_{FE}	f_T
BC182L	NPN	T092	300 mW	200 mA	50 V	100–480	150 MHz
ZTX653	NPN	Eline	1.5 W	2 A	100 V	100	175 MHz

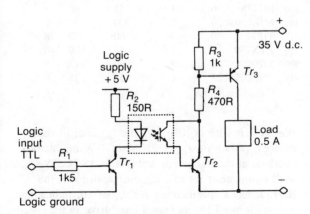

Fig. 2.15 Isolated power switch (BJT)

with typical, maximum and minimum values,

(f) useful characteristics, i.e. graphs showing how currents vary with applied voltage, how the output is affected by the input and so on.

Before going on to consider those parameters, ratings and characteristics that become important for specific devices under particular conditions, let us work through a typical selection procedure. The circuit for the example is shown in Fig. 2.15 and consists of a TTL controlled isolated power switch to enable a logic level 1 signal from, say, a micro-computer output port, to switch a 35 V d.c. supply to a resistive load of 500 mA. The operation is straightforward: a logic 1 state (2.4 V for TTL) supplies base current to Tr_1 via R_1. Tr_1 conducts and forces the LED inside the opto-isolator to send an infrared beam across the gap to the phototransistor. This transistor switches base current drive to Tr_2, forcing it to conduct and to pull base current out of Tr_3. The base current to Tr_3 is limited to about 50 mA by R_4. Tr_3 is switched hard on and connects nearly the full 35 V across the load. When the logic level input is 0 (i.e. 0.4 V or less) Tr_1, the opto-isolator, Tr_2 and Tr_3 are off so that there is zero volts across the load.

In this case, assume that we are considering suitable transistors for the Tr_3 position only. Let us work through the steps.

1 Defining the task

A pnp transistor operated as a switch in common emitter mode to connect a 35 V d.c. supply to a 500 mA resistive load. Ambient temperature range 0 °C to +35 °C.

2 Required parameter values

Since the transistor is being operated as a switch, there are three possible states — 'on', 'off' and the transition state.

(i) 'On' state parameters

I_c to I_B ratio taken as 10:1 (this is a usual rule-of-thumb for a transistor switch in CE mode to ensure that it fully saturates). At lower values of collector current ($I_c \leq 50$ mA), a 20:1 ratio is more often assumed. We can therefore state that Tr_3 should have an $h_{FE(min)}$ value of 20 at $I_c = 500$ mA.

The 'on' state voltage between collector and emitter, called $V_{CE(sat)}$, must be as low as possible to give efficient switching and to keep the switch power losses to a minimum.

$V_{CE(sat)}$ at $I_c = 500$ mA to be 1 V or less.

(ii) 'Off' state parameters

Leakage current between collector and emitter must be low. In this case, there is a resistor R_3 between base and emitter so the parameter of interest is I_{CER}.

I_{CER} at V_{CE} of 35 V to be less than 100 μA.

(iii) Transition state

When a BJT is switched from 'off' to 'on' the parameters of interest are:

t_d = delay time
and t_r = rise time

Normally these are specified as:

$t_{on} = t_d + t_r$.

When the BJT is switched from the fully 'on' state to the 'off' state, the turn 'off' delays are larger and are specified as:

t_s = storage time (caused by minority charge storage in the base region)

and t_f = fall time.

Thus, $t_{off} = t_s + t_f$.

For a medium current switch values of t_{on} might be 200 ns and t_{off} up to 1 μs.

Alternatively, since fast switching implies a high value of f_T, we could initially specify a value for this parameter.

Therefore, $f_{T(min)} = 10$ MHz.

Fast switching speed is important in ensuring that power losses during the on/off and off/on transitions are kept to a minimum. When the transistor is switching there will always be a finite time when it is half on with half the supply voltage (17.5 V in this case) across it. This is where the additional power loss arises.

3 A statement of the maximum expected values of current, voltage and power (all at 35 °C).

These are the absolute minimum values for the device; to allow for derating, the chosen device must have values well in excess of these.

$I_{c(max)} = 500$ mA   negative values
$V_{CER} = 35$ V   negative values
$P_C = 0.5$ W (assuming $V_{CE(sat)} = 1$ V).

4 Either t_{on} and $t_{off} \leq 1$ μs or $f_T = 10$ MHz min.

5 Mechanical limitations — no particular constraints.

From available short-form data, a list of possible pnp devices can be made up (NB: all currents and voltages are negative).

From Table 2.5 we can eliminate the following for the reasons given:

(e), on the limit for I_c;

(d), (f), (h) and (i), all with values of f_T below our specified 10 MHz. This, however, does not indicate that each of these devices would not function adequately in the circuit. They might, but we are eliminating them on grounds of low switching speed.

Table 2.5

	Type	P_{tot} (W)	I_c (A)	V_{CE} (V)	h_{FE}	f_T (MHz)
(a)	BC461	1	2 (peak)	60	40	50
(b)	BD132	15	3	45	20	60
(c)	BD136	12.5	1.5	45	40	75
(d)	BD438	36	4	45	40	3
(e)	MJE350	20	0.5	300	30	n.q.
(f)	TIP32A	40	3	60	10	8
(g)	ZTX750	1.5	2	45	100	140
(h)	TIP30A	30	3	60	15	3
(i)	PNP3054	25	4	55	25	0.8

We are left with (a), (b), (c) and (g) and, of these devices, (a) with a P_{tot} at 25 °C of 1 W might well overheat at the maximum ambient of 35 °C. We shall eliminate it for this reason. Device (b), the BD132, has a specification for h_{FE} of 20, indicating a possible need for increased base drive in the circuit. Thus, we are left with a choice between (c) the BD136, and (g) the ZTX750. The full data sheets of these will have to be examined before the final decision is made. However, so far we have not considered other constraints such as *availability*, *cost* and even the *preference* for certain suppliers within an organisation. Quite often these may force the designer either to modify his design to suit an available device, or to continue his search for the best fit component among a preferred range.

From a study of the full data sheets for the BD136 and the ZTX750, the following information can be extracted (see Table 2.6).

For both transistors, I_{CBO} (the collector base leakage current) is the only leakage parameter quoted.

In practice, I_{CER} is less than I_{CEO}, where

$$I_{CEO} = I_{CBO} (1 + h_{FE})$$

For the two transistors, I_{CER} would therefore be less than 10 μA, a value well within that required.

It follows from a close study of the data that the ZTX750 would be a suitable choice for the application. It is designed for this sort of task, has a high value of h_{FE}, a low $V_{CE(sat)}$ and reasonable switching performance. But one last point concerning its power dissipation and the effect on junction temperature at 35 °C ambient needs to be checked.

At 25 °C ambient $V_{CE(sat)} = -0.3$ V at $I_c = -\frac{1}{2}$ A
Therefore $P_c \approx 150$ mW

Table 2.6

Parameter/rating	BD136	ZTX750
h_{FE}	50 min at $I_c = -500$ mA	100 min at $I_c = -0.5$ A
$V_{CE(sat)}$	-0.5 V at $I_c = -500$ mA	-0.3 V at $I_c = -1$ A, $I_B = 0.1$ A
I_{CBO}	-100 nA at -30 V(V_{CB})	-100 nA at -45 V(V_{CB})
t_{on}	Not quoted	40 ns } $I_c = -500$ mA
t_{off}	$f_T = 50$ MHz(min) at $I_c = -500$ mA	450 ns } $V_{CC} = -10$ V
$V_{(BR)CEO}$	-45 V	-45 V
P_c	8 W	1.5 W at $T_{amb} = 25$ °C, derate by 5.7 mW °C^{-1}
$R_{Th(j\text{-}amb)}$	100 °C W^{-1}	175 °C W^{-1}

Allowing for a rise in $V_{CE(sat)}$ with temperature to, say, -0.4 V at 35 °C,

$$P_c \text{ at } 35 °C \approx 200 \text{ mW}$$

The junction temperature at 35 °C will be given by:

$$T_j = T_{amb} + R_{\theta(j\text{-}amb)}P_c$$
$$= 35 + 175 \times 0.2$$

Therefore, $T_j = 70$ °C.

At this junction temperature the ZTX750 could dissipate approximately 1.8 W, showing that there is no need for any heat sink to be provided.

2.8 FIELD EFFECT TRANSISTORS

An alternative arrangement for switching the 35 V d.c. supply to the 500 mA load using a powerFET is shown in Fig. 2.16. In this case, a suitable P channel powerFET has to be selected. The circuit is simpler in design since the voltage drive to the

powerFET can be derived from a resistor connected in the collector circuit of the phototransistor. When a logic 1 is applied at the input, the LED and phototransistor conduct, current is drawn through R_3 and R_4 and an approximate 12 V level is developed across R_4. This is applied to the gate of F_1 and the powerFET is forced to switch hard on to connect the 35 V d.c. to the load.

1 The parameters of interest are:

(i) For the 'on' state

$V_{GS(th)}$: the value of gate to source threshold voltage that will initiate drain current

g_{fs} : the forward conductance of the powerFET measured in siemens (or A/V) ($g_{fs} = I_d/V_{gs}$)

$R_{DS(on)}$: the drain to source resistance when the FET is conducting.

In this case, the requirements are:

$V_{GS(th)}$: not greater than -4 V
g_{fs} : not less than 100 mS
$R_{DS(on)}$: not greater than 5 Ω

(ii) For the 'off' state
Leakage current specified by I_{DSS}, the zero gate voltage drain current.

I_{DSS} not greater than 1000 μA

(Note that the leakage of a powerFET is sometimes higher than that of an equivalent BJT.)

(iii) Transition state
Specified by turn on and turn off delay times. These have values that are much lower than a BJT switch.

t_{on} and t_{off} both better than 200 ns.

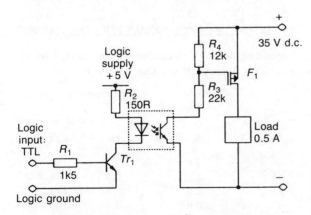

Fig. 2.16 Isolated power switch (powerMOSFET)

2 The maximum expected values of current, voltage and power are:

$$I_D : 500 \text{ mA}$$
$$V_{DS} : 35 \text{ V}$$
$$P_D : 1.5 \text{ W}$$

In this case, the power dissipated by the FET is given by:

$$P_D = I_d^2 R_{DS(on)}$$

and will therefore have a typical value of 1.25 W if $R_{DS(on)}$ is 5 Ω. It would be best to select a powerFET with a value of $R_{DS(on)}$ lower than this.

P-channel powerFETs are not as readily available as n-channel types which means that there is a limited set of suitable devices to choose from for the F_1 position. Some of the possibles, presented in short-form format, are given in Table 2.7. (NB: all voltages and currents are negative.)

Of these, (c), the IRF9513, seems the best choice. Both (a) and (d) have been eliminated for the reason that they have a much higher power rating than is required, and (b) for the opposite reason (i.e. its power rating and $I_{d(max)}$ values are low). Device (e) has a relatively high value of $R_{DS(on)}$ which would entail a dissipation in the circuit of nearly 1.7 W and its value of g_{fs} is also much lower than the other devices. Thus, (e) is also eliminated.

From the full data sheet on the IRF9513, the following information is obtained for the various stages.

(i) For the 'on' state
At $I_D = 500$ mA, $g_{fs} \approx 0.6$ S ($T_j = 125$ °C), and $V_{GS(th)} = -4$ V.

Thus, the drive signal of -12 V is more than adequate to ensure that the FET fully switches on.
$R_{DS(on)}$ is quoted as 1 Ω at $I_d = 500$ mA.

But we need to check that the value of $R_{DS(on)}$ does not rise excessively and cause thermal runaway at high junction temperatures. This is always a possibility when a powerFET is being used as a switch because $R_{DS(on)}$ has a positive temperature coefficient. The ambient temperature is 35 °C max (see original specification) and the IRF9513 has a quoted junction to ambient thermal resistance of 80 °C W^{-1}. (This is the no-heat-sink condition.)

Assuming $P_D = 1$ W

$$T_j = 35 + 80 = 115 \text{ °C}$$

where T_j is junction temperature.
From the data sheet $R_{DS(on)}$ at $T_j = 150$ °C is 1.5 Ω. Thus, $P_D = I_d^2 . R_{DS(on)} = 375$ mW.

This shows that the IRF9513 can be operated without a heat sink and that there is no danger of a thermal runaway situation. In fact the FET's junction temperature will be almost 50 °C lower than the 115 °C estimated above.

(ii) For the 'off' state
BV_{DSS}, the drain to source breakdown voltage, is quoted as -60 V at $V_{GS} = 0$ V. Therefore, the FET will easily withstand the 35 V between drain and source.

$$I_{DSS} = 1 \text{ mA max at } V_{DS} = 48 \text{ V and } V_{GS} = 0 \text{ V}.$$

Therefore, in the off state the FET will dissipate only 35 mW.

(iii) Transition state

$$t_{on} = 90 \text{ ns } (V_{DD} = -50 \text{ V}, I_d = 1.5 \text{ A})$$
$$t_{off} = 80 \text{ ns } (V_{DD} = 50 \text{ V}, I_d = -1.5 \text{ A})$$

The fast switching speed is another of the advantages that the powerFET has over the BJT.

2.9 DISCRETE DEVICE PARAMETERS AND RATINGS

Depending on the application, only a selected set of a device's parameters become important to the

Table 2.7

	Type no.	P_D (W)	I_D (A)	V_{DDS} (V)	$V_{GS(th)}$ (V)	$R_{DS(on)}$ (Ω)	g_{fs}	t_{on}/t_{off} (ns)
(a)	MTM8P08	75	8	80	4	0.4	2	150
(b)	IRFD9110	1	0.7	100	4	1.2	0.8	50
(c)	IRF9513	20	2.5	60	4	1.6	1.1	130
(d)	IRF9520	40	6	60	4	0.6	2	200
(e)	BD512	10	1.5	60	1.7	6.5	0.15	100

Table 2.8 Parameters and ratings for discrete semiconductors

Signal diodes	Power diodes (rectifiers)	Zener and regulator diodes	Bipolar transistors	JFETs	PowerFETs	Thyristors
V_F forward	V_F (I_F)	V_Z (I_Z)	h_{FE} d.c. current gain (I_C, V_{CE})	$V_{DS(max)}$	$V_{DS(max)}$	$I_{T(av)}$
$I_{F(av)}$ average forward current	$I_{F(av)}$	r_Z slope resistance (I_Z)	h_{fe} small signal current gain (I_C, V_{CE})	V_p pinch off voltage	$I_{D(max)}$	I_{TSM} peak forward current (t)
I_R reverse leakage current (V_R)	I_{FSM} peak forward current (t)	Temperature coefficient of I_Z in mV $°C^{-1}$	$I_{C(max)}$	I_{DSS} drain current with $V_{GS} = 0$ V	$V_{GS(th)}$ threshold voltage at which drain/current is initiated (I_D)	V_{GT} gate trigger voltage
V_{RRM} peak reverse voltage	I_R (V_R)	P_{tot}	V_{CEQ} maximum collector emitter voltage base open	Y_{fs} or g_m	Y_{fs} or g_m	I_{GT} gate trigger current
T_{rr} reverse recovery time (I_F)	V_{RRM}		I_C leakage current with emitter open		$R_{DS(on)}$	P_{tot}
	P_{tot}		$V_{CE(sat)}$	P_{tot}	Drain source on resistance	
			(I_C:I_B = 10:1) f_T(I_C, V_{CE}) P_{tot}		P_{tot}	

Given conditions are shown in brackets. In all cases temperature is assumed to be 25 °C.

designer. From the previous sections we can see that when a transistor is operated as a switch the parameters of interest are:

$$V_{CE(sat)}, h_{FE}, I_{CER}, BV_{CER}, t_{off} \text{ and } P_c$$

Whereas if the device is to be used as a linear amplifier, parameters such as:

$$h_{fe}, h_{ie}, f_T, N \text{ (noise figure) and } C_{TC} \text{ (collector capacitance)}$$

will be more important.

Some of the most important parameters and ratings for various devices are shown in Table 2.8. In each case the given conditions of frequency, current, voltage and temperature are quoted.

Some indication concerning the choice of devices for linear applications can be seen from the circuit given in Fig. 2.17. This is an audio frequency preamplifier formed around a d.c. coupled pair of transistors. Each stage has local series negative feedback provided by the undecoupled emitter resistors R_3 and R_7 which gives the circuit an overall

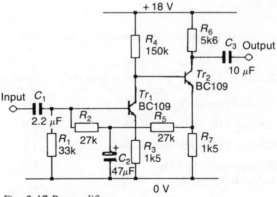

Fig. 2.17 Preamplifier

voltage gain of approximately 300 (i.e. 50 dB). In this case we shall consider the performance parameters required for the transistor used in the Tr_1 position. In order of importance, these are:

(a) a high value of h_{fe} at low values of d.c. collector current; in the circuit the I_c for Tr_1 is about 100 μA;

(b) a noise figure that is as low as possible;

(c) a bandwidth of 10 Hz to 30 kHz;

(d) a $V_{CE(max)}$ of 18 V.

Note that in this application parameters and ratings such as f_T, $V_{CE(sat)}$, I_{CER} and P_{tot} are not relevant.

N-p-n transistors which would be suitable for the Tr_1 position are:

BC109C : $h_{fe} = 100$ at $I_c = 10$ μA,
$N = 4$ dB max, 30 Hz-15 kHz
and BC549 : $h_{fe} = 150$ at $I_c = 10$ μA,
$N = 4$ dB max, 30 Hz-15 kHz.

2.10 SELECTING ICs

Choosing ICs for a design, particularly the digital types, may appear to be a completely different task to that of selecting a discrete component. It is somewhat different, for in many cases the designer must decide on a particular family of ICs suitable for the whole design, not just on one IC. But the approach to the selection is much the same. The task the ICs are required to perform has to be defined, the necessary values of important parameters must be specified and notes made of maximum ratings.

For digital ICs the important parameters are going to be:

1 noise margin,
2 propagation delay time,
3 power dissipation (usually quoted per gate) and possibly also fan-out and logic levels.

In any random logic system design, the choice has to be from the standard logic families of TTL, CMOS and ECL with the power-to-speed trade off being the dominant factor. ECL, which is one of the fastest logic families available, will only be used in specialised high speed designs, which leaves the logic designer in all other cases to decide between TTL (with all its variants) and CMOS. Here we are considering relatively low volume production. An alternative design solution could be to implement the random logic in a PLA (Programmable Logic Array) or in a custom made IC. However, for small production quantities, where several logic ICs must be used, the choice is between TTL and CMOS. CMOS has good noise immunity, a lower static power consumption than TTL and the ability to work with a wide power supply range. TTL, on the other hand, has generally higher speed, a higher tolerance to current-injected noise (because its output impedance is low) and better drive capability. The main features of the various logic types are given in Table 2.9. Note that 74HC is a CMOS version TTL.

There are no absolute rules concerning the specification of TTL or CMOS for a design; a grey area

Table 2.9 Performance characteristics of logic families

Family	Propagation delay time (ns)	Noise immunity	Fan-out	Power dissipation per gate	Power supply (V)
Standard TTL 54/74	10	1 V	10	10 mW	5 ± 0.25
Schottky TTL 54S/74S	3	1 V	10	19 mW	5 ± 0.25
Schottky TTL 54LS/74LS	9.5	1 V	20	2 mW	5 ± 0.25
Advanced Schottky TTL 54AS/74LS	1.5	1 V	10	20 mW	5 ± 0.25
Advanced low power Schottky TTL	4 (3 with buffer output)	1 V	20	1 mW (2 mW with buffer output)	5 ± 0.25
ECL 10100/10200	2/1.5	400 mV	30	40 mW	−5.2
CMOS 4000B series	40 (5 V) 20 (10 V) 15 (15 V)	45% of supply	50	10 nW static 1 mW Hz^{-1}	5−15
High speed CMOS 74HC 74HCT	8	45% of supply	50	27 nW	2−6

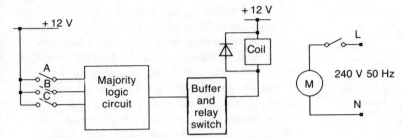

Fig. 2.18 Majority logic circuit

exists between them. CMOS would be an obvious choice for a relatively low speed system required to work in an electrically noisy environment (a power supply of 15 V would give almost 7 volts of noise margin). But normally the choice between the logic families is not as clear cut as this.

There is no reason either why a design should not use a mix of TTL and CMOS ICs, but extra care over interfacing between the different types would be necessary.

As an example of the specification of logic ICs, let us consider the following problem:

A small engineering works requires a fan to be operated if a *majority* of three switch inputs to a circuit are at a high state. The switches are single pole types which connect to a +12 V supply and the fan is a mains operated motor which is to be isolated from the logic by an electromagnetic relay. An outline of the circuit is shown in Fig. 2.18.

The Boolean expression for the logic, which can be readily proved by truth table and minimisation techniques, is:

$$F = A \cdot B + A \cdot C + B \cdot C$$

For a NAND only solution, De Morgan's rule $(\overline{A + B} = \overline{A} \cdot \overline{B})$ can be used as follows:

$$\overline{F} = \overline{A \cdot B + AC + BC}$$

Therefore, $F = \overline{\overline{A \cdot B} \cdot \overline{A \cdot C} \cdot \overline{B \cdot C}}$.

The two logic circuits, both of which will give a logic 1 output if a majority of the inputs are at 1, are shown in Fig. 2.19.

Suppose the designer decided initially to implement the logic using TTL. At first sight he would need one 7400 (a quad 2-input NAND IC) and a 7410 (a triple 3-input NAND IC), but he would then encounter some problems.

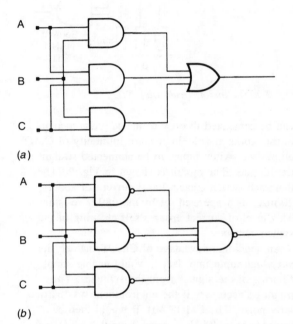

(a)

(b)

Fig. 2.19 (a) Logic circuit using AND—OR gates;
(b) Logic circuit using NAND gates only

The TTL specification has:

V_{CC} (supply voltage) 4.75 Vmin, 5.25 Vmax.
V_{IH} (input voltage) 5.5 Vmax.

This means that the TTL ICs require a 5 V regulator supplied from the +12 V and that the input signals from the switches must be reduced to below 5.5 V. One method is outlined in Fig. 2.20 where resistors are used to reduce the input level and the 7400 IC has been replaced by a 74132 which has Schmitt type NAND gates. However, before that stage was reached the designer would either attempt to change the switch supply to +5 V by negotiating with the factory staff, or turn to a CMOS logic to perform the task. The 4000 series CMOS would be ideal for the design since the supply rail to the logic

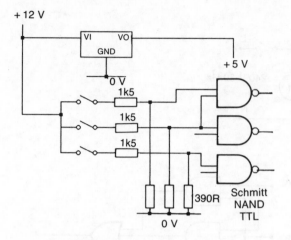

Fig. 2.20 Outline of circuit using TTL

can be connected directly to the 12 volts available in the works and the high noise immunity of CMOS allows the switch inputs to be connected straight to the IC pins. The circuit is shown in Fig. 2.21. Note that each switch contact has a current of about 20 mA when operated set by the 680 Ω resistor. This level of current ensures self-cleaning of the switch contacts.

An additional advantage of CMOS, namely its very high input impedance, would enable simple filtering of the signals from the switches. This might be necessary if the environment was particularly noisy. The CMOS 4011B would then be replaced by a 4093B, a quad 2-input NAND Schmitt IC.

Since CMOS outputs can only source or sink a relatively low output current (typically 1.1 mA at

$V_{DD} = 10$ V and T_{amb}), a high gain interface is used between the MOS output and the relay. In this case a ZTX600B Darlington ($P_{tot} = 2.5$ W) has been specified with the 15 kΩ resistor limiting the output current from the 4023B chip to just under 1 mA.

One last point: with CMOS all unused inputs must either be connected to 0 V, V_{DD} or to another input. In this case, the unused NAND gate in the 4011B and the two 3-input NAND gates in the 4023B must be disabled by connecting their inputs to 0 V.

The term *linear IC* (also called *analog IC* by many manufacturers) covers components such as op-amps, comparators, phase locked loops, ADCs, DACs, regulator chips and so on. The selection process in most cases follows the procedure outlined in section 2.8 and, without detailing the various parameters for all possible devices, the process will be illustrated for two of the more commonly used linear ICs, the op-amp and the ADC. The circuit is shown in Fig. 2.22 and consists of a non-inverting amplifier with a voltage gain of approximately 50 linking the signal from a low frequency low-level sensor to the input of an ADC. The sensor gives an output in the range 1 to 50 mV and, since the ADC has 8 bits, one LSB change referred to the op-amp input is 195 μV.

First, let us consider the important parameters concerning op-amps. These are:

A_{vol} : the open loop differential voltage gain
R_{in} : the output resistance under open loop conditions
R_o : output resistance
V_{io} : the input offset voltage

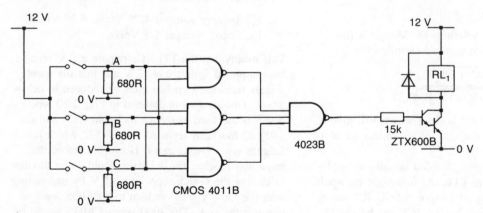

Fig. 2.21 The full logic circuit using CMOS gates

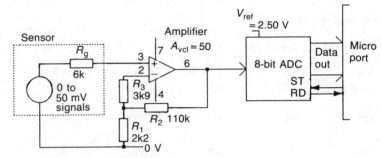

Fig. 2.22 Sensor interface circuit

dV_{io}/dT : the temperature coefficient of input offset voltage

Ib : the input bias current (the average value of $Ib+$ and $Ib-$)

I_{io} : the input offset current (the difference between $Ib+$ and $Ib-$)

dI_{io}/dT : the temperature coefficient of input offset current

CMRR (common mode rejection ratio) : the ratio of differential to common mode voltage gain

PSRR (power supply rejection ratio) : the ratio of the change in V_{io} to power supply voltage change

Slew rate : the average time rate of change of the output signal for a step input under closed loop unity gain conditions.

Values of these parameters for a few popular op-amps are given in Table 2.10.

For the circuit in question, the most important parameters to be specified for the op-amp are the input offsets (V_{io} and I_{io}) and the input offset temperature coefficients dV_{io}/dT and dI_{io}/dT. These must all be as low as possible to avoid errors in the amplification of the sensor signal. Parameters such as slew rate and CMRR are of secondary importance in this case.

Assume that the specification requires:

(a) an offset at 25 °C ambient that is less than LSB referred to the input, i.e. less than 97.5 μV,

(b) a drift with temperature, referred to the input, of less than 0.5% per °C, i.e. less than 9.75 μV °C^{-1}.

The d.c. error introduced by V_{io} and I_{io} at the input is given by:

$$\text{offset error} = V_{io} + I_{io}.Rg \text{ volts}$$

and the drift error with temperature is given by:

$$\text{drift error} = dV_{io}/dT + (dI_{io}/dT).Rg \text{ V } °C^{-1}$$

For a 741 V_{io} = 1 mV

I_{io} = 20 nA
dv_{io}/dT = 5 μV °C^{-1}
dI_{io}/dT = 0.5 nA °C^{-1}

Thus, offset error = 1.12 mV, a value well outside the specified 97.5 μV. This would make it essential to include some offset nulling components in the circuit.

Drift error = 8 μV °C^{-1}. This is just within the specified 9.75 μV °C^{-1}, but results in an error of 4.1% per °C per 1 LSB step.

Obviously an op-amp with much lower values of offsets and offset drifts is required. Consider the use of an OP-07. For this op-amp the parameter values are:

V_{io} = 0.06 mV I_{io} = 0.8 nA
dV_{io}/dT = 0.5 μV °C^{-1}
dI_{io}/dT = 12 pA °C^{-1}

Thus, offset error = 64.8 μV, which is well within the specified value, and offset drift with temperature = 0.572 μV °C^{-1}. An error of only 0.3% per °C per 1 LSB step. Even if the ambient temperature changed by 40 °C, the error would only be 12% of one LSB step. The OP-07 is therefore a good choice for applications requiring low drift and low offset.

The features and parameters of an ADC are described by:

(i) *Input span:* the range of analog input values from 0 V to $+V$ that result in the minimum and maximum digital output.

(ii) *Resolution:* the number of bits (n) used in the conversion.

(iii) *Conversion time 't_c'* (measured in microseconds): the time between the 'start

Table 2.10 Specifications for some commonly used op-amps

	Bipolar 741	*Bipolar 741S*	*Bipolar 531*	*MOSFET 3130*	*JFET 351*	*Op-07*
Supply voltage range (V)	± 3 ± 18	± 5 ± 18	± 5 ± 22	± 5 ± 8	± 5 ± 18	± 3 ± 18
Max. power dissipation (mW)	500	625	300	630	500	500
Max. differential input voltage (V)	30	30	15	± 8	± 30	± 30
Max. input voltage, either input to 0 V	15 V	15 V	15 V	$\pm V$	$\pm V$	± 22 V
Open-loop gain A_{vol} (dB)	106	100	96	110	110	132
Input resistance (Ω)	2 MΩ	1 MΩ	20 MΩ	1.5×10^{12} Ω	10^{12} Ω	33 MΩ
Input bias current	80 nA	200 nA	400 nA	5 pA	50 pA	2.2 nA
Input offset current I_{io}	20 nA	30 nA	50 nA	0.5 pA	25 pA	0.8 nA
Input offset voltage V_{io} (mV)	1	2	2	8	5	0.06
Temp. coeff. of input offset voltage dV_{io}/dT	5 μV °C^{-1}	3 μV °C^{-1}	—	10 μV °C^{-1}	10 μV °C^{-1}	0.5 μV °C^{-1}
Temp. coeff. of input offset current dI_{io}/dT	0.5 nA °C^{-1}	0.5 nA °C^{-1}	0.6 nA °C^{-1}	Doubles for every 20 °C rise	Doubles for every 20 °C rise	12 pA °C^{-1}
CMRR (dB)	90	90	100	80	100	120
PSRR (μV V^{-1})	30	10	10	300	30	0.16
Output voltage swing (V)	± 13	± 13	± 15	± 6.5	± 13.5	± 13
Frequency compensation	Int.	Int.	Ext.	Ext.	Int.	Int.
Slew rate (V μs^{-1})	0.5	20	35	10	13	0.17

conversion' command being given to the ADC and the instant that valid digital data are presented at the ADC's output.

(iv) *Linearity:* the amount of deviation from a straight line transfer characteristic.

(v) *Reference voltage V_{ref}*: usually provided internally.

(vi) *Clock frequency.*

For most applications the key parameters are *conversion time*, since t_c will decide the speed at which samples of the analog input can be taken, and *resolution*. For a reasonable representation of the analog in digital form many bits are required. The more bits used in the conversion process, the finer will be the resolution and the closer the accuracy. For example:

n	Resolution
6	1.5625% (1 part in 64)
8	0.3906% (1 part in 256)
10	0.0976% (1 part in 1024)
12	0.0244% (1 part in 4096)

Let us assume that in this case the specification requires:

Resolution : better than 0.5% (1 part in 200)
Conversion time t_c : 100 μs
Input span : 0–2.5 V
Linearity : 0.5 LSB

An 8-bit ADC is necessary and the available types are:

- ramp and counter
- tracking
- successive approximation
- flash.

The two extremes in speed performance result from using either the ramp and counter, where the conversion time might be as high as several milliseconds, or the flash ADC. The latter is a relatively high cost, ultra fast converter with nanosecond conversion time. The choice is thus narrowed to either the tracking or successive approximation types.

The successive approximation method would be more suitable in this case since the system is not required to follow high frequency signals. Eight-bit ADCs which fit the specification are the GEC Plessey ZN 427E-8 and ZN 448E, both of which are designed to easily interface with a microprocessor.

ZN 427E-8 specification

Resolution : 8 bits
Conversion time : 10 μs max (depends on external clock frequency)
Linearity : 0.5 LSB (typ)
Internal reference V_{ref} : 2.55 V ± 5 mV
V_{refTC} : 50 ppm °C^{-1}

ZN 448 specification

Resolution : 8 bits
Conversion time : 9 μs (internal clock)
Linearity : 0.5 LSB (typ)
Internal reference V_{ref} : 2.55 V ± 5 mV
V_{refTC} : 50 ppm °C^{-1}
On-chip clock frequency : 1 MHz

Interfacing directly to the system bus is allowed, since both ADC chips have a built-in tri-state output buffer which can be enabled by a *read* signal.

2.11 DESIGN EXERCISES

1 A potential divider using two resistors is shown in Fig. 2.23. If the input voltage is 20 V d.c., R_1 is 18 kΩ and the required output is 6 V, suggest the n.p.v. (E24 series) for R_2. Then

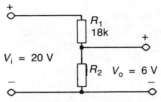

Fig. 2.23 Potential divider

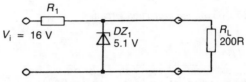

Fig. 2.24 Regulator

calculate the actual output voltage with this resistor value in circuit.

2 For the simple voltage regulator circuit shown in Fig. 2.24, DZ_1 is a 5.1 V Zener diode with its current I_z set to 5 mA when the load R_L is connected. Calculate the value and power rating for R_1 taking into consideration an output short-circuit condition. What type of resistor should be specified?

3 A CMOS 4047B chip is connected in astable mode with $C_T = 2.2$ nF (see Fig. 2.24). The required frequency is 6 kHz nominal. Suggest the n.p.v. for R_T and estimate the error in f_o caused by using this fixed value of resistance.

4 A silvered mica capacitor of 2.2 nF is used for C_T in the oscillator of question 3. These types of capacitor have the following specifications:

Selection tolerance : $\pm 1\%$
Temperature coefficient : +35 ppm °C^{-1}

Assuming all other temperature effects are ignored what drift could occur, due to this capacitor, for a 20 °C change in ambient temperature?

5 A 6 VA miniature mains transformer intended for pcb mounting has two equally rated 15 V secondary windings. The regulation is quoted as 15%. Determine

(a) the off-load secondary voltage,
(b) the rated secondary current.

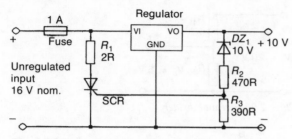

Fig. 2.25 Overvoltage protection circuit

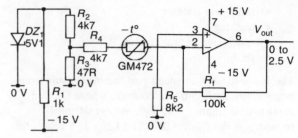

Fig. 2.26 Temperature sensing circuit

Table 2.11

Device no.	V_{DRM} (V)	V_{RRM} (V)	$I_{T(av)}$ (A)	I_{GT} (mA)	V_{GT} (V)
C103YY	60	60	0.32	0.2	0.8
BTX18-400	400	500	1.0	5	2
BT105	500	700	1.0	50	3.5
C106	400	400	2.55	0.2	0.8
2N4443	400	400	5.1	30	1.5
2N4444	600	600	5.1	30	1.5
BTY79-400R	400	400	6.4	30	3
BTY79-800R	800	800	6.4	30	3
THY500-12	500	500	12	60	3
THY800-12	800	800	12	60	3
THY1200-12	1200	1200	12	60	3
THY500-26	500	500	26	40	3
THY800-26	800	800	26	40	3
THY500-40	500	500	40	60	2.5

6 Selection of a thyristor for a crowbar circuit (see Fig. 2.25). This crowbar is designed to protect a sensitive load on a pcb from an over-voltage on the power supply output leads. The d.c. voltage on the power supply output is normally 10 V ± 100 mV, but if a fault condition in the power supply causes this voltage to rise above 12 V, the thyristor must conduct and blow the fuse.

Work through the selection process for the thyristor and, from the devices listed in Table 2.11, choose a *best fit* device. Give reasons for rejecting the other devices.

7 Selection of an op-amp and reference device for a temperature sensing circuit (Fig. 2.26). In this example, a thermistor with resistance R_T of 4700 Ω at 25 °C is connected in the input lead of an inverting amplifier. The output of the amplifier is given by:

$$V_o = V_{in} \frac{R_f}{R_T + R_4}$$

With this connection method the linearity of the output voltage with temperature over a limited range is good.

State the parameters that would be important for both the 5 V reference device and the op-amp. Support your statements with estimates of errors caused by changes in ambient temperature assuming that the temperature being measured by the thermistor remains constant. Ambient temperature changes are not more than 10 °C. The thermistor has a resistance of 1100 Ω at 70 °C. Errors should be less than 0.25 °C total.

3 DESIGNING D.C. POWER SUPPLIES

3.1 POWER SUPPLY FEATURES

All electronic instruments and systems need stable sources of d.c. power and it follows that the design or specification of the power unit itself needs careful consideration if the whole system is to operate satisfactorily. In the majority of cases, the power is derived from the single phase a.c. mains supply and the power unit has to be designed to accept the 240 V 50 Hz (or 110 V 60 Hz) a.c. mains input and, after rectification, smoothing and regulation, deliver the required d.c. output voltages to the loads. It is the design of such power supplies that is described in this chapter.

The characteristics of a power unit and the way in which the d.c. power is distributed to the various parts of a system have a direct effect on system performance. Symptoms such as excess noise, over-heating, crosstalk between circuits and oscillations are typical of a poorly designed or underspecified power unit. The design of the power supply is not something to be undertaken as a last step. It is an integral and vital part of the system and its design should be considered very early on in the overall plan, and not just as an *add on* to the system.

ESSENTIAL FEATURES OF A REGULATED POWER SUPPLY

The important features of the type of power unit being considered here are:

- isolation from the a.c. mains supply,
- efficiency,
- regulation (at the load),
- noise and ripple,
- transient response,
- overload and overvoltage protection,
- stability.

A typical specification for a bench power supply is given in Table 3.1. Let's briefly consider each of these features.

Isolation

For personal safety and system protection it is essential that the d.c. outputs are isolated from the mains supply. In the most basic, and usual, arrangement a transformer provides this function. The primary side must be fitted with a suitably rated

Table 3.1 Triple output power supply specification

Mains input:	220–240 V, 50–400 Hz a.c. 110–115 V versions also available
Outputs:	5 V at 1 A and ±15 V at 200 mA
Line regulation:	Less than 0.05% + 2 mV output change for a ±10% mains change
Load regulation:	Less than 0.1% + 5 mV (5 V output) Less than 0.02% + 2 mV (±15 V output) (zero to full load)
Ripple and noise:	At full load (Δf = 80 kHz) Less than 2 mV pk–pk (5 V output and ±15 V output)
Transient recovery time:	Less than 300 μs typical for output to recover within 50 mV following a step full load change of 1 μs rise time
Output impedance:	Less than 0.5 Ω at 100 kHz
Temperature coefficient:	0.02% per °C
Maximum ambient temp:	40°C (derate linearly to 60°C)
Overload protection:	Foldback current limiting on all outputs Overvoltage protection on 5 V with trip set to 7 V

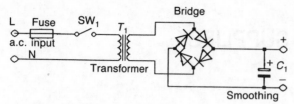

Fig. 3.1 Unregulated power supply

fuse and an on/off switch, both of which must be wired in the live lead (see Fig. 3.1).

Efficiency

Efficiency is the ratio of output power to input power and is given by:

$$\eta = \frac{\text{Power taken by load}}{\text{a.c. power input}} \times 100\%$$

The highest possible efficiency is normally desirable since the difference between the input and output power has to be dissipated as heat by the power unit. A low efficiency unit will require a larger than normal heat-sink, additional space or even a fan to get rid of this unwanted heat. Linear regulators have efficiencies in the range 60% to 70% which means, for example, that a linear design supplying 30 W (say 10 V at 3 A) might need to dissipate 20 W itself (see Fig. 3.2). Switch mode power units (SMPU) are much more efficient, with typical values being in the range 80% to 95%. Thus, an SMPU takes up much less space than an equivalent linear regulator and saves expenditure on heat sinks.

Regulation

Regulation refers to the power unit's ability to hold its output voltage constant irrespective of changes both in load current and in supply voltage. These

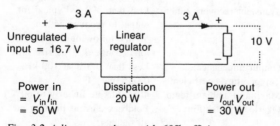

Fig. 3.2 A linear regulator with 60% efficiency

are referred to as *load regulation* and *line regulation* where:

Load regulation

$$= \frac{V_o \text{ (off-load)} - V_o \text{ (full load)}}{V_o \text{ (off-load)}} \times 100\%$$

and

Line regulation

$$= \Delta V_o \text{ (full load) per volt change in supply.}$$

A decent medium power regulator should have a load regulation performance of better than 0.1% and a line regulation of, say, better than 1 mV V^{-1}.

Noise and ripple

Full wave and bridge rectification produces a ripple frequency of $2f_s$, where f_s is the supply frequency. Thus some ripple at 100 Hz (or 120 Hz for units connected to 60 Hz supplies) will always appear at the output of a mains driven power supply, the amplitude of this ripple increasing with load current. In addition, components in the regulator will generate high frequency noise which will also appear across the load. Noise and ripple amplitude should be typically less than a few millivolts at the specified value of load current.

Transient response

Transient response refers to the power unit's ability to react to rapidly changing load conditions. Suppose the load on a power supply is switched suddenly from 1 A to 3 A; a power supply regulator cannot immediately compensate for this change and its output voltage must fall briefly. The speed with which it recovers, usually to within some tens of millivolts of its original value, is called the *transient response*. Power supplies for digital logic therefore reuqire a low value in this parameter and additional decoupling capacitors at the point of load.

Protection circuits

All power units require protection from an overload or short-circuit condition. This is referred to as a

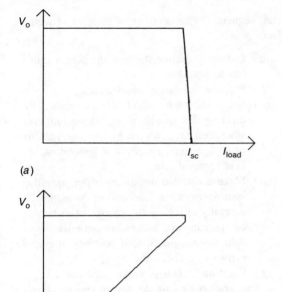

(a)

(b)

Fig. 3.3 (a) Simple current limit characteristics;
(b) Foldback current limit characteristics

current limit, which can have either a simple limiting characteristic (Fig. 3.3(a)) or preferably a foldback characteristic (Fig. 3.3(b)). The simple limit can be effective for low power units (less than 10 W), but it must be realised that the full voltage is across the power supply under short-circuit conditions. The power unit's components must be capable of dissipating this power. Take the example of a linear regulator with $V_{in} = 12$ V, $V_o = 9$ V and a current limit set to 2 A (see Fig. 3.4(a)). Under normal operating conditions with the load current at, say, 1.8 A the regulator will be dissipating 5.4 W.

Normal regulator internal dissipation
$$= (V_{in} - V_o)I_L \text{ W}$$
$$= (12 - 9) \times 1.8$$
$$= 5.4 \text{ W}$$

When the output is shorted, and the limit operates, the power being dissipated by the regulator rises to 24 W (see Fig. 3.4(b)).

Short-circuit regulator dissipation
$$\approx V_{in}I_{sc} \text{ W}$$
$$= 12 \times 2$$
$$= 24 \text{ W}$$

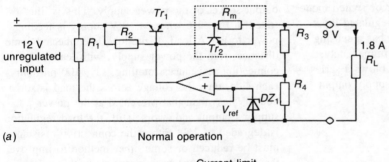

(a)   Normal operation

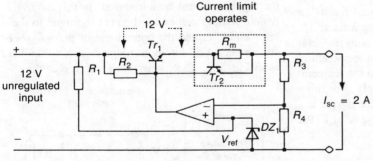

(b)   Short circuited output

Fig. 3.4 (a) Series element (Tr$_1$) dissipation ≈ 5.4 W; (b) Series element dissipation with output shorted is ≈24 W

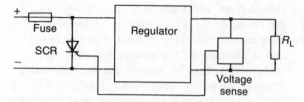

Fig. 3.5 Overvoltage protection circuit (crowbar)

The series element has to be fitted on a heat sink large enough to take care of this overload condition and this can take up unnecessary space. On the other hand, the foldback current limit, once tripped, will switch the power unit into a condition where it will only supply a very restricted value of current or, in some cases, no current at all. The power loss caused by a short circuit is then only a fraction of the normal dissipation; the penalty of a slightly more complicated trip circuit is clearly worth it.

A current trip is used to prevent damage to the power supply from an overload, and also limits the current that can be supplied to the load. Another important feature is an overvoltage protection circuit (usually called a *crowbar*) which prevents a fault condition in the power unit from placing a damaging voltage across load devices. This could occur if a short in the series element (linear or switch mode type) of the unit forced the full unregulated input voltage across the load. A crowbar has a sensing circuit that detects an overvoltage, immediately forces the voltage to zero and then blows a series fuse to fully disconnect the power supply output from the load (see Fig. 3.5).

STABILITY

Stability is any change of output voltage from its set value, while the power unit is supplying a fixed load current, over a period of time or with temperature. In the short term, the effects with temperature will predominate and are mostly due to the temperature characteristic of the reference supply. For this reason, the choice of a suitable reference device is very important. This will be further discussed in the design examples later in this chapter.

3.2 DESIGNING POWER SUPPLIES

As with any other electronic circuit design the task is best carried out by working through a proper

design sequence. This consists of a series of well defined stages.

(a) Carefully outline the task the power unit has to perform.
(b) Prepare the design specification.
(c) Select the most suitable circuit method for meeting this specification, taking into consideration factors such as cost, availability of components, space, heat generation, heat removal, etc.
(d) Make a detailed design on paper, usually starting from the load end of the supply, carefully checking the ratings of critical components and estimating parameter values for regulation. If possible, use CAD software to check the figures.
(e) Build and test a prototype and check operation against the design specification.
(f) Carry out any necessary modifications.
(g) Retest against the specification.

For a system power supply the method in which the power is to be distributed and the position of the load with respect to the power supply output must also be taken into consideration. Regulation of the voltage at the load is what is required, not at the output socket of the power supply. This is illustrated in Fig. 3.6 where a 10 V supply is feeding power to a 1 A load. If the load is connected some distance from the power supply, with lead and connection resistances totalling, say, 100 milliohms each side, then the voltage across the load is some 200 mV less than that presented at the power supply's output and, worse still, the load regulation is degraded to 2%. Either the connection resistance must be reduced or some other method to improve the regulation must be introduced. In this case, *remote sensing* can be used where the input to the error amplifier and the bottom end of the reference are connected by low power signal leads to the load as in Fig. 3.7. The connection resistance of the

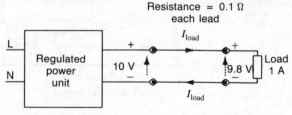

Fig. 3.6 Illustration of the loss of regulation to a distant load

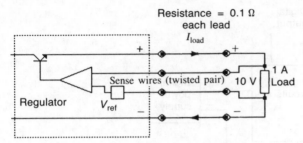

Fig. 3.7 An improvement using remote sensing

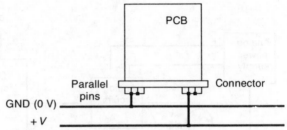

Fig. 3.9 Connecting a pcb to power

supply leads is then included within the feedback loop of the regulator and the voltage at the load is regulated correctly. But this method of remote sensing to improve regulation at the load cannot be used when there is more than one load to be supplied. For this more general case, either a well designed bus system has to be constructed or individual point-of-load regulators should be fitted on each sub-system pcb. In the latter case, a semi-regulated d.c. value is set up and distributed round the system (see Fig. 3.8).

A well designed power distribution system, which will minimise internally generated noise and therefore cut down interference between the various parts of the system, should have the following features:

- A low inductance and impedance for the supply and ground return lines — use heavy gauge wire and parallel several pins on connectors. See Fig. 3.9.
- An analogue circuit ground return line that is separate from any digital ground. See Fig. 3.10.

- Careful layout of ground and supply tracks on pcbs. Preferably, use a comb pattern and if possible position supply and ground patterns on opposite sides of the pcb. See Fig. 3.11.
- Adequate decoupling on pcbs — particularly for digital circuits.

3.3 TEST STRATEGIES

Having built a prototype unit, the next task facing the designer is to work out a test strategy, that is, the best method of testing to ensure that all important aspects of the unit's actual performance are checked against the target specification. Let us suppose that a mains driven regulated supply to give 15 V at 2 A has been designed and awaits its first tests. Here is the designer's target specification:

V_{in} : 240 V ± 10 V 50 Hz a.c. mains
V_{out} : 15 V ± 25 mV
Load current : 2 A

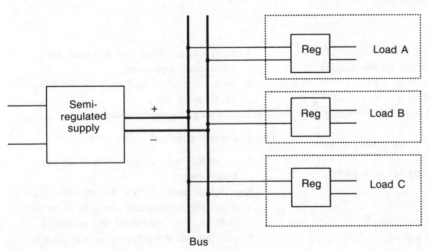

Fig. 3.8 Point-of-load regulation

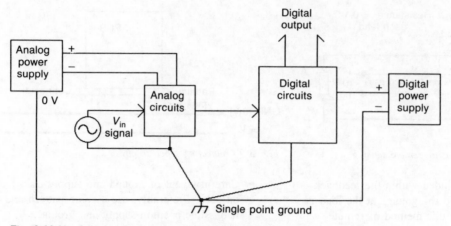

Fig. 3.10 No shared paths between analog and digital supplies

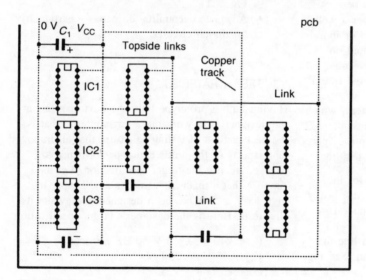

Fig. 3.11 Supply and ground pattern for a pcb

Overload current trip : 2.2 A ± 5% foldback to 0.5 A max. under short-circuit conditions

Load regulation : better than 0.15%

Line regulation : less than 3 mV V^{-1} of V_{in}

Ripple and noise at full load : not greater than 10 mV pk−pk

Temperature coefficient : not greater than ±0.025%/°C

Temperature range : −10 °C to +35 °C.

The test strategy should be to:

1 list all necessary test equipment,
2 design a suitable test circuit,
3 carry out an initial test to check for satisfactory operation,
4 with a specified load of 2 A, set V_o to 15 V ± 25 mV,
5 test all performance parameters.

The equipment required is listed as:

- a variable a.c. supply such as an auto-transformer
- a digital meter with a display of at least $4\frac{1}{2}$ digits to enable small changes in output voltage to be measured and recorded
- two current meters; one an a.c. type to

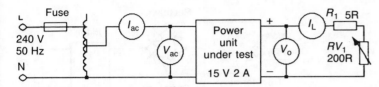

Fig. 3.12 Power supply test circuit

monitor the a.c. current, the other a d.c. meter to record load current

- a variable, high wattage, load resistor
- a sensitive oscilloscope and/or a.c. meter to measure ripple and noise
- some form of temperature enclosure to enable the temperature characteristic to be evaluated.

The test set up is shown in Fig. 3.12. Note that it is very important to connect the digital multimeter used to record V_o across the power supply output socket connectors, not on the other side of the meter measuring load current. Otherwise, the volt drop of the ammeter will distort the voltage readings and make the regulation seem particularly poor.

Now for details of each test. With a light load connected to the supply output, say all the 200 Ω load in circuit, the a.c. supply is gradually increased from zero up to 240 V. As the a.c. input rises, both the a.c. input current and the d.c. output voltage should be monitored, checking that they stay well within reasonable limits, i.e. I_{in} less than 50 mA and V_{out} not greater than 17 V. In fact, as the a.c. supply is increased the d.c. output should rise linearly until the regulation point is reached. Then the output voltage should remain almost constant even though the a.c. input is increasing.

If a variable a.c. supply is not available the same set up is used, except that the full 240 V a.c. mains input is applied — this is often called a *smoke-test* for the obvious reasons!

Assuming the unit passes this first test, it is then possible to set the output voltage to the specified value. With the full 240 V a.c. input applied, the load current should be increased gradually up to the maximum of 2 A. Then V_o is adjusted to be 15 V ± 25 mV. This is why a $4\frac{1}{2}$ digit multimeter is necessary. The current taken from the a.c. supply during this test should not exceed 150 mA.

The load regulation is then measured. For this test, the mains input voltage is held constant at 240 V and the change in d.c. output voltage measured from zero to full load. In this case, the change in V_o must be less than 22 mV (0.15%).

To test the line regulation the load current is held fixed at 2 A and the a.c. input voltage varied from 230 V to 250 V. The change in d.c. output voltage is recorded; this must be less than 30 mV.

With the full 2 A load connected, the peak-to-peak amplitude of the output ripple voltage can be measured using a sensitive oscilloscope, one with a vertical sensitivity of 2 mV/div. But it has to be remembered that the reading of a CRO is subject to an error of at least ±3%. An additional check can be made using a digital meter on a.c. volts range; this will read r.m.s. ($V_{pk-pk} = 2\sqrt{2}V_{rms}$).

The check on the temperature characteristic is the most time consuming and difficult to make. The full test requires a temperature enclosure which can be set from −10 °C up to +35 °C. The unit under test is placed in the enclosure; the mains input is held at 240 V and the load current at 2 A. The temperature is varied over the required range and the change in V_o monitored and recorded. This must not be greater than ±169 mV.

A final test is to check correct operation of the overcurrent trip. The output current is gradually increased above 2 A and the point at which the output voltage begins to *fold* is recorded. This should be between 2.189 A and 2.211 A. A digital multimeter is required in the ammeter position. Then, with a short across the output, the current supplied must not be greater than 500 mA.

Up to this point it has been assumed that all the specialised test gear is readily available. This is obviously not always the case, but there are means of testing the key performance parameters with a more modest range of test instruments. The minimum requirement is:

- a variable or switched load,
- an analog multimeter which can be used to

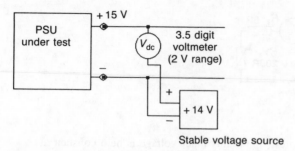

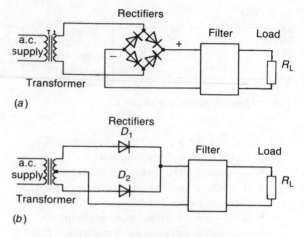

Fig. 3.13 Using a backing-off technique

Fig. 3.14 (a) Basic unregulated supply using a bridge rectifier; (b) Unregulated supply using a full-wave rectifier and a centre-tapped transformer

check the a.c. input current and then moved to record changes in d.c. load current,
• a digital voltmeter to record changes in V_o.

These would enable the unit to be set up and the load regulation to be measured.

Suppose that only a $3\frac{1}{2}$ digit multimeter is available for voltage measurement. On the 20 V range this would have a resolution of ± 10 mV (full scale = 19.99 V) which is just sufficient to allow V_o to be set to the required 15 V, but insufficient for the load regulation test. However, the sensitivity can be increased if the meter is placed in series with a stable d.c. source (see Fig. 3.13). If this d.c. voltage is set to 14 V then the voltmeter can be switched to the 2 V range to measure the 15 V output. This increases the sensitivity to ± 1 mV. A backing-off technique such as this can be useful, especially when the requirement is to record a small change in a voltage rather than its absolute value.

3.4 THE UNREGULATED D.C. SUPPLY

TRANSFORMERS AND RECTIFIERS

For units that derive their power from the a.c. main supply (and as stated previously this is the normal arrangement for most electronic instruments and systems), a transformer, rectifiers and a smoothing filter are essential elements. These enable a suitable d.c. voltage level with minimum superimposed ripple to be set up prior to the regulator circuit. Two of the most basic circuit arrangements are shown in Fig. 3.14.

The transformer, which provides the vital electrical isolation and change in voltage level, has three important parameters:

• its secondary voltage (or voltages if several windings are used),
• its power rating,
• the regulation.

The secondary voltage, quoted as the r.m.s. value, is the a.c. voltage across the secondary at the rated (*full load*) secondary current.

The power rating, or VA rating, of the transformer is the product of this a.c. secondary voltage and the full load a.c. secondary current (both r.m.s. values). For example, a 100 VA rated transformer could have two secondary windings of 20 V at 2.5 A each, or one secondary winding of 20 V at 5 A, or some other combination.

The regulation of a transformer refers to its ability to hold the secondary voltage at its rated level irrespective of changes in load current, i.e.

Regulation
$$= \frac{(\text{off-load voltage} - \text{full-load voltage})}{\text{off-load voltage}} \times 100\%$$

Values in the range 5% to 10% are typical. Thus, a 100 VA transformer with one secondary of 20 V and a regulation of 7% would have an off-load secondary voltage of 21.5 V.

All mains transformers have laminated cores to reduce eddy current losses and therefore have low magnetising current and high efficiencies. The toroidal transformers have the added advantages of a low profile and low stray magnetic field. But it is not advisable to use these types with a half-wave rectifier because there could then be problems with saturation.

In Fig. 3.14(b), a full-wave bridge is shown for the rectifier circuit. The half-wave type is inefficient and the full-wave circuit, which has two rectifiers, requires a centre tapped secondary winding on the transformer with double the turns. This puts up both the costs and space required. It is usually best to use a bridge rectifier circuit. The four silicon power diodes forming the bridge rectifier will cause a volt drop of about $2V_D$ at the load (where V_D is typically in the range 0.7 to 1.5 V depending on the value of the current) and each rectifier must be capable of passing an average current equal to the value of the d.c. load current. Heat sinks may be required for the diodes because the forward volt drop with the forward current sets up a power loss for each rectifier. The rectifier data sheet should be consulted to determine the power rating. Two other important points concerning the rectifier diodes are:

(a) the peak inverse voltage across any diode in the bridge will be $2V_p$ (where V_p is the peak value of the secondary voltage),

(b) with the capacitive input filter a large switch-on surge current will occur. The value of this current will be limited only by the resistance of the secondary winding and the bulk resistance of the diode and may be tens of amps. A small series resistance is often necessary to restrict the surge current to within the rated value for the rectifiers used.

FILTERS

For the smoothing circuit either a choke input or capacitive input filter can be used. See Fig. 3.15.

For the choke input filter:

$$V_{DC} = 0.9V_{AC}$$
$$I_{DC} = 0.94I_{AC}$$

and for the capacitive input filter:

$$V_{DC} = 1.41V_{DC}$$
$$I_{DC} = 0.62I_{AC}$$

NB: For the d.c. output voltage given above no

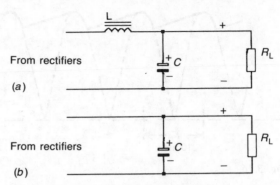

Fig. 3.15 (a) Smoothing filter — choke input;
(b) Smoothing filter — capacitive input

allowance has been made for the volt drop across the rectifiers. In practice, subtract at least 1.5 V from the d.c. output values obtained from these equations.

For units operating from the 50/60 Hz mains the choke input filter is a relatively expensive option since a coil with an inductance of several henries will be necessary. We shall therefore concentrate on the capacitive input filter design.

The relatively large value electrolytic capacitor used in this position must have three important parameters specified:

- the value of capacitance
- the ripple current rating
- the working voltage.

The filter capacitor is charged during the time interval just before the peak level of the a.c. voltage is reached and then partially discharged by the load after the peak value, see Fig. 3.16. This results in the d.c. voltage being very nearly equal to the peak value of the a.c. secondary voltage but with a small superimposed a.c. ripple at a frequency of $2f_s$. The value of the capacitor determines the peak-to-peak value of this ripple. As a rule of thumb:

$$C_{min} \approx \frac{I_{dc}t}{V_{R(pk-pk)}}$$

$$C_{min} \approx \frac{1}{2\sqrt{2}f_R KR_L}$$

where f_R = ripple frequency ($2f_s$)

$$K = \text{ripple factor} = \frac{\text{r.m.s. ripple voltage}}{\text{d.c. output voltage}}$$

and R_L = load resistance.

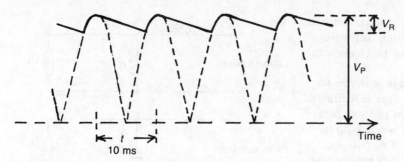

Fig. 3.16

Thus, a circuit to give an output of 12 V at 500 mA with 1 V pk−pk ripple would require a 5000 μF electrolytic capacitor. Since the tolerance on electrolytics is particularly wide (typically −10% + 50%) the value calculated from the above rule-of-thumb should be treated as a minimum and a higher capacitance, such as the next n.p.v. up, specified for actual use.

Since the capacitor is being alternately charged and discharged a large ripple current flows. This ripple current is larger than the d.c. load current. For example, if the d.c. current is 500 mA the capacitor's ripple current is typically 700 mA. It is very important that the capacitor is physically large enough to cope with the maximum ripple current in the circuit. The ripple current flows through the effective series resistance (ESR) of the capacitor causing a power loss, and the heat generated must be dissipated by the surface area of the capacitor. Specifying a capacitor with a ripple current rating below the value set up in the circuit could result in unpleasant effects. It is a good rule to specify a capacitor with a ripple current rating of at least $1.5I_{dc}$ or preferably $2I_{dc}$.

The d.c. voltage across the capacitor is equal to the peak value of the secondary voltage and the working voltage rating of the capacitor must therefore exceed this peak value. Allow a good safety margin in specifying the working voltage since this will prolong the life of the capacitor.

DESIGN EXAMPLE FOR AN UNSTABILISED D.C. SUPPLY

Design method — start at the load end.

1. Specify:
   (*a*) the required d.c. output voltage (V_{DC}),

   (*b*) the load current (I_{DC}),
   (*c*) the ripple voltage (V_R).

2. Determine the value for the smoothing capacitor.

3. For the capacitor check:
   (*a*) the ripple current rating (I_R),
   (*b*) the working voltage rating (V_R).
   Then specify the type and value to be used.

4. For the bridge rectifier check:
   (*a*) the current rating (I_F),
   (*b*) the PIV (V_{RRM}),
   (*c*) the power dissipation (P_D),
   (*d*) the surge current rating (I_{sm}).

5. Specify the rectifiers to be used.

6. Calculate for the transformer:
   (*a*) the required secondary voltage (V_{AC}),
   (*b*) the secondary current (I_{AC}),
   (*c*) the VA rating.

7. Calculate the rating for the primary fuse. For this design, see Fig. 3.17.

The calculations for these steps are as follows.

1. Requirements/target specification
   (*a*) output voltage $V_{DC} = +20$ V
   (*b*) load current $I_{DC} = 2$ A
   (*c*) ripple voltage $V_R = 1$ V pk−pk

2. $C_{min} \approx \dfrac{I_{dc}.t}{V_{R(pk-pk)}} = 20\ 000\ \mu$F

3. (*a*) ripple current ≈ 3 A min.
   (*b*) working voltage ≥ 20 V
   suitable capacitors are:
   (i) Mullard 106/107 series
        22 000 μF, 25 V wkg $I_R = 11.6$ A
        tolerance −10 to +50%,

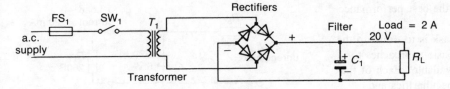

Fig. 3.17 Unregulated power supply to give 20 V d.c. at 2 A

(ii)   STC ALP/ALT series
22 000 μF, 25 V wkg $I_R = 6.8$ A,

(iii)   two 10 000 μF Mullard type 071
wired in parallel both 25 V wkg
with $I_R = 4.3$ A each.

4.   (a)   Each rectifier must be capable of passing
a minimum of 2 A and withstanding a
reverse voltage of 43 V.

(b)   The power dissipation for each diode will
be approximately 2 W.

(c)   The surge current (I_{FS}) flowing at switch
on would depend on the series resistance
of the secondary winding and any
resistance of the rectifier (R_S).
Therefore $I_{FS} = V_{DC}/R_S$
Assuming $R_S \approx 0.35$ Ω, $I_{FS} \approx 60$ A.

5.   Recifiers required must have rating in excess of
the following:
$I_F \geq 3$ A
$V_{RRM} \geq 50$ V
$I_{FSM} \geq 60$ A
Suitable types are:
(i)   four IN5401 rectifier diodes
$I_F = 3$ A $T_{amb} = 25$ °C
$V_{RRM} = 50$ V
$I_{FSM} = 200$ A

(ii)   four Motorola MR500 rectifier diodes
$I_F = 3$ A $T_{amb} = 95$ °C
$V_{RRM} = 100$ V
$I_{FSM} = 100$ A

(iii)   bridge rectifier — type MD970A2 — each
rectifier
$I_F = 4$ A $T_{amb} = 25$ °C
$V_{RRM} = 100$ V
$I_{FSM} = 100$ A
The bridge unit is probably the most
suitable.

6.   Required secondary voltage:
(a)   Allowing for voltage drop across rectifiers
(say 1.5 V) the secondary voltage required
is just over 15 V r.m.s.

(b) $I_{AC} = I_{DC}/0.62 = 3.23$ A
(c)   VA rating of transformer $\approx$ 50 VA

7.   Fuse rating:
The normal primary current when secondary is
fully loaded is given by

$$I_p \approx \frac{I_s V_s}{V_p} \text{ (assuming zero losses)}$$

$$I_p \approx 0.21 \text{ A}$$

A short-circuit condition on the secondary
would cause this primary current to rise just
over 1.5 A. An anti-surge fuse with a rating of
500 mA should be fitted.

3.5   LINEAR REGULATOR DESIGN

The function of the power supply regulator is to
hold the output voltage almost constant irrespective
of changes in both the load current and in the
unregulated input. These two important parameters
are called *load regulation* and *line regulation* (the
latter is also sometimes called stability factor). Any
changes in output voltage due to these parameters
should be typically less than a few millivolts. For
example a 5 V, 2 A regulator with load regulation
of 0.1% would experience a change in output
voltage of only 5 mV as the demand for power by
the load changes from zero to the full load current
of 2 A.

It is true to say that for many applications the
availability of three terminal regulator ICs, such as
the 78/79 series and the 317K/338K, have made the
regulator design task a fairly simple matter.
However, these IC regulators can be used only in
the more commonly required power supply
situations, for example a 5 V on-board regulator to
supply TTL logic with, say, 0.5 A of load current.
There are many other applications that require a
different design approach. Apart from this a good
understanding of regulator principles and operation

is essential if one is to get the best performance from an IC regulator.

For any design the first task is to draw up the target specification. What basic approaches to regulator design are then available? Each of the following, with their own peculiarities and advantages, could be used:

1. Shunt regulator
2. Linear series regulator
   (a) using discretes
   or (b) using a three-terminal linear regulator IC
3. A switched mode design

SHUNT REGULATORS

The first of these, the shunt regulators, can be useful for low power applications, i.e. up to a few watts, and they have the advantages of simplicity and built-in overload protection. However, the efficiency is not high and the off-load condition results in a maximum dissipation in the shunt element.

The principle of operation is illustrated in Fig. 3.18. The regulating device is in parallel with the load and if the load current increases the additional current required is taken from the shunt element. As long as the shunt element has a low dynamic impedance the output voltage will remain constant. The shunt element must therefore have a low slope resistance, so that if the load is completely disconnected all the current $(I_R + I_L)$ flows through the element but only a small change of voltage occurs across it. If the load is made a short circuit, no current at all passes through the element. It is therefore automatically protected from an overload and the circuit can only supply a maximum short-circuit current given by:

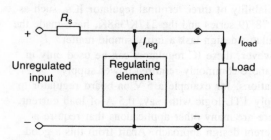

Fig. 3.18 Basic shunt regulator

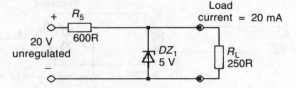

Fig. 3.19 Simple shunt regulator circuit

$$I_{SC} = V_{in}/R_S.$$

Naturally, the series resistor R_S must be capable of dissipating the power set up by a short-circuit condition or alternatively a fuse may be provided in series with the supply line.

The simplest shunt regulator circuit consists of one resistor and a Zener or voltage regulating diode, Fig. 3.19. Suppose a 5 V regulator diode is used to give a 5 V supply from a 20 V d.c. input, and that the maximum load current is 20 mA. If the Zener diode current is set to 5 mA (a typical value) when maximum load current is being supplied the value of R_S is:

$$R_S = \frac{V_{in} - V_{out}}{I_Z + I_L} = 600 \ \Omega.$$

The load regulation can be estimated from a knowledge of r_z, the diode's slope resistance,

$$\Delta V_{out} = \Delta I_Z.r_Z$$

where ΔV_{out} = the change in output voltage from zero to full load, and ΔI_Z = the change in Zener current from zero to full load. Suppose $r_Z = 50 \ \Omega$. Then $\Delta V_{out} = 20 \times 10^{-3} \times 5 = 100 \ mV$ and the load regulation $\approx 2\%$.

A simple shunt regulator such as this will not have very good regulation nor will it provide much load current. An improved arrangement is shown in Fig. 3.20 using a *pnp* transistor, wired as an emitter follower as the shunt element (Tr_2), and an *npn* transistor (Tr_1) as an error amplifier. Tr_1 has its emitter tied to a reference voltage set up by a 3.6 V Zener diode and its base connected via a potential divider to the output voltage. If the output falls, the base voltage of Tr_1 also falls, which forces Tr_1 collector to rise. Since Tr_1 collector is connected directly to Tr_2 base, the output voltage is automatically corrected. With the values given the circuit can provide 60 mA at 5 V and has a load regulation of about 0.5%.

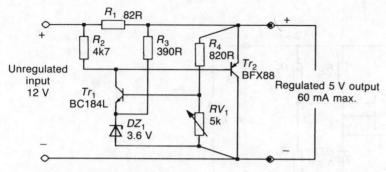

Fig. 3.20 Improved shunt regulator

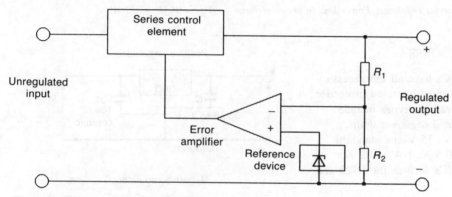

Fig. 3.21 The basic linear series regulator

LINEAR SERIES REGULATORS

The linear series regulator (Fig. 3.21) is the classic method for providing stable and well regulated output voltages. The basic circuit consists of a series element, a voltage reference and an error amplifier. One input of the error amplifier is tied to the reference voltage while the other is connected either directly or via a potential divider to the output. The error amplifier then drives the control input of the series element and in this way any change in output voltage is automatically compensated by a change in drive to the series element. For example, if the output falls due to an increase in load current the error amplifier output rises and forces the series element to conduct more to supply the necessary current. With a good stable reference and a high gain in the error amplifier a load regulation of better than 0.01% is possible. But great care over layout is essential to achieve such excellent performance. The series regulator has two major defects:

(*a*) The efficiency is not high since power is wasted in the series element. A voltage across this element of at least 3 V is usually necessary for correct operation, and therefore, since all the load current flows through this device, its power dissipation can be high. For example suppose a +6 V, 3 A regulated supply has an unregulated output of 10 V. This leaves 4 V across the series element (Fig. 3.22) and in this case the series element is dissipating 12 W at full load.

$$\text{Efficiency} = \frac{\text{output power}}{\text{input power}} \times 100\% \approx 60\%$$

(*b*) Any overload condition at the output can easily damage the series element. This means that some form of overcurrent limit or trip is essential.

A typical circuit with an overcurrent trip is discussed later.

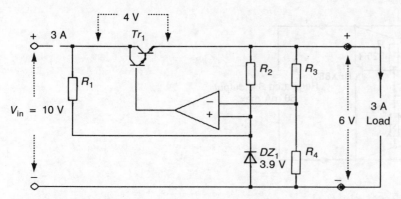

Fig. 3.22 Power losses in a series regulator. Power loss in series element $= (V_{in} - V_o)I_L = 12 \ W$

THREE-TERMINAL IC REGULATORS

Three-terminal regulator ICs have all the necessary series regulator parts, including overload protection, built into one package. Available types include fixed regulators (positive and negative) with voltages of 5 V, 6 V, 12 V, 15 V and standard current ratings of 0.1 A, 0.5 A, 1 A and 3 A, adjustable regulators and ICs such as the L723 and the 317M/K.

The fixed regulator ICs have the advantages of:

- ease of use (few external components are required)
- reliable operation
- built-in short circuit protection
- internal thermal trip.

However, no precise adjustment can be made to the output voltage and the initial accuracy is not high. For example, a 7805 has $V_0 = 5$ V $\pm$ 0.2 V, and a 7815 has $V_0 = 15$ V $\pm$ 0.6 V.

Typical performance for the 78/79 range is (7805):

> Input: 7 V to 25 V
> Output voltage: 5 V $\pm$ 0.2 V
> Output current: 1 A
> Load regulation: 0.2%
> Line regulation: 0.2%
> Ripple rejection: 70 dB
> Noise (10 Hz to 100 kHz): 0.04 mV
> Short-circuit current: 750 mA

The positive regulators have a BJT as the series element, connected as an emitter follower, whereas the negative types have the BJT in common emitter mode with the load in the collector circuit. The

Positive regulator

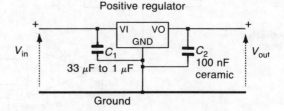

Negative regulator

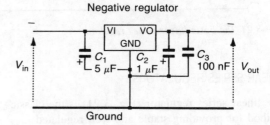

Fig. 3.23 Bypass/decoupling for 3-terminal IC regulators

latter are therefore less stable and must have external bypass capacitors fitted. This is good practice in any case and in Fig. 3.23 the typical bypass component values are shown. These capacitors must be wired as close to the regulator terminals as possible.

Adjustable regulator ICs allow the user to set the output voltage over a fairly wide range or to set it to a precise value. The 317k (1.5 A) and the 338k (5 A) are typical. The input voltage can be from 4 V up to 40 V and the output set from 1.25 V up to 37 V maximum. Load regulation is typically 0.1% and line regulation 0.02%.

The output current of most IC regulators can be increased by using an external higher current pass

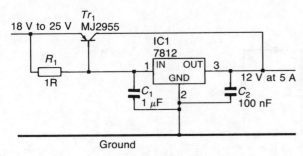

Fig. 3.24 Current boost (5 A) for an IC regulator

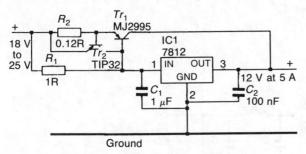

Fig. 3.25 Adding protection for the boost transistor

transistor. The standard circuit for this current boost with short-circuit protection is shown in Fig. 3.24. R_1 is wired in series with the regulation IC and it has a value such that at low currents the voltage across it is insufficient to turn on Tr_1. At higher currents, say, above 600 mA, the voltage across R_1 exceeds 600 mV and Tr_1 starts to conduct. In this way any current in excess of 600 mA is supplied to the load by Tr_1. This boost transistor is outside the protection loop of the regulator and therefore requires its own current limit. The simplest arrangement to provide this additional protection is given in Fig. 3.25.

3.6 SWITCH MODE REGULATORS

Switch mode regulators are highly efficient and therefore take up far less space than the linear types. They are the obvious choice for supplying higher power requirements (i.e. above 20 W). The operation is based around a fast electronic switch (a BJT or powerFET) which is driven on and off at a frequency above audio to connect a d.c. voltage to the load via an LC filter, see Fig. 3.26. When the switch is on, full power is applied to the load; and when the switch is off, zero power is applied to the load.

Apart from the brief periods between the on and off states, the switch itself will dissipate very little power, hence the high efficiency of a SMPU. The switching frequency, at 15 kHz or more, is usually held constant and the output voltage can be altered by varying the mark-to-space ratio of the switching waveform. Regulation of the output voltage can be achieved by controlling the duty cycle of the switch. The output voltage, or a portion of it, is compared with a stable reference and the error signal generated is used to alter the duty cycle.

The most efficient and space saving SMPU uses what is termed primary or *direct-off-line* switching (Fig. 3.27) where the a.c. supply itself is rectified and then switched at a high frequency across the primary winding of a transformer. Since a high frequency is used this transformer will be a ferrite core type, which takes up much less space than an iron-cored transformer. The secondary output voltage is then rectified and smoothed before being applied to the load. Regulation at the load is achieved as described previously by comparing the output voltage against a reference and using the error to control the duty cycle of the primary switches. Naturally the design and construction of direct-off-line SMPU is fairly complex. An alternative method, which is still very efficient, is called secondary switching. The a.c. mains supply is fed to the input of a normal mains transformer and the secondary voltage is rectified and smoothed to give an unregulated d.c. supply. This d.c. level is then switched using a fast BJT or powerFET as outlined above. The relatively complex circuit required is available in IC form and the design work only involves the calculation and specification of a few external components. An example is given later.

3.7 REGULATOR DESIGN EXAMPLES

1 SHUNT REGULATOR USING A POWERFET
(see Fig. 3.28)

The modern powerFET with its high input impedance and high value of g_m (this is often greater than 500 millisiemen) can be used in simple, low cost and effective shunt regulators. In this

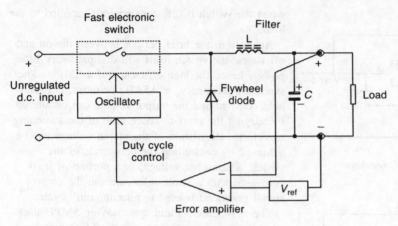

Fig. 3.26 Basic circuit for a switching regulator

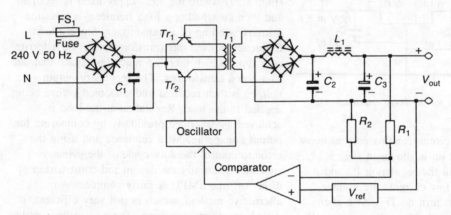

Fig. 3.27 Direct off-line switching regulator

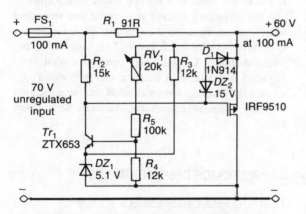

Fig. 3.28 Shunt regulator using a powerFET

example a circuit is required to give a regulated +60 V output at load currents up to 100 mA from a 70 V d.c. unregulated input. A Zener diode is used to set up the reference voltage and, for simplicity, the design uses a single transistor for the

error amplifier. The collector of Tr_1 drives the gate of the FET directly, and this connection, because of the FET's high input impedance, allows the error amplifier to operate at high gain. Also, since the g_m of the FET is large, only very small changes in Tr_1 collector voltage and current will occur as the load is varied. This means that changes in the reference voltage are also kept to a very low level. However, because the error amplifier is based on a single transistor and not a differential stage, the temperature stability of the circuit will not be high. This can be improved by selecting a Zener diode that has a positive temperature coefficient of about 2 mV $°C^{-1}$. In this way the rise in reference voltage with temperature will counteract the fall in V_{BE} of Tr_1.

Target specification

Unregulated input voltage : 70 V nominal
Output voltage : 60 V ± 0.5 V

Output current : up to 100 mA
Load regulation : better than 0.1%
Line regulation : better than 20 mV V^{-1}
Temperature range : 10 °C to 35 °C

Design procedure

   (i)   Select a suitable powerFET and check worst case conditions.

  (ii)   Determine the value and rating for R_1.

 (iii)   Choose a reasonable value for the collector current for Tr_1. Hence determine the value and power rating for R_2.

 (iv)   Select the transistor type for Tr_1. Check conditions.

  (v)   Select a Zener diode type and choose a suitable Zener current. Check conditions.

 (vi)   Determine the value and power rating for R_3.

(vii)   Determine the value and power rating for R_4, R_5 and RV_1.

(viii)   Select values and types for any protection devices.

(i) Selection of the powerFET

A p-channel FET operated in linear mode is required. The expected ratings are:

$V_{DS(max)} = -70$ V
$I_{D(max)} = -110$ mA
$I_{D(min)} = -10$ mA
$P_D \approx 6.6$ W at $T_{amb(max)}$ of 35 °C

An IRF9510, which has the following characteristics and ratings, is suitable.

$V_{DS(max)} = -100$ V
$I_{D(max)} = -3$ A
$P_D = 20$ W at $T_{case} + 25$ °C

This device must be mounted on a suitable heat sink which can be calculated as follows. The maximum dissipation of the FET occurs when the load is removed from the circuit since that is when the whole of the load current is forced to flow through the FET. Under no load conditions $I_D = -110$ mA and $V_{DS} = 60$ V. The dissipation is therefore 6.6 W. The thermal resistances quoted for the IRF9510 are:

$R_{th(j-c)} = 6.4$ °C W^{-1}
$R_{th(c-h)} = 1$ °C W^{-1}

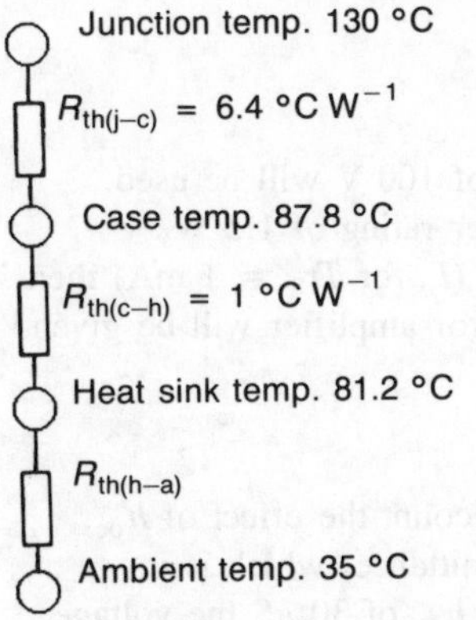

Junction temp. 130 °C

$R_{th(j-c)} = 6.4$ °C W^{-1}

Case temp. 87.8 °C

$R_{th(c-h)} = 1$ °C W^{-1}

Heat sink temp. 81.2 °C

$R_{th(h-a)}$

Ambient temp. 35 °C

Fig. 3.29 Heat sink calculations for the FET dissipating 6.6 W

$$R_{th(h-a)} = \frac{T_h - T_a}{P_{tot}} = 7 \text{ °C } W^{-1}$$

When the device is dissipating 6.6 W and assuming the junction temperature is allowed to rise to 130 °C a heat sink with a thermal resistance of at least 7 °C W^{-1} is required. (See Fig. 3.29.)

(ii) Value and power rating for R_1

Current through $R_1 = I_L + I_d = I = 110$ mA.

$$\text{Therefore } R_1 = \frac{V_{in} - V_0}{I} = 91 \text{ } \Omega.$$

Power dissipated for R_1 under normal operating conditions $= I^2 R_1 = 1.01$ W. Therefore use a 2.5 W rated wirewound resistor.

(iii) Collector current for Tr_1

A reasonable value for I_c of Tr_1 is somewhere in the range of 0.5 mA up to say 5 mA. Too low a value will result in low gain in the error amplifier whereas too high a value will increase the dissipation of Tr_1. Let us assume a value for collector current of 1 mA.

$$R_2 = \frac{V_{in} - (V_0 - V_{GS(TH)})}{I_c}$$

where $V_{GS(TH)}$ = the threshold voltage for the IRF9510 (4 V).

$$\text{Therefore } R_2 = \frac{70 - (60 - 4)}{1} \text{ k}\Omega \approx 14 \text{ k}\Omega$$

Therefore R_2 is 15 kΩ (n.p.v.).

(iv) Transistor for error amplifier

This must be an n-p-n transistor with the following expected ratings:

$V_{CE(max)}$: +70 V
$I_{(max)}$: 1 mA
P_c : 70 mW

A ZTX653 with a V_{CEO} of 100 V will be used. This transistor has a power rating of 1.5 W.

Assuming g_m = 38 mS (I_c for Tr_1 = 1 mA) then the voltage gain of the error amplifier will be given by:

$$A_v \approx g_m R_2 \approx 570$$

This does not take into account the effect of h_{oe}, the transistor's output admittance, which is in parallel with R_2. With an h_{oe} of 30 μS the voltage gain reduces to just over 400.

(v) Zener diode

The reference is to be set to approximately 5 V and should have a positive temperature coefficient of about +2 mV °C^{-1}.

A 5.1 V ± 5% type BZX85 with temperature coefficient of +2 mV °C^{-1} is chosen. The Zener current will be set at 5 mA which will result in a power dissipation of only 26 mW.

(vi) Value and power rating of R_3

$$R_3 = \frac{V_o - V_z}{I_z - I_c} = \frac{60 - 5.1}{(5-1)\text{ mA}} = 13.7 \text{ k}\Omega$$

Therefore R_3 = 12 kΩ (n.p.v.)
Power dissipation = 200 mW
Therefore a $\frac{1}{2}$ W rating resistor is specified.

(vii) Values and power ratings for R_4, R_5 and RV_1

Since I_C has been set to 1 mA a current of 500 μA will be suitable for the R_4, R_5 and RV_1 resistor divider. This value should effectively swamp the base current requirement of Tr_1.

$$R_4 = \frac{V_z + V_{BE}}{I} \text{ where } I = 500 \text{ }\mu\text{A}$$

Therefore R_4 = 12 kΩ

$$R_5 + RV_1 = \frac{V_o - (V_z + V_{BE})}{I} = 108 \text{ k}\Omega$$

Suitable values for R_5 and RV_1 will then be 100 kΩ and 20 kΩ respectively. The power dissipation of all three resistors is under 50 mW so 125 mW rated components can be used. RV_1, the preset used to adjust the output voltage, should be a cermet type.

(viii) Protection devices

If the output is suddenly short circuited an overload current will flow, limited only by the series resistor R_1,

$$I_{sc} = V_{in}/R_1 \approx 770 \text{ mA}$$

If no series fuse is fitted the dissipation of R_1 will rise to over 50 W! A fuse is obviously essential and one which is rated at 100 mA will be suitable. A fuse will normally blow at twice the rated current (although the characteritics depend on the fuse construction and the length of time the overload current flows). Therefore in this circuit an overload current of 200 mA should blow the fuse. At this value of current the dissipation of R_1 is approximately 3.6 W, which does not represent a severe overload for the wirewound resistor chosen in the design.

If the output is taken low during an overload the reverse rating of the V_{GS} voltage for the IRF9510 may be exceeded. For example, under short-circuit load conditions the voltage between gate and source could rise to nearly 70 V for the short time before the fuse blows. To avoid damage to the FET a 15 V protection Zener (DZ_2) together with a series diode is fitted between the gate and source connections. This will prevent the gate voltage from rising more positive than 15 V with respect to the source under any conditions.

Predicted performance

An estimate of the load regulation can be made as follows.

If the change in load current is assumed to be the full 100 mA then the change in the FET current is also 100 mA. The g_{fs} of the IRF9510 is approximately 100 mS at I_D = 50 mA. Therefore, since $g_{fs} = \Delta I_d / \Delta V_{gs}$,

$$\Delta V_{gs} \approx 1 \text{ V}.$$

This is the voltage change at Tr_1 collector (the output of the error amplifier) for a zero to full load step. Since the voltage gain of the error amplifier is approximately 400 the input error must be:

Input error at Tr_1 base = $\Delta V_{gs}/A_V$
$$\Delta V_B = 2.5 \text{ mV}$$

Thus the change in output voltage is:

$$\Delta V_o = \frac{(R_4 + R_5 + RV_1)}{R_4}.\Delta V_B = 20.5 \text{ mV}.$$

Therefore predicted load regulation $= (\Delta V_o / V_o) \times 100\% = 0.034\%$.

This does not take into account any change of V_o due to changes in the reference voltage or variation in error amplifier gain. When these are considered the regulation should still be within 0.1% but care over layout would be necessary to achieve this performance. For example, as indicated in the diagram the bottom end of R_4 and DZ (the reference) should be connected as near as possible to the negative return rail from the load, and similarly the top end of RV_1 should be connected as near as possible to the positive output point.

2 SERIES REGULATOR USING AN OP-AMP AS THE ERROR AMPLIFIER

Target specification

Unregulated input : 22 V ± 1 V
Output voltage : 18 V ± 100 mV
Output current : 500 mA
Short-circuit output current : 600 mA
Load regulation : better than 0.1%
Line regulation : better than 10 mV V^{-1}

Quite high performance regulators can be designed using a standard op-amp, such as the 741 or OP-07, as the error amplifier with a general purpose Darlington as the series element. The good regulation performance results from the inherent

high gain of the op-amp. In this example a regulated 18 V output to supply load currents up to 500 mA is provided from an unregulated 22 V input. A simple current limit will be described. The initial circuit design, with the simple limit formed by Tr_2 and R_7, is shown in Fig. 3.30.

Design procedure

(i) Select the device to be used for the series element. This entails a check on the maximum dissipation of this element and a determination of heat sink requirements.
(ii) Design the current limit.
(iii) Select suitable device(s) for the reference supply and determine resistor values.
(iv) Calculate values for feedback resistors and any preset if required.
(v) Select a suitable op-amp.

(i) Series element

The requirement is for a high value of current gain so that current drawn from the op-amp is kept to a minimum. A Darlington transistor would be the most suitable.

In the basic circuit the maximum values of current, voltage and power for the series device will occur when the output is short circuit. Under these conditions:

$$V_{CE(max)} = 23 \text{ V}$$
$$I_c = 600 \text{ mA}$$
$$P_{tot(max)} = 13.8 \text{ W}$$

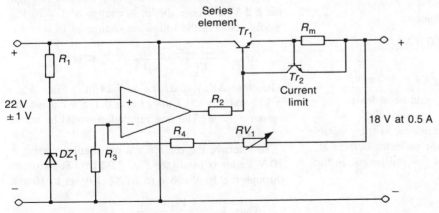

Fig. 3.30 Starting point for the linear regulator design

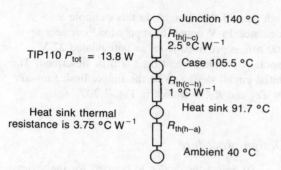

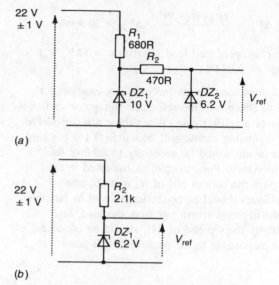

Fig. 3.31 Heat sink requirements for the Darlington

Note that a foldback limit would reduce the maximum expected power dissipation to just 3 W.

Consider the TIP110. The short-form data for this Darlington are:

V_{CE} = 60 V
$I_{c(max)}$ = 4 A
P_{tot} = 50 W at 25 °C case temperature
$h_{FE(min)}$ = 500

This would be a suitable choice since the maximum current required from the op-amp is then only 1 mA. Assuming an ambient temperature of 40 °C max, and allowing for a junction temperature rise to 140 °C (150 °C is the maximum allowed), the required thermal resistance of the heat sink can be calculated using:

$$R_{th(h-a)} = \frac{T_j - T_a}{P_{tot}} - [R_{th(j-c)} + R_{th(c-w)}]$$

where $R_{th(j-c)}$ = 2.5 °C W^{-1} and $R_{th(c-w)}$ = 1 °C W^{-1} for the TIP110. Therefore $R_{th(h-a)}$ = 3.75 °C W^{-1}. (See Fig. 3.31.)

(ii) Design of the current limit

Since I_{SC} is to be set to 600 mA,

$R_7 = V_{BE}/I_{sc}$ = 1 Ω
Power dissipation = $I_{sc}^2 R_7$ = 360 mW.

The power rating for R_7 should be at least 500 mW, preferably 1 W.

Any small signal n-p-n transistor will be suitable for the Tr_2 position since the collector current at overload will only rise to a few milliamps. In this case a BC107 will be used.

(iii) Reference supply

In order to meet the regulation performance the reference circuit must be stable. A IN821 reference

Fig. 3.32 (a) Basic reference ΔV_{ref} = 7 *mV* V^{-1};
(b) Improved reference ΔV_{ref} = 0.4 *mV* V^{-1}

diode has been chosen for this position. This diode has the following data:

V_Z = 6.2 V ± 5%
at I_Z = 7.5 mA
r_Z = 15 Ω
Temp. coeff. = 0.01%/°C

Note the excellent temperature stability obtained with this diode.

However, since the slope resistance of the diode is 15 Ω, if R_2 were to be directly connected to V_{in} any changes in V_{in} would cause a relatively large variation in V_{ref}. See Fig. 3.32(a).

Here R_2 is set to 2100 Ω giving 7.5 mA through the 6.2 V reference diode. A change of 1 V in V_{in} would result in the following change in V_{ref}:

$$\Delta I_Z = \frac{\Delta V_{in}}{R_2} = \frac{1}{2.1 \text{ k}} = 0.47 \text{ mA}$$

Therefore $\Delta V_{ref} = \Delta I_Z r_Z$ = 7.14 mV. Since $V_o \approx$ 3 V_{ref}, ΔV_o = 20.7 mV, i.e. a 0.115% change in output voltage. The line regulation would be out of specification.

To improve the reference a pre-regulator using a 10 V Zener is used (see Fig. 3.32(b)). The current through the 10 V diode (a BZX61) is set to 10 mA.

$$\text{Thus, } R_1 = \frac{V_{in} - V_{Z1}}{I_Z - I_{Z2}}$$

$$= 685 \text{ Ω} \qquad 680 \text{ Ω is n.p.v.}$$

The dissipation of R_1 is just over 200 mW, therefore a 500 mW resistor should be used.

$$R_2 = \frac{V_{Z1} - V_{ref}}{I_{Z2}}$$

$$= 506 \; \Omega \quad 470 \; \Omega \text{ is n.p.v.}$$

A 470 Ω 250 mW resistor is specified.

Changes in V_{ref} caused by variations in V_{in} are now kept to a very low value, a 1 V change in V_{in} causing only a 400 μV change in V_{ref} (i.e. 0.007% of V_{out}).

(iv) Feedback resistor values

The input to the non-inverting pin of the op-amp will be 6.2 V ± 5% (i.e. V_{ref}). Since the output voltage has to be 18 V ± 0.56% a preset must be included in the feedback to enable V_{out} to be set accurately.

The current through this network is set to approximately 1.3 mA by choosing R_4 to be 4.7 kΩ. It is important to keep these resistors at relatively low values, i.e. in the range 1−10 kΩ. If they are made too high additional drift with temperature will occur, caused by the input offset current temperature coefficient of the op-amp.

With R_4 set to 4.7 kΩ,

$$R_5 + RV_1 = \frac{(V_{out} - V_{ref})}{V_{ref}} R_4$$

where RV_1 is mid-setting of the preset.

$$\text{Therefore } R_5 + RV_1 = \frac{(18 - 6.2)}{6.2} \times 4.7 \text{ k}$$

$$= 8.95 \text{ k}\Omega$$

Make $R_5 = 6.8$ kΩ and RV_1 a 2.5 kΩ preset.
The power dissipation of all three components is

only a few milliwatts. Therefore 125 mW devices can be used.

(v) Choice of op-amp

The main parameters of interest are:

A_{vol} : the open loop gain
dV_{io}/dT : input offset voltage drift with temperature
dI_{io}/dT : input offset current drift with temperature and slew rate.

To improve temperature stability a resistor R_3 has been included in the non-inverting input. This resistor must have a value equal to the resistance in the inverting lead.

$$R_3 = R_4 \,||\, (R_5 + RV_1) \approx 3.3 \text{ k}\Omega$$

Then the drift with temperature at the output caused by the op-amp's offset temperature coefficients is as follows (assuming a 741 is used):

$$\Delta V_o/°C = \left[1 + \frac{(R_5 + RV_1)}{R_4}\right] \cdot \left[\frac{dI_{io}}{dT} R_3 + \frac{dV_{io}}{dT}\right]$$

$$= 2.904[0.5 \times 10^{-9} \times 3.3 \times 10^3 + 5 \times 10^{-6}]\text{per °C}$$
$$= 19.3 \; \mu\text{V °C}^{-1}$$

From this it can be seen that the temperature stability of the circuit is primarily determined by the temperature coefficient of the reference diode and should therefore be only just slightly worse than 0.01% per °C.

In order to improve the transient response and to increase stability, two capacitors are shown wired across the output pins. The 64 μF 50 V working electrolytic is to reduce low frequency (100 Hz) ripple and the 100 nF (ceramic) to improve the transient response. The complete circuit is shown in Fig. 3.33.

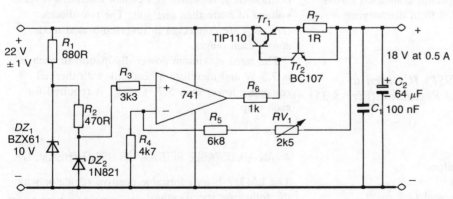

Fig. 3.33 Completed regulator design

3 DESIGNS USING 'FIXED' 3-TERMINAL REGULATOR ICS

These ICs are particularly useful for on-board regulators and small power supply units. Some precautions need to be observed.

(a) Bypass capacitors

Positive regulators normally have an n-p-n transistor as the series element in emitter-follower configuration, a connection that is fairly stable. Negative regulators, on the other hand, since p-n-p transistors are difficult to create in IC form, use an n-p-n in common-emitter mode with the load in the collector circuit. These regulators are therefore more prone to instability. Typical bypass arrangements should be as follows:

Positive regulators
    1 μF on the input terminals
    100 nF ceramic on the output terminals

Negative regulators
    5 μF on the input terminals
    1 μF electrolytic in parallel with a
    100 nF ceramic on the output terminals

These capacitors must be connected as near as possible to the regulator IC pins.

(b) Reverse bias protection

To prevent damage to the IC under conditions when the circuit becomes reverse biased, an additional diode must be connected as shown in Fig. 3.34. Then if the input side is accidentally shorted or crowbarred the bypass capacitor connected across the output can be prevented from discharging through the regulator IC.

Example 78S15 and 79S15 ICs used to provide a ±15 V Dual Regulator (Fig. 3.35)

Specification
V_{in} : ± 20 V
V_{out} : ± 15 V
Tolerance : $\pm 5\%$ each output
Load current : 1.5 A max
Load regulation : 0.1% typical (2% max)

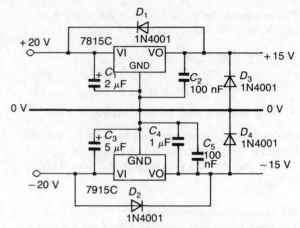

Fig. 3.34 ±15 V regulator using fixed three-terminal regulator ICs

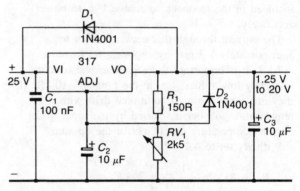

Fig. 3.35 Variable regulator using a 317

Line regulation : 0.5 V V^{-1} typical
Temperature stability : -1 mV °C^{-1}

This dual power supply requires additional protection to prevent *latch-up*. This can occur because most regulator ICs cannot tolerate a reverse voltage of more than one volt. The two diodes (D_3, D_4) are connected in reversed-biased mode across each output.

The rated maximum power dissipation of each IC is 7.5 W and therefore a heat sink with thermal resistance lower than 5.7 °C W^{-1} is required for each chip.

4 AN ADJUSTABLE REGULATOR USING THE LM317K

The LM317 is an adjustable positive regulator with the following specification:

Input voltage range : 4 V to 40 V
Output voltage range : 1.25 V to 37 V
Output current rating : 15 A
Line regulation : 5 mV typical (25 mV max)
Load regulation : 0.2%/V typical (0.07%/V max)
Ripple rejection : 64 dB
Thermal resistance $R_{\text{th}(j-c)}$: 4 °C W^{-1}

The circuit in Fig. 3.35 illustrates a typical use of this IC. The input is set to 25 V and the output is adjustable over the range 1.25–22 V.

$$V_{\text{out}} = 1.25 \ (1+RV_1/R_1)$$
Therefore $R_1 = 150 \ \Omega$ with $RV_1 = 2.5 \ \text{k}\Omega$

D_1 is the reverse diode fitted in the event of an input short circuit.

The ripple rejection is increased by using a decoupling capacitor across RV_1 and this 10 μF tantalum necessitates another protection diode D_2. Then, if the output is short circuited, C_2 will be safely discharged without reverse biasing the IC.

Load currents up to 1.5 A are possible but since the input is held at 25 V a relatively large IC power dissipation occurs at low outputs. For example, with V_{out} set to 1.25 V, if I_L was 1.5 A the power dissipation of the IC would rise to

$$P_{\text{tot}} = (25-1.25) \ 1.5 = 35.6 \ \text{W}$$

The dissipation derating curve given in Fig. 3.36 shows that maximum dissipation is 20 W at a case temperature of 70 °C. This limits the output current at $V_{\text{o}} = 1.25$ V to 842 mA. The current available at various voltages can be found using the formula:

$$I_{\text{L(max)}} = \frac{P_{\text{d}}}{(V_{\text{in}}-V_{\text{o}})}$$

Note the above calculations assume a heat sink of better than 1.25 °C W^{-1} at ambient temperatures up to 40 °C.

5 A SLOW SWITCH-ON POWER UNIT USING A 317K IC REGULATOR

Delayed switch-on of power to certain loads is often required and an example, based on a 317K regulator IC, is illustrated in Fig. 3.37. When the unregulated input voltage is first applied C_1 will be uncharged and the voltage across it will be zero volts. Tr_1 will be on, holding the adjust pin of the 317K at zero volts. C_1 then charges slowly via R_1 and R_3 so that Tr_1 gradually turns off allowing the output voltage to rise to the value set by R_1 and R_2.

With $R_1 = 220 \ \Omega$ and V_{out} required $= 20$ V, R_2 value can be calculated using:

$$V_{\text{out}} = 1.25 \ (1+R_2/R_1)$$

rearranging gives $R_2 = R_1[(V_{\text{out}}/1.25)-1]$
Therefore $R_2 = 3.3 \ \text{k}\Omega$.

6 SWITCHING REGULATOR DESIGNS USING A STANDARD IC

There are several standard ICs available that contain the elements required to create simple secondary mode switching regulators. The Motorola type 78S40 is a typical example and will be used here to illustrate the technique involved. The IC consists of a stable 1.25 V voltage reference, a controlled duty-cycle oscillator with an active current limit circuit, a comparator, a series switch capable of 1.5 A and 40 V, and a power diode, see Fig. 3.38. Also included on the chip is an uncommitted operational amplifier. All that is required from the designer is to calculate and fit certain external components, these being a timing capacitor to set the oscillator

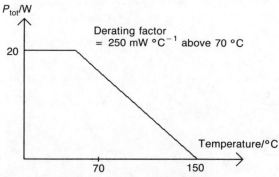

Fig. 3.36 Derating graph for the LM317K

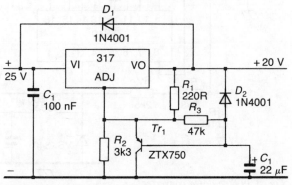

Fig. 3.37 Slow turn-on regulator

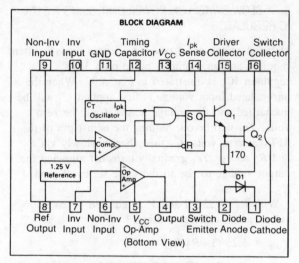

Fig. 3.38 The μA 78S40 switching regulator IC

frequency, a current sense resistor, feedback resistors to fix the voltage and L and C filter components.

The main features of the 78S40 can be listed as follows:

- Maximum input voltage 40 V
- Output voltage adjustable from 1.25 V to 40 V
- Peak output current 1.5 A (This can be increased by using an external transistor)
- Power dissipation of 1.5 W at $T_A = 25 \, ^\circ C$

- Internal reference 1.245 V ± 65 mV

The IC can be used to create step-down, step-up and inverting regulators but care has to be taken over layout to achieve optimum performance.

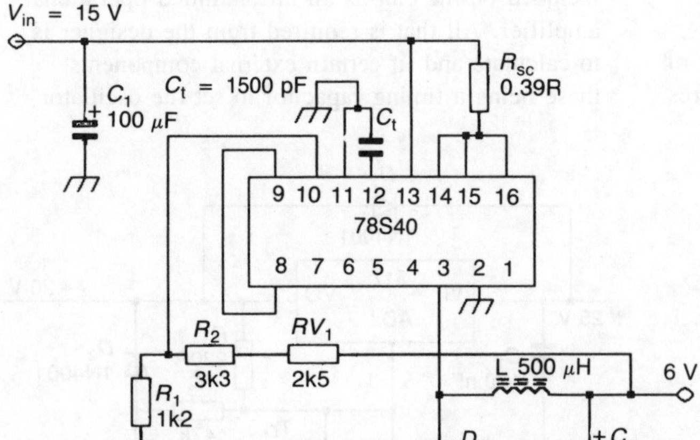

(a) Step-down convertor (Fig. 3.39)

Target specification

V_{in} : 15 V ± 2 V
V_{out} : 6 V ± 50 mV
I_L : 400 mA
I_{SC} : 450 mA ± 20 mA
Ripple : less than 2%
f_{min} : 15 kHz

Design formulas

$$t_{on}/t_{off} = \frac{V_{out} + V_F}{V_{in(min)} - (V_{sat} + V_{out})}$$

$$f_{min} = \frac{1}{t_{on} + t_{off}} \text{ Hz}$$

$$C_t = 4 \times 10^{-5} \cdot t_{on} \text{ F}$$

$$I_{pk(switch)} = 2I_{out(max)} \text{ A}$$

$$R_{sc} = 0.33/I_{pk(switch)} \ \Omega$$

$$L_{(min)} = \frac{V_{in(min)} - (V_{sat} + V_{out})}{I_{pk(switch)}} \cdot t_{on(max)} \text{ H}$$

$$C_o = \frac{I_{pk(switch)} \cdot (1/f_{min})}{8V_{r \, pk-pk}} \text{ F}$$

Fig. 3.39 Step-down converter

$V_{out} = 1.25[1 + (R_2/R_1)]$ V

where $V_{r\,pk-pk}$ is the tolerated ripple voltage, V_{sat} = the saturation voltage of the internal switch and V_F = the volt drop across the flywheel diode.

Calculations

(i) $\dfrac{t_{on}}{t_{off}} = \dfrac{V_{out} + V_F}{V_{in(min)} - (V_{sat} + V_{out})}$

In this case $V_{out} = 6$ V, $V_F = 1.25$ V and $V_{sat} = 1.3$ V.

Therefore $\dfrac{t_{on}}{t_{off}} = \dfrac{6 + 1.25}{13 - (1.3 + 6)} = 1.27$

Since $f_{min} = 15$ kHz, $t_{on} + t_{off} = 66$ μs
Therefore $t_{on} = 37.5$ μs
and $\quad t_{off} = 29.5$ μs
Therefore $C_t = [4 \times 10^{-5}]\, t_{on} = 1500$ pF

(ii) $I_{pk(switch)} = 2I_{0(max)} = 0.9$ A
therefore $R_{sc} = 0.33/I_{pk(switch)} = 0.37$ Ω
use 0.39 Ω (n.p.v.)

(iii) $L_{min} = \dfrac{[13 - (2.55)]}{0.9} \times 37.5 \times 10^{-6}$ H $= 435$ μH

(iv) $C_o = \dfrac{I_p(1/f_{min})}{8V_r}$

In this case $V_r = 120$ mV

therefore $C_{o(min)} = \dfrac{0.9}{8 \times 0.12 \times 15 \times 10^3} = 62.5$ μF

We shall use a 100 μF.

(v) Since $V_{out} = 1.25[1 + (R_2/R_1)]$ and the sampling network current is to be set to 1 mA (this current can be as low as 0.1 mA),

$R_2 = 1.2$ kΩ
and $R_1 + R_2 = 6$ kΩ.

Therefore $R_2 = 4.8$ kΩ — use a 3k3 resistor in series with a 2k5 potentiometer (preset).

The inductor of 435 μH(min) should be wound, using insulated copper wire, on a ferrite pot core such as an RM6 or RM10. The procedure is:

(a) Calculate $LI^2_{(pk)}$ to give the magnetic energy in mJ. Then use a core that has an $LI^2_{(sat)}$ value equal to or greater than $LI^2_{(pk)}$. To keep d.c. losses to a minimum use a core with a large inductance factor.

(b) Number of turns required is given by

$n = \sqrt{L/A_L}$

where L is in nH and A_L is the inductance factor.

(c) Select the largest diameter wire, for the number of turns required, that can be fitted onto the bobbin.
In this case: $LI^2_{(pk)} = 0.43$ mJ and therefore an RM10 core ($L^2_{(sat)} = 1.082$ mJ) should be used. For the RM10 $A_L = 400$ nH/turns^2.

$n = \sqrt{(L/A_L)} = \dfrac{437 \times 10^3}{400} = 33$

The coil can be wound using almost 1 mm diameter insulated copper wire.

The layout of the circuit is critical if the best performance is to be achieved, and an oscilloscope is essential for checking that spurious oscillations are not set up. For the layout keep all lead lengths to a minimum and use one solid earthpoint, preferably at the *anode* end of the flywheel diode. Note that an external diode (a fast Schottky 3 A type) has been used instead of the IC's internal diode to increase circuit efficiency.

Even when great care is taken over the layout some voltage spikes will appear across the output, especially at maximum load. Use additional 100 nF ceramic decoupling capacitors to reduce these transients.

Prototype performance
V_{in} set to +15 V
V_o at $I_o = 100$ mA set to 6.050 V
V_o at $I_o = 400$ mA measured as 6.022 V
Ripple 50 mV pk−pk at $I_o = 400$ mA
Load regulation: 0.5%
Efficiency at full load: 82%

(b) Step-up convertor using the 78S40 (Fig. 3.40)

The step-up switching regulator has the switch connected in parallel after the inductor (see Fig. 3.40(a)). This arrangement ensures that the output voltage is always higher than the input voltage. When the switch closes, current flows through the

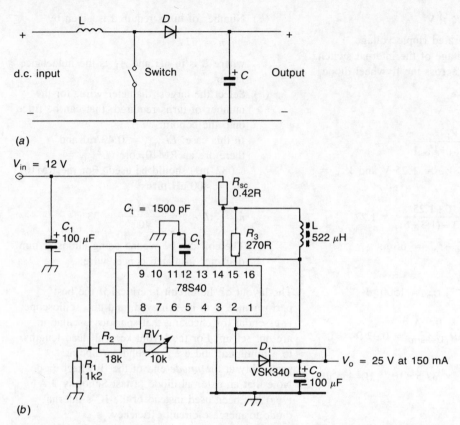

Fig. 3.40 (a) Connections for step-up conversion; (b) 78S40 connections for a step-up switching regulator

inductor and energy is stored in the inductor's magnetic field. When the switch opens the voltage across the load then equals the d.c. input voltage plus the back e.m.f. due to the energy being released from the inductor as the field collapses. In this way power is delivered to the load:

$$P_{out} = LI^2f/2$$

The voltage can be regulated by controlling the duty cycle of the switching frequency f. The 78S40 chip is therefore connected as shown in Fig. 3.40(*b*).

Target specification
V_{in}: 12 V
V_{out}: 25 V $\pm$ 100 mV
$I_{out(max)} = 150$ mA
$I_{sc} = 165$ mA
Ripple: less than 100 mV pk–pk
f_{min}: 15 kHz

Design formulas

$$\frac{t_{on}}{t_{off}} = \frac{V_{out} + V_F - V_{in(min)}}{V_{in(min)} - V_{sat}}$$

$$f_{min} = \frac{1}{t_{on} + t_{off}} \text{ Hz}$$

$$C_t = 4 \times 10^{-5} t_{on} \text{ F}$$

$$I_{pk(switch)} = 2I_{0(max)} \frac{t_{on} + t_{off}}{t_{off}} \text{ A}$$

$$R_{sc} = 0.33/I_{pk(switch)} \text{ }\Omega$$

$$L_{min} = \frac{V_{in(min)} - V_{sat}}{I_{pk(switch)}} t_{on} \text{ H}$$

$$C_o = \frac{I_{out} t_{on}}{V_R}$$

$$V_{out} = 1.25(1 + R_2/R_1) \text{ V}$$

Here $V_F = 1.25$ V
and $V_{sat} = 1.3$ V.

Calculations

1. $\dfrac{t_{on}}{t_{off}} = \dfrac{V_{out} + V_F - V_{in(min)}}{V_{in(min)} - V_{sat}} = \dfrac{25 + 1.25 - 12}{12 - 1.3} = 1.33$

   Since $f_{min} = 15$ kHz, $t_{on} + t_{off} = 67$ μs

   $t_{on} = 38.25$ μs
   and $t_{off} = 28.75$ μs

2. $C_t = 4 \times 10^{-5} \times t_{on} = 1.5$ nF

3. $I_{pk(switch)} = 2I_{o(max)}[(t_{on} + t_{off})/t_{off}] = 0.78$ A
   Therefore $R_{sc} = 0.42$ Ω

4. $L_{min} = \dfrac{V_{in(min)} - V_{sat}}{I_{pk(switch)}} t_{on}$

   $= \dfrac{(12 - 1.3)}{0.78} \times 38 \times 25$ μH $= 525$ μH

   Therefore $L = 525$ μH

5. $C_O = \dfrac{I_O t_{on}}{V_R}$

   $= \dfrac{0.15 \times 38.25}{0.1}$ μF

   $= 57.4$ μF — use 100 μF

6. Make $R_1 = 1.2$ kΩ

   $R_2 = R_1 \left(\dfrac{V_{out}}{1.25} - 1 \right)$

   $= 22.8$ kΩ

   R_2 will be an 18 kΩ resistor in series with a 10 kΩ cermet trimpot.

7. R_3 is selected to be a value that provides sufficient base current drive for Q_1. The use of this external resistor reduces the power dissipation. Assume that Q_1 has a current gain of 20. Then the peak current required through Q_2 is given by

   $I_{C2} = I_{pk(switch)}/h_{FE(sat)} = 0.78/20 = 39$ mA
   Therefore $R_3 = (V_{in} - V_{sat})/I_{C2}$
   $= 270$ Ω

Prototype results
   $V_o = 25.01$ V
   $I_o = 150$ mA
   Load regulation: 0.5%
   Ripple: 80 mV pk−pk at full load

3.8 REFERENCE SUPPLIES

BASIC REQUIREMENTS

Since it is often the performance of the reference circuit that is a key factor in determining the overall regulation of a power supply, the design of the reference circuit itself needs careful consideration. The important features of any voltage reference are:

- stability of the reference voltage with time,
- stability of the reference voltage with temperature (i.e. a low temperature coefficient is a must),
- a low dynamic impedance, so that changes in current through the device do not set up changes in V_{ref},
- a low noise factor.

Close accuracy of the reference value may not in itself be important since this can usually be trimmed by some external potentiometer. However, the stability of the trimming component has then to be taken into consideration. Nor is the ability to pass large currents and to dissipate relatively high power (i.e. more than a few milliwatts) an essential feature of the circuit since the reference itself can be buffered to any external load by an op-amp follower or other arrangement.

The two main methods for generating a reference voltage are by using:

(a) a Zener or voltage regulating diode, or
(b) a band-gap device.

Designs using both of these devices will be investigated.

DESIGNING REFERENCE CIRCUITS USING ZENER DIODES

A true Zener is a diode with a reverse breakdown voltage of less than approximately 5 volts. These diodes have a *soft* breakdown characteristic and have a negative temperature coefficient. For example a 3.3 V 500 mW Zener would have a dynamic resistance of at least 100 Ω and exhibit a change in V_Z of about -2 mV °C^{-1}. As the breakdown voltage moves higher, i.e. for Zener diodes of 5 V and upwards, the knee in the characteristic becomes sharper thus reducing R_Z,

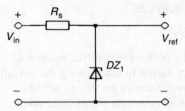

Fig. 3.41 Simple Zener diode reference circuit

and the temperature coefficient moves positive. The reason for this is due to the changing mechanism of the breakdown characteristic from the true Zener effect to avalanche.

The simplest reference can be created by using a Zener in series with a fixed resistor (see Fig. 3.41) and to get the best temperature performance a diode within the range 4.3–5.6 V should be used. These values exhibit the lowest temperature drifts. This can be seen from Table 3.2 for a commonly used Zener diode, the BZY88. For the simple circuit of Fig. 4.1 R_S can be calculated using:

$$R_S = \frac{V_{in} - V_{ref}}{I_Z}$$

I_Z, the diode current, should be a value that ensures

Table 3.2 Device: BZY88 Tolerance: ±5% P_{tot}: 500 mW.
Temperature = 25 °C and I_Z = 5 mA for the figures given.

V_Z Zener voltage (V)	r_Z Dynamic resistance (Ω)	TC Temp. coefficient (mV °C^{-1})
2.7	120	−1.8
3.0	120	−1.8
3.3	110	−1.8
3.6	105	−1.8
3.9	100	−1.4
4.3	90	−1.0
4.7	85	+0.3
5.1	75	+1.0
5.6	55	+1.5
6.2	27	+2.0
6.8	15	+2.7
7.5	15	+3.7
8.2	20	+4.5
9.1	25	+6.0
10	25	+7.0
12	35	+9.0

the diode dissipation is well within its rated maximum value, typically no more than 20% of $P_{Z(max)}$. For the BZY88 range I_Z should be set to approximately 5 mA.

In the formula above the load presented to the circuit is assumed to be very light, i.e. I_Z is much greater than I_L. Suppose we use a BZY88 4V7 diode to provide a reference from a 16 V ± 1 V supply.

Then $R_S = (16 - 4.7)/5$ kΩ ≈ 2k2

Apart from the poor tolerance of the reference voltage (±5% selection tolerance is typical for the BZY88 range) the main defect of this circuit is that the relatively high value of the Zener's dynamic impedance (r_Z = 85 Ω) will set up changes in V_{ref} as V_{in} changes.
Here

$$\Delta V_{in} = \pm 1 \text{ V}.$$

Therefore

$$\Delta V_{ref} = \frac{\Delta V_{in} r_Z}{R_s + r_Z} = \pm 37.2 \text{ mV}$$

This represents a change of nearly ±1% in V_{ref}, which can hardly be described as stable.

Improvements to the basic circuit can be made by supplying the Zener diode from a constant current source (see Fig. 3.42). In this way changes in V_{in} will not greatly affect the reference voltage. Here the Zener diode current is set by the value of R_2 and the V_{BE} of Tr_1. Since the V_{BE} of a silicon transistor is typically 600 mV,

$$R_2 = 600 \text{ mV}/I_Z$$
For I_Z = 5 mA, R_2 = 120 Ω.

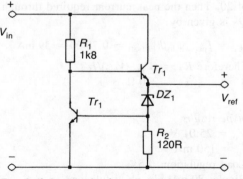

Fig. 3.42 Improved reference circuit using a constant current

Another advantage of this circuit is that changes in V_{BE} with temperature, typically -2 mV °C^{-1}, can be offset by using a Zener diode that has a positive temperature coefficient. For example, if a 6.2 V BZY88 is used, the two temperature coefficients should cancel, giving a reference that is very stable with temperature. (However, it must be pointed out that the TC figures quoted for the BZY88 are the typical ones — it would be unlikely that a true zero TC would result in practice.)

Assuming that $V_Z = 6.2$ V and $V_{in} = 16$ V $\pm$ 1 V as before, then $V_{ref} = V_Z + V_{BE(Tr1)} \approx 6.8$ V.

R_1 value is calculated using:

$$R_1 = \frac{V_{in} - (V_Z + 2V_{BE})}{I_{C1}}$$

If I_{C1} is set to 5 mA to match the Zener diode current then:

$$R_1 = \frac{16 - (6.2 + 1.2)}{5} \approx 1.720 \text{ k}\Omega$$

Therefore a 1k8 will be specified.

An estimate of the effect of ΔV_{in} on V_{ref} can be made by determining the change in collector current of Tr_1 and then referring this to a V_{BE} change. The change in Zener current is assumed to be negligibly small.

$$\Delta I_C = \Delta V_{in}/R_1 \qquad (1)$$

$$\Delta I_C = g_m \cdot \Delta V_{BE} \qquad (2)$$

Therefore

$$\Delta V_{BE} = \Delta V_{in}/g_m R_1$$

Since the collector current is set to 5 mA the g_m of Tr_1 will be approximately 200 mS. (For a transistor $g_m \approx 40$ mS mA^{-1} of I_C.)

Therefore

$$V_{BE} = \frac{1}{200 \times 10^{-3} \times 1.8 \ 10^{-3}} = 2.8 \text{ mV V}^{-1}$$

Therefore since V_{BE} is added to V_Z the reference will change by about $+3$ mV per volt of V_{in}. This is more than a tenfold improvement on the previous circuit.

An alternative technique that can be used to prevent changes in V_{ref} due to V_{in} is to use another Zener diode as a pre-regulator to drive the

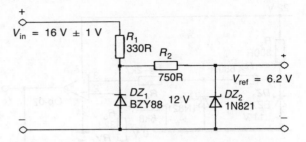

Fig. 3.43 Zener diode used as pre-regulator for the reference

reference (see Fig. 3.43). It may also be a cheaper method of producing the constant current than using the two transistors. However, in this case temperature compensation may be more difficult to achieve and therefore a Zener reference diode with a low TC should be used for the DZ_2 position. The 1N821 or 1N827 temperature compensated reference diodes are ideal. These are 6.2 V $\pm$ 5% devices which have 15 Ω dynamic impedance and temperature coefficients of 0.01%/°C and 0.0001%/°C respectively at $I_Z = 7.5$ mA. For the circuit $ZD_1 > ZD_2$.

Therefore make ZD_1 a 12 V device with $I_Z = 5$ mA.

$$R_1 = \frac{V_{in} - V_{Z1}}{I_{Z1} + I_{Z2}}$$

$$R_2 = \frac{V_{Z1} - V_{Z2}}{I_{Z2}}$$

For $V_{in} = 16$ V $\pm$ 1 V, $R_1 = 330$ Ω (n.p.v.) and $R_2 = 750$ Ω (n.p.v.).

An estimate of the change in V_{ref} due to a 1 V change in V_{in} can be made as follows:

$$\Delta V_{Z1} = \Delta I_{Z1} r_{Z1} \approx \frac{V_{in} r_{Z1}}{R_1}$$

For the BZY88 12 V Zener, $r_Z = 35$ Ω. Therefore $\Delta V_{Z1} = 106$ mV V^{-1}.

$$\Delta V_{ref} \approx \frac{\Delta V_{Z1} r_{Z2}}{R_2}$$

$$= (106 \times 15)/750 \text{ mV} = 2.12 \text{ mV V}^{-1}$$

A line stability of better than 0.035% per 1 V change in V_{in}.

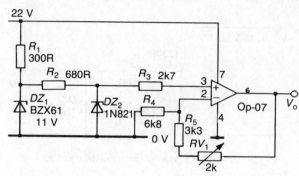

Fig. 3.44 10 V reference

DESIGN EXAMPLE USING A ZENER DIODE TO PROVIDE A REFERENCE OF 10 V (See Fig. 3.44)

Target specification

V_{ref} : 10 V ± 50 mV
V_{in} : 22 V ± 10%
Load current : between 1 mA and 2 mA
Line stability : better than 1 mV V^{-1}
Temperature coefficient : better than ±0.015%/°C

Since the output is required to supply 10 V at 2 mA a buffer amplifier is essential. This can be a non-inverting amplifier with a trimpot used in the feedback loop to allow accurate output voltage setting.

A 1N821 reference diode will be used with a pre-regulator Zener as described earlier.

The pre-regulator will be a BZX61 11 V diode which has r_Z = 10 Ω and TC = 5.5 mV °C^{-1}, both at I_Z = 20 mA.

Therefore

$$R_1 = \frac{V_{in} - V_{Z1}}{I_{Z1} + I_{Z2}} = \frac{22 - 11}{27.5} \text{ k}\Omega = 0.4 \text{ k}\Omega$$

$$R_2 = \frac{V_{Z1} - V_{Z2}}{I_{Z2}} = \frac{11 - 6.2}{7.5} = 0.64 \text{ k}\Omega$$

Therefore R_1 = 390 Ω (n.p.v.)
and R_2 ≈ 680 Ω (n.p.v.)

The op-amp must be a type with low offset drift with temperature. The OP-07 is suitable. This op-amp has:

dV_{io}/dT = 0.5 μV °C^{-1}
and dI_{io}/dT = 12 pA °C^{-1}

To give 10 V output the gain of the non-inverting circuit must be 1.613.

Voltage gain = 1 + (R_f/R_4) where R_f = (R_5 + RV_1)

If RV_1 is made a 2 kΩ cermet trimpot and R_5 a 3k3 resistor, then R_4 can be a 6k8 fixed resistor. This gives a maximum gain (RV_1 at max) of

A_{Vmax} = 1.78

and a minimum gain (RV_1 at min) of

A_{Vmin} = 1.48

which should ensure that the tolerance of the 1N821 can be accommodated.

R_3 is included in the circuit to compensate for drift of input bias current with temperature. Its value should be equal to the parallel value of R_4 and R_f.

Therefore R_3 ≈ 2k7.

Questions

1   Given that r_Z for the BZX61 is 10 Ω, estimate the change in V_{ref} per volt change of V_{in}.
2   What is the contribution in mV/°C of the DZ_1 temperature coefficient to the reference temperature coefficient?
3   Given that output voltage drift of the op-amp is given by:

$$\Delta V_O = A_V \left[\frac{dI_{io}}{dT} R_3 + \frac{\Delta V_{io}}{dT} \cdot \frac{R_f + R_4}{R_f} \right] \text{V per °C},$$

Estimate the drift in reference voltage due to the op-amp. [Answers are given in Section 8.3.]

REFERENCE CIRCUITS USING BAND-GAP DEVICES

The band-gap reference is based on the predictable base-emitter voltage of silicon integrated circuit transistors. The usual arrangement is shown in Fig. 3.45 where the reference voltage is developed from the energy band-gap voltage of the silicon semiconductor material; this is typically 1.204 volts.

From the circuit

$$V_{ref} = V_{BE(T3)} + I_2 R_2 \quad (1)$$

The values of the internal resistors R_1 and R_2 are

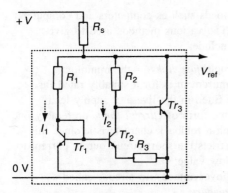

Fig. 3.45 Basic circuit internal to a band-gap device

set during fabrication so that the collector currents of the two transistors Tr_1 and Tr_2 are significantly different. In practice I_1 is made equal to $10I_2$. This current difference means that the V_{BE} of Tr_1 will always be larger than the V_{BE} of Tr_2. Thus the voltage across R_3 is:

$$V_{R3} = V_{BE(Tr1)} - V_{BE(Tr2)}$$

Therefore

$$I_2 = \frac{V_{BE(Tr1)} - V_{BE(Tr2)}}{R_3} \quad (2)$$

Substituting (2) in (1) gives:

$$V_{ref} = V_{BE(Tr3)} + [(V_{BE(Tr1)} - V_{BE(Tr2)})R_2/R_3]$$

By careful choice of I_1 and the ratio of R_2 to R_3 (which is carried out during manufacture) the band-gap device can be made to have a very low temperature coefficient. Without going further into any proof of this you can see that this effect will result if the temperature coefficient of the term in the bracket is of opposite sign (positive) to that of $V_{BE(Tr3)}$. This will be the case because of the slightly different coefficients of the two V_{BE} drops and the multiplier $R_2:R_3$.

Let's consider a typical general purpose band-gap reference such as the REF25Z. For this device:

V_{ref} : 2.5 V ± 2% (a ± 1% tol. version is also available)
Dynamic resistance : 2 Ω max
I_{knee} : 40 μA
I_{ref} : 60 μA to 5 mA
TC : 35 ppm/°C typical*

*ppm = parts per million, i.e. 50 ppm = 0.005%

To operate the device a series resistor R_s is used to limit the current:

$$R_s = (V_{in} - V_{ref})/I_{ref}$$

To give a reference of 2.5 V from an input of 5 V the reference current should be set to about 1 mA (5 mA is the maximum value).

Then R_s = 2.5 kΩ (use 2k4 n.p.v.).

The stability of the reference with respect to changes in V_{in} is given by:

$$\Delta V_{ref} = \frac{\Delta V_{in} r_f}{R_s + r_f}$$

where r_f = band-gap dynamic resistance.

Therefore for the REF25Z the stability is 1.2/2402 ≈ 0.83 mV V^{-1}

Other band-gap devices are available that allow the user to programme the reference voltage externally. The Texas Instruments TL431 is a good example. This programmable reference (see symbol and diagrams Fig. 3.46) has the following specification:

V_{in} : 2.5 V to 36 V
V_{ref} : nominally 2.5 V
r_{ref} : 0.2 Ω
TC : 100 ppm/°C typical

Three external resistors are required, see Fig. 3.47.

$$R_s = \frac{V_{in} - V_{out}}{I_K + I_R}$$

where I_K is the current allowed by the designer to flow through the device.

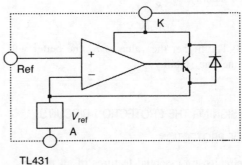

Fig. 3.46 Programmable band-gap device

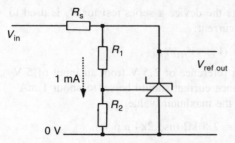

Fig. 3.47 Using the programmable band-gap reference

I_R should be set to about 1 mA to swamp the small current I_{ref}. Then:

$$V_{out} = V_{ref}[1+(R_1/R_2)]$$

where $V_{ref} = 2.5$ V

DESIGN EXAMPLE USING THE TL431

$V_{out} : 5$ V
$V_{in} : 15$ V $\pm$ 2 V

1. Set I_K to 2 mA and I_R to 1 mA.

   Then $R_s = \dfrac{V_{in} - V_{out}}{I_K + I_R}$

   $= 10/3$ k$\Omega = 343$

2. Since $V_{out} = 5$ V

   $R_1 = R_2$
   $R_2 = V_{ref}/I = 2k5$

   Therefore R_1 and R_2 can be 2k2, 2k4 or 2k7 value resistors.

   Line stability $= \dfrac{\Delta V_{in} r_z}{R_s + r_z}$

   ≈ 61 μV V^{-1}

NB: The higher the value of R_s the better will be the line stability.

3.9   DESIGNING THE PROTECTION CIRCUITS

TYPES OF PROTECTION

These circuits are essential features of all power supplies. They minimise the risk of fire, prevent damage to sensitive loads, protect the power supply components from short circuits, and are also used to give the virtual uninterruptable supplies required by volatile loads such as computers and computer memories. The various methods used to give protection include:

(a) simple *fuse links* — the minimum requirement is for a suitably rated fuse to be fitted in the live a.c. supply lead;
(b) some form of *current limit*, preferably one with a foldback characteristic since this restricts the short-circuit output current to a low value;
(c) an overvoltage trip circuit, called a *crowbar*;
(d) a *thermal* sensor and *shut down* circuit;
(e) the use of psu *supervisory ICs*.

The main points about the design of protection circuits revolve around the consideration of effectiveness and reliability. Close accuracy of any trip point is not usually necessary but reliable operation is. For most of the power unit's active life the protection circuits just *sit back* monitoring conditions and are only required to take some action if and when a fault occurs. This means the design needs to be simple, consume very little power, and have the minimum of interference on the unit's performance. It follows that a simpler design will probably have the edge in terms of actual reliable and effective operation over a more complex circuit, even though the latter might well have closer tolerance trip points and more desirable characteristics. Sometimes, of course, a compromise is necessary between these two approaches.

DESIGNING THE BASIC CURRENT LIMIT

The circuit (Fig. 3.48) consists of a current monitoring resistor placed in series with the supply

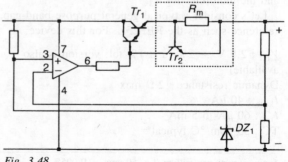

Fig. 3.48

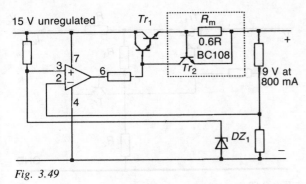

Fig. 3.49

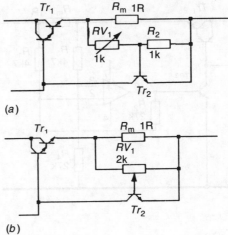

(a)

(b)

Fig. 3.50

lead, *but within the feedback loop of the regulator,* and one transistor. The resistor is connected within the loop to prevent the output resistance and load regulation of the power supply being degraded. This simple circuit is quite effective for light to medium load currents. If the load current rises above a predetermined level, set by the value of R_m, the voltage across R_m exceeds the base-emitter voltage of the transistor Tr_2 which then conducts to divert base drive from the series pass transistor. The short-circuit output current is given by:

$$I_{sc} \approx V_{BE}/R_m \approx 600/R_m \text{ mA}$$

For the example in Fig. 3.49 the output current will be limited to:

$$I_{sc} = 600/0.6 \text{ mA} \approx 1 \text{ A}$$

Transistor Tr_2 is only required to pass the few milliamps necessary to restrict the base drive to the Darlington. Therefore most small signal general purpose n-p-n transistors, such as the BC108, BC182L or BC184L, will be adequate for the purpose.

The defects of the simple circuit are:

(a) Under short-circuit conditions the dissipation of the series transistor in the regulator rises to a much larger value than its normal maximum operating dissipation.

In the circuit at the maximum load current of 0.8 A the power dissipation of Tr_1 is:

$$P_c \approx (V_{in} - V_{out})I_L = 5 \text{ W}$$

While under short-circuit conditions with $I_{sc} = 1 \text{ A}$,

$$P_{sc} = V_{in}I_{sc} = 15 \text{ W}$$

(Here we have neglected the small volt drop across R_m.)

It can be seen that the series transistor's dissipation under short-circuit conditions is some three times higher than its normal value. Either the available load current must be restricted or a relatively large heat-sink is required for Tr_1.

(b) The limiting point is not accurately set and depends upon the tolerance of R_m and the variation in V_{BE} of Tr_2.

The first point can only be overcome by changing the protection circuit to give foldback characteristics, but an improvement to allow more precise setting of the limit can be made using the circuits given in Fig. 3.50. In this case R_m has to be a slightly higher value than that previously calculated so that at I_{sc} a voltage of about 1 V is developed across it.

Therefore

$$R_m \approx 1/I_{sc}.$$

A potential divider consisting of a trimpot and a fixed resistor is used to connect a portion of the voltage across R_m to the base emitter junction of the transistor Tr_2.

Since

$$V_{BE} = \frac{V_{sc}R_2}{RV_1 + R_2}$$

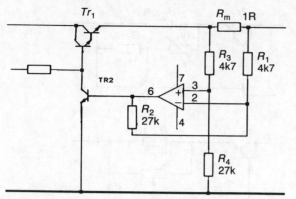

Fig. 3.51

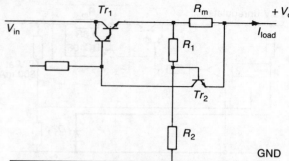

Fig. 3.52

and

$$V_{sc} = I_{sc}R_m$$

$$I_{sc} = \frac{V_{BE}(RV_1+R_2)}{R_mR_2} \text{ A}$$

With the values given I_{sc} can be set between 0.6 A and 1.2 A.

The trimpot can of course be connected in R_2 position, or R_2 can be omitted and the trimpot wiper connected directly to Tr_2 base.

The relatively high value necessary for R_m in these basic circuits means that some extra power is lost and that usually a 1 W or higher rated resistor must be fitted. If R_m is 1 Ω as in Fig. 3.50 at $I_L =$ 0.8 A the voltage across it is 800 mV and its power loss is 800 mW. Using an amplifier to increase the signal across R_m as in Fig. 3.51 allows a much lower value of monitoring resistor to be used.

In this case since the op-amp is connected as a differential amplifier with gain of $-R_2/R_1$,

$$I_{sc} = (V_{BE}/R_m)(R_1/R_2)$$

Using the values as suggested $I_{sc} = 1$ A. The current monitoring resistor now dissipates only 100 mW. The 0.1 Ω value can be made using a few turns of resistance wire, e.g. 16SWG manganin wire which has a resistance of about 3 Ω per metre.

FOLDBACK CURRENT LIMITS

There are several ways of implementing this useful circuit. Foldback characteristics are essential on high current systems to prevent excessive heat dissipation in the series element when the output is

overloaded or short circuited. A typical circuit is shown in Fig. 3.52. If a predetermined knee current I_K is exceeded, feedback is used to *reduce* the load current as the output voltage falls to zero. At short circuit the current I_{sc} is then limited to a much lower value than the maximum load current rating of the power supply. For the circuit the V_{BE} of Tr_2 is given by:

$$V_{BE} = I_LR_m - (V_o+I_LR_m) \cdot \frac{R_1}{R_1+R_2}$$

Re-arranging to make I_L the subject gives:

$$I_L = \frac{V_{BE}(R_1+R_2+V_oR_1}{R_mR_2}$$

Thus

$$I_K = \frac{0.6(R_1+R_2)+V_oR_1}{R_mR_2}$$

where I_K is the knee current.

When the output is short circuited $V_o = 0$ and $I_K = I_{sc}$.

$$I_{sc} = \frac{0.6(R_1+R_2)}{R_mR_2}$$

Let's take a design example for a 5 V, 2.25 A supply. We shall set I_K, the knee current, to be 2.5 A and make R_m 1 Ω.

Since

$$I_K = \frac{0.6(R_1+R_2)+V_oR_1}{R_mR_2}$$

We have:

$$2.5R_2 = 0.6R_1 = 0.6R_2 + 5R_1$$

Therefore $R_2 \approx 3R_1$.

With $R_1 = 910$ Ω, R_2 should be 2k7.

Check:

$$I_K = \frac{0.6(3.61)+5\times0.91}{2.7} = 2.5\ \text{A}$$

Using these values for R_1 and R_2 gives a short-circuit current of:

$$I_{sc} = \frac{0.6(0.91+2.7)}{2.7} \approx 0.8\ \text{A}$$

The power dissipation of the series transistor at I_{sc} is only 8 W instead of nearly 25 W which would result if the simple current limit had been used.

The same technique to give foldback current limiting can be applied to IC regulators such as the 723. The internal portions of the 723 (see Fig. 3.70) are a stable reference of 7.2 V, a comparator, a series pass transistor and a current limiting transistor. Simple current limiting can be set up using one external resistor R_m, but this method restricts the maximum available output current. An example is shown in Fig. 3.53(a) for a 5 V output from a nominal 9 V unregulated input. Short-circuited output current is given, in this case, by:

$$I_{sc} \leq P_{max}/V_s$$

Therefore $I_{sc} = 660/9\ \text{mA} = 73\ \text{mA}$.

Thus the maximum load current for this 5 V current limited design must not exceed 70 mA. An additional series pass transistor would be necessary if more load current was required.

Now let's consider the foldback circuit of Fig. 3.54(b). Only two extra resistors are required. First let us calculate the maximum load current:

$$I_{Lmax} = \frac{P_{max}}{V_s - V_o} = 160\ \text{mA}$$

But we shall restrict this to, say, 140 mA to give a reasonable safety margin. This is still double the output of the previous circuit.

Set I_K to be 150 mA. With $R_m = 12\ \Omega$, a suitable value that allows a reasonable volt drop for sensing purposes without reducing the voltage across the series transistor excessively,

$$I_K = \frac{0.6(R_1+R_2)+V_oR_1}{R_mT_2}$$

Rearranging to make R_2 the subject gives

$$R_2 = \frac{(0.6+V_o)R_1}{(R_mI_K-0.6)}$$

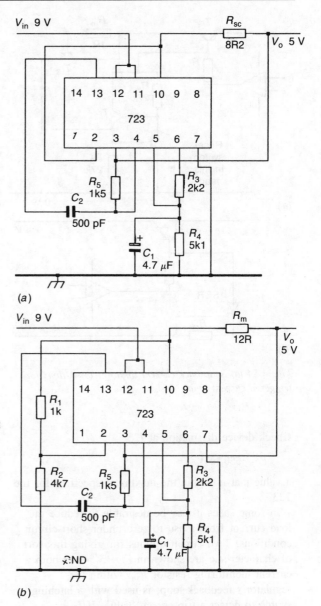

(a)

(b)

Fig. 3.53 (a) Simple current limiting used with the 723;
(b) Foldback current limiting used with the 723

Therefore $R_2 = 4.7R_1$.

Make $R_1 = 1\ \text{k}$ and $R_2 = 4\text{k}7$.

Determine I_{sc}:

$$I_{sc} = \frac{0.6(R_1+R_2)}{12R_2} = 60\ \text{mA}$$

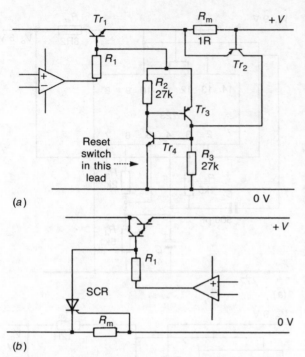

Fig. 3.54 (a) Snap-back current limiting; (b) A thyristor triggered current limit

flows through the two transistors. But when the trip current is exceeded Tr_2 conducts and passes current to Tr_4 base. Tr_4 amplifies this current and pulls base current out of Tr_3. Since Tr_3 and Tr_4 are connected in a positive feedback loop both rapidly switch fully on, taking the base of Tr_1, the series element, to the same potential as the negative return rail. In this way Tr_1 is held off and the short-circuit load current is zero. The reset switch breaks the loop in Tr_3 and Tr_4 to allow power to be restored.

The circuit in Fig. 3.54(*b*) uses the same technique but has a thyristor as the trigger device. The load current sensing resistor R_m is placed in the supply return lead. If a certain value of trip current is exceeded the voltage across R_m is sufficient to trigger the thyristor which then switches into a forward conduction state. The potential at the base of the series element (the Darlington) is reduced to less than 1 V which forces it to cease conducting. Thus I_{sc} is zero.

The trip current is given by:

$$I_{trip} = V_{GT}/R_m.$$

A sensitive low power thyristor such as the C203YY is required. The important requirements are:

V_{GT} (gate trigger voltage) : less than 1 V
I_{GT} (gate trigger current) : less than 1 mA
and I_H (holding current) : less than 10 mA.

The last point is important because the thyristor must stay latched-on once the trip current is exceeded. If the holding current rating for the thyristor is higher than the drive available to the base of the series Darlington the thyristor will not latch and the current limit will not be effective.

Consider a design using the C203YY to give foldback protection. I_{trip} is to be 2 A and this value is to be preset using the resistors as shown. (See Fig. 3.55.)

For the C203YY:

$V_{GT} = 0.8$ V
$I_{GT} = 0.2$ mA
$I_H = 5$ mA typical

In this case the voltage across R_m must exceed V_{GT}, therefore $R_m = 1.5\ V_{GT}/I_{trip}$. Use a 0.6 Ω.

Make the current through RV_1 and R_2 at least 10 times greater than I_{GT}. Therefore $R_2 = V_{GT}/10I_{GT}$ = 400 Ω (390 Ω n.p.v.); RV_1 can be a 500 Ω cermet

Check device dissipation at I_{sc}:

$P = 550$ mW,

a value that is within the maximum specified for the 723.

In some cases it may be desirable to reduce the load current from a psu to zero under short-circuit conditions. Two circuit options for giving this sort of characteristic are shown in Fig. 3.54. In both a current monitoring resistor R_m, within the regulator's feedback loop, is used with a latching switch to detect a trip current value. If I_T is exceeded the trigger device operates and the power supply is shut down. A *reset* facility must usually be incorporated which is operated to restore power once the overload has been located and removed.

For the example given in Fig. 3.54(*a*) the trip current is as follows:

$$I_{trip} = V_{BE(Tr2)}/R_m$$

The two additional transistors Tr_3 and Tr_4 form a snap-action switch which under normal load conditions is off, i.e. only a tiny leakage current

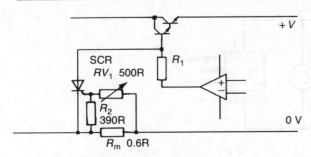

Fig. 3.55 Values for a thyristor triggered current limit; I_{trip} *is 2 A*

trimpot since the nominal value of RV_1, i.e. the value to which it will be set in the circuit, is:

$$RV_1 = \frac{V_{RM} - V_{GT}}{10 I_{GT}} = 200 \ \Omega$$

OVERVOLTAGE PROTECTION – THE CROWBAR

A *crowbar* is a circuit that protects the load being supplied from an overvoltage should a fault occur in the power supply itself. The common causes of an overvoltage at the output of a regulator are:

   (i) a short circuit in the series element,
   (ii) an open circuit in the feedback loop,
   (iii) an open circuit reference device.

The essential parts of a crowbar are a voltage sensing circuit connected across the power supply output terminals or directly across the load and a fast acting trigger device. It is usually good practice to use a latching trigger device that also blows a series fuse on the input side of the regulator to fully disconnect the supply from the load. In this way full protection is ensured.

A circuit outline is given in Fig. 3.56. The

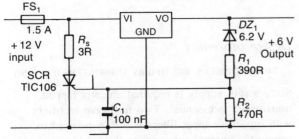

Fig. 3.56 Crowbar overvoltage protection circuit. Trip voltage

voltage sensing circuit can be a Zener diode in series with a potential divider. When the output voltage, caused by a fault condition, rises above a trip value V_T the Zener conducts and the voltage across R_2 just exceeds the V_{GT} value of the thyristor. The thyristor needs to be a sensitive device with low values of V_{GT} and I_{GT}.

Design values to give $V_T = 8$ V.

$$V_{GT} = (V_T - V_Z) . \frac{R_2}{R_1 + R_2} \qquad (1)$$

Rearranging gives

$$V_T = V_Z + V_{GT} \frac{R_1 + R_2}{R_2} \qquad (2)$$

and

$$\frac{R_1 + R_2}{R_2} = \frac{V_T - V_Z}{V_{GT}} \qquad (3)$$

Let's assume that a TIC106 thyristor is to be used. This has $V_{GT} = 0.8$ V and $I_{GT} = 0.2$ mA.

From (3) $R_1 = 1.25 R_2$ $\qquad (DZ_1 = 6.2$ V)

Make the current through R_1 and R_2 at least 10 times greater than I_{GT}.

Therefore $R_1 = V_{GT}/10 I_{GT} = 390 \ \Omega$ and $R_2 = 470 \ \Omega$, these being the nearest preferred values.

Check V_T using equation 2:

$$V_T = 6.2 + 0.8 (2.205) = 8 \text{ V}$$

C_1 is a 100 nF ceramic capacitor fitted to prevent short duration transients or noise from falsely triggering the thyristor.

If the normal load current is, say, 1 A the series fuse should be rated at 1.5 A. When the trip voltage is exceeded the TIC106 will fire, taking the unregulated input of the regulator to nearly 0 V. R_s is used to limit the maximum current through the thyristor to a value that will be sufficient to blow the fuse. For the TIC106 the continuous on-state current is specified as 5 A (at a case temperature of 80 °C) and the surge current for 10 ms is quoted at 30 A. R_s should therefore be a value that restricts the forward current to about 4 A.

$$R_s = V_{in}/I \approx 3 \ \Omega$$

A wirewound resistor with a power rating of greater than 10 W should be used.

The operation of the circuit can be tested by

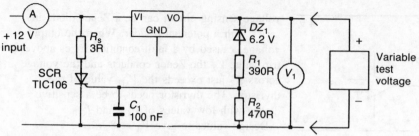

Fig. 3.57 Test circuit for the crowbar

removing the regulator and applying a test voltage across the sensing circuit. *The load must be disconnected.* The fuse can be removed and replaced by a suitable d.c. ammeter (10 A range), see Fig. 3.57. The test voltage is increased until the thyristor fires. At this point V_1 should be 8 V and the ammeter should indicate about 3 A.

3.10 WORKED DESIGN PROBLEMS

OPTIONS

The choices available for the design of power supply systems can be listed as:

- (*a*) fixed three-terminal IC regulators,
- (*b*) variable or special function IC regulator chips such as the 723,
- (*c*) switched mode designs using either primary or secondary switching,
- (*d*) linear series regulators using discretes, i.e. powerFETs, Darlingtons and op-amps,
- (*e*) shunt regulators.

The particular advantages and disadvantages of these various approaches are given in Table 3.2, and clearly for the maximum efficiency and minimum space usage some form of switched design is best. On the other hand the highest performance in terms of regulation and stability can only be gained by using a linear series regulator. Often, however, the choice is not clear cut and perhaps several different solutions can be effective in meeting the same target specification. There is no need for arguments over this. The important criteria are

- (i) that the design works,
- (ii) that it meets the specification,
- (iii) that it is economical in use of space and components.

This final section is included to give some worked design examples showing how the various steps in the design sequence are made, illustrating the choice of the best approach and introducing other standard techniques.

TRACKING REGULATOR

Many op-amp and other linear circuits require split supplies, in other words a supply that provides both a positive and a negative rail with a centre zero. The range required is typically from ± 4 V u⌐ ± 18 V max. In this example the requireme⌐ a tracking regulator, one in which the suppɩ⌐ varied and where the negative closely follows oɩ tracks the setting of the positive rail.

Design specification

V_{in} : 240 V 50 Hz a.c. mains (or 110 V at 60 Hz)
V_{out} : ± 5 V to ± 15 V continuously variable
I_L : 150 mA max
Tracking error : Less than ± 50 mV
Load regulation : Better than 0.1%
Line regulation : Less than 2 mV V^{-1}
Ripple and noise : Less than 10 mV pk–pk

(For circuit outline see Fig. 3.58.)

Design procedure

I TRANSFORMERS, RECTIFIERS AND FILTERS (Fig. 3.59)

Since a split supply is required a centre tapped transformer is essential. Two full-wave rectifiers with capacitive input filters will then be used to supply the unregulated input to the tracking regulator. To enable the regulator to reach the

Table 3.3 Advantages and disadvantages of regulators

Option	Advantages	Disadvantages
Fixed 3-terminal regulator ICs	Easy to use, compact and with built in protection	The output voltages are not precise and only fair to medium regulation is provided. The higher power types are expensive
Variable and special function regulator ICs	Precise output setting is possible over a wide range. Good regulation	More complicated than fixed types with additional components such as resistors, potentiometers and pass transistors required
Switched mode designs	Highly efficient, space saving units with low heat loss	Relatively complex and can be noisy since switching spikes are generated. Greater care over layout is essential
Linear regulators using discretes	Excellent regulation performance is possible	Efficiency is not usually better than 70%. Therefore large heat sinks are required for higher power designs. Overcurrent protection must be designed in
Shunt regulators	Simple circuits with inherent overload protection	Relatively inefficient and therefore only suitable for low power applications

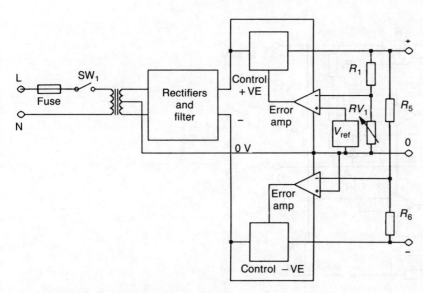

Fig. 3.58 Circuit outline for tracking regulator

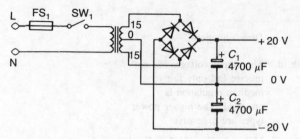

Fig. 3.59 The unregulated ±20 V d.c. supply

specified maximum of ±15 V the unregulated input needs to be set at approximately ±20 V d.c. Allowing for a small volt drop across the rectifiers suggests that each half of the transformer's secondary winding should produce 15 V r.m.s. at an a.c. load current of about 200 mA. ($I_{a.c.} \approx 1.5 I_{d.c.}$).

The VA rating of the 15 V−0−15 V transformer is therefore 6 VA. There are several small transformers of this type available off-the-shelf, many of them suitable for pcb mounting. Good choices would be the RS207-598 or RS208-282.

The full-wave rectifiers can be wired using four IN5401 diodes, or a small bridge unit such as the General Instruments W005 can be used. The rectifiers must have a V_{RRM} rating in excess of 50 V and be capable of passing 0.5 A of continuous current.

The two filter capacitors should have a working voltage of at least 25 V. The value can be estimated using:

$$C_{min} \approx \frac{I_{dc}t}{V_{R(pk-pk)}}$$

where $t = 10$ ms for 50 Hz operated units. Suppose the maximum peak to peak ripple is to be 0.5 V.

Then

$$C_{min} \approx \frac{0.2 \times 10 \times 10^{-3}}{0.5}$$

Therefore $C_{min} \approx 4000$ μF.

Suitable capacitors are as follows:

Dubilier CEA series 25 V, 4700 μF
Panasonic TSU series 35 V, 4700 μF pcb mount electrolytic.

Both these capacitors have ripple current ratings well in excess of the 300 mA expected in the circuit ($I_R \approx 2$ A).

2 REGULATOR SECTION

Since the power requirement is relatively modest (6 W) the best approach for this task is to use a linear series regulator. An outline of the circuit is given in Fig. 3.60. The positive portion is a standard circuit with a reference, an error amplifier and a series pass transistor. The negative regulator

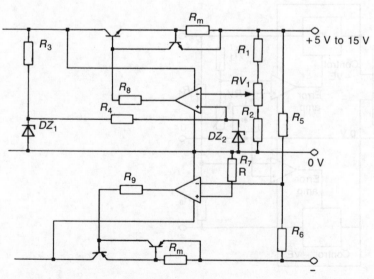

Fig. 3.60 Circuit design of the regulator section

is referenced to zero volts and its output is set by the gain of the inverting amplifier, i.e. $A_{vcl} = R_6/R_5$. Thus if R_5 and R_6 are made equal value close tolerance resistors, the negative rail will track the positive rail.

Circuit design and calculations

(a) Begin with the *reference*. In this case the actual value of V_{ref} must be less than the minimum output voltage (5 V), therefore standard 2.5 V devices such as the ZN404 or REF25Z are suitable. The reference diode could be supplied via a resistor connected to the regulator's output, but because the output is variable from +5 V up to +15 V this connection would result in an unnecessary shift in V_{ref} as V_o was changed. Instead the reference is driven from a pre-regulator connected to the unregulated input. A 10 V Zener is a practical value for this pre-regulator, and both diode currents can be set to a value of, say, 5 mA.

Then

$$R_3 = \frac{V_{in} - V_{Z1}}{I_{Z1} + I_{ref}} = 1 \text{ k}\Omega$$

R_4 value is given by

$$R_4 = \frac{V_{Z1} - V_{ref}}{I_{ref}} = 1.5 \text{ k}\Omega$$

(b) *Divider chain*. A potentiometer RV_1 is to be used to vary the positive rail from +5 V to +15 V. To find the values required we have to consider two conditions:

(i)   when the otuput is to be +5 V. In this case all of the pot is associated with R_2.
(ii) when the output is to be +15 V. Here all the pot is linked with R_1.

For condition (i)

$$\frac{V_o}{V_{ref}} = \frac{R_1 + RV_1 + R_2}{R_2 + RV_1}.$$

Therefore since $V_o = 5$ V and $V_{ref} = 2.5$ V,

$$R_2 + RV_1 = R_1 \quad (1)$$

For condition (ii)

$$\frac{V_o}{V_{ref}} = \frac{R_1 + RV_1 + R_2}{R_2}$$

Therefore since $V_o = 15$ V,

$$5R_2 = R_1 + RV_1 \quad (2)$$

We now have two equations which can be used to find the ratios of the three components. Assume R_2 is 1 kΩ.

From equation (1)

$$1 + RV_1 = R_1 \quad (3)$$

and from (2)

$$5 = R_1 + RV_1 \quad (4)$$
(where all values are in kΩ).

Subtracting (3) from (4) gives

$$2RV_1 = 4$$

Therefore $RV_1 = 2$ kΩ and by substituting this value in (3)

$$R_1 = 3 \text{ k}\Omega$$

The values of R_1, RV_1 and R_2 are in the ratio 3:2:1 to allow the voltage range from 5 V to 15 V to be set up.

The actual values used should not be too low so that excessive current is taken from the supply line nor high enough to cause excessive drift with temperature from the op-amp. The total resistance should lie in the region of 5 kΩ to 10 kΩ.

Therefore R_1 = 3k3 ± 1% 250 mW metal film RV_1 = 2k2 cermet pot with linear track and R_2 = 1k1 ± 1% 250 mW metal film.

(c) *The error amplifier*. This can be a standard op-amp such as the 741 (the dual version 747 cannot be used because the supply voltage across the op-amp used in the positive regulator could then be nearly 44 V).

Drift using a 741 would be approximately 7 mV °C^{-1} which is an acceptable figure. Alternatively, op-amps such as the OP-07 can be used.

(d) *Series transistors*. A relatively modest current of just 150 mA max. is required from this transistor. But in order to keep the current taken from the op-amp to a low value, say less than 1 mA, a Darlington is specified. A low current drain at the op-amp output will ensure that it will provide the necessary voltage drive to the series pass transistor when the regulator is set to give the maximum output of 15 V. It is unlikely that any single transistor would have a minimum h_{FE} of 150 at an I_c of 150 mA.

A TIP110 Darlington is a suitable choice. This has:

$V_{(BR)CE}$: 60 V
$h_{FE(min)}$: 750 at $I_c = 4$ A
P_c : 50 W at 25 °C case temperature, 2 W at 25 °C free air temperature

At first sight the use of a TIP110 might seem to be a case of overspecifying. But this Darlington, and its p-n-p complement the TIP105, are readily available and inexpensive. An alternative arrangement such as using a BC108 to drive a BD131 would also be suitable but more costly.

Since the maximum dissipation of the Darlington could rise to 3.5 W under short-circuit output conditions a small heat sink is essential. One with a thermal resistance of less than 20 °C W^{-1} is suitable.

(e) *The current limit*. A simple current limit will be quite effective in this circuit.

$R_m = 600/I_{sc}$ Ω where I_{sc} is in mA
Therefore $R_m = 3.43$ Ω

A 3.3 Ω (3R3) is the n.p.v. and the rating should be 250 mW. The limiting transistor can be any general purpose small signal n-p-n type such as a ZTX300 or BC108.

(f) *The negative regulator*. For this part of the circuit the input is derived from the output of the positive regulator. An inverting amplifier using another 741 or OP-07 has its non-inverting input tied to zero volts via a temperature compensating resistor R_7 and its output drives the p-n-p Darlington TIP105. In order for the negative output to track the positive output with minimum error the two resistors R_5 and R_6 must be exactly equal in value. Suitable values are 10 kΩ with a selection tolerance of ±0.1%. If close tolerance resistors are not available the two resistors can be matched using a bridge or digital multimeter. This will ensure that the tracking error is within the specified limit of ±50 mV. R_7 is a resistor with a value equal to the parallel combination of R_5 and R_6; a 5k1 is the n.p.v.

The design is now complete; see Fig. 3.61. Try these design modifications:

1. Change the current limit to give foldback characteristics. The trip current is to be 175 mA and short-circuit current less than 50 mA.
2. Suggest simple changes that would allow

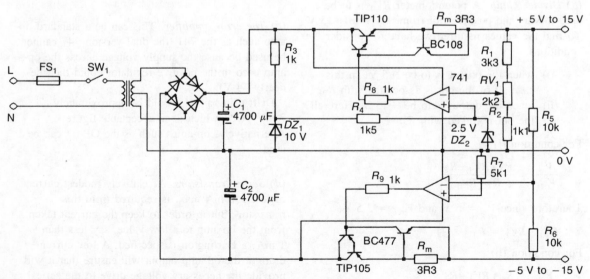

Fig. 3.61 Completed design for the ±5 V to ±15 V tracking regulator

the outputs to be set from ± 4 V up to ± 12 V.

3. Use an LM317M adjustable IC regulator for the positive portion of the circuit.

PROGRAMMABLE CMOS SUPPLY

A programmable regulator is required that can be used under microcomputer control to output three fixed voltages of 5 V, 10 V and 15 V as required by an ATE controller. This enables tests to be made on boards containing CMOS logic. The load current is a maximum of 200 mA and a supply of 24 V d.c. is available. A block diagram of the unit is shown in Fig. 3.62.

Target specification

V_{in} : 24 V
V_{out} : switchable 5 V, 10 V, 15 V $\pm 1\%$
I_L : 200 mA maximum
Load regulation : Better than 1%

One possible circuit design approach to this problem (Fig. 3.63) is to use a constant current source and three equal value resistors. Two switches are then required to allow the three values of voltage to be set up:

S_0	S_1	V_0
0	0	$3IR$ (15 V)
0	1	$2IR$ (10 V)
1	0	$1IR$ (5 V)

A power op-amp such as the 759, which can deliver up to 325 mA, can be used as a non-inverting amplifier to supply the output. The absolute value

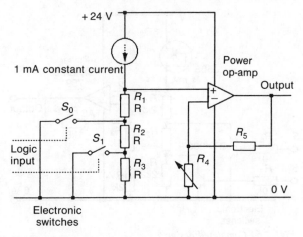

Fig. 3.63 Possible circuit arrangement

of the voltage across the resistor network is not important since a gain control can be incorporated in the op-amp circuit. However, it is important that the three resistors R_1, R_2 and R_3 are equal in value.

Circuit design

A suitable constant current source is the J505. This delivers a constant 1 mA (tolerance $\pm 20\%$) output current for a range of voltages from 2.1 V to over 40 V. The maximum allowed voltage across the diode is 50 V. The typical dynamic impedance is 1.9 MΩ which means that the 10 V change expected in the circuit would only result in a 5.3 μA variation in the current supplied.

The three resistors could have values of 5 kΩ each, giving a 5 V, 10 V or 15 V output from the op-amp, if this is wired as a unity gain follower. But since the J505 has a tolerance on its 1 mA output current of $\pm 20\%$ some form of trim is needed to set the output voltage. This can be one potentiometer fitted in the feedback loop of the amplifier, rather than an adjustment fitted to all three resistors connected in the diode circuit. These three resistors are therefore made 2k2 each with a tolerance of $\pm 1\%$ or better. The voltage to the input of the amplifier will then be 2.2 V, 4.4 V or 6.6 V depending on the switch positions. The amplifier gain has to be

$$A_{Vcl} \approx 2.27$$

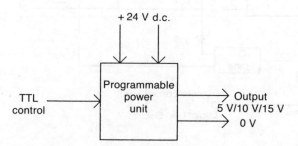

Fig. 3.62 Programmable CMOS supply

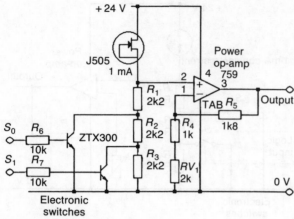

Fig. 3.64 Completed design

For the non-inverting amplifier

$$A_{Vcl} = 1 + \frac{R_5}{R_4 + RV_1}$$

Therefore R_5 is made 1k8, R_4 is made 1 kΩ and Rv_1 a 2k cermet trimpot. These will ensure that the output voltages can be set to within specification.

The switches can either be logic powerFETs, straightforward n-p-n transistors such as the ZTX300 or BC107, or TTL open-collector invertors. The completed design is shown in Fig. 3.64.

Try these modifications to the design:

1. Use a standard 723 IC regulator.
2. Redesign the circuit to give outputs of 3 V, 6 V, 9 V, 12 V and 18 V. A 3-to-8 decoder chip may be used.
3. Replace the J505 by a transistor (p-n-p) constant current circuit.
4. Increase the output current to 2 A.

A REMOTELY CONTROLLED 5 V, 1 A REGULATOR

An unregulated 30 V supply has to be switched remotely to a regulator which then provides 5 V at 1 A to some TTL. A standard 7805 fixed IC regulator chip can be used but both the TTL load being supplied and the regulator chip must be protected against an overvoltage. The remote control input is a TTL level with a logic 1 enabling the 5 V output.

Target specification

V_{in} : 30 V nominal
V_{out} : 5 V at 1 A
V_{out}max : 7 V for TTL
V_{in}max : 25 V for the 7805

One approach to this problem is to use a switching device driven with a fixed mark−space ratio waveform to reduce the 30 V unregulated input to a voltage of approximately 9 V at the IC regulator's input. The outline of this method is shown in Fig. 3.65. The oscillator is enabled by a logic 1 on the control input and the pulse output from the oscillator is then used to drive a power switch. The duty cycle of the oscillator is set to about 30% so that the 30 V input is reduced to 9 V. A standard

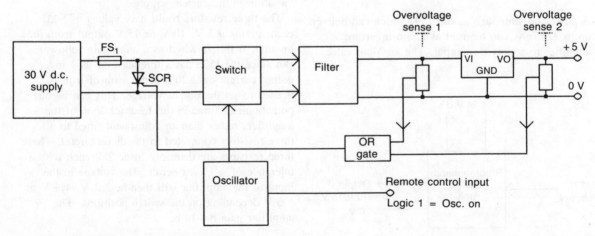

Fig. 3.65 Block diagram of remotely controlled 5 V supply

SMPU filter circuit then provides a d.c. input to the 7805 regulator. Overvoltage sensing circuits are provided at the input and the output of the 7805, set to 12 V and 6.5 V respectively, and either of these sensing circuits is used to give a trip signal to a thyristor connected across the 30 V unregulated input.

The overall system design is best completed by considering the blocks one by one, starting with the switch. Once this portion of the design is settled the filter, oscillator, regulator and overvoltage protection circuits can be finalised.

(a) The switch (see Fig. 3.66)

A series switch using either a powerFET or a BJT is required. This switch must be fast in operation and have a low value of on resistance. Possible circuit configurations are also shown in Fig. 3.66. The powerFET version (Fig. 3.66(c)) will be the

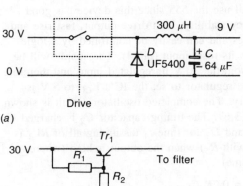

(a)

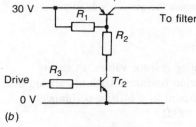

(b)

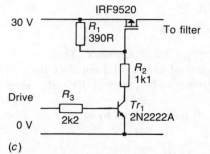

(c)

Fig. 3.66 Switch circuits

most efficient since it is a voltage driven device. The transistor would require a base drive current of nearly 200 mA (since $I_{pk} = 2I_{dc}$ and the $I_c{:}I_B$ ratio of a BJT used as a switch is usually taken as 10:1). This means that either power has to be wasted in R_2 or Tr_1 must be a Darlington.

Let's consider the design using a powerFET. The IRF9520 is a suitable p-channel device. This has:

$$V_{DDS} : -60 \text{ V}$$
$$I_{D(max)} : -6 \text{ A}$$
$$R_{ds(on)} : 0.6 \ \Omega$$
$$P_D : 40 \text{ W}$$
$$g_{fs} : 2 \text{ S}$$
$$V_{GT(th)} : 4 \text{ V}$$

The drive signal should be above audio at, say, 20 kHz with a mark-to-space ratio determined by the input and output voltage:

$$t_{on}/t_{off} \approx \frac{V_{out}}{V_{in} - V_{out}}$$

(here I have neglected the volt drop across the FET and the flywheel diode).

Therefore $t_{on} : t_{off} \approx 1 : 2.5$
With $f = 20$ kHz

$$t_{on} + t_{off} = 50 \ \mu s$$

Therefore $t_{on} = 14.5 \ \mu s$ and $t_{off} = 35.5 \ \mu s$

The peak current will be

$$I_{pk} = 2I_{dc}$$

Therefore $I_{pk} = 2$ A.

In order to fully switch this value of current to the load the FET will need a gate voltage of:

$$\text{Gate drive} \approx V_{GS(th)} + \Delta V_{GS}$$

where ΔV_{GS} is the increase necessary above the threshold value.

$$\Delta V_{GS(min)} = I_{pk}/g_{fs}$$

Therefore $\Delta V_{GS(min)} \approx 1$ V

Thus the pulse height at the gate of the powerFET must be equal to or greater than 5 V. This is the minimum value that will ensure a 2 A drain current. To allow a safety margin we shall set the gate drive amplitude to about 7 V. The values of the two resistors R_1 and R_2 can now be determined. With Tr_1 on, the full 30 V will appear across R_1 and R_2

and since we require 7 V across R_1 there must be 23 V across R_2. The resistors are in the ratio 1:3. The actual values must not be too low so that a relatively high power loss occurs resulting in poor efficiency, nor too high so that switching speed is impaired. A high value in R_1 and R_2 will not allow the FET gate capacitance to be rapidly charged and discharged. Suppose we fix the current through R_1 and R_2, when Tr_1 is on, to 20 mA (a value that should ensure fast turn on and turn off). Then:

$$R_1 + R_2 \approx 30/20 \text{ k}\Omega$$

$$= 1.5 \text{ k}\Omega$$

Therefore make R_1 390 Ω and R_2 1k1.

The power loss in these resistors will be:

$$P \approx 0.3V_{in}I_R \qquad (30\% \text{ duty cycle})$$

Therefore $P \approx 200$ mW.

Both resistors should be 0.5 W rating.

Tr_1 can be any general purpose n-p-n small signal switching transistor with a V_{CEO} rating in excess of 35 V. Suitable transistors for Tr_1 are BC107, BC182L or 2N2222A.

For a transistor switch the I_C to I_B ratio is assumed to be 10:1.

Therefore

$$R_3 \approx \frac{V_{OSC} - V_{BE}}{I_B}$$

Where V_{OSC} is the amplitude of the drive signal from the oscillator. Assuming this is 5 V R_3 value is 2k2.

(b) Filter design

The values of inductance and capacitance can be estimated using the following formula:

$$L_{min} \approx \frac{V_{dt}}{dI} \approx \frac{(V_{in} - V_{out})t_{on}}{I_{pk}}$$

Therefore $L_{min} \approx 152 \ \mu$H.

This inductor should be wound on a ferrite pot core using an RM6 or RM10.

$$C_{min} \approx I_{pk}/8fV_{r(pk-pk)}$$

For 500 mV pk−pk ripple

$$C_{min} \approx 25 \ \mu\text{F}$$

These are the minimum values to be used; in

practice make the inductance 300 μH and fit a 64 μF, 30 V wkg electrolytic for C_1.

A fast recovery diode must be used for the flywheel and it must be capable of passing the peak switch current. A UF5400 is suitable.

(c) Oscillator design

The target specification for this portion of the system is:

f_o : 20 kHz $\pm$ 1 kHz
Duty cycle : 30% preset
Pulse height : 5 V
Control : TTL 1 = ON

Possible options are:

   (i) a 555 astable,
  (ii) using a CMOS IC such as the 4011B,
 (iii) using TTL Schmitt gates.

We shall use the 555 since this device has good frequency stability, high drive output, fast rise and fall times and can easily be controlled by a logic level on its reset input (pin 4). The supply will be taken from the 30 V unregulated input and therefore a simple regulator to set the IC's V_{CC} to 5 V is necessary. The completed oscillator circuit is shown in Fig. 3.67. The timing capacitor C_2 is charged via R_4 and D_1 for time t_1 (assuming all of RV_1 is linked with R_5) when the output is high (where t_1 = on time).

$$t_1 = 0.7R_4C_2$$

For a 555 the timing resistor values, to ensure satisfactory operation free from latch-up, should be in the range 1 kΩ(min) to 1 MΩ(max). Initially assume R_4 to be 10 kΩ.

$$C_2 = t_1/0.7R_4$$

Therefore $C_2 = 2.14$ nF

C_4 can therefore be a 2.2 nF capacitor. This implies an R_4 value of nearer 9 kΩ but since the mark-to-space ratio is to be preset by RV_1, R_4 value will be 6k8.

Since t_2, the off time, is given by $t_2 = 0.7(RV_1 + R_5)C_2$,

$$RV_1 + R_5 = 23 \text{ k}\Omega$$

Therefore R_5 will be made a 15 kΩ and RV_1, to

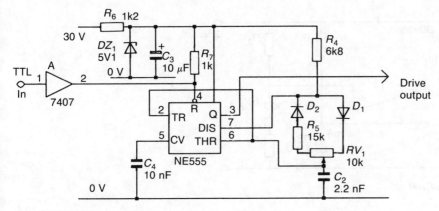

Fig. 3.67 Oscillator section

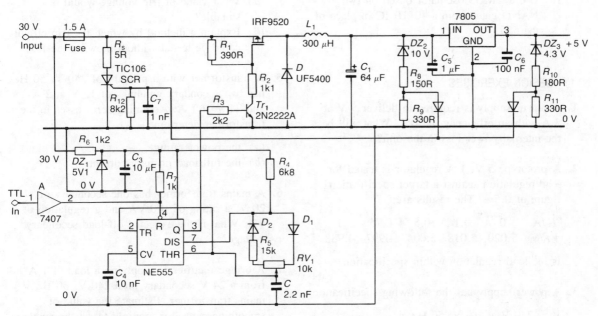

Fig. 3.68 Completed design

allow precise setting of the 30% duty cycle, will be a 10 kΩ cermet.

The 5 V nominal supply to the 555 is obtained using a simple Zener shunt regulator. DZ_1 is a 5.1 V BZX85 or other similar 1.3 W device. Since the 555 supply current is specified as 10 mA and the diode current is also 10 mA

$$R_6 \approx \frac{V_{in} - V_Z}{I_S + I_Z}$$

Therefore $R_6 = $ 1k2 n.p.v., 1 W rating.
Check diode maximum dissipation:

$$P_{Zmax} \approx (I_{Zmax}).V_Z = 100 \text{ mW}$$

The enable input will be applied to pin 4, the reset input of the 555, using a TTL open-collector buffer.

The only remaining portions of the design to be completed are the 7805 regulator and the protection circuits. Values of components are given in the final completed circuit, Fig. 3.69, and it is left as a reader exercise to check/modify these.

Other design modifications:

1. Redesign the switch circuit using a BJT in place of the powerFET. A ZTX750 is most suitable. Check the power losses in this circuit and compare it to the original design.

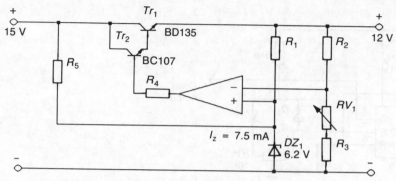

Fig. 3.69 Series regulator 12 V at 200 mA

2. Use a CMOS oscillator based on two NAND gates from a 4011B IC in place of the 555.

3.11 DESIGN EXERCISES

1. A power supply is required to deliver 9 V at 3 A with an efficiency of 70%. What will be the internal power loss in the unit?

2. A prototype 5 V, 1 A regulator is tested for load regulation against a target specification figure of 0.5%. The results are:

I_L/A	0	0.1	0.5	0.75	1
V_O/V	5.020	5.018	5.004	4.997	4.988

Is the load regulation within specification?

3. A power supply has the following specification:

V_{in} : 240 V $\pm$ 10 V, 50 Hz a.c.
V_o : 24 V
I_L : 0.6 A
Load regulation : 0.1%
Line regulation : 5 mV V^{-1} of V_{in}
Temperature coefficient : +0.008%/°C

Estimate the total change in output voltage if simultaneously

(a) the load is reduced by 200 mA,
(b) the mains voltage rises by 6 V,
(c) the ambient temperature increases from 15 °C to 32 °C.

4. A regulator used to supply some TTL logic is to be fitted with an overvoltage trip.

(a) What value of trip voltage would be suitable?
(b) Explain a method by which the trip circuit could be tested without blowing the fuse.

5. A transformer with a primary of 240 V, 50 Hz has two secondary windings of 12 V at 2 A and 24 V at 1 A. Assuming zero losses in the transformer determine

(a) the power rating,
(b) the full load primary current.

6. A mains transformer has one secondary of 20 V, a rating of 100 VA and a regulation of 9%. What is the expected off-load secondary voltage?

7. A bridge rectifier is supplying a load of 1 A from a 24 V secondary on a 240 V, 50 Hz mains transformer. Estimate the value of smoothing capacitor required to set the ripple voltage to no more than 750 mV pk–pk. What should be the ripple current and voltage rating of the capacitor?

8. A simple Zener diode shunt regulator is to be designed using a 5.1 V Zener diode type BZY88 to the following specification:

V_{in} : +15 V
V_{out} : 5 V nominal
Load : 260 Ω
I_Z : to be 5 mA under maximum load conditions.

(a) Calculate a suitable value and power rating for the series resistor. The power rating must be able to withstand a short-circuit output condition.

(b) Calculate the maximum power dissipation for the Zener diode.

(c) Given that the Zener has a dynamic resistance of 75 Ω estimate

    (i) the change in output for a 5 mA change in load current and
    (ii) the change in output, under full load conditions, for a 1 V change in input voltage.

9. A series regulator, shown in Fig. 3.69, is required to deliver a regulated 12 V output at a maximum load current of 200 mA.

(a) Design a suitable transformer, rectifier and filter circuit to produce the 15 V d.c. required with only 1 V pk–pk ripple.

(b) Calculate values for all resistors in the regulator section.

(c) Design a simple current limit to operate at 220 mA.

(d) A BD135 is specified for the series element. Calculate the maximum power dissipated by this transistor under short-circuit output conditions and estimate the thermal resistance of the heat sink if T_{amb} = 50 °C and the junction temperature is not allowed to rise above 100 °C. Assume $R_{th(j-c)} = 1.5$ °C W^{-1} and $R_{th(c-h)} = 1$ °C W^{-1}.

10. A 723 IC regulator (see Fig. 3.70) is to be

```
          NC ⊏ 1   ∪  14 ⊐ NC
Current limit ⊏ 2      13 ⊐ Frequency compensation
Current sense ⊏ 3      12 ⊐ V+
Inverting input ⊏ 4    11 ⊐ V_c
Non-inverting input ⊏ 5  10 ⊐ V_out
           V_ref ⊏ 6    9 ⊐ V_z
             V− ⊏ 7     8 ⊐ NC
```

(a) Pin configuration

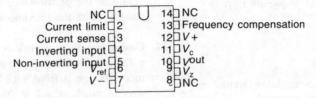
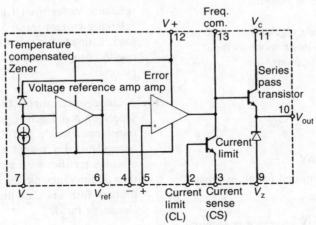

(b) Equivalent circuit

Parameter	Test conditions	Typical value
Line regulation	V_{in} = 12 V to 15 V	0.01%
	V_{in} = 12 V to 40 V	0.02%
Load regulation	I_L = 1 mA to 50 mA	0.03%
Ripple rejection		86 dB
Reference voltage		7.15 ± 0.2 V
Long-term stability		0.1% per 1000 hrs
Input voltage range		9.5 V to 40 V
Output voltage range		2 V to 37 V
Average temp. coefficient	V_{in} = 12 V to 15 V	0.002% per °C
	I_L = 1 mA to 50 mA	

(c)

Fig. 3.70 Pin-out and specifications for the 723

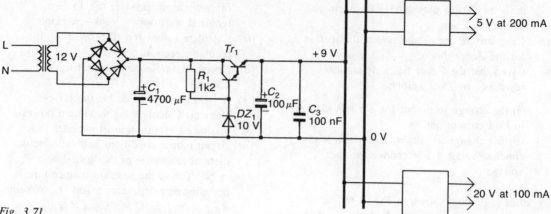

L
N
12 V

C_1
4700 µF

R_1
1k2

Tr_1

DZ_1
10 V

$+C_2$
100 µF

C_3
100 nF

+9 V

0 V

5 V at 200 mA

20 V at 100 mA

Fig. 3.71

used in the design of a regulator to the following specification:

V_{in} : 30 V unregulated (1 V pk–pk ripple)
V_{out} : 25 V preset
I_o : 1 A
Line regulation : 0.03%
Load regulation : 0.05%

Outline the design of the regulator circuit. An external pass transistor is essential.

11. A 78S40 switched mode regulator IC is to be used to design in step-down mode to the following target specification:

V_{in} : 18 V ± 1 V
V_{out} : 5 V ± 50 mV
I_{out} : 300 mA
I_{SC} : 350 mA
f_{min} : 17 kHz
Ripple : less than 75 mV

Calculate the values required for all external components.

12. (*a*) An 18 V ± 100 mV reference is required for industrial use from a nominal 30 V supply. By applying the technique described on pp. 77–82, design a suitable circuit. A IN821 temperature compensated reference diode is available.

(*b*) For your circuit estimate the change in reference voltage if the nominal 30 V input drops by 10%.

13. Repeat the above exercise using a Ferranti

REF25Z or similar band-gap as the reference element. No pre-regulator is to be used. Compare the performance in terms of line stability with the previous circuit.

14. Design a 6 V ± 50 mV reference circuit using a TL430 programmable band-gap device. The input voltage is from a 12 V battery which can vary as much as ±2 V. The load to the reference varies from 1 to 3 mA with the reference current set to 5 mA at minimum load. Estimate the worst case change in V_{out} due to changes in input voltage and load current.

15. An unregulated supply used in a bus system to supply on-board pcb regulators has a mains transformer with a 100 VA rating. The unregulated d.c. output is nominally 9 V from a bridge rectifier with a ripple content of less than 300 mV pk–pk. Estimate the rating of the primary fuse and state the type of fuse that should be fitted.

16. Two parts of an electronic system have point-of-load regulators, see Fig. 3.71, which require a common overvoltage protection cut-out. The first regulator provides some TTL ICs with 5 V at 200 mA and the other a display driven via a SMPU step-up regulator with a voltage output of 20 V at 100 mA. The crowbar must operate a current limit fitted to the 9 V pre-regulator. Design both the overvoltage protection and a simple current limit for the pre-regulator.

4 DESIGNS USING OP-AMPS

4.1 ANALOG AND LINEAR DESIGN METHODS

Although the major portion of electronics uses digital type circuits there are still several specialised areas that require analog components and analog design techniques. An obvious example of this is in the interfacing of signals between transducers that are measuring temperature, pressure and light level to a microcomputer-based control system. The weak electrical signals from the sensors must be amplified, filtered and then converted before being suitable for the computer's use. Real world quantities are nearly always analog and this type of design, which can pose tricky problems, is a vital and important area of work. The problems of this sort of design work are usually those of linearity, gain control, bandwidth limiting, noise reduction, offset nulling and, not least, reducing drift caused by temperature changes. Suppose one of the sensor signals is in the range $50 \mu V$ to $500 \mu V$: the drift and noise level caused by the amplifier, and referred to that input, would have to be less than $10 \mu V$ in order that the integrity of the signal is maintained. The analog parts of a system can be just as important as the digital parts, and there are obviously some critical decisions to be made by the designer at the planning stage of such a circuit.

What then distinguishes a linear IC from its digital brother? An accurate definition would probably include a statement that any variation in the output of the IC must have the same proportional relationship as the change in its input. But the classification has become rather looser than that, and manufacturers have a tendency to describe an IC as *linear* or *analog* if it can't be seen to fit neatly into the digital logic or microprocessor categories. Thus we have timer ICs, CMOS switches, multiplexers, comparators, display drivers, waveform generators, converters (ADC and DAC) and regulators all linked with the more obviously linear ICs, the operational amplifiers.

Design techniques using regulator ICs, both linear and switched types, are discussed in Chapter 3 and the use of ADCs and DACs appears in Chapter 7. This leaves us, in this present chapter, with the not inconsiderable design area using op-amps, OTAs. This, as we shall see, will provide plenty of scope for design problems.

APPLICATIONS OF LINEARS

The standard areas where linear ICs still predominate can be listed as follows:

- signal processing,
- waveform generation and timing,
- level detection and comparators,
- instrumentation and measurement circuits,
- interface circuits,
- amplifiers — operational, audio, video and wideband,
- alarm and monitoring circuits,
- power control and voltage regulation.

Analog processing typically involves the linear amplification of a weak input, often in the presence of a high common mode signal. A bandwidth limiting filter may be necessary to remove high frequency noise and low frequency drift and this will be followed by a sample-and-hold circuit so that the signal can be held constant for measurement. A system block diagram to do this is shown in Fig. 4.1. An instrumentation amplifier, a special version of an op-amp that has a very high common mode rejection ration (CMRR) will be used and the filter can be some form of active circuit using a standard op-amp. Sample-and-hold ICs can be bought off-the-shelf or quite effective units to provide this function can be created using op-amps and switches with a high quality hold capacitor.

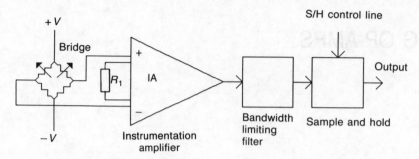

Fig. 4.1 Analog system block diagram

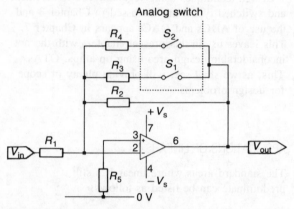

Fig. 4.2 Simple programmable amplifier

Another application example, relatively simple in this case, shows how two linear ICs can be used to provide programmable voltage gain in an amplifier circuit — see Fig. 4.2. The op-amp is connected as an inverting amplifier where the gain is given by:

$$A_{vc1} = -R_F/R_1$$

The CMOS analogue switch IC is used to vary R_F. If both S_1 and S_2 are open

$$R_F = R_2$$

whereas if S_1 is closed and S_2 is open

$$R_F = R_2R_3/(R_2 + R_3)$$

By suitable choice of resistor values the voltage gain can be set as desired by external control signals. As we shall see later the *on* resistance of the switches cannot always be ignored and will have some effect on the gain setting, that is unless R_2, R_3 and R_4 are relatively high value resistors, i.e. above 10 kΩ.

Before we move on to discuss circuit design in more detail, consider a final example of a linear application given in Fig. 4.3. This is an audio distribution circuit, the sort of arrangement that is often necessary in audio work where one input from a pick-up or microphone is required to drive more than one output. In this case a quad op-amp IC, the TL084, is used to provide drive to three outputs.

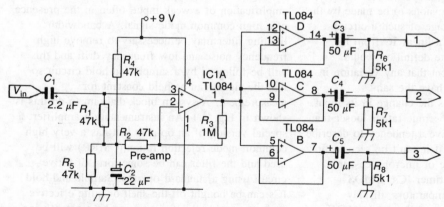

Fig. 4.3 Audio distribution circuit

One of the four op-amps in the IC, which have a channel separation of 120 dB, is used as an a.c. non-inverting amplifier with a voltage gain set to approximately 20 and input impedance of 50 kΩ. Single supply operation is arranged by connecting both of the op-amp's inputs via resistors to $\frac{1}{2}V_S$. The other three op-amps in the package are wired as voltage followers. These unity gain followers have very high input impedance and therefore present only a light load to the pre-amplifier, and low output impedance to give sufficient drive signals to any power amplifiers connected to each channel. Since the full power bandwidth of the TL084 op-amp is 150 kHz the frequency response of the distribution system can easily cover the audio range and will be flat from at least 15 Hz to over 30 kHz. The response and other performance parameters of this type of circuit were analysed, to illustrate the use of a CAD software tool, in Section 1.3.

The three simple examples of analog applications just given are, of course, only a small selection of the large number of circuit and system possibilities that can be created with linear ICs. In this chapter and the next some of these other circuits, and in particular design techniques and methods, will be investigated.

Different design problems occur in linear circuits to those in digital circuits. With digital circuitry two of the main design preoccupations are with timing and the prevention of false or bad data. Usually if the noise level on data leads in a digital system can be kept within the noise margin of the logic, and this margin can often be 1 V or more, then the system will be safe from false data. This obviously isn't the case with linear circuits where noise entering the system at the input and added to by system components can always pose interference problems. Special care over shielding, decoupling and filtering is often called for.

If we divide linear design into its main areas the particular problems that require attention in these applications can be listed.

D.C. Amplifiers (usually differential)
- drift with temperature
- reduction of offsets and gain errors
- achieving a high common mode rejection ratio
- accuracy and linearity

A.C. Amplifiers
- stability of operation, i.e. no oscillations, or ringing
- noise reduction
- distortion level
- band-width setting

Waveform generators
- stability of frequency and amplitude; particularly with changes in temperature
- range
- output distortion level
- accuracy of frequency and amplitude

Comparators
- accuracy of trip point
- stability of trip point
- jitter free operation (most important with slowly changing inputs)

These particular problems will be discussed in later design examples and are in addition to the standard requirement of designing circuits so that no rating of a particular IC is exceeded. For example, most general purpose op-amps have supply voltage rating of up to ±18 V (some up to ±22 V) so the power supply design may need attention to ensure that this basic rating is not exceeded. In any case it is always good practice to design circuits so that all devices and components are operated well within their maximum ratings of voltage, current, power and temperature. This *derating* technique reduces stress-related failures and therefore markedly prolongs the life of the circuit and improves its reliability. Typical MIL-SPEC derating for active devices is to lower circuit voltages and currents to 75% of maximum ratings and to hold any junction temperatures to no greater than 110 °C.

Another problem can arise if a split supply is inadvertently reversed, a condition that will usually destroy an IC. A simple over-voltage circuit is shown in Fig. 4.4(a) and reserve polarity protection for op-amps in Fig. 4.4(b). In the latter case the diodes must have a forward current rating that is larger than the power suppply's short-circuit output current and the power supply itself must have an over-current limit.

The mechanical layout of designs is also very important, especially where feedback is used. The layout should always be compact with minimum

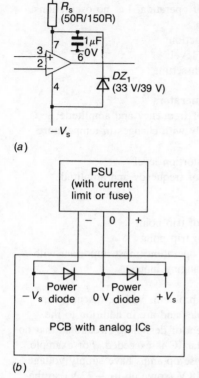

(a)

(b)

Fig. 4.4 Simple protection circuits: (a) overvoltage;
(b) reverse supply

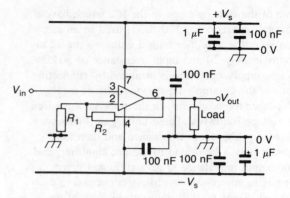

Fig. 4.5 Decoupling an analog IC

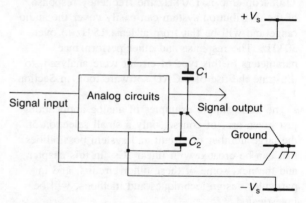

Fig. 4.6 Single point grounding

lead lengths and with a good ground plane or
ground return line. A ground plane on a pcb, where
all available copper is used as the ground, will give
this return path a low resistance and inductance and
will reduce additional noise. Local power line
decoupling is also good practice; at the least the pcb
supply point should be bypassed with a $1\,\mu F$
tantalum in parallel with a 100 nF disc ceramic, but
where circuits have a GBP above 10 MHz each IC
itself should be decoupled using 100 nF disc
ceramics. These should be wired as close as is
practical to the IC pins so that the capacitor closes
the signal current loop by the shortest available part
— see Fig. 4.5.

Where a ground plane is not available, single-
point grounding should be used, in other words the
input signal return, the load signal return and the
power supply common should all be connected at
the same point. This star connection will reduce
ground loop and common current paths which
would cause interference and unwanted feedback

between different parts of the system, see Fig. 4.6.
This applies particularly to situations where a mix
of digital and analog circuit is used, i.e. there
should be a separate ground return for each part.

Noise in systems, and particularly in amplifiers,
where the amount of noise present reduces the
system's ability to detect useful signals, is
dependent upon the source resistance and the input
stage. On any data sheet the noise of the device is
normally specified as 'equivalent input noise'.
Thermal noise in the source resistance and the
internal noise voltage and noise current generators
in the op-amp will be the limiting factors, and
therefore it is important to use shielding for low
level signal inputs to avoid additional noise and
interference being picked up on the input lead. It is
always best to use a differential amplifier (see next
section) since these have the highest common mode
rejection ratios (CMRR). Both signal lines will then
be run as a twisted pair picking up the same
common mode interference signals and enclosed in

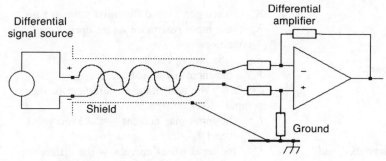

Fig. 4.7 Shielding for a differential source

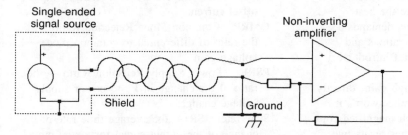

Fig. 4.8 Connections for a shield from a single-ended source

a shielded cable. The shield is then connected to ground *at only one point* as shown in Fig. 4.7. If a single-ended signal source has to be used then the shield should not be allowed, if it can be avoided, to carry signal current. Use a separate ground return lead inside the shield — see Fig. 4.8. Having got the best shield arrangement the noise level is then dependent on the value of the source resistance and the type of amplifier. In general, a bipolar operational amplifier will add less equivalent input noise for source resistances of below 10 kΩ. Above this value the low input current types such as the BIFET and CMOS op-amps, which have lower noise currents, will tend to be quieter.

Designs using linear ICs tend to use more passive components than digital circuits, and since it is often the capacitors and resistors that are used to set timing, frequency, bandwidth, gain and so on, the type of passive used will have an important bearing on the tolerance and stability of the circuit parameters. When using capacitors avoid electrolytics, apart from decoupling and coupling at l.f., since tolerances are wide and leakage currents can be high. For timing and frequency generation use polystyrene or silvered mica for low values (up to 10 nF), and monolithic ceramic (up to 1 μF) or polycarbonate and polyester (up to 10 μF). Disc

ceramics should be used for decoupling h.f. and tantalums for decoupling/coupling l.f. and for low frequency generation and timing.

Resistors for general purpose biasing can be carbon film, but metal film or metal glaze (cermet) should be used for feedback, attenuation, filter and comparator applications. These have high stability and low temperature coefficient, and can be purchased with close tolerances. Carbon composition resistors or cracked-carbon resistors, since they have little or no spiral grinding which would put up their self inductance, can be operated at high frequencies. The latter, if specially manufactured, can operate up to and above 100 MHz. However, metal film or metal glaze resistors, although having a spiral film, are suitable for frequencies up to 50 MHz or more. In general for an h.f. or wideband application use low value film types and ensure that all connections to the resistor are as short as possible.

4.2 OP-AMP CIRCUITS

OP-AMP PRINCIPLES

The operational amplifier is one of the key components in analog design and for this reason the

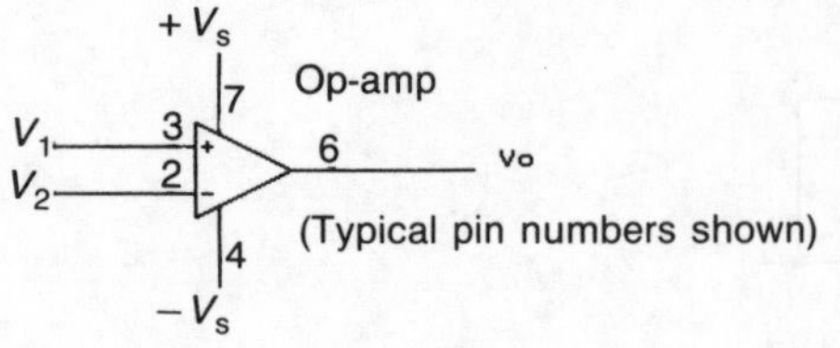

Fig. 4.9 Op-amp

principles of its operation are well established and covered in many texts. What concerns us here is how to select an op-amp for a particular task and how to optimise a design to achieve the best performance. However, because this demands a good understanding of parameters, ratings and limitations of the devices, some brief introductory notes will be included.

Basically the op-amp is a very high gain, directly coupled, differential amplifier; in other words it produces an output which is a much magnified copy of the difference between the voltages on its two inputs.

Thus from Fig. 4.9 we get

$$V_o = A_{vol}(V_1 - V_2)$$

where A_{vol} is the open loop differential voltage gain and $(V_1 - V_2)$ is the differential input voltage. Since A_{vol} is typically 100 dB (100 000 as a ratio) it takes only a fraction of a millivolt difference between V_1 and V_2 to give a large output (NB: here we have assumed that offsets are zero).

The ideal op-amp, which is often a useful guide in deciding which type to use in a design, would have:

- an open loop differential voltage gain of nearly infinity,
- zero common mode gain,
- an infinitely high input resistance,
- almost zero output resistance,
- an infinitely wide bandwidth,
- zero offset (both I_{io} and $V_{io} = 0$).

This concept is useful since specialised op-amps are designed to have almost the ideal performance parameters in one or two key areas, e.g. low offset, or wide bandwidth. How close does an ordinary general purpose op-amp come to the ideal? and how do we decide which op-amp to use for a particular application? First let us define the most important op-amp parameters:

A_{vol} : the open loop differential voltage gain

R_{in} : the input resistance under open loop conditions

R_{out} : the output resistance

V_{io} : the input offset voltage

dV_{io}/dT : the temperature coefficient of the input offset voltage

I_B : the input bias current — the average of I_B+ and I_B-

I_{io} : the input offset current — the difference between I_B+ and I_B-

dI_{io}/dT : the temperature coefficient of input offset current

CMRR : Common Mode Rejection Ratio — the ratio of differential to common mode voltage gain

PSRR : Power Supply Rejection Ratio — the ratio of the change in V_{io} to power supply voltage changes

Slew rate : SR — the average time rate of change of the output signal for a step input under closed loop unity gain conditions

GBP : Gain Bandwidth Product — the frequency at which the small signal open loop differential gain has fallen to unity

I_{os} : the maximum output current that the op-amp can deliver into a short circuit

V_{opp} : the maximum peak-to-peak output voltage swing that the op-amp can deliver to a defined load without saturation or clipping occurring (typically 5% THD)

PBW : the Full Power Bandwidth, i.e. the frequency at which the voltage gain is 3 dB down while the op-amp is delivering V_{opp} into a stated load

At d.c. and low frequencies a simplified equivalent circuit, shown in Fig. 4.10, can often be useful in analysing a design, particularly when looking at offset and offset drift effects. This shows the two input bias currents as current generators I_B+ and I_B- and the input offset voltage V_{io} as a voltage generator in series with the input. The output circuit is a voltage generator $A_{vol} V_{in}$ in series with an output resistance R_o.

When designing circuits to amplify low level d.c. voltages, care has to be taken to prevent the input bias currents from producing additional input offset voltage errors and excessive input drift with temperature. These errors and drifts occur because the input bias currents must flow through the

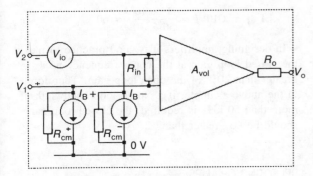

Fig. 4.10 Simplified op-amp equivalent circuit

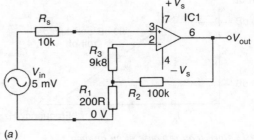

(a)

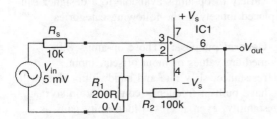

Fig. 4.11 Example of a non-inverting design

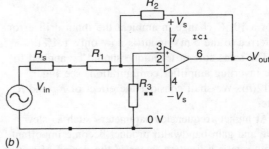

(b)

Fig. 4.12 (a) Improving the circuit with drift compensating resistor R_3; (b) Drift compensating resistor R_3 in an inverting design

resistance connected in the two input leads. As long as the resistances in the input leads are equal, the voltage errors set up will cancel, leaving only the small error and drift due to I_{io}, where I_{io} is the difference between I_B^+ and I_B^-. The balancing of the resistance in both the inverting and non-inverting inputs is vital if low drift with temperature is required. Take the example shown in Fig. 4.11 of a non-inverting d.c. amplifier with closed loop gain of 500 amplifying signals of typically 5 mV from a 10 kΩ source. Suppose the op-amp used has:

$V_{io} = 1\,mV$
$I = 100\,nA$
$I_{io} = 20\,nA$
$dV_{io}/dT = 2\,\mu V\,°C^{-1}$
$dI_{io}/dt = 0.5\,nA\,°C^{-1}$

which are values of these parameters for a typical general purpose bipolar op-amp.

Since the resistances in the two leads are unbalanced (R_s in the non-inverting lead and $R_1//R_2$ in the inverting lead) the static input error is:

$V_e \approx V_{io} + I_B R_s \approx 2\,mV$

This, of course, could be nulled out by applying a suitable fixed input voltage of the opposite polarity. Most op-amps are provided with an offset

null facility that does this. But the drift error with temperature would still be large and is given by:

$\Delta V = dV_{io}/dT + (dI_B/dT)R_s\,V\,°C^{-1}$

Suppose the input bias current changes by 10 nA per °C, and this is a rather conservative estimate, the drift error is:

$\Delta V \approx 102\,\mu V\,°C^{-1}$

For a 10 °C change in ambient temperature the input drift error referred to the 5 mV input is 20%.

To balance the circuit, and thereby reduce the drift, a resistor R_3 is added to increase the resistance in the inverting lead. See Fig. 4.12(a).

$R_3 = R_s - R_1//R_2$

Therefore $R_3 \approx 8\,\Omega$

With the resistances balanced the static error is:

$V_e \approx V_{io} + I_{io}R_s \approx 1.2\,mV$

i.e. nearly half the previously estimated value, and the drift error becomes:

$\Delta V = dV_{io}/dT + (dI_{io}/dT)R_s\,V\,°C^{-1}$
$= 7\,\mu V\,°C^{-1}$

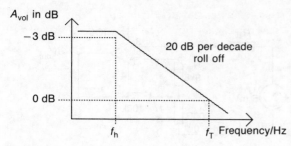

Fig. 4.13 Open loop response of an op-amp

For a 10 °C change in ambient the input drift error referred to the 5 mV input is now only 1.4%.

The same sort of technique should be applied to the inverting amplifier configuration, see Fig. 4.12(b). We shall consider the effect of R_{in} and R_o later.

At higher frequencies parameters such as slew rate and gain bandwidth product become important. Slew rate is a limiting factor in the design of square and triangle wave generators, whereas for small-signal a.c. amplifiers GBP allows the designer to calculate the probable bandwidth for his gain setting. A typical response curve for an op-amp is given in Fig. 4.13 showing how the open loop voltage gain varies with frequency. At d.c. the open loop gain has a very high value, say 100 dB, but as the signal frequency is increased a point is reached where the gain starts to roll off. Any further increase in frequency causes the gain to fall by 20 dB per decade (or 6 dB per octave). This roll-off is normally set by the IC manufacturer to ensure stability. At some high value of frequency the open loop voltage gain is unity. This frequency is called f_T.

GBP = gain × bandwidth
Therefore
GBP = $A_{vol}f_h$

where f_h is the frequency at which the open loop gain begins to roll off, i.e. when it is 3 dB down on its d.c. value.

The magnitude of A_{vol} at any frequency between f_h and f_T is given by

$$|A_{vol}| \approx GBP/f$$

where f is the signal frequency.

Suppose an op-amp has a GBP of 3 MHz and an A_{vol} value at d.c. of 100 dB. Then $f_h = 300$ Hz. What is $|A_{vol}|$ at 50 kHz?

$$|A_{vol}| = GBP/f = \frac{3 \times 10^6}{50 \times 10^3} = 60$$

In designing amplifiers it is good practice to make the closed loop gain at the upper frequency no greater than 20% of the open loop gain. Therefore in the above example, if a closed loop bandwidth of more than 50 kHz is required, the closed loop gain should be no greater than 12.

SELECTING OP-AMPS

The variety of op-amps available to a designer can be placed loosely in the following categories:

(a) **General purpose:** Those op-amps with medium values of input offsets, input resistance, slew rate and bandwidth. Most will have built-in frequency compensation so that stability, even at closed loop unity gain, is assured. The obvious example is the popular 741 (the 747 is the dual version). The 741 has the following typical specification values:

Open loop voltage gain A_{vol} : 106 dB
Input offset voltage V_{io} : 1 mV
Input offset current I_{io} : 20 nA
Input resistance R_{in} : 2 MΩ
Slew rate SR : 0.5 V μs^{-1}
Full power bandwidth PBW : 9 kHz
Gain bandwidth product GBP : 1 MHz

(A 741S is a 741 with a higher slew rate of 20 V μs^{-1}, and a 741N is a low noise version of the 741.)

(b) **High input resistance:** Op-amps with field effect transistors in the input stage. These include BIFET, CMOS and FET types. A typical example is the 351 (353 is the dual version). The 351, which is pin compatible with the 741, has the following typical specification values:

A_{vol} = 110 dB
V_{io} = 5 mV
I_{io} = 25 pA
R_{in} = 10^{12} Ω
SR = 13 V μs^{-1}
BW = 150 kHz

These high input resistance types have very low

input bias currents with consequent low values of I_{io}, but relatively high input offset voltages.

(c) **Low offset and low drift:** Sometimes these are called *precision op-amps* because offset nulling may not be necessary. They feature very low offset voltages and offset currents and in particular have low offset temperature coefficients. Examples are the 725CN, OP-07, OP-27 and the OP-77. Take the OP-07 specification:

$A_{vol} = 132\,dB$
$V_{io} = 0.06\,mV$
$dV_{io}/dT = 0.5\,\mu V\,°C^{-1}$
$I_{io} = 0.8\,nA$
$dI_{io}/dT = 12\,pA\,°C^{-1}$
$R_{in} = 33\,M\Omega$
$SR = 0.17\,V\,\mu s^{-1}$

Note the trade-off between speed and the excellent low drift. The equivalent drifts with temperature for a 351 op-amp, previously mentioned, are $10\,V\,°C^{-1}$ for input offset voltage and a doubling of I_{io} for every 20 °C rise in temperature.

(d) **High speed:** Op-amps that have high values of slew rate and can therefore cope with rapidly changing signals. The NE5539 is a good example:

$A_{vol} = 52\,dB$
$V_{io} = 2.6\,mV$
$I_{io} = 2\,\mu A$
$R_{in} = 100\,k\Omega$
$SR = 500\,V\,\mu s^{-1}$
$PBW = 4.8\,MHz$

(e) **Low noise and distortion:** Typical examples are the 071 and the OP-27. The 071 specification is:

$A_{vol} = 106\,dB$
$V_{io} = 3\,mV$
$I_{io} = 5\,pA$
$R_{in} = 10^{12}\,\Omega$
$SR = 13\,V\,\mu s^{-1}$
$N = 18\,nV\,Hz^{-1}$
$THD = 0.01\%$ (10 V r.m.s. output at 1 kHz)

(f) **Specialised amplifier** such as OTA, the operational transconductance amplifier, that

delivers an output current proportional to the differential input voltage (the 3080E is typical of this type) and the Norton or Current Differencing Amplifier, which produces an output voltage proportional to the difference in its input currents.

(g) **Power op-amps:** Devices designed to deliver larger output currents. The 165 is typical, it can output up to 3 A into a 5 Ω load. A heat sink is usually required.

(h) **Ultra low offset amplifiers:** These are either trimmed or 'chopper' stabilised internally so that offset voltages and currents are almost negligible.

So where does this place us in selecting an op-amp for a particular application? If the op-amp is required to amplify the signal from an audio source, say a microphone or a cartridge, then a low noise op-amp such as the OP-27G may be required. On the other hand an application to amplify low level d.c. signals would indicate the choice of a low drift (precision) op-amp such as the OP-27, an oscillator circuit to produce square waves at 50 kHz would require a high SR wide bandwidth op-amp, and so on. The important steps in device selection are to:

1. Decide the type of op-amp required.
2. Write down the detail of the probable specification values required for the application.
3. Make a list of possible types by studying short-form data.
4. Select from the short-form data the most suitable types and then, having made a detailed study of their full specification, choose the best fit device.

NB: Other constraints such as availability, cost and preferences will usually apply.

USING OP-AMPS

Op-amps can be used in a wide variety of applications, both linear and non-linear, but the most common use is as straightforward amplifiers. The standard configurations together with their features are shown in Fig. 4.14 but before we

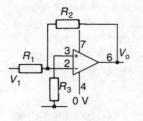
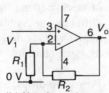
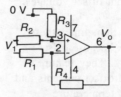
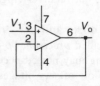

(a) **Inverting amplifier**
- $A_{vc1} = -R_2/R_1$
- $R_1 = R_1$
- No common mode error
- $R_3 = R_2/R_1$ for temperature drift reduction
- Include any source resistance with R_1

(b) **Non-inverting amplifier**
- $A_{vc1} = 1 + R_2/R_1$
- R_1 is very high $= R_{in}(1 + A_{vol}\beta)$
- There is a small common node error

(c) **Differential amplifier**
- $A_{vc1} = R_4/R_1$
(providing R_1 and R_2 include source resistance)
- Resistors should be matched
$R_1 R_4/(R_1 + R_4) = R_2 R_3/(R_2 + R_3)$
- Full common mode rejection is difficult to achieve — better to use an IA

(d) **Voltage follower**
- $A_{vc1} =$ unity
- R_1 can be as high as 100 M

Fig. 4.14 Standard configurations

continue with a discussion of their merits and the effects of op-amp parameters on circuit performance we need a short review of negative feedback.

An amplifier with negative feedback will have a voltage gain given by:

$$A_{vcl} = \frac{A_{vol}}{1 + A_{vol}\beta} \qquad (1)$$

where A_{vcl} is the closed loop gain, i.e. the gain with negative feedback applied, A_{vol} is the open loop gain, i.e. the gain before negative feedback is applied, β is the fractional gain of the feedback network, i.e. the amount of signal feedback, and $A_{vol}\beta$ is called the loop gain.

If the loop gain ($A_{vol}\beta$) is made sufficiently large compared to unity, the closed loop gain equation reduces from (1) to

$$A_{vcl} \approx \frac{1}{\beta}$$

In other words, the magnitude of the closed loop gain is entirely dependent on β, which is itself normally set by the ratio of two resistors. When designing amplifiers one of the first tasks is to ensure that the loop gain is much greater than unity over the required frequency range. Suitable values for the resistors can be determined later.

Consider the use of an op-amp which has an A_{vol} = 100 dB and GBP = 1 MHz in the design of a non-inverting amplifier to give a voltage gain of 150. The circuit is given in Fig. 4.15.

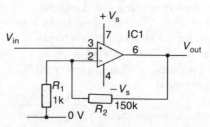

Fig. 4.15 Non-inverting circuit with voltage gain set to 150

$$A_{vcl} = V_o/V_i$$
and $\beta = V_f/V_o$

$$V_f = \frac{V_o R_1}{R_1 + R_2}$$

Therefore

$$\beta = \frac{R_1}{R_1 + R_2}$$

As long as the loop gain $A_{vol}\beta \gg 1$,

$$A_{vcl} = \frac{1}{\beta} = \frac{R_1 + R_2}{R_1}$$

This is more commonly written as:

$$A_{vcl} = 1 + R_2/R_1$$

In this case the ratio R_2 to R_1 to give the required closed loop gain is 149 (in practice R_2 would be made 150 kΩ and R_1 1 kΩ since these are the nearest preferred values).

Assuming this R_2 to R_1 ratio of 149; $\beta = 1/150$.

With $A_{vol} = 100\,000$ (100 dB)

$$A_{vcl} = \frac{100\,000}{1 + 100\,000/150} = 149.77$$

One of the major advantages of negative feedback is the improvement in the stabilisation of voltage gain. This can be clearly demonstrated if we now imagine a 50% reduction in open loop gain from 100 000 down to 50 000. The new value of closed loop gain is:

$$A'_{vcl} = \frac{50\,000}{1 + 50\,000/150} = 149.55$$

which is a fall in closed loop gain of only 0.15%.

Other important benefits from negative beedback are:

(i) a wider bandwidth

$$f_{hcl} = f_{hol}(1 + A_{vol}\beta)$$

where f_h represents the upper cut-off frequency,

(ii) a reduction in internally generated noise and distortion

$$D' = D/(1 + A_{vol}\beta)$$

where D = THD under open loop conditions and D' = THD under closed loop conditions,

(iii) a change in input and output impedance. For series applied feedback as in the non-inverting configuration.

$$R_i = R_{in}(1 + A_{vol}\beta)$$

where R_i is the input resistance under closed loop conditions and R_{in} is the op-amp input resistance, and for shunt applied feedback as in the inverting configuration

$$R_i = R_{in}/(1 + A_{vol}\beta).$$

For both circuits, where the feedback is derived in parallel with the output

$$R_{out} = R_o/(1 + A_{vol}\beta)$$

where R_{out} is the closed loop output resistance and R_o is the op-amp output resistance.

The wider bandwidth results from the gain-stabilising effect of negative feedback. In the

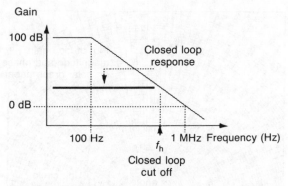

Fig. 4.16 Closed loop response

example the op-amp is assumed to have a GBP of 1 MHz. In other words, its open loop gain begins to roll off at 100 Hz — see Fig. 4.16. The response of the closed loop gain will be contained within the open loop plot but, because changes in A_{vol}, while $A_{vol}\beta$ remains larger than 1, have little effect on closed loop gain, the response of A_{vcl} will remain flat over a much wider bandwidth. For a closed loop gain of 150 the bandwidth will be nearly 6.7 kHz.

Some errors and drawbacks occur with negative feedback. A rearrangement of equation (1) gives

$$A_{vcl} = \frac{1}{\beta}\left[\frac{1}{1 + 1/A_{vol}\beta}\right]$$

Since $A_{vcl} \approx 1/\beta$ the term $[1/(1 + 1/A_{vol}\beta)]$ must be an error multiplier.

Suppose for an amplifier $\beta = 0.01$ giving an apparent A_{vcl} of 100 (40 dB). If the open loop gain is 80 dB (10 000) the error is

gain error multiplier = $[1/(1 + 1/100)] = 0.99$

The actual closed loop gain is 99 and the error is 1%.

Instability can also occur in amplifier circuits when the op-amp is uncompensated. This is because phase shifts in the amplifier and in external components can convert the negative feedback signal at some frequencies into positive feedback. The result will be oscillations or ringing at that frequency.

A study of the formula for closed loop gain given earlier shows that if the loop gain $A_{vol}\beta$ changes sign (i.e. shifts in phase and approaches unity) then the denominator in the equation becomes almost zero and the closed loop gain rockets towards

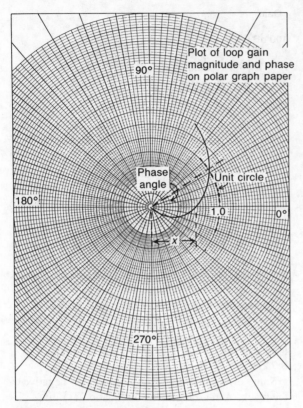

Plot of loop gain magnitude and phase on polar graph paper

90°

Phase angle

Unit circle

180°

1.0

0°

x

270°

Fig. 4.17 Typical Nyquist plot

infinity. This is the classic condition for oscillations.

The criterion for ensuring *conditional stability* in a negative feedback amplifier is to keep the phase shifts round the loop below 180° while the magnitude of the feedback signal is such that $A_{vol}\beta$ is greater than or equal to unity. Stability is measured by two parameters, plotted on a *Nyquist diagram* or a *Bode diagram*.

  (a) *phase margin*, which is the amount of phase shift less than 180° when the loop gain is exactly unity,
  (b) *gain margin*, the reciprocal of the loop gain magnitude when the phase shift of the feedback signal is at 180°. This is normally expessed in dB.

$$\text{GM} = 20 \log(1/x)$$

These points are illustrated in Fig. 4.17.

For an amplifier to be stable with negative feedback a phase margin of 45° and a gain margin of 20 dB are normally required. If these values are

lower a peak will occur in the high frequency closed loop response causing ringing, distortion or oscillation.

Most general purpose op-amps have built in frequency compensation which causes the open loop gain to roll off from a low frequency at a constant rate of 20 dB/decade. Thus even with 100% negative feedback, circuits using these op-amps cannot become unstable. But naturally the bandwidth is restricted. Uncompensated op-amps allow the designer to fix the roll-off point by wiring a small-value capacitor between IC pins or form an IC pin to ground, so that response is tailored to fit the amount of negative feedback used in the circuit. As long as the rules stated by the manufacturer are followed no instability should occur.

EFFECT OF OP-AMP INPUT RESISTANCE

It might appear that R_{in}, the input resistance of the op-amp, would affect the performance of the inverting amplifier since it appears in parallel with the feedback signal, see Fig. 4.18. However, providing A_{vol} is large the effect of R_{in} will remain negligible. A simple proof of this is as follows:

$$I_1 = I_2 + I_3 \tag{1}$$
$$\text{and } V_x = V_o/A_{vol} \tag{2}$$

From (1) $\dfrac{V_i - V_x}{R_1} = \dfrac{V_x - V_o}{R_2} + \dfrac{V_x}{R_{in}}$

Using (2) $\dfrac{V_i - V_o/A_{vol}}{R_1} = \dfrac{V_o/A_{vol} - V_o}{R_2} + \dfrac{V_o}{A_{vol}R_{in}}$

Rearrangement gives:

$$\frac{R_2}{R_1}V_i = V_o\left[-1 + \frac{1}{A_{vol}} + \frac{R_2}{A_{vol}R_{in}} + \frac{R_2}{A_{vol}R_1}\right]$$

Therefore $\underbrace{\dfrac{V_0}{V_i} = \dfrac{R_2}{R_1}}_{\text{actual gain}} . \underbrace{\left[-1 + \dfrac{1}{A_{vol}} + \dfrac{R_2}{A_{vol}R_{in}} + \dfrac{R_2}{A_{vol}R_1}\right]}_{\text{error caused by } R_{in}}$

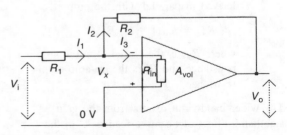

Fig. 4.18 Analysing the effect of R_{in}

If both A_{vol} and R_{in} are large the error in the gain equation will be insignificant and therefore the effect of R_{in} can be neglected.

EFFECT OF OP-AMP OUTPUT RESISTANCE

All op-amps will also have a finite value of output resistance, typically in the range of 50 Ω up to 500 Ω. This has the effect of placing a limit on the lowest values that can be used for the feedback resistors and on the load. In both feedback configurations, where voltage derived feedback is used, the circuit output resistance is given by the formula:

$$R_{out} = \frac{r_o}{1 + A_{vol}\beta}$$

where R_{out} = the output resistance with feedback and r_o = the op-amp's internal output resistance. Suppose a 741 op-amp (r_o = 75 Ω) is used to give a closed loop voltage gain of 40 dB (100 as a ratio). Then the circuit output resistance is:

$$R_{out} = \frac{75}{1 + \dfrac{100\,000}{100}} \approx 0.075\ \Omega$$

But this very low output resistance of the circuit is only effective if the output is lightly loaded and also if the feedback resistors have not been set by the designer at values that require large currents. In other words, the low output resistance of the circuit does not imply that the op-amp can source a relatively high current. The effect of r_o is to reduce the output-voltage swing since output and feedback current will flow through r_o and set up a signal volt drop across it. A rather extreme example of this effect is shown in Fig. 4.19. Here a non-inverting amplifier has a closed loop gain of 3 but the load

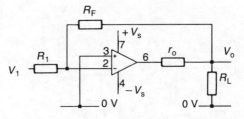

Fig. 4.20 Analysing the effect of r_o on open loop gain

and feedback resistors have been deliberately made low values. Suppose the input is +2 V, which should result in an output of +6 V. With the *excessively low* values the current in the load and the feedback network totals 20 mA resulting in a large voltage drop across r_o (2 V if we asume r_o = 100 Ω). This forces the op-amp into positive saturation and the output voltage will be in error. As a rule-of-thumb always ensure that the parallel combination of load and feedback resistor is a value that is *at least ten times greater* than r_o. In the circuit in question R_1 should be 1 kΩ and R_2 and R_L both 2 kΩ as absolute minimum values.

Another effect of r_o is to introduce a small error into any gain equation. A study of the inverting amplifier of Fig. 4.20 shows that r_o and R_L reduce the open loop voltage gain:

$$A'_{vol} = \frac{A_{vol}}{1 + r_o \dfrac{(R_L + R_F)}{R_F R_F}}$$

Since the closed loop gain is given by:

$$A_{vcl} = \frac{A'_{vol}}{1 + A'_{vol}\beta}$$

the change in A_{vol} will have a small effect on A_{vcl}. However, this effect will usually be insignificant if R_L and R_F are large compared to r_o. For example, suppose r_o = 100 Ω and R_F and R_L are made 4 kΩ.

$$A_{vol} = \frac{A_{vol}}{1 + 0.1(8/16)} = 0.952\, A_{vol}$$

Before we move onto the next section let's consider the design of a simple non-inverting amplifier to the following specification (see Fig. 4.21):

Input : 0 to +1 V sawtooth at 50 Hz
Output : 0 to +6 V sawtooth
Load : 3 kΩ
Op-amp to be used : 741 with r_o = 75 Ω

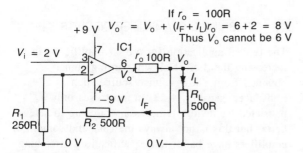

If r_o = 100R
$V_o' = V_o + (I_F + I_L)r_o = 6 + 2 = 8\ V$
Thus V_o cannot be 6 V

Fig. 4.19 Analysing the effect of r_o on external resistor values

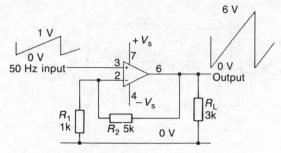

Fig. 4.21 A design example

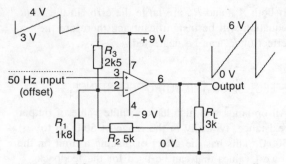

Fig. 4.22 Modifications to compensate for signal offset

Since $R_L = 3$ kΩ we can calculate the minimum value for R_F using:

$$R_L // R_F \geq 10 r_o$$

Therefore $\dfrac{R_L R_F}{R_L + R_F} = 750$ Ω.

Therefore $\dfrac{3 R_F}{3 + R_F} = 0.75$ where R_F is in kΩ.

Therefore $R_F = 1$ kΩ.

This, of course, is the absolute minimum resistance that should be used for R_F and since no design should be on the minimum but always have a safety margin we shall set R_F to 5 kΩ.

The gain required is 6 so the value of R_1 can be found using the formula

$$A_{vcl} = 1 + \frac{R_F}{R_1}$$

Therefore $R_1 = 1$ kΩ.

Imagine now a change to the specification that brings a further complication to the design. The input now has an offset of +3 V. Another resistor is required (R_3) connected between the +9 V rail and the inverting input so that the output is forced to start at 0 V as required, see Fig. 4.21. This is one of the general offset control problems which often occur in design. it should be tackled, not by simply fitting a trimpot in circuit to the +9 V rail and adjusting for best fit, but by calculation based on the requirement.

There are two conditions to be met:

(a) The gain of the circuit must still be 6.
(b) The offset control must set the inverting input to +3 V to balance the offset on the non-inverting input.

From (a) we get:

$$(R_1 R_3)/(R_1 + R_3) = 1 \quad \text{since } R_2 = 5 \text{ kΩ}$$
Therefore
$$R_1 R_3 = R_1 + R_3 \tag{1}$$

and from (b):

$$3 = \frac{9(5R_1)/(5 + R_1)}{R_3 + (5R_1)/(5 + R_1)}$$

$$3R_3 + (15R_1)/(5 + R_1) = 45R_1/(5 + R_1)$$
$$3R_1 R_3 = 30R_1 - 15R_3$$
Therefore
$$R_1 R_3 = 10R_1 - 5R_3 \tag{2}$$

From these two equations:

$$R_1 + R_3 = 10R_1 - 5R_3$$
$$6R_3 = 9R_1$$
Therefore $R_3 = 1.5R_1$

Substitute this result in equation (1):

$$1.5R_1^2 = R_1 + 1.5R_1$$
Therefore $\quad R_1 = 1.667$ kΩ
Using $R_3 = 1.5R_1$ gives $R_3 = 2.5$ kΩ.

This is a general design method that can be applied to any d.c. signal offset problem and is the best way to meet the two initial requirements. Other examples will be given in the next section.

4.3 DESIGNING D.C. AMPLIFIER CIRCUITS

The typical application for a d.c. amplifier is in increasing the d.c. or slowly varying signal obtained from a low voltage source such as a transducer, see Fig. 4.23. In most uses only a restricted bandwidth is necessary, i.e. up to a few hertz; but this is not always the case and some d.c. amplifiers have bandwidth specifications stretching up to several megahertz. What the label 'd.c.

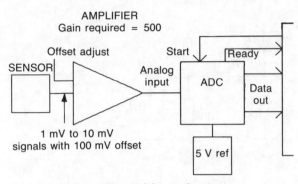

Fig. 4.23 Typical d.c. amplifier application

amplifier' implies is that direct coupling must be used. There can be no coupling capacitors.

Naturally, the most important characteristics of a d.c. amplifier are the offset voltage and current and the temperature coefficients of these offsets. Offset nulling for either, or both, the offsets inherent in the signal and at the input of the op-amp (V_{io}, I_{io}) will usually be required, and of even more importance is achieving low drift with temperature. In the example of Fig. 4.23, suppose we are amplifying a 1 mV signal with offsets totalling 100 mV and that the drift of offsets in the amplifier is 20 μV °C^{-1}. It is a relatively easy task to set up a stable and opposite 100 mV level to null the offset, but the drift would cause an error, relative to the signal being amplified, of 2% per °C. The ambient temperature would only have to change by 5 °C to give an input error of 10%. Problems such as this may not be immediately apparent at the design stage but care over the selection of the op-amp, the circuit configuration and the value and type of resistors will enable an optimum circuit to be engineered.

As an illustration of the above restriction let us consider the design of an amplifier used to increase the signal level from a simple temperature detector to a level suitable to drive an ADC or a bar graph display. The detector is to be a forward biased silicon diode. A 1N4148, or similar, will do. The diode is to be biased with a forward current of 1 mA and will exhibit the typical 2 mV fall in V_F per °C change in temperature. The range is to be from 0 °C to 50 °C with the output of the amplifier giving a 0 V to +2.5 V signal change. Some signal offset must therefore be provided so that when the detector is at 0 °C the diode's forward bias of about

600 mV is nulled, giving an output of zero from the amplifier.

The gain required is:

$$A_{vcl} = V_o/V_{in}$$

where $V_{in} = 2$ mV $\times$ 50 = 100 mV

Therefore $A_{vcl} = 25$.

Three configurations for the circuit are possible:

(1)   an inverting amplifier,
(2)   a non-inverting amplifier,
(3)   a simple differential amplifier.

1   The Inverting Amplifier Design (Fig. 4.24)

The diode, used to sense the temperature, is supplied with a nominal forward current of 1 mA via R_1 connected to the +9 V supply. Since R_2 sets the input resistance of this configuration it must be a value that is much greater than the diode's static forward resistance in order to minimise errors. With R_2 made 33 kΩ the input current to the amplifier is restricted to a value of 18 μA which is only a small percentage of I_F. To give a voltage gain of 25 the feedback resistor must be 825 kΩ (an 820 kΩ is the n.p.v.).

When the detector is at 0 °C there will still be a forward bias of some 600 mV across the diode. To

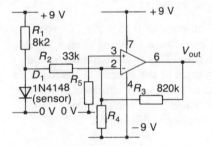

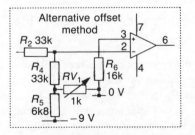

Fig. 4.24 Inverting amplifier design

null this offset a resistor R_4 could be connected from the inverting input of the op-amp directly to the -9 V rail. The value is given by:

$$R_4 \approx 9R_3/0.6\,\text{k}\Omega$$

Therefore $R_4 \approx 12.3\,\text{M}\Omega$

This is an excessively high value and an alternative nulling technique must be used. This entails an extra component to set up the 600 mV negative voltage which is then fed to the summing point by R_4.

A resistor R_6 is required to minimise drifts due to the op-amp's input bias current changes with temperature, and this must be a value equal to the resistance in the inverting lead. A $16\,\text{k}\Omega$ is the nearest value.

The problem with this investing configuration is that relatively high value resistors must be used. This has the effect of increasing errors caused by temperature drifts of the op-amp. In the circuit the drift at the op-amp's input is given by:

$$\Delta V_{\text{in}} = \frac{dV_{\text{io}}}{dT} + \frac{dI_{\text{io}}}{dT}\,R_6\ \text{V}\,°\text{C}^{-1}$$

For a general purpose op-amp typical values of the two important parameters are:

$$dV_{\text{io}}/dT \approx 5\,\mu\text{V}\,°\text{C}^{-1}$$
$$dI_{\text{io}}/dT \approx 0.5\,\text{nA}\,°\text{C}^{-1}$$
$$\Delta V_{\text{in}} = 5\times10^{-6}+0.5\times10^{-9}\times16\times10^3\ \text{V}\,°\text{C}^{-1}$$

Therefore $\Delta V_{\text{in}} = 13\,\mu\text{V}\,°\text{C}^{-1}$.

This represents an error of 0.65% per °C when referred to the 2 mV input resulting from a 1 °C change at the sensor. This is not large but would restrict the resolution of the system. A precision op-amp could be used to virtually eliminate drift but a better approach would be to redesign the circuit using the non-inverting configuration.

2   The Non-Inverting Amplifier Design (Fig. 4.25)

With this circuit the resistors can be kept to low values. The diode sensing the temperature is forward biased via R_1 to the -9 V rail with a current of 1 mA. At 0 °C the input will be typically -600 mV and as the temperature being sensed rises the diode voltage will also rise positively towards 0 V. Offset is provided using resistors R_2 and R_3,

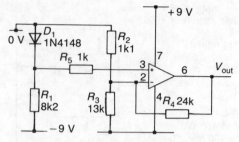

Fig. 4.25 Non-inverting circuit

which with R_4 also set the gain. The gain is to be 25 as before and a suitable value for R_4 is chosen. Let this be 24 kΩ. To calculate values for R_2 and R_3 take the following two conditions:

(a) Since $A_{\text{vcl}} = 25$ and $R_4 = 24\,\text{k}\Omega$

$$R_2//R_3 = 1$$

Therefore $R_2R_3 = R_2+R_3$ \hfill (1)

(b) With the output equal to zero volts the voltage set up on the inverting terminal must be -0.6 V.

$$\frac{9\,R_2R_4/(R_2+R_4)}{R_3+(R_2R_4)/(R_2+R_4)} = 0.6$$

With $R_4 = 24\,\text{k}\Omega$ we get:

$$216R_2/(24+R_2) = 0.6R_3+(24R_2)/(24+R_2)$$

which gives:

$$R_2R_3 = 320R_2-24R_3 \hfill (2)$$

Therefore using equations (1) and (2):

$$R_2 + R_3 = 320R_2 - 24R_3$$

Therefore $R_3 = 12.76R_2$.

Substitute this value in equation (1):

$$12.76R_2^2 = R_2 + 12.76R_2$$

Therefore $R_2 = 1.078$ kΩ (1kl is n.p.v.)

and $R_3 = 12.94$ kΩ (13k is n.p.v.)

In practice R_2 could be 1kl and R_3 made a 10 kΩ in series with a trimpot of 5 kΩ to enable an exact null to be achieved.

The non-inverting configuration has a very high input resistance and therefore will not load the diode. In order to minimise drifts R_5 is included in the non-inverting lead. Its value is given by:

$$R_5 = R_4//R_3//R_2.$$

Therefore $R_5 \approx 1 \text{ k}\Omega$.

Drift referred to the input is then:

$$\Delta V_{\text{in}} = \frac{dV_{\text{io}}}{dT}\left[\frac{1+R_2}{R_4}\right] + \frac{dI_{\text{io}}}{dT}R_5$$

Therefore ΔV_{in}, using the typical parameter values, would be approximately $6\ \mu\text{V}\ {}^\circ\text{C}^{-1}$ which is twice as good as the previous circuit.

The only possible drawbacks to this configuration are:

(i) a small common mode error will be set up, and
(ii) since a single input line is used the circuit will be susceptible to interference, especially if the diode is located more than 50 cm from the amplifier.

For point (i), since most op-amps have CMRR values of 90 dB or higher the common mode error will be very small.

$$\text{CMRR} = A_{\text{vd}}/A_{\text{vcm}}$$

In this case:

$$A_{\text{vcm}} = 25/32 \times 10^3 \approx 0.8 \times 10^{-3}$$

For an input of 2 mV the error will be a mere 0.0033%.

Point (ii) can only be overcome by using some form of differential amplifier.

3 The Differential Amplifier Design (Fig. 4.26)

The diode sensor is supplied with the 1 mA of forward current and an offset value to null the diode's 600 mV at 0 °C is set up using a simple resistor network R_2 and R_3. A twisted pair of leads then carry the signal to the input of the differentially connected op-amp. As with the inverting circuit, the input resistance of the amplifier must be reasonably high to avoid loading the diode, therefore both R_4 and R_6 are made 33 kΩ and R_5 and R_7 are 820 kΩ to set the voltage gain to 25.

With this type of circuit the resistors must be close tolerance, i.e.

$$R_5/R_4 = R_7/R_6$$

otherwise common mode errors will occur. The

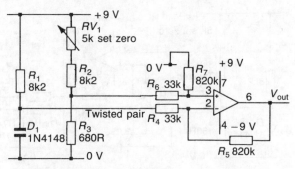

Fig. 4.26 The differential solution

drift with temperature, referred to the input, is given by:

$$\Delta V_{\text{in}} = \frac{dV_{\text{io}}}{dT} + \frac{dI_{\text{io}}}{dT}\frac{R_4 R_5}{R_4+R_5}\ \text{V}\ {}^\circ\text{C}^{-1}$$

For our typical op-amp this would add up to a drift of about $21\ \mu\text{V}\ {}^\circ\text{C}^{-1}$, which is much higher than the previous circuits.

The defects of the simple differential configuration can be overcome by using an instrumentation type amplifier, see Fig. 4.27. This circuit has:

• very high input resistance,
• high common mode rejection,
• an easy method for gain variation.

The gain is given by:

$$A_{\text{V}} = 1 + \frac{2R_2}{R_1}$$

By making R_1 a variable component the gain can be simply adjusted, something that cannot easily be achieved with the one op-amp differential circuit.

The discussion on d.c. amplifiers, so far as offset nulling is concerned, has focused on removing unwanted signal offset. In cases where the offset present in the signal is zero it is only the op-amp's offset voltage, caused by V_{io} and I_{io}, that must be nulled. This can be particularly important in situations where the signal level is small, say only some tens of millivolts, since the value of op-amp offset may then be significant. Either the designer has to specify a precision type op-amp where the offsets are very small or some offset nulling circuit must be designed. Most general purpose op-amps are provided with an offset nulling facility which simply entails connecting a 10 kΩ trimpot between two pins of the IC with the wiper connected to the

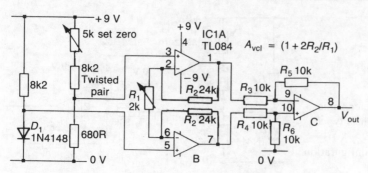

Fig. 4.27 *An improved circuit using an instrumentation amplifier*

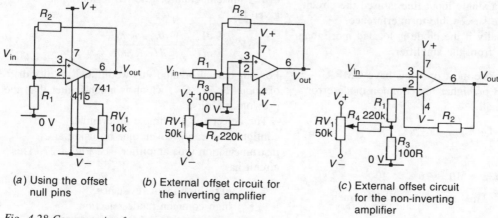

(a) Using the offset
null pins

(b) External offset circuit for
the inverting amplifier

(c) External offset circuit
for the non-inverting
amplifier

Fig. 4.28 *Compensating for op-amp input offset*

negative supply rail, Fig. 4.28(*a*). This trimpot must obviously be a reasonably high quality component with good stability; a 4 or 10 turn cermet type is suitable. In situations where no offset null facility is provided at the op-amp's pins other circuit techniques must be used. Two circuits for use in the inverting and non-inverting configurations are given in Fig. 4.28(*b*) and Fig. 4.28(*c*) respectively. The values given are typical and would need to be adjusted to take account of the resistances in the other input lead, otherwise excessive drift with temperature might result. For example, if an inverting amplifier has $R_1 = 1$ kΩ and $R_2 = 100$ kΩ the nulling components should be 1 kΩ for R_3 and 1 MΩ for R_4.

In the non-inverting configuration the nulling components give an error to the gain. In practice R_3 must therefore be a very low value compared to R_1, typically 100 times less.

EFFECT OF HIGH SOURCE RESISTANCE

Often in d.c. circuits the requirement will be to increase the signal from a high resistance source. The non-inverting configuration is the best choice since this itself has a very high input resistance (10 MΩ or greater) and will therefore not load the source. An additional resistor, to balance the offset caused by bias currents, is then required, see Fig. 4.12(*a*).

$$R_3 = R_S - \left[\frac{R_1 R_2}{R_1 + R_2} \right]$$

Design example

A d.c. amplifier is required to increase a nominal 25 mV level from a sensor to 5 V. The sensor has a source resistance of 10 kΩ. Estimate the input drift error if the op-amp has:

$$dV_{io}/dT = 3\,\mu V\,°C^{-1}\ \text{and}\ dI_{io}/dT = 0.2\,\text{nA}\,°C^{-1}$$

The circuit is similar to that given in Fig. 4.12(a). Since $A_{vcl} = 1 + R_2/R_1$, to give a nominal gain of 200 we can set R_2 to 180 kΩ and R_1 to 910 Ω.

To balance the resistances in both input leads:

$$R_3 = R_S - 180k//910k$$

Therefore $R_3 \approx 9kl$

$$\Delta V_{in} = \frac{dV_{io}}{dT}\left[1 + \frac{R_1}{R_2}\right] + \frac{dI_{io}}{dT}R_S$$

Therefore $\Delta V_{in} \approx 5\,\mu V\,°C^{-1}$.

4.4 DESIGNING A.C. AMPLIFIERS

The main considerations in the design of a.c. amplifiers are typically:

- the closed loop gain,
- the bandwidth,
- the input impedance,
- the output amplitude (into a stated load).

As we have seen before, the value of closed loop gain at frequencies near the closed loop cut-off point should, as a rule, not exceed 20% of the open loop gain. For any amplifier the magnitude of the open loop gain is given by:

$$|A_{vol}| = GBP/f$$

where f is the signal frequency above f_h.

For example, if an op-amp has a GBP of 10 MHz the magnitude of the open loop gain at 200 kHz is:

$$|A_{vol}| = (10 \times 10^9)(200 \times 10^3) = 50$$

A closed loop gain of 10 will have a bandwidth of about 200 kHz.

The closed loop bandwidth and gain are therefore trade-offs that can be made in any design. If in the previous example we reduced the bandwidth to 40 kHz, the closed loop gain can be as high as 50. Unless very high value resistors are used in the feedback path or the amplifier has to drive a capacitive load, it is the op-amp GBP itself that restricts the upper cut-off frequency of the final circuit.

At low frequencies the coupling capacitors set the

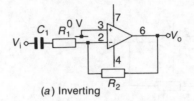

(a) Inverting

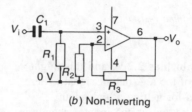

(b) Non-inverting

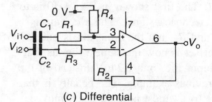

(c) Differential

Fig. 4.29 A.c. amplifier configurations

gain roll-off, and the value required will be dictated by the input resistance of the configuration used. Fig. 4.29 illustrates the basic a.c. amplifier circuits using the inverting, non-inverting and differential amplifier modes. For the first two circuits the input resistance will be set by the value of R_1. This gives a low frequency cut-off of:

$$f_L = \frac{1}{2\pi C_1 R_1}$$

In other words, when the reactance of C_1 is equal to R_1 the gain will be 3 dB down on its mid-band value. For an inverting design with $R_1 = 5\,k\Omega$ and $R_2 = 100\,k\Omega$, giving an a.c. gain of 25, the value of C_1 to set the low frequency cut-off to 15 Hz is:

$$C_1 = 1/2\pi f_L R_1 = 2.122\,\mu F\ (2.2\,\mu F\ \text{n.p.v.})$$

R_1 in the non-inverting circuit is simply a signal return path that prevents C_1 from charging up and causing a latched output condition. It does not affect the gain and can therefore be a high value as long as it doesn't set up too much d.c. offset. Suppose R_1 is made 220 kΩ and the op-amp has an input bias current of 100 nA, and d.c. offset at the input is then 22 mV. If the amplifier has a gain of 100 the variation of the operating point at the output

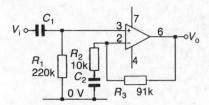

Fig. 4.30 Increasing input resistance

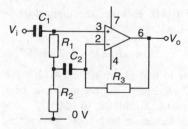

Fig. 4.31 Bootstrapping

could easily be as high as 2.2 V, and this might lead to distortion of the a.c. output signal. There are two techniques for getting a high input resistance without setting up too great a change in operating point. The first shown in Fig. 4.30 is to a.c. couple the feedback signal. The a.c. gain is still set by R_2 and R_3, but the d.c. gain is unity.

The output offset is now the same value as that set up on the input, i.e. only 22 mV instead of the 2.2 V in the previous example. The penalty is that the roll off due to C_2 must now be taken into account and C_2 must be a non-polarised capacitor.

The two low frequency cut-offs are:

$$f_{L1} = 1/2\pi C_1 R_1$$
and $f_{L2} = 1/2\pi C_2 R_2$

Only one of the reactive networks should be allowed to set the low frequency cut-off. If they are selected to be values that make f_{L1} equal to f_{L2} the roll-off at low frequencies will be excessive — 40 dB per decade instead of 20 dB per decade.

With $R_1 = 220\,\text{k}\Omega$, $R_2 = 10\,\text{k}\Omega$ and $R_3 = 91\,\text{k}\Omega$ (a.c. voltage gain 20 dB), let us calculate C_2 to set the low frequency cut-off point to 33 Hz:

$$f_{L2} = 1/2\pi C_2 R_2$$

Therefore

$$C_2 = 1/2\pi f_{L2} R_2 \approx 500\,\text{nF}$$

If C_1 is made a 22 nF the value of f_{L1} is also near 33 Hz and roll-off is 40 dB per decade. By selecting C_1 to be a value that moves f_{L1} to less than a tenth of f_{L2}, the roll-off is less sharp, at only 20 dB per decade.

The other technique for increasing input resistance is called *bootstrapping*, Fig. 4.31. This uses positive feedback at just less than unity gain to the bottom end of R_1. When an input signal is applied, at frequencies within the pass band of the amplifier

where C_2 can be considered as an a.c. short, the bottom end of R_1 will 'follow' the input signal. Thus there is effectively very little signal voltage across R_1 and its a.c. resistance therefore appears to be a much higher value than it actually is. Effective a.c. input resistances of 10 MΩ or higher are possible even with R_1 equal to a few kΩ. With this circuit d.c. stability is also high since the d.c. gain is unity. Both C_1 and C_2 will set the low frequency cut-off and the rule of not allowing both to give the same corner frequency applies.

A.c. coupling also allows the designer to operate the op-amp with a single supply rail and this is a very useful feature in many applications. The method is to provide bias, usually at half the supply voltage, to *lift* the inputs off ground. A single supply inverting amplifier with a.c. gain set by R_1 and R_2 is shown in Fig. 4.32(a). Two equal resistors R_3 and R_4 bias the non-inverting input to $\frac{1}{2}V_s$ and since R_2 gives unity gain d.c. feedback, the inverting input and the output will also be at $\frac{1}{2}V_s$. A.c. coupling must be used on both the input and output. C_3 can be omitted if the power supply is well regulated; it is there to provide noise and ripple decoupling. R_3 and R_4 should be values that preferably set up the same resistance in both input leads, i.e. $R_3//R_4 \approx R_2$. This will avoid drift of the operating point with temperature.

Circuits for single supply follower, non-inverting and differential amplifiers are also shown in Fig. 4.32. In the last circuit the parallel combination of R_3 and R_4 should be made equal to R_2.

In some single supply circuits the additional noise introduced by the bias can be overcome by having low value bias resistors, which are decoupled, and stand-off resistors from the bias point to the op-amp's inputs. Circuits for both the follower and the non-inverting versions are shown in Fig. 4.33.

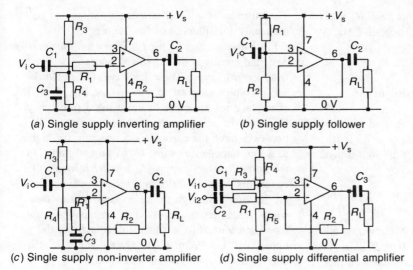

(a) Single supply inverting amplifier   (b) Single supply follower

(c) Single supply non-inverter amplifier   (d) Single supply differential amplifier

Fig. 4.32 Single-supply a.c. amplifiers

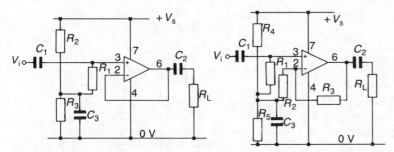

Fig. 4.33 Using stand-off resistors

Design example

An a.c. inverting amplifier is required to the following specification:

Supply : +12 V
R_{in} : 10 kΩ ± 10%
Voltage gain : 25 dB ± 1 dB
Bandwidth : 20 Hz to 20 kHz

See Fig. 4.34 for the circuit diagram.

(1) $R_1 = 10$ kΩ since R_1 is the input resistance.
(2) Converting 25 dB into a ratio gives 17.78.
     Since $A_{vcl} = R_2/R_1$,

     $R_2 = 177.8$ kΩ (180 kΩ is n.p.v.)

(3) For best temperature stability of the operating point $R_3//R_4 = R_2$.

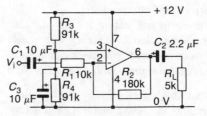

Fig. 4.34 Design example of an a.c. inverting amplifier

Therefore $R_3//R_4 \approx 180$ kΩ

$R_3 = R_4 = 91$ kΩ

This will give an operating point of +6 V.

(4) Let C_2 set the low frequency cut-off.

$f_L = 1/2\pi C_2 R_L$

Therefore $C_2 \approx 1.6$ μF (use a 2.2 μF).

(5) C_1 must now be chosen so that with R_1 it gives a low frequency cut-off that is about 2 Hz. Therefore

$$C_1 = 1/4\pi R_1 \approx 8\,\mu F \text{ (use a 10 }\mu F\text{).}$$

(Both C_1 and C_2 can be electrolytics if necessary.)

(6) The decoupling capacitor C_3 is used to reduce any ripple (100 Hz) from the power rail. It should have a value that gives a low reactance, say 1/20 of R_4, at this frequency. Therefore

$$C_3 \approx 20/200\pi R_4 \approx 0.2\,\mu F \text{ (use a 220 nF).}$$

(7) An op-amp with a GBP of 1 MHz would allow a closed loop gain of up to 50 at 20 kHz. Thus the upper cut-off frequency will be well in excess of 20 kHz; a small capacitor can be fitted in parallel with R_2 to shape the high frequency response if required.

4.5   INTRODUCTION TO ACTIVE FILTER DESIGN

Filter circuits, which heavily attenuate signals of certain frequencies while passing others, are often needed in electronic systems. If we just consider the simple example of a 50 Hz (60 Hz for the USA) notch filter used to kill mains hum in an audio system the parameters and characteristics of a filter become plain to see. These are:

1. a sharp cut-off characteristic,
2. high levels of attenuation for any signals not in the pass band frequency range, and
3. a flat response with minimum ripple and overshoot for signals within the pass band.

Filter circuits of high performance can be built using an op-amp, as the active element, and a few carefully selected resistors and capacitors. Low-pass, high-pass, band-pass and band-stop (notch) circuits are all possible and, since no inductors are necessary, the circuits are less bulky and cheaper than those using just passive components. Also the op-amp provides gain so there is no insertion loss over the pass band and the active filter has good isolation. This isolation results from the op-amp's high input impedance and low output impedance. The only drawback is that designs are limited by the frequency characteristics of the op-amp.

Therefore most general purpose op-amps can be used only for filters at audio frequencies.

For low-pass and high-pass filters the most easily designed circuit is the equal component 'Butterworth' type. These have two CR networks and a voltage gain set to 4 dB — see Fig. 4.35; the characteristics are close to those listed previously. Consider the low-pass circuit. Here the two CR networks have the capacitors connecting the signal to a low impedance point, C_2 to ground and C_1 to the output of the op-amp. At low frequencies these capacitors will have a high reactance which allows all the signal through to the op-amp. But as the signal frequency is increased the capacitors shunt more and more of the signal to ground and the output will fall. With $C_1 = C_2$ and $R_1 = R_2$ the attenuation beyond cut-off will increase by 40 dB/decade.

For the circuit:

$$f_c = 1/2\pi\sqrt{(R_1 R_2 C_1 C_2)}$$

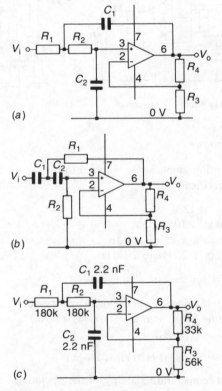

Fig. 4.35 Active filters: (a) Low-pass; (b) High-pass; (c) Low-pass design with 400 Hz cut-off

But with $R_1 = R_2$ and $C_1 = C_2$, which is the most convenient design condition, this simplifies to:

$$f_c = 1/2\pi RC \qquad (1)$$

To set the gain to 1.586 (4 dB) R_4 must be made just over half the value of R_3.

Therefore
$$R_4 = 0.586R_3 \qquad (2)$$

Design method

Low-pass filter with a cut-off frequency of 400 Hz.

Select a standard value for the capacitors. In this case 22 nF will be suitable. Rearrange equation (1) to make R the subject:

$$R = 1/2\pi f_c C$$

Therefore $R = 18.08\,\text{k}\Omega$ (18 kΩ is n.p.v.)
Make $R_3 = 56\,\text{k}\Omega$.
Therefore $R_4 = 0.586R_3 = 32.82\,\text{k}\Omega$ (33 kΩ is n.p.v.)

To get the best results from these circuits good quality close tolerance components must be used. Since capacitors are relatively bulky and expensive the values in this design could be reduced to, say, 2.2 nF, allowing the use of ±2.5% tolerance polystyrene types. In that case the two resistors R_1 and R_2 would have to be 180 kΩ ±1% metal film.

Unless a wide-band op-amp is used the attenuation level will fall above 100 kHz. This is because the open loop gain of the op-amp falls as the frequency is increased. In other words, the low-pass active filter built with a general purpose op-amp, such as the 351, has inferior high frequency rejection. This can be overcome by attenuating the high frequency components of the signal using a passive filter as shown in Fig. 4.36. This initial low-pass filter has its cut-off frequency set to ten times that of the active filter and is then buffered to

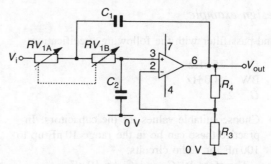

Fig. 4.37 Tuning a Butterworth filter

the filter by a unity gain follower. For the above example typical values for the passive filter could be 15 kΩ and 1 nF.

Tuning, or fine trimming, of the cut-off frequency of the Butterworth active filter means having a twin ganged potentiometer that varies all or part of R_1 and R_2 together, see Fig. 4.37.

To design a high-pass filter, use the same design procedure and simply interchange the positions of the capacitors and resistors in the R_1C_1 and R_2C_2 networks. Leave the voltage gain at 4 dB.

The band-pass filter, which allows a range of signal frequencies to pass while heavily attenuating frequencies above and below the pass band, can be designed using a variety of techniques. With this type of filter the centre frequency, f_o, and bandwidth are related by the Q factor.

$$Q = f_o/\text{BW}$$

With a single op-amp used in the multiple-feedback circuit of Fig. 4.38 the value of Q is usually restricted to 5. The gain of the circuit is set by R_3 and R_1, and the centre frequency can be trimmed by R_2. The formulas for the design are:

$$f_o = \frac{1}{2\pi C}\sqrt{\left[\frac{R_1 + R_2}{R_1 R_2 R_3}\right]} \quad \text{where } C = C_1 = C_2$$

$$R_1 = Q/2\pi fCG$$
$$R_2 = Q/2\pi fC(2Q^2 - G)$$
$$R_3 = Q/\pi fC$$

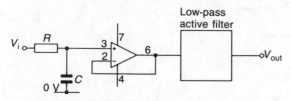

Fig. 4.36 Using a passive filter to improve h.f. rejection

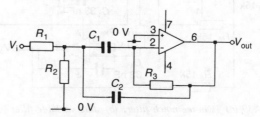

Fig. 4.38 A simple band-pass filter

Design example

Band-pass filter with the following specification:

f_o : 1.25 kHz
BW : 500 Hz
G : 2

(1) Choose suitable values for the capacitors. In practice these can be in the range 10 nF up to 100 nF for audio circuits.
    Therefore let C_1 and C_2 be 10 nF.
(2) Since the BW required is 500 Hz the circuit must have a Q of 4.

Therefore R_1 = 15.0 kΩ
R_2 = 3.183 kΩ
and R_3 = 63.66 kΩ

The *twin-tee circuit* can also be used within the feedback of an op-amp to give band-pass or band-stop (notch) characteristics. An active twin-tee notch circuit is shown in Fig. 4.39.

For this circuit:

$Q = R_2/2R_1 = C_1/C_2$
$f_o = 1/2\pi R_1 C_1$

Consider a 50 Hz notch filter with a Q of 5.
Letting C_1 = 100 nF,

R_1 = 31.83 kΩ

Since $Q = 5$, $R_2 = 10R_1$.
Therefore R_2 = 318.3 kΩ
Finally, since $C_2 = C_1/Q$,

C_2 = 20 nF

The *state variable filter* is a circuit using three op-amps and passive components that can simultaneously give low-pass, high-pass and band-pass characteristics. Basically the circuit consists of a difference amplifier and two integrators — see Fig. 4.39. The formulas required for a design are

$f_o = 1/2\pi R_1 C_1$

and $R_2 = (3Q - 1)R_3$

With this circuit it is possible to achieve a narrow pass band or good high-pass and low-pass response, but not both together.

Design example

State variable filter with high Q band-pass response. Specification:

Centre frequency : 20 Hz
Q : 11

(The gain of the pass band output is equal to Q.)
    As a first step choose a suitable value for the

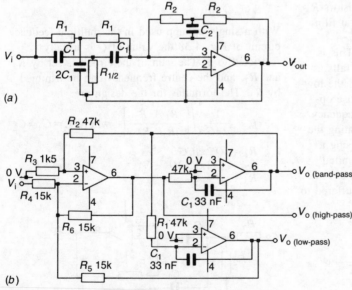

(a)

(b)

Fig. 4.39 (a) Twin-tee notch filter; (b) state variable filter (values for 200 Hz band-pass)

capacitor C_1. This can be in the range 10 nF to 500 nF.

Let $C_1 = 33$ nF.
Then $R_1 = 1/2\pi f_o C$
Therefore $R_1 = 24\,114\,\Omega$ (24 k is n.p.v.)

For a Q of 11, which will give a nominal bandwidth of 18 Hz, the value of R_2 is:

$$R_2 = (3Q-1)R_3$$

Therefore $R_2 = 32R_3$

Thus if R_3 is made a 1k5, R_2 can be a 47 k resistor. These two values will give a Q of 10.8.

Resistors R_4, R_5 and R_6 which set the gain of the difference amplifier and the input resistance should all be the same value. A suitable size is 15 kΩ. The circuit is shown in Fig. 4.39(b).

4.6 OTHER OP-AMP APPLICATIONS

OSCILLATOR CIRCUITS

An op-amp with a few selected components can be used to generate square, sine and triangle waves and in many cases this proves a cheap alternative to the waveform generating ICs that are available. The limitations to bear in mind are:

(1) The slew rate of the op-amp will limit the maximum frequency.
(2) The value of the op-amp's input bias current will restrict the lowest frequency that can be generated.
(3) Stability of the operating frequency may not be high, especially if the op-amp is allowed to saturate.

The *astable* multivibrator shown in its basic form in Fig. 4.40 can be used to generate square waves. The circuit will always self start because of the

small offsets present in the op-amp and the positive feedback via R_3 and R_2. Assume that the output initially switches to positive saturation. A portion of this level is fed back to the non-inverting pin to hold the output in saturation. C_1 charges via R_1 towards V_o^+(sat) and when the voltage across it just exceeds the voltage across R_2 the op-amp is forced to switch its output to negative saturation. C_1 is now discharged until its voltage falls below that presented on the non-inverting input. Thus square waves will be generated at the output with an amplitude of $\pm V_{o(\text{sat})}$. The total time period is given by:

$$T = 2R_1 C_1 \ln\left[1 + \frac{2R_2}{R_3}\right]$$

This can be simplified if R_2 is made equal to $0.325R_3$ to give:

$$T = R_1 C_1$$
and $f = 1/R_1 C_1$

To design an oscillator to give 100 Hz $\pm$ 10 V amplitude square waves the following values can be used:

$$R_3\ 10\ \text{k}\Omega \qquad R_2\ 3\ \text{k}\Omega \qquad R_1\ 100\ \text{k}\Omega \qquad C_1\ 100\ \text{nF}$$

Any general purpose op-amp with a supply of ± 12 V will be suitable. To change the frequency simply vary R_1 or switch in other values of capacitor. If frequencies higher than 1 kHz are required use a high slew rate op-amp. At 1 kHz with a 741, which has a slew rate of 0.5 V s^{-1}, the rise and fall times of the waveform will be 40 μs.

Mark-to-space ratio can be altered by using diodes in series with two timing resistors so that the charge and discharge of C_1 can be different. See Fig. 4.41 where a mark-to-space ratio of 1:9 is set at the frequency previously required.

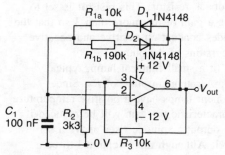

Fig. 4.41 Generator (100 Hz) with a 1:9 mark-to-space ratio

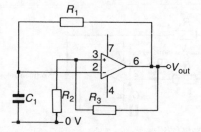

Fig. 4.40 Basic op-amp square wave generator

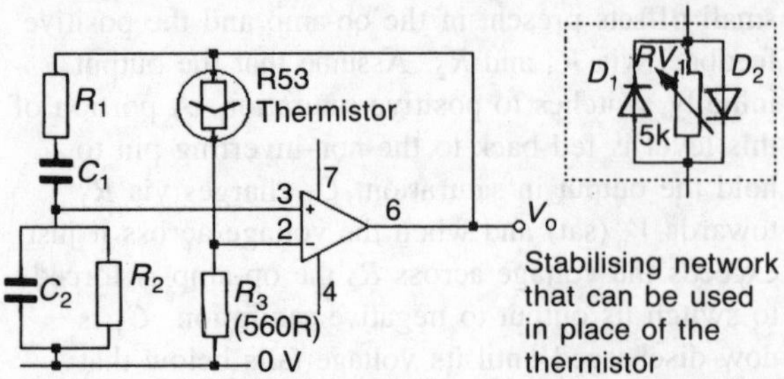

Fig. 4.42 Wien bridge oscillator

Stabilising network that can be used in place of the thermistor (change R_3 to 1k8)

Popular *sine wave oscillators*, which consist of an amplifier and a frequency determining network within the feedback, are the phase shift and the Wien Bridge. The latter, if properly designed, can be capable of giving a stable, high quality, low distortion output. The circuit given in Fig. 4.42 shows the standard Wien Bridge arrangement. At one frequency the phase shift from the output back to the non-inverting input via the CR phase-shifting network will be exactly zero. The circuit will therefore oscillate at this frequency because of the positive feedback.

$$f_o = 1/2\pi CR$$

Since the losses in the network are one-third, the amplifier must have a gain of 3 *exactly* to maintain oscillations. Negative feedback with an amplitude sensing device is used to do this. Usually this is a sealed thermistor type R53 as shown. This device has a resistance that falls if the output amplitude increases. In this way the gain is stabilised and the output will be a near perfect sine wave with an amplitude of 1 V r.m.s. Distortion can be less than 0.05%. Other alternatives for the stabilising circuit are:

(1) To use two diodes in parallel with a feedback resistor. This resistor is set to give a gain of just more than 3 so that the diodes conduct on positive and negative excursions of the output.

(2) To fit a small filament lamp, typical 50 mA rating, in place of R_2. Since filament lamps have a positive temperature characteristic the gain will be reduced if the output amplitude rises above a set level. Although this is claimed to be a standard method it can be very difficult to

set up and to get it to give reliable operation.

If a low distortion output (less than 2%) is required use a sealed thermistor as the stabilising element, otherwise use the two-diode circuit.

Design example

Wien bridge oscillator:

Frequency : 600 Hz ± 50 Hz
THD : not critical

Since $f_o = 1/2\pi CR$

$$R = 1/2\pi fC$$

Select a suitable value for C, say 22 nF. Then:

$$R = 1/(2\pi \times 600 \times 22 \times 10^{-9}) = 12.057 \text{ k}\Omega \text{ (use 12 k}\Omega\text{)}$$

To give a voltage gain of just over 3, R_2 must be at least twice R_1.

Therefore make $R_1 = 4k7$
and $R_2 = 10 k$

Diodes can be any general purpose types such as the 1N4148.

In order to reach the specification limit of ± 50 Hz the components in the frequency determining network should be close tolerance. Use ± 1% metal film resistors and ± 2.5% capacitors.

The function generator, Fig. 4.43, is a two op-amp circuit that produces simultaneous triangle and square waves. The first op-amp is wired as a comparator with its reference at 0 V and the second as an integrator. Unless some limiting is used the square wave amplitude is set by the saturation levels of the first op-amp, while the ratio of R_1 to R_2 determines the amplitude of the triangle.

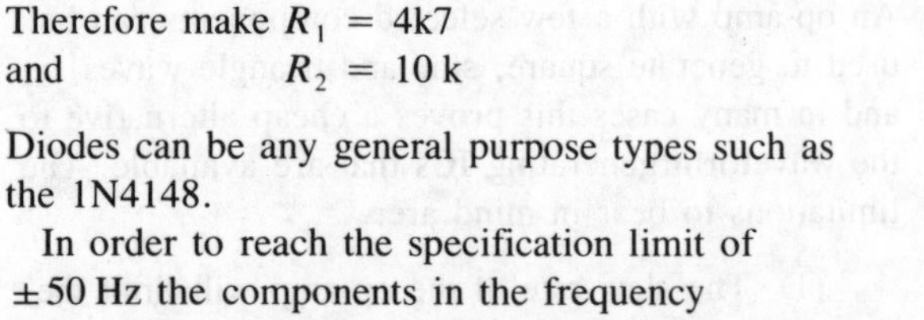

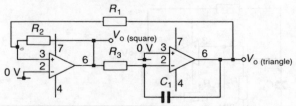

Fig. 4.43 Function generator

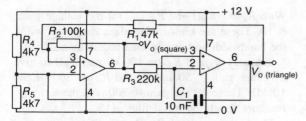

Fig. 4.44 Single supply function generator circuit

$$f_o = \frac{1}{4R_3C} \cdot \frac{R_2}{R_1}$$

A single supply version of this circuit is shown in Fig. 4.44. Designed to operate from a +12 V supply the generator will oscillate at approximately 240 Hz and give a triangle amplitude of 5 V pk−pk.

4.7 WORKED DESIGN PROBLEMS

PROGRAMMABLE A.C. AMPLIFIER

An automatic test machine needs an a.c. amplifier which can be readily programmed to give voltage gains of unity, 10, 50 and 200. In each case the bandwidth is to be from 40 Hz to 4.5 kHz. Input signals are in the range 5 mV pk−pk up to 1 V pk−pk and the supply is a single, well regulated, +15 V. The available current is 10 mA maximum. Switching signals are TTL.

Design specification

Power supply : +15 V at 10 mA
Input signal : 5 mV pk−pk to 1 V pk−pk
Input resistance : 20 kΩ
Gains : Unity, 10, 50 and 200
Gain tolerance : ±5%
Output resistance : Less than 10 Ω
Bandwidth : 40 Hz to 4.5 kHz
Switch drive : TTL High = 2.4 V
                    Low = 0.4 V

Options

(a) An inverting op-amp circuit with an analog switch wired to select the required

feedback resistor values (similar to Fig. 4.2).

(b) A non-inverting op-amp circuit using an analog switch IC wired to connect selected portions of the output back to the inverting input.

(c) An OTA with its I_{ABC} current programmed by external switches.

(d) A standard programmable gain IC such as the PGA 102KP.

Option (a) has two design snags:

(i) Since the input resistance of the circuit is specified as 20 kΩ a feedback resistor of 4 MΩ would be necessary for the ×200 gain. This is excessively large.

(ii) The switches in the IC will have to be in series with the feedback resistors and the switch 'on' resistance, which can be as high as 300 Ω, could cause additional errors at low gain.

Option (d) is a good approach but the IC can be relatively expensive and for the device mentioned only 3 gains (×1, ×10 and ×100) are provided. The OTA version could be a possibility, but non-linearity at low signals might be a problem.

For this design, option (b) is probably the best choice since this will not suffer from the defects listed above. The circuit is shown in Fig. 4.45. The switches are used to connect a portion of the output signal back to the inverting input and therefore do not affect the feedback fraction. The switch 'on' resistance will simply set up a tiny d.c. offset voltage which can be neglected in this case since the amplifier is a.c. coupled.

The op-amp must have a GBP of at least 3 MHz. This is because the bandwidth under closed loop conditions is required to be 4.5 kHz. At ×200 gain the open loop gain should be at 10 000. An op-amp such as the 351 is suitable.

The switch IC is a Quad SPST where the switches are closed by a logic 1 input. A DG308 or 4066B are suitable types. These CMOS analog switches can be operated with the 12 V supply and will accept TTL compatible switch drive inputs. However the DG308 requires an additional −12 V supply. Therefore the 4066B is selected. In this circuit the switch drive signals should be buffered

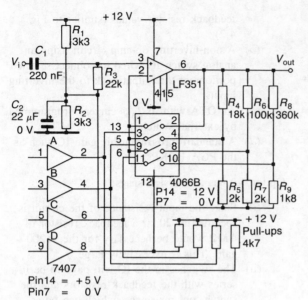

Fig. 4.45 Programmable a.c. amplifier

to the switch IC using open-drain or open-collector, non-inverting gates.

Design calculations

Since a single supply of $+12\,$V is specified the input must be biased to 6 V. A potential divider R_1 and R_2 is used for this. With the current through these resistors set to 2 mA, 8 mA of current is still available for the op-amp and switch.

$$R_1 = R_2 = 3k3$$
$$R_3 = 22\,k \text{ (n.p.v. to } 20\,k\Omega)$$

To fix the low frequency cut-off to 40 Hz, C_1 has to have a reactance of 22 kΩ at that frequency.

$$C_1 \approx 10/2\pi f_L R_3$$

Therefore $C_1 \approx 0.181\,\mu$F (220 nF is n.p.v.).

C_2 must be set to give a cut-off frequency of 4 Hz, i.e. one tenth of that given by $C_1 R_3$.

$$C_2 \approx 10/2\pi f_L R_9$$

therefore $C_2 \approx 22.1\,\mu$F (22 μF will be used).

The gain setting resistors for $\times 10$ are calculated using the formula:

$$A_{vcl} = 1 + R_4/R_5$$

With $R_4 = 18\,$kΩ and $R_5 = 2\,$kΩ the voltage gain is 10. These are reasonable values consistent with the bandwidth and output load requirements.

Similarly R_6 and R_7 are 100 kΩ and 2 kΩ to give a voltage gain of 50 and R_8 and R_9 are 360 kΩ and 1.8 kΩ. These set the gain to 200. All these resistors should be metal film $\pm 1\%$.

The bottom ends of R_5, R_7 and R_9 are all connected back to the 6 V bias level set up by R_1 and R_2 so that the inverting pin of the op-amp is held at the same reference level as the non-inverting pin.

TTL logic levels are specified as the switch drive, so an open collector TTL buffer IC (7407) is used with pull-up resistors of 4k7 to the $+12\,$V rail.

1. What changes would be required to give a bandwidth of 20 Hz to 15 kHz?
2. Modify the circuit so that it can be switched by logic 0 signals.
3. Gain changes of $\times 2$, $\times 16$, $\times 100$ and $\times 1000$ are requested. Redesign the circuit, taking into account bandwidth requirements, to do this.

LOW FREQUENCY POWER SINE WAVE OSCILLATOR WITH SWEEP FACILITY

The requirement in this example is for a sine wave oscillator which can be varied from 0.5 Hz to 10 Hz and deliver 3 A pk–pk output into a 5 Ω load. The THD is to be less than 3%. A $\pm 12\,$V supply is available and ambient temperatures of up to 35 °C must be catered for.

Design specification

Frequency : 0.5 Hz to 10 Hz
Frequency tolerance : $\pm 10\%$
Output amplitude : 15 V pk–pk $\pm 5\%$ into 5 Ω
THD : Less than 3%
Ambient temperature : 0 °C to $+35$ °C
Power supply : $\pm 12\,$V at 5 A

Circuit options

The proposed power oscillator will consist of two sections: a variable low frequency oscillator and a

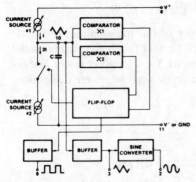

Functional diagram

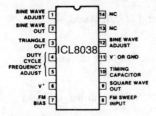

Pin configuration

Fig. 4.46 ICL 8038

power amplifier. The choices available for the oscillator include:

(*a*) a Wien bridge oscillator,
(*b*) a VCO circuit using two op-amps and a sine wave shaping circuit,
(*c*) a waveform generating chip such as the ICL 8038.

The power amplifier can either be a discrete circuit or be based on a power op-amp such as the 165.

Option (*a*) would need a ganged potentiometer for frequency variation and relatively high values of capacitor. The design of option (*b*) might give difficulties in meeting the specification on distortion. Therefore an ICL 8038 IC will be used. This waveform generating IC can produce sine, sawtooth and square waves over the frequency range 0.001 Hz to 100 kHz and has provision for an externally applied sweep voltage. A typical THD on the sine wave output is claimed to be 1% and the stability with temperature is quoted as 250 ppm/°C. The block diagram, given in Fig. 4.46, shows that it consists of two current sources charging and discharging a timing capacitor. Two external resistors set the value of the currents and the user also fits the capacitor. With the resistors equal in value a triangle wave is generated with an almost 50% duty cycle. The IC has a sine wave shaping circuit to convert the triangle to a low distortion sine output. The user can reduce THD by external resistors and potentiometers.

Component calculations

A well-regulated supply will be needed for the 8038 and this can be provided from the ± 12 V using two linear regulator ICs type 78LO5 and 79LO5 to give ± 5 V rails (Fig. 4.47).

The frequency is set by two external resistors and

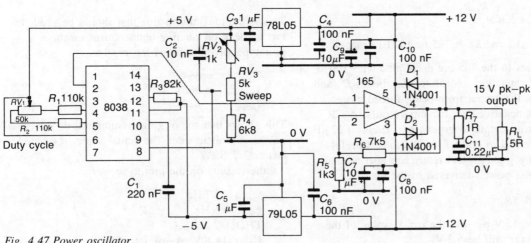

Fig. 4.47 Power oscillator

a capacitor. The two resistors are connected from $+V_{CC}$ to pins 4 and 5 and the capacitor from pin 10 to $-V_{CC}$.

$$f \approx \frac{0.3}{RC} \text{ where } R = R_1 = R_2$$

With $C = 220 \text{ nF}$, $R = 136 \text{ k}\Omega$

To give duty cycle adjustment of 50%, potentiometer RV_1 is made 50 kΩ and R_1, R_2 are fixed at 110 kΩ.

For low distortion output a resistor (part variable) of about 100 kΩ is recommended from pin 12 (sine wave adjust) to pin 9 ($-V_{CC}$). In this case, to keep the number of trimpots to a minimum only an 82 kΩ fixed resistor R_3 is specified.

The sweep input is to pin 8 and has a range given in the 8038 data sheet as:

$$V_{sweep} : V_{CC} \text{ maximum to } \tfrac{2}{3}V_S + 2 \text{ V minimum}$$

where $V_S = 10 \text{ V}$ (in the case).

These voltage levels are generated by the divider chain RV_2, RV_3 and R_4. With values of 500 Ω, 5 kΩ and 6.8 kΩ respectively the requirements on V_{sweep} are met. RV_3 sets the low frequency value and RV_3 is used to sweep the frequency over the required range.

The power amplifier has to increase the output level from the 8038 to 15 V pk–pk. For the waveform IC the sine wave amplitude is specified as $0.22V_S$. Since $V_S = 10 \text{ V}$ the output is therefore 2.2 V pk–pk.

Gain required is 6.8.

Since $A_{vcl} = 1 + R_6/R_5$
$\quad\quad R_6 = 5.8 \, R_5$

$\quad R_5 = 1k3$ and $R_6 = 7k5$ ($\pm 1\%$ E12 range)

The supplies to the 165 are decoupled with 100 nF and 10 μF capacitors and protection diodes D_1 and D_2 prevent the output from being forced more positive or negative than the supply rails. A CR network from output to ground of 1 Ω and 0.22 μF is also essential to kill h.f. oscillations. Careful layout and a good ground return are also needed.

The r.m.s. power delivered to the load is:

$$P_o = V^2/R_L$$

Since $V_o = 15 \text{ V}$ pk–pk, the r.m.s. value of the output voltage will be 5.3 V.

Therefore $P_o = 5.3^2/5 = 5.62 \text{ W}$

Taking the efficiency of the 165 amplifier to be approximately 60% (in fact this is the figure quoted at an output current of 3 A so a good safety margin is allowed), we can now find the power dissipation of the IC.

$$\text{Efficiency} = \frac{P_{out}}{P_{in}}$$

Therefore $P_{in} = \dfrac{5.62}{0.6} = 9.37 \text{ W}$

Power loss in the op-amp $= P_{in} - P_{out} = 3.75 \text{ W}$

A heat sink is necessary and is calculated as follows:

(i) Find the thermal resistances of junction to case and of case to heat sink:

   $R_{th(J-C)} = 3 \text{ °C W}^{-1}$ (from the 165 data sheet)
   $R_{th(C-h)}$ assumed to be about 2 °C W^{-1}

(ii) Decide on a maximum safe junction temperature for the 165 output transistors. Let $T_j = 100$ °C. This should give a satisfactory derating factor.

(iii) Since the ambient temperature can rise to 35 °C the required thermal reistance of the heat sink is calculated using:

$$R_{th(h-a)} = \frac{T_j - T_a}{P_{tot}} - [R_{th(J-C)} + R_{th(C-h)}]$$

Therefore $R_{th(h-a)} = \dfrac{65}{3.75} - (3+2) = 12 \text{ °C W}^{-1}$

This is the maximum value that should be used. In fact a check on running temperatures on the prototype gave the following results:

T_{case} = 66 °C
$T_{heat \, sink}$ = 56 °C
$T_{ambient}$ = 22 °C

This shows that the original assumption of $R_{th(C-h)}$ is on the optimistic side. The actual value in circuit is nearer 2.7 °C W^{-1}.

Other results on the prototype were:

f_{max} : 10.7 Hz
f_{min} : 0.6 Hz
THD : 2.8%
V_{out} : 14.8 V pk–pk into 5 Ω

Modify the circuit to:

1. Provide a low impedance triangle wave output of 10 V pk−pk into a 2.5 kΩ load. The output amplitude from pin 3 of the 8038 is stated as $0.33 V_S$.
2. Give an 18 V pk−pk sine wave output into the 5 Ω load. Resistor values and the heat sink will have to be recalculated.
3. Change the frequency specification to give a range from 20 Hz to 2 kHz.

LIGHT LEVEL CONTROL CIRCUIT

This final example is of a partly completed design which is left to be finished or modified as necessary. Although no one likes taking on an unfinished task (many engineers prefer to scrap the design and start again), this is not an uncommon situation in industry, when an engineer either leaves or is moved to another project.

The problem is to hold the light level over a work area relatively constant at a value adjusted by an operator. Lamps are mains driven and typical light intensities are to be from 100 up to 1000 lux.

Brief target specification:

Output circuit
Incandescent lamps : 750 W, 240 V a.c.

Light intensity level : 100 lux to 1000 lux
Control circuit : continuously variable
isolated from mains

Design outline

The designer has opted for a phase control system using an opto-isolated triac to switch on a main triac at a selected point in the mains half cycle (Fig. 4.48). This sets the illumination level given by the lamps. Feedback is via an opto-sensor which generates a d.c. voltage proportional to light level. This is compared with a preset value, and the resulting signal is used, together with a ramp synchronised to the mains, to give the switching pulse to the output triac. Since the control circuit must be fully isolated from the mains, a step-down transformer with centre-tapped secondary has been used. This is rectified and used to provide the regulated supplies for the control circuits (±9 V nominal) and also the synchronising signal for the ramp generator. In this way the ramp always starts from the zero-crossing point in the mains waveform. Depending on the setting of the intensity control and the feedback signal, the pulse to operate the opto-isolated triac from the comparator occurs early or later in the mains half cycle.

More detail of the design, the parts that have been completed, is given in Fig. 4.49. Options for the sensor circuit include devices such as

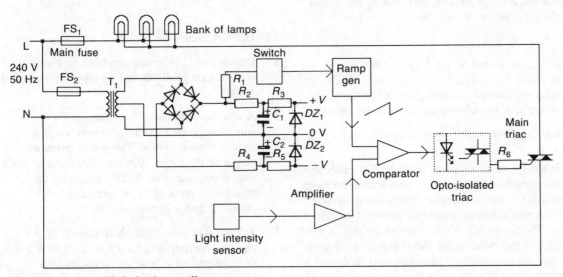

Fig. 4.48 Outline of light level controller

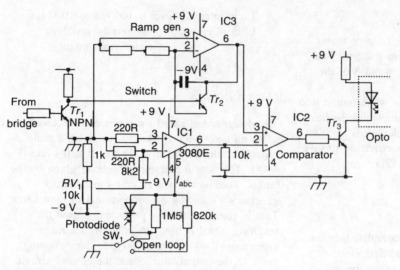

Fig. 4.49 Detail of OTA and other circuit design

photodiodes, phototransistors and light dependent resistors. In this case a large area photodiode has been chosen, one with a sensitivity of about $50 \, nA \, lx^{-1}$. This is placed in the bias current (I_{ABC}) control circuit of a 3080 OTA. The input to the OTA is derived from RV_1 which sets the initial intensity level. The voltage level from this potentiometer is reduced to a few hundred millivolts and applied to the inverting input. As the light intensity at the output varies, the diode current will modulate the g_m of the OTA and produce a varying output voltage. For example, with a light level of 200 lx and RV_1 set to, say, give $-4 \, V$, the output of the OTA across R_1 will be:

$$V_o = V_{in} \, g_m R_1$$

where $g_m \approx 20 \, mA \, V^{-1}$ at $I_{ABC} = 1 \, mA$.

At 200 lx $I_D \approx 10 \, \mu A$ and since the 1M5 in parallel with the photodiode gives a bias level of $6 \, \mu A$ the total modulating current will be $16 \, \mu A$.

There $V_o = 100 \times 10^{-3} \times 0.32 \times 10^4$
$\approx 3.2 \, V$

This level is then compared with the 5 V ramp and at the point in the mains half cycle where the ramp equals 3.2 V the comparator switches and sends a pulse across the opto-coupler to turn on the main triac. The lamps will receive power for only a small portion of the mains cycle and if the intensity rises or falls the diode current variation will be forced to modulate the OTA and vary the control voltage. In

this way the intensity set by RV_1 should remain constant. A switch is provided so that the feedback can be turned off and a standard bias for I_{ABC} of about 10 μA selected by the 820 kΩ resistor set up.

This is as far as the detailed design goes, except for the circuit outline of the ramp generator, its switch and the comparator. Complete the design so that the ramp has a 5 V amplitude with a time period of 10 ms. Specify the types of opto-coupler, triac and all other components used in the design. Modifications are going to be necessary, therefore prepare a *test strategy* for the unit.

4.8   DESIGN EXERCISES

1   Design a d.c. inverting amplifier to give a voltage gain of 40 dB and an input resistance of 3.3 kΩ.

2   A non-inverting amplifier using an OP-07 op-amp is required to amplify slowly varying signals from a sensor. The sensor gives an output in the range 10 mV to 100 mV and has a source impedance of 50 kΩ. Assuming the maximum output is to be nominally $+5 \, V$ outline a design for the circuit.

3   A 2 Hz sine wave with an amplitude of 3 V pk−pk superimposed on a d.c. level of 1.5 V is to be amplified to give an output of 10 V pk−pk offset from 0V by less than $\pm 250 \, mV$.

Use a non-inverting design with offsetting resistors to achieve this.

4 An a.c. amplifier is required to the following specification:

Voltage gain : 33 dB ± 1 dB
R_{in} : 25 kΩ ± 5%
BW : 10 Hz ± 2 Hz to 100 kHz ± 10 kHz
Supply : +9 V

Design a suitable circuit. Assuming that the op-amp used has an open loop voltage gain of 100 dB, state the GBP necessary to meet the specification.

5 A control system must be fitted with a low-pass filter to limit the bandwidth to 30 Hz. Design a Butterworth active filter to do this. 100 nF capacitors are available and resistors can be n.p.v.

6 A state variable band-pass filter (see circuit, Fig. 4.39(b)) has the following values:

R_1 100 kΩ R_2 100 kΩ R_3 2.2 kΩ
$R_4 R_5 R_6$ 10 kΩ C_1 4.7 nF

Determine the centre frequency and the bandwidth.

7 (a) An op-amp is to be used as a square wave generator to operate at a frequency of 1500 Hz with a mark-to-space ratio of 3:1.

The power supply is ± 9 V. Assuming that a 10 nF capacitor is used for the timing suggest suitable n.p.v. for all other components.

(b) Modify the design so that the frequency can be accurately set.

(c) Convert the circuit to single supply operation.

8 (a) Design and test a sine wave oscillator based on the Wien bridge circuit to operate at 100 Hz. Use diodes as the stabilising elements.

(b) The design above is to be modified to operate at 80 kHz. Specify the type of op-amp required.

(c) Research other methods of sine wave generation using op-amps and redesign the circuit of (a) using two alternatives.

9 A standard 8-bit DAC IC has a maximum output of 2.490 V, a settling time of 2 μs and an output resistance of 4 kΩ. Design an amplifier that can be used to increase this level to give 0 V to 9.960 V output. Both the zero and maximum outputs must be made adjustable to within ± 20 mV. State:
(i) the type of configuration,
(ii) any important parameter(s) of the op-amp that must be considered.

5 COMPARATORS AND TIMER CIRCUITS

5.1 COMPARATOR CHARACTERISTICS

Whenever it is necessary to sense a voltage level, the use of a comparator circuit is indicated. The basic analog comparator is a circuit that compares the two voltages presented on its inputs and gives an output state that signals when one input is above or below the other. Usually one of the inputs is a stable known reference.

Any differential amplifier, i.e. an op-amp, operated in open-loop mode can be used for this function, but certain parameters, as discussed later, need to be optimised for best performance. A comparator IC is really a special form of op-amp designed for high speed operation with fast slew rate and high open loop gain, but in addition it also has an output stage that comes out of saturation quickly and neatly.

The high open loop gain of a differential amplifier means that its output will saturate at one state when the input being sensed is less than the reference level, but will switch to the opposite saturation state when the input just exceeds the reference. The polarity of the output depends on whether the input being sensed is connected to the inverting or non-inverting pin of the comparator; see Fig. 5.1.

For many applications the important parameters required from a comparator are:

- wide bandwidth,
- fast slew rate,
- high open-loop gain,
- low values of input offset drift.

It follows that uncompensated op-amps, for example the 531 with a slew rate of $30 \, \text{V} \, \mu\text{s}^{-1}$, can be used to give the fast response necessary. On the other hand, standard comparators usually have a purpose-designed output stage that can directly interface with TTL and/or be capable of driving relays, lamps and other loads. The industry standard 311 is typical; see Table 5.1 for the specification details. Note that this IC has a response time, the normal way of specifying comparator speed, of better than 200 ns and is designed to operate from a single supply rail ($+5 \, \text{V}$ to $+36 \, \text{V}$) or from a dual supply ($\pm 2.5 \, \text{V}$ to $18 \, \text{V}$). It has a switching transistor as its output which has both the emitter and collector unconnected. This essentially open-collector output can drive loads of up to 50 mA at voltages up to 40 V, see Fig. 5.2.

The high gain inherent in most comparators means that only a very small difference is necessary between the two inputs to cause the output to switch. A device such as the 319 (a dual, high speed, single supply comparator) has a voltage gain quoted as $40 \, \text{V} \, \text{mV}^{-1}$. This means that the input difference need only be 0.25 mV to cause a 10 V change at the output. This sort of performance may often be desirable but it can lead to problems when there is a slowly varying input and where the source resistance is high. It is all too easy to get oscillations or 'jitter' at the switch-over point (Fig. 5.3). If a bipolar comparator is used the input bias current is typically between 200 nA and 10 μA. At the point where the comparator switches, the input bias current usually also changes from one of the

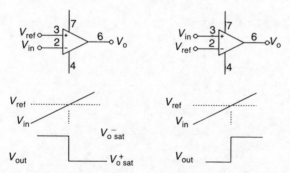

Fig. 5.1 Comparator connections and operation

Table 5.1 Standard comparator ICs

Parameter	LM311	LM319	TLC339	LM392
Supply voltage (V)	5 to 36 or ± 2.5 to ± 18	5 to 36	3 to16	3 to 32 or ± 1.5 to ± 16
Max. diff. input voltage (V)	± 30	5	± 18	32
Max. power dissipation	500 mW at $V_S = \pm 15$ V	500 mW at $V_S = 5$ V	875 mW at $V_S = 5$ V	570 mW at $V_S = 5$ V
Open loop voltage gain (dB)	106	92	not quoted	166
I_B	100 nA	250 nA	5 pA	50 nA
Response time	200 ns	80 ns	2.5 μs	1.3 μs
Output swing	$\pm V_S$	0 to $+V_S$	0 to $+V_S$	$\pm V_S$

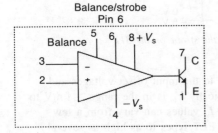

Fig. 5.2 The 311 comparator

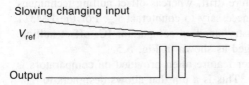

Fig. 5.3 Jitter caused by a slowly varying input

inputs to the other. If the source resistance is relatively high this switch in the bias current will change the input level and cause the comparator's output to switch back and forth before settling to its new state. Suppose the bias current change is 200 nA and the source resistance is 5 kΩ. As a slowly varying signal approaches the trigger point and just passes it, the 'step' induced on the input will be:

$$V_{in} = R_S I_b$$

Therefore $V_{in} = 1$ mV.

This is more than sufficient to cause the comparator to switch back to its previous state.

There are three possible solutions to this problem:

(a) introduce some hysteresis into the circuit,
(b) specify a FET input or CMOS comparator, or
(c) buffer the input.

Each of these methods has merits for different applications. Hysteresis can often be a desirable feature since it introduces a 'dead band'. Once the input has passed a fixed threshold level (V_t^+) the comparator output will not switch back to its previous state until the input has fallen back below a lower threshold value (V_t^-). By setting the difference between these two threshold levels to be greater than the expected signal changes or noise at the trigger point, it is possible to eliminate jitter. The hysteresis is the difference between the two thresholds and is typically set to values in the range 5 mV to 500 mV.

Where hysteresis has to be kept low the FET or CMOS comparators with their very low bias currents, typically 10 pA or less, can be used. But the response will often be slower than the bipolar equivalent.

The third method is to buffer the source with an amplifier so that the resistance presented at the comparator's input is low. Some ICs are available, such as the LM392, which have an op-amp and a comparator in the same package. These are ideal for this sort of application.

Suppose we opt for the hysteresis method to eliminate the jitter. This is introduced by using some positive feedback in the circuit. A portion of the output level is fed back to the non-inverting

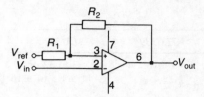

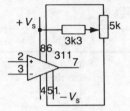

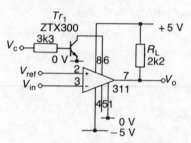

Fig. 5.4 Introducing hysteresis

Fig. 5.5 Offset adjustment for the 311

Fig. 5.6 Using the strobe on the 311

input as shown in Fig. 5.4. This sets up the two trip points:

V_t^+ the positive going threshold
V_t^- the negative going threshold.

Hysteresis $V_h = V_t^+ - V_t^-$

For the circuit:

$$V_t^+ = V_{ref} + [V_{o(sat)}^+ - V_{ref}]R_1/(R_1 + R_2) \quad (1)$$
$$V_t^- = V_{ref} + [V_{o(sat)}^- - V_{ref}]R_1/(R_1 + R_2) \quad (2)$$

where $V_{o(sat)}$ is the comparator's output saturation level (either positive or negative).

The hysteresis is found by subtracting equation (2) from equation (1).

$$V_h = [V_{o(sat)}^+ - V_{o(sat)}^-]R_1/(R_1 + R_2)$$

The reference level does not affect the hysteresis.

Take the example of a comparator which switches between ± 5 V and has $R_1 = 1$ kΩ and $R_2 = 9$ kΩ. $V_{ref} = +3$ V.

$$V_t^+ = 3 + (5-3)\, 1/10 = 3.2 \text{ V}$$
$$V_t^- = 3 + (-5-3)\, 1/10 = 2.2 \text{ V}$$
$$V_h = [5-(-5)]\, 1/10 = 1 \text{ V}$$

If low values of hysteresis are wanted R_1 should be made much less than R_2. Then

$$V_h = [V_{o(sat)}^+ - V_{o(sat)}^-]R_1/R_2$$

Thus for a comparator that has TTL compatible outputs, $V_{o(sat)}^+$ is about 3.4 V and $V_{o(sat)}^-$ is 0.4 V, the formula for V_h could be rewritten as:

$$V_h = 3R_1/R_2$$

Suppose we require the hysteresis to be 30 mV then:

$$R_2 = 100R_1$$

with $R_1 = 10$ kΩ, $R_2 = 1$ MΩ.

When hysteresis is small V_t^+ will be essentially equal to the value of the reference voltage.

Comparator ICs will also have errors at the

threshold due to the input offset voltages and currents. Typically V_{io} is in the range ± 1 mV to ± 10 mV and I_{io} values can vary from a few picoamps for FET types to as high as several microamps for bipolars. Keeping source resistance low will minimise the effects of I_{io} and its temperature drift, whereas offset nulling techniques will be necessary to counteract V_{io}. For the LM311, the industry standard comparator IC, offset nulling is arranged as shown in Fig. 5.5.

Another feature often provided on comparators is a strobe. This is a pin that allows designers to incorporate test and synchronising signals. In this way the output state of the comparator can be tested by a control signal. In Fig. 5.6 the typical arrangement for driving the strobe on an LM311 is shown. Pin 6 (balance/strobe) is connected to the collector of a transistor switch (BC107, 2N2222 or similar) which has its emitter at ground. A TTL control signal via the 3k3 resistor will turn this transistor on and off. A high state TTL will force the strobe input pin to go low which will put the output into the off state irrespective of the comparator's input conditions. Since the output transistor is off its output will be at $+5$ V in the example.

Output stages are usually different in design to those in op-amps and may not withstand indefinite short-circuit conditions. Always check the data sheet. Typically the types of output stage fall into three categories.

   (a) An uncommitted transistor with both its emitter and collector unconnected.

   (b) An open collector or open drain output transistor.

   (c) A push–pull totem pole type output that can be interfaced directly with TTL and CMOS logic.

Both (a) and (b) allow the circuit connected at the output to be at a much higher voltage than the actual supply of the comparator and the output transistor can usually sink several milliamps.

The totem pole outputs are designed for high speed and may have a limited fan-out capability. For example, the TL810 can only drive one standard TTL load. A check of the full data is often necessary.

5.2 USING OP-AMPS AS COMPARATORS

From the preceding section it will be apparent that for many general purpose comparator applications, particularly those where high speed is not an important requirement, there is no reason why an ordinary op-amp cannot be used. If speed is a critical factor, either use an uncompensated (i.e. wide bandwidth) op-amp or turn to a comparator IC.

A low temperature detector circuit will serve as an example, Fig. 5.7. In this, the requirement is for a high voltage output level to be given greater than $+5\,V$ but less than $+10\,V$, if the temperature being sensed falls below 4 °C. The tolerance on the trip point is ± 1 °C. The sensor is to be a thermistor type GL23 which has a quoted resistance of 2000 Ω

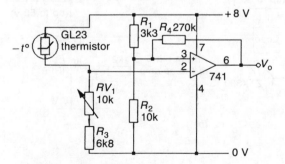

Fig. 5.7 Low temperature trip circuit

at 20 °C. For a n.t.c. thermistor the resistance at any temperature within its range is given by

$$R_2 = R_1 e^{B(1/T_2 - 1/T_1)}$$

where R_1 is resistance at temperature T_1, R_2 is resistance at temperature T_2 and B is a constant (3200 for the GL23).

(NB: Temperature in this formula is in kelvin. To convert from °C to K simply add 273.)

Therefore at 4 °C:

$$R_2 = 2000 e^{3200(1/277 - 1/293)}$$
$$= 2000 e^{0.631}$$
$$\approx 3760\ \Omega$$

However the quoted value for R_1 at 20 °C has a tolerance of $\pm 20\%$ and the constant B a tolerance of $\pm 5\%$. Taking both these variations into account means that the calculated value of 3760 Ω can have an error of $\pm 900\,\Omega$. It is essential to allow for this spread by including some adjustment in the design.

Another factor to be considered is the trip limit of ± 1 °C.

At 3 °C $R_2 = 3919\,\Omega$
and at 5 °C $R_2 = 3605\,\Omega$

In other words a ± 1 °C change around the trip point causes the thermistor resistance to change by $\pm 155\,\Omega$. This is a fairly large change and means that the sensitivity of the circuit can be high. For example, if we pass 1 mA of current through the thermistor a 0.1 °C change near the trip point will set up a voltage change of 15 mV. This would be more than sufficient to cause a switch at the op-amp's output. It also means that any drifts of the op-amp's offset voltages and currents are swamped. If a 741 is used with dV_{io}/dT of 5 μV °C^{-1} and dI_{io}/dT of 0.5 nA °C^{-1} the drift error at the circuit's input will be less than 10 μV °C^{-1} of ambient temperature.

When using thermistors for temperature sensing it is also important to keep the current through the device to a relatively low value. The GL23 has a dissipation constant of 1.2 mW °C^{-1}. In other words, the thermistor's temperature will be raised 1 °C above that which it is measuring if it is dissipating 1.2 mW. In the circuit I have set the current through the sensor to be approximately 0.6 mA which reduces the sensitivity to about half that previously calculated but restricts the thermistor's dissipation to about 1.2 mW.

The error caused by the self-heating effect is not more than 1 °C.

In the circuit the supply to the op-amp is set to 8 V and two resistors R_1 and R_2 are used to set up the reference:

$$V_{ref} = V_S R_2/(R_1 + R_2)$$

With $V_{ref} = 6$ V and $I_{ref} = 0.6$ mA, R_2 must be 10 kΩ. Therefore R_1 can be 3k3. These resistors need not be close tolerance since adjustment of the trip point will be made using R_3 and RV_1. To enable the 'spread' of values previously calculated for the thermistor to be accepted, R_3 is made a 6k8 and RV_1 a 10 kΩ.

Note that the thermistor is fitted in such a way that the circuit operation is *fail safe*. If the sensor goes open circuit (the more usual failure mode) the output voltage of the op-amp will switch high.

Some hysteresis is built into the circuit using R_4. From the previously determined formula,

$$V_h = [V_{o(sat)}^+ - V_{o(sat)}^-] R'/(R' + R_4) \qquad (1)$$

where $R' = R_1//R_2$ (about 2k5)

The hysteresis, in this case, should be made equal to or greater than the change in voltage generated across the thermistor for a 0.5 °C change.

At the trip point the GL23 resistance changes by about 75 Ω for 0.5 °C giving a voltage change of:

$$\Delta V = \Delta R_t I \approx 45 \text{ mV}$$

Therefore set the hysteresis at 50 mV.

From equation (1):

$$50 \times 10^{-3} = (7-2)\ 2.5/(2.5 + R_4)$$

Therefore $R_4 \approx \dfrac{12.5}{50}$ MΩ

$$\approx 250 \text{ kΩ (270k is n.p.v.)}$$

Any general purpose op-amp can be used but because of the single supply the output level from a 741 in the off state can be as high as +2 V. This rather high value means that some level shifting of the output is required if it is to drive a transistor switch. A suitable arrangement is shown in Fig. 5.8 where a 4.7 V Zener in series with a 1k5 resistor is used to drive the base of a simple BJT switch. The transistor can be a ZTX 300, BC 107 or similar and is capable of driving loads up to 50 mA and 24 V. The 2 V low state output from the op-amp is insufficient to bias the Zener and therefore the transistor is off. When the output switches to the +7 V, the high state, the Zener conducts and supplies about 2 mA of base drive to the transistor to force it into saturation. The load can be a piezoelectric buzzer, a relay coil or the LED in an opto-isolator.

This rather over-complicated output circuit can be avoided by using an op-amp that is specifically designed for single supply operation and will therefore give a low level output that is much closer to zero volts. The LinCMOS op-amps such as the TLC251 and TLC271 are examples that could be used. Alternatively the output could be used to drive a power FET as shown in Fig. 5.8(b). Here the output of the 741 (or other general purpose op-amp) is connected to the gate of an IRF511 Hexfet. Since this power FET has a gate-to-source threshold voltage of typically 4 V the low state output from the comparator will not cause it to switch on. To allow a safety margin two resistors are used to

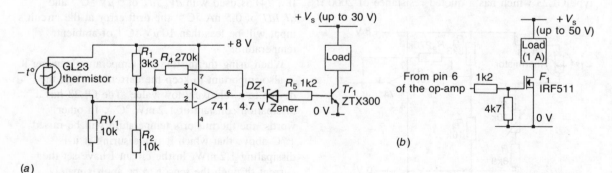

(a)

Fig. 5.8 Output circuits

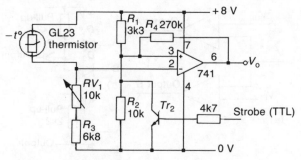

Fig. 5.9 Adding a strobe

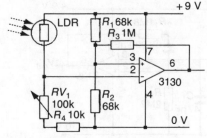

Fig. 5.10 Dark level sensing circuit

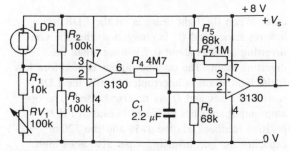

Fig. 5.11 Light sensor with delay

ensure that the gate voltage is less than 2 V under these conditions. When the output of the comparator circuit switches high the available drive to the gate of the FET is 5.5 V, which will enable loads of up to 1 A to be switched in the drain circuit. Since the typical on resistance ($R_{ds(on)}$) of the IRF511 is quoted as a maximum of $0.6\,\Omega$, the power dissipation of this device will be only 600 mW at maximum output current. A heat sink should not be necessary.

If a 351 op-amp is tried in the circuit instead of the 741 as specified, the two output levels will be about 0.75 V (low) and 7.5 V (high). This means that the level shifting is simpler to design and the Zener diode can be omitted. The 351 is a JFET op-amp with fast slew rate and is pin for pin compatible with the 741.

A 'strobe' feature can be added to the circuit to allow remote sensing. One gating method would be to connect a switch to the reference point as shown in Fig. 5.9. An n-p-n transistor is connected across R_2 and is held 'on' by a logic level applied via R_5. With this input high the reference voltage will be clamped to near zero volts and the comparator output will be low irrespective of the temperature level being sensed. When a low level, less than 0.5 V, is applied to the strobe the comparator will be enabled and its output will rise positive to +7 V as long as the temperature at the sensor is at or below the 4 °C level. There are, of course, several other methods that can be used to provide a strobe.

BIFET, JFET and CMOS op-amps are also useful in comparator circuits, especially where the source resistance is high. The MOSFET input types 3130 and 3140 also give almost zero volts output in the low state when used with a single supply. Consider a light sensing circuit using an LDR. The simplest arrangement for detecting a low ambient (i.e. dusk)

level is shown in Fig. 5.10, which is simply a variation of the temperature sensing circuit but using higher value resistors. With the 3130 the maximum differential input voltage is ± 8 V which means that for higher supplies some form of protection must be provided at the input pins of the op-amp. With this circuit R_1 and R_2 set up a reference level of +4.5 V on the non-inverting input and while the LDR is in light its resistance is lower than the setting of the potentiometer RV_1. At low light levels the LDR resistance rises, causing the inverting input to fall below the 4 V reference. The output switches from zero to just above 7 V.

Some hysteresis is essential and is provided by R_3. With R_3 equal to 1 MΩ the hysteresis should be approximately 300 mV.

A variation of this circuit shown in Fig. 5.11 prevents passing shadows from causing the circuit to trip. A dual MOSFET input op-amp, the 3240, is used with one op-amp providing a buffer between the LDR and a CR delay network. The second op-amp is the comparator with its reference again set to +4 V. The 4M7 resistor has to charge the 2.2 nF tantalum capacitor and this provides a delay before the trip is exceeded.

If the opposite effect is required, in other words only rapid input changes are to cause an output swing, a circuit similar to that in Fig. 5.12 can be

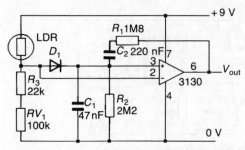

Fig. 5.12 Circuit for detecting rapid changes only

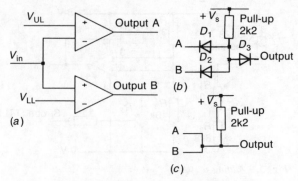

Fig. 5.14 Basic 'window' comparator circuit

used. When the light beam is on the LDR has a low resistance and C_1 is charged so that the non-inverting input is about 0.7 V lower than the inverting input. The op-amp output is therefore low. If the light beam is interrupted briefly the LDR resistance rises and D_1 is reverse biased. The op-amp output switches high and because of the positive feedback via the 1M8 and the 220 nF capacitor the non-inverting input also goes high. This is a semi-stable condition. When C_2 has discharged sufficiently the diode D_1 will again conduct and the output will return to the low level. This circuit will therefore produce a pulse, with a width determined by the CR components, every time the light beam is broken but not if the light level changes slowly.

5.3 APPLICATION AND DESIGN EXAMPLES

WINDOW COMPARATOR

This is a circuit designed to give an output change of state only when the input is between two well defined limits, i.e. within a voltage 'window'. The two levels are usually referred to as V_{UL} and V_{LL} and the circuit has the transfer characteristic indicated in Fig. 5.13. When the input level is

below V_{LL} the output is in the low state; it switches to the opposite state when the input is between V_{LL} and V_{UL}, and returns to the low state when the input exceeds V_{UL}. The basic circuit, shown in Fig. 5.14(a), uses two comparators such as the Dual LM193 which have open collector or open drain outputs. The outputs can then be combined using a variety of circuits. Let's first consider the basic circuit and the three possible input conditions.

(i) V_{in} less than V_{LL} A=High   B=Low

(ii) V_{in} greater than V_{LL} but less than V_{UL} A=High   B=High

(iii) V_{in} greater than both V_{LL} and V_{UL} A=Low   B=High

Only when V_{in} is within the 'window' will both outputs be high. These can be combined using a diode AND circuit, Fig. 5.14(b) or, if open collector transistors are provided in the comparators, by simply wiring the two outputs together to a common pull-up resistor, Fig. 5.14(c). For high speed operation this pull-up resistor must be a reasonably low value, say in the range 680 Ω to 2.2 kΩ.

The window comparator is a very useful circuit for limit detection, i.e. for testing components and system signals.

Design example

A window comparator is required to the following specification (Fig. 5.15):

$$V_{in} : 0\,V \text{ to } +10\,V$$
$$V_{LL} : 4\,V \pm 5\%$$

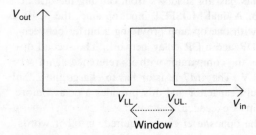

Fig. 5.13 Transfer characteristic for a 'window' comparator

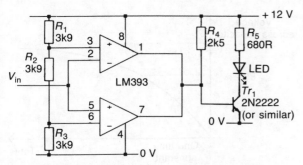

Fig. 5.15 Design example of a 'window' comparator

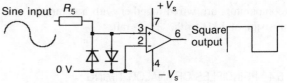

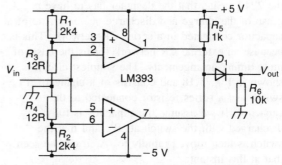

Fig. 5.16 Simple zero-crossing detector

Fig. 5.17 Design example of a zero-crossing detector

Window : 4 V ±5%
V_{CC} : 12 V
Output : To switch on an LED
Source resistance : 2 kΩ

Since the tolerance on the window is ±5% the two voltage levels can be set up using ±1% (or ±2% if necessary) fixed resistors. These three resistors should be kept to low values consistent with the available current. This will ensure that drifts on the trip voltages with temperature are minimised. By setting the supply to +12 V equal value resistors are required to give $V_{UL} = 8$ V and $V_{LL} = 4$ V. A suitable choice is 3k9 which requires only 1 mA of current from the supply. A dual comparator type LM393 which has open collector outputs and is designed to run from a single supply is specified in the circuit, but other types can be used. The two outputs are wired AND with a common resistor R_4. The value of this resistor has to be set so that it fully saturates the LED driver Tr_1. With the LED current set to 15 mA by R_5 the base current of Tr_1 must be 1.5 mA to ensure saturation.

$$R_4 = \frac{V_{CC} - V_{BE(sat)}}{I_{B(sat)}} \approx 7.5 \text{ k}\Omega$$

ZERO CROSSING DETECTOR

This is a useful comparator application, where the input is an a.c. signal and the output is a short duration pulse only when the input passes through zero. The simplest arrangement is based on a comparator which has one input tied to a reference voltage of zero (ground), see Fig. 5.16. As the a.c. signal moves through zero the comparator output will switch from one level of saturation to the other. In this way the output is a square wave at the

same frequency as the input. Apart from the fact that it has 'edges' that are generated at the crossing points, not a pulse, the circuit also has the defect of 'jitter' at the switching point. A better method is to use two comparators based on the 'window' circuit, see Fig. 5.17. Here two bias levels are set up to give a narrow window about zero. This window is usually set to some tens of millivolts, then as the input moves positive or negative through zero, comparator outputs will only be high for the brief period when the input is within the two reference levels.

Design example

See Fig. 5.17.

V_{in} : 100 Hz, 20 V pk−pk a.c. signal
V_{out} : +5 V ±10% amplitude
V_{trip} : ±25 mV

Again an LM393 dual comparator will be suitable and no input protection should be necessary since this chip has a differential voltage rating of ±36 V (otherwise use the circuit option indicated on the input of Fig. 5.16).

The supply is a standard ±5 V and the two levels of +25 mV and −25 mV can be set up by fixed resistors in the ratio 1:200. R_1 and R_2 can be 2.4 kΩ and R_2 and R_3 12 Ω. The outputs of the two comparators are wired together with a common resistor of 1 kΩ to the +5 V rail.

5.4 PRINCIPLES OF ANALOG TIMING

Using timer ICs such as the 555, the ZN1034 or the 2240 means that the designer has to have a grasp of the charge and discharge characteristic of a capacitor connected in a series CR network. This is because an external CR network forms the basis of most timing arrangements. The simplest circuit is shown in Fig. 5.18 and consists of a changeover switch and a series resistor connected to the capacitor. If we assume the capacitor is fully discharged with the switch at 'B', and that the switch is then moved rapidly to 'A' it can be seen that at this instant:

$$V_C = 0\,\text{V} \qquad \text{at } t = 0$$
$$i_C = V/R$$

As the capacitor charges, the voltage across the resistor falls and the current at any time t is given by:

$$i_C = \frac{V - V_C}{R}$$

Thus the charging, or circuit, current falls exponentially towards zero as the capacitor charges. The voltage across the capacitor at any time t is given by:

$$V_C = V(1 - e^{-t/CR})$$

where CR is called the time constant in seconds (C in farads, R in ohms) (see Fig. 5.19).

When $t = CR$
$$V_C = 0.632\,V$$

In other words, the voltage across the capacitor changes by 63.2% over a period of one time constant and it takes several time constants before the voltage aross the capacitor reaches the supply voltage V. Typically this time for the capacitor to

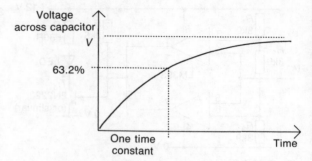

Fig. 5.19 Capacitor charging characteristic

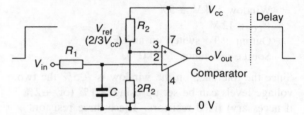

Fig. 5.20 Simple delay circuit

fully charge is taken to be about 4 to 5 time constants.

If we assume the capacitor is fully charged to voltage V and the switch is then moved rapidly from 'A' to 'B', the capacitor will then discharge via R towards zero volts. In this case:

$$V_C = Ve^{-t/CR}$$

Again when $T = CR$ the voltage across the capacitor will have fallen 63.2% from its initial value V.

Most timing circuits, which naturally require repeatable accurate delays, use changes of voltage across the capacitor of not greater than 60% to 70%, since these points on the charge/discharge characteristic can be more easily defined. For example, in the popular 555 the external timing capacitor charges from 0 V to 2/3 V_{CC} to define the timing period in the monostable mode. The principle is illustrated in Fig. 5.20 where a comparator has one input tied to a reference voltage set to 2/3 V_{CC} and the capacitor is charged from zero towards V_{CC}. When the voltage across the capacitor exceeds 2/3 V_{CC} the comparator output switches states. The timing period for this, relative to the CR value, can be found using:

$$V_C = V(1 - e^{-t/CR})$$

where, in this case, $V_C = 2/3\,V_{CC}$ and $V = V_{CC}$.

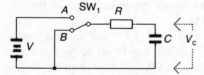

Fig. 5.18 Basic timing circuit

Therefore $\dfrac{2}{3} = 1 - e^{-t/CR}$

$e^{-t/CR} = \dfrac{1}{3}$

Therefore $t = 1.0986CR$.

This is usually rounded up as: $t = 1.1CR$.

By using the two formulas for charge and discharge it is possible to calculate values of time delays for changes of voltage between defined points. This can be done using any scientific calculator. As an exercise, calculate the time constant for a 220 nF capacitor and a 47 kΩ resistor and the time taken for the capacitor to discharge from 2/3 V_{CC} to 1/3 V_{CC}. (Answers at foot of page.)

If the 'trip' points used to define the timing are derived from the same supply voltage as that charging the capacitor, changes to timing should not be caused by changes to the voltage rails supplying the circuit. It is the CR network which will primarily determine the accuracy and stability of the timing. With standard capacitors the tolerance is typically ±2% up to ±10%, whereas resistors of ±1% tolerance are readily available. This means that it is often the capacitor that is the limiting factor on accuracy, and if accuracies of better than ±3% are required part of the timing resistance must be made adjustable. Cermet trimpots are best for this purpose. Another important factor to consider early in the design is the long term stability and the temperature stability of the circuit. The IC used will have a quoted temperature coefficient showing how the trip points change with temperature, and this is often much better than the performance from the timing components. If good stability is required, and this is usually the case, then components such as silvered mica or polystyrene capacitors and cermet or metal film resistors will prove the best choices. Typical temperature coefficients for good quality capacitors are ±50 ppm/°C and for resistors ±100 ppm/°C.

Consider an example using a 100 nF capacitor with a 200 kΩ timing resistor.

The time constant $CR = 20$ ms

The temperature stability is found by adding together the two coefficients.

Answers: time constant = 10.34 ms, $t = 7.17$ ms

Therefore timing drift = ±150 ppm/°C

For a 10 °C change in ambient the timing would drift by ±1500 ppm or ±30 μs.

Although long term changes of power supply rails, when the trip points are defined from them, will not cause timing errors, it is still important to have a well regulated and ripple free supply. This is especially important when short term changes occur relative to the timing period. It is always wise to have good decoupling at the timer IC pins to eliminate noise and switching spikes, otherwise there will be timing jitter. For example, the popular 555 timer can generate switching current spikes of up to 200 mA peak. Decoupling becomes essential.

5.5 TIMER ICs

The most popular timer ICs can be grouped under general headings as follows:

Medium delay times
microseconds to minutes: NE555
dual version is the NE556
low power versions ICM 75551PA and the LinCMOS TLC555

Long time delays
milliseconds to days: ZN1034

Programmable delays
microseconds to days: 2240

With these ICs and careful choice of external timing components it is possible to generate delays, waveforms (square, triangle and sawtooth) with accuracies of better than ±2% and in some cases better than ±0.5%. As we shall see the basic circuits can also be used in a wide variety of other applications.

The 555 is a good starting point and a block diagram of it is given in Fig. 5.21. It has two fast comparators whose trip points are set to 1/3 V_{CC} and 2/3 V_{CC} by an equal component (5 kΩ) resistor chain. The outputs of the comparators are connected to the set and reset inputs of a bistable with the $\overline{Q}$ output of this bistable driving both a discharge transistor and an output buffer stage. In the monostable mode (one fixed duration output pulse for one trigger input) an external CR network is

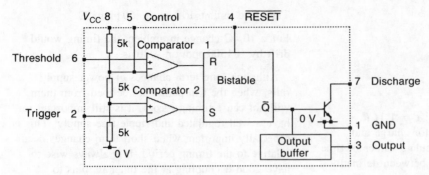

Fig. 5.21 555 timer block diagram

connected with the capacitor wired from pin 6 and pin 7, the discharge transistor's collector, to ground. The resistor is connected from pins 6/7 (threshold trip point equal to 2/3 V_{CC}) to V_{CC}. When power is applied the bistable assumes a high state on $\bar{Q}$ so the internal transistor clamps the capacitor to zero volts and the output is low. A short duration trigger pulse to pin 2 taking the inverting input of comparator 2 momentarily low causes the bistable to be set. The internal discharge transistor turns off and the output of the 555 switches high. The timing capacitor now charges and the voltage across it rises exponentially towards V_{CC}. When this voltage just exeeds 2/3 V_{CC} comparator 1 switches high and resets the bistable. This forces the capacitor to be rapidly discharged and the output to return to near zero volts. A wide range of supply voltages (5 V to 15 V) can be used. As we have seen in Section 5.1 the time delay generated by charging a capacitor from 0 V to 2/3 V_{CC} is:

$$t = 1.1CR$$

This is the timing period for the 555 monostable.
   The main points of the 555 are:

   Timing error : $\pm 1\%$
   Drift with supply voltage : 0.01%/volt
   Temperature coefficient : ± 50 ppm $^{\circ}$C^{-1}
   Rise/fall time of output : 100 ns
   Output current (sink or source) : 100 mA
   Maximum power dissipation : 600 mW

There are some other pins on the 555 that allow the designer flexibility in circuits. These are:

   (a) Pin 4 RESET: A low level applied here will always override the timing and reset the output low. This input can be used with a

pulse to interrupt timing or it can be held low to clamp the output to its low state. In this condition it acts like an enable input. If not used it should be tied high to V_{CC}.

   (b) Pin 5 CONTROL: This allows direct access to the threshold voltage level of 2/3 V_{CC}. Thus this trip level is available as a reference or an external control voltage can be applied which will force the threshold level to a new value. This allows modulation of the timing. The threshold level can also be trimmed by an external resistor network. This can be useful in compensating for the tolerance of the timing capacitor, especially in designs where several switched time delays have to be selected. Close tolerance resistors can be used and only one trimpot is required for timing adjustment. The principle is shown in Fig. 5.22. When not used this pin should be decoupled with a 10 nF capacitor to improve the timer's noise immunity.

   What then are the limitations in design work? For timing components the resistor should be a

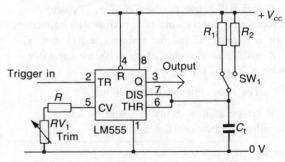

Fig. 5.22 One use of the control pin on the 555

minimum of 1 kΩ and a maximum of 10 MΩ. But these are the extremes. It is best to keep timing resistor values in the range 5 kΩ to 1 MΩ.

A practical minimum value for the timing capacitor is 100 pF. If lower values are used any stray capacitance will affect the accuracy. For the upper value the only limitation is leakage current and capacitor size. This should rule out the use of aluminium electrolytics which, apart from wide tolerances, have relatively high values of leakage current. The leakage current of a capacitor can be represented by an equivalent resistor in parellel with the capacitance. If this leakage is appreciable with respect to the current charging the capacitor, errors in timing will occur. Take the case of a capacitor with a leakage current of 1 μA and a timing resistor of 1 MΩ connected to a 10 V supply. The initial charging current is 10 μA of which 9 μA is available for charging the capacitor. But when the voltage across the capacitor has risen to 2/3 V_{CC} the current available is 3.33 μA, leaving 2.33 μA for the capacitor. The timing error will be large and temperature dependent. If the leakage current is very high in comparison to the available charging current ($R = 10$ MΩ, say) the voltage across the capacitor may never reach the trip point and the output, once triggered, will remain continuously high. This is obviously an extreme case but it could occur with a very high value 'leaky' electrolytic capacitor. Tantalum electrolytics should be used for the higher values in timing circuits.

If we allow for some error in the timing, in addition to that caused by the capacitor's tolerance, a practical limit on the capacitor is about 50 μF. With a timing resistor of 5 MΩ this gives a maximum possible time delay of about 5 minutes. For delays above a few minutes a timer such as the ZN102E will be a better choice than the 555.

The trigger pulse width to a 555 should not be less than 1 μs and the minimum recommended output pulse width or time delay is 10 μs. This sets an upper frequency limit of about 100 kHz when the 555 is used in the astable mode but it is possible to stretch this a bit. The trigger pulse width should be well below the output pulse time, otherwise retriggering will occur. This fact can be put to good use in 'missing pulse' detector circuits.

The main differences in performance between the standard bipolar 555 and the CMOS versions are:

1.   CMOS types have lower power

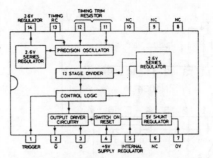

Fig. 5.23 ZN1034 block diagram

consumption. Quiescent current is typically 300 μA as opposed to the 6 mA for the standard 555.

2.   Input bias to the threshold and trigger inputs is reduced to 10 pA. These high impedance inputs allow the CMOS version to give more accurate delays with relatively low cost and smaller timing capacitors since higher value timing resistors can be used.

3.   The output stage, which can source 10 mA and sink 100 mA, generates a much reduced current spike. The need for large decoupling capacitors is minimised.

4.   Typical rise and fall times are 40 ns. The CMOS 555 is therefore capable of oscillations up to 2 MHz.

The *longer duration timer* ICs use a mix of analog and digital circuitry. The block diagram of the ZN1034 timer is typical, Fig. 5.23. It has a precision oscillator, running at a frequency set by an external CR network, feeding a 12-stage binary counter. When a trigger pulse is applied the oscillator is gated to the counter input. The counter output will change state only after 4095 pulses. A simple calculation will show that if the oscillator is running at 1 Hz the output will not change state until about 1 hour has elapsed. The ZN1034 also has an on-chip regulator allowing it to run from a wide range of supply voltages with a suitable series resistor. Its output driver can sink or source 25 mA. The timing function can be set, with a simple CR network, Fig. 5.24(*a*), where the periodic time of the oscillator is $0.68CR \pm 10\%$. Since the divider is 4095 the timing period is then given by the formula:

$$T = KC_t R_t \text{ seconds}$$

where $K = 2800 \pm 10\%$.

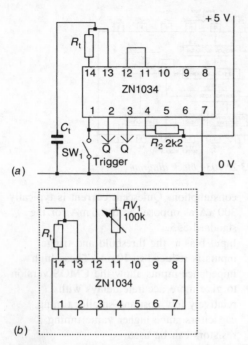

Fig. 5.24 (a) Basic timing for the ZN1034; (b) Using the trim facility

The minimum and maximum recommended values for the timing components are:

C_r 1 nF to 100 μF
R_t 3.3 kΩ to 5 MΩ

With the maximum values the time delay using this mode is about 16 days.

To allow for trimming of the time period an external resistor can be fitted between pins 11 and 12, Fig. 5.24(b). With a 100 kΩ trimpot connected and set at mid point the time multiplying factor K_{50} is typically 3700 ± 10%. A 100 kΩ potentiometer allows a trim of ± 25%.

Triggering is on a Schmitt trigger input which has a hysteresis of about 300 mV. This input should normally be held high with a pull-up resistor of a few kΩ. Triggering can then be achieved using either switch contacts, from a transducer or from TTL and CMOS logic.

The 2240 and 7240, Fig. 5.25, are bipolar and CMOS versions of a programmable timer which is similar in operation to the previous device but with additional programming capability. An external CR network sets the frequency of the timer's oscillator with the basic time period equal to 1RC. After a

trigger (active high) pulse is received the time base oscillator is enabled and its output is fed to an 8-bit counter. The outputs of this counter are open-collector (2240) or open-drain (7240) which are normally high. All are set low by the trigger and only change to a high state as the count advances. The timing is only completed by a reset pulse which is applied using a combination of counter outputs, selected by the user, in a wired-AND configuration. For example, if a divider of 15 is required, outputs 1, 2, 3 and 4 would be wired together and connected back to the reset (pin 10) see Fig. 5.26. In this way the total time delay can be set using the formula:

$$T = NRC$$

where N is a number between 1 and 255. Typical accuracies, excluding the tolerance of the RC components, are ± 0.5% for the 2240 and ± 5% for the 7240.

Recommended timing values are:

R 1 kΩ to 10 MΩ
C 5 nF to 200 μF

Again, a low leakage capacitor is essential and for higher values tantalum types should be used.

With the 2240 and the 7240 the threshold levels are set to 21.3% and 71% of V_{CC}. But this, like the 555, can be modified by applying a voltage to the MOD input on pin 12.

Although the discussion on the various timer chips has focused on monostable operation all of them can be connected as astables. Some examples are included after the next section.

5.6 MONOSTABLE DESIGNS

Having considered the limitations imposed by the various timer ICs we can now look at some typical designs.

EXAMPLE 1

Design specification

Power supply : +5 V
Output pulse height : TTL compatible
Output pulse width : 50 μs ± 10%

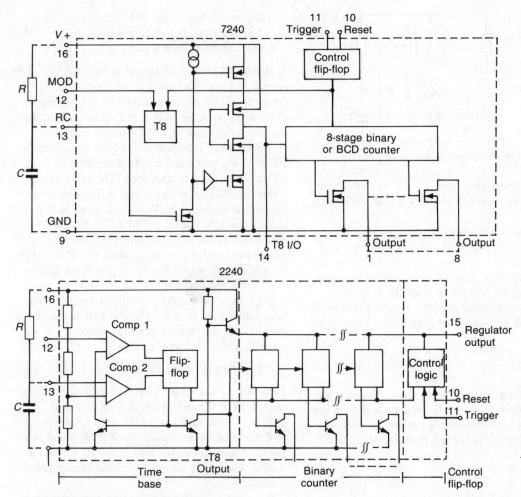

Fig. 5.25 2240 and 7240 block diagrams

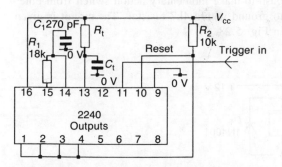

Fig. 5.26 Wiring the 2240 to divide the timing by 15

Load : 2 standard TTL gate inputs
Power consumption : Less than 10 mW
Trigger input : 2 μs TTL positive pulse

A CMOS 555 is the most obvious choice since

these devices require less than 1 mW in the quiescent state.

The next component to fix is the timing capacitor, and because the output pulse width is only $50\,\mu s$ a reasonable value for C_t is between 500 pF and 5 nF. Initially we shall set C_t to be 1 nF.

Using the formula:

$$T = 1.1\,C_tR_t$$
$$R_t = T/1.1C_t$$

Therefore $R_t = 45.45\,k\Omega$

The n.p.v. is 47 kΩ which, if used with the 1 nF capacitor, gives a nominal $51.7\,\mu s$ pulse width. This is 3.4% high but within the ±10% limit. If the tolerance on the timing resistor is ±2% and that on the capacitor 2.5% the maximum error on T is just over $4\,\mu s$ which is still within the 10% limit.

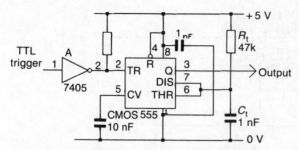

Fig. 5.27 Monostable design to give a 50 μs pulse

Therefore C_t will be a 1 nF ±2.5% silvered mica or polystyrene capacitor and R_t a 47 kΩ ±2% metal film.

Pin 5 is decoupled using a 10 nF polyester capacitor and the supply decoupling can be a 1 nF ceramic disc.

The trigger input must be converted to negative going. An open collector or open drain invertor gate is used to connect the TTL trigger pulse to pin 2 with a pull up resistor of 1 kΩ to V_{DD}, Fig. 5.27.

EXAMPLE 2

The requirement is for a timer circuit that operates a 12 V, 100 mA relay for 12 seconds ±0.5 s when two contacts are momentarily closed. A reset facility, which is also switch contacts, must be provided.

Target specification

> Power supply : +12 V
> Time period : 12 s ±0.5 s

Output current : 100 mA
Trigger input : switch contacts
Reset input : switch contacts

A standard 555 is suitable and at first sight it might appear that the relay coil can be connected directly from the output pin to ground with a protection diode to prevent the back e.m.f. generated by the coil from damaging the 555's output circuit. However, even though the IC can source up to 200 mA, the maximum power dissipation of 600 mW must not be exceeded. The relay current of 100 mA would cause the power dissipation to be grossly exceeded. A buffer switch using an n-p-n general purpose transistor (ZTX300, BC108, BFY50) is essential to link the 555's output to the relay. The current now taken from the 555's output is only 10 mA, which holds the power dissipation well below the 600 mW.

Since the time period is relatively long and the limit rather tight at ±4.17% it is best to decide on the value of R_t rather than the capacitor C_t. If we make R_t 1 MΩ the value of C_t is:

$$C_t = T/1.1R_t = 10.91 \ \mu F$$

Therefore C_t can be a 10 μF low leakage tantalum capacitor (16 V working) with a tolerance of ±20%. To take account of the wide tolerance, part of R_t must be made adjustable. With R_t equal to an 820 kΩ resistor in series with a 500 kΩ trimpot a ±20% adjustment on the 12 second timing period is allowed.

The reset facility is arranged by connecting the push-to-make momentary action switch from pine 4 to ground with a 4k7 resistor. The circuit is given in Fig. 5.28.

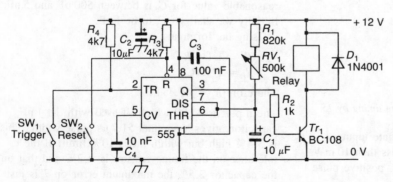

Fig. 5.28 Design for a 12-second timer

EXAMPLE 3

A timer is required that generates a high state 2 hours after power is applied. The power supply is a partially regulated +24 V. An LED is to be used to indicate that timing is in progress and the output is also to drive an opto-isolator with a current of 10 mA.

Design specification

>   Power supply : +24 V ± 15 %
>   Timer period : 2 hours ± 5 %
>   Trigger : at power up
>   Output : (i) 10 mA LED during timing
>   (ii) 10 mA to the input of an opto-
>   isolator after time period has
>   elapsed.

A ZN1034 will be used for this design. It has its own +5 V internal regulator, can be trimmed to give the timing required and has two complementary outputs Q and $\overline{Q}$. The circuit is given in Fig. 5.29.

Calculation of R_S value

The value of this resistor is found using:

$$R_S = \frac{V_{S(min)} - V_{R(max)}}{I_{S(min)}}$$

$V_{R(max)} = 5.3 \text{ V from ZN1034 data sheet}$
$V_{S(min)} = 20.4 \text{ V } (24 \text{ V} - 15\%)$

$$I_{S(min)} = I_{CC(max)} + I_{R(min)} + I_{O(max)}$$
$$I_{S(min)} = 5 + 2 + 10 = 17 \text{ mA}$$

Therefore $R_S = \dfrac{(20.5 - 5.3)}{17} = 888 \,\Omega$

$$(910 \,\Omega \text{ is n.p.v.})$$

The power rating should be 500 mW. This resistor is connected from V_S, the nominal 24 V suppply, to pin 5 the regulator input on the ZN1034. This pin is connected with a short link to pin 4 and decoupled using a 100 nF ceramic capacitor.

Timing components

To meet the ± 5 % tolerance on the 2-hour timing period a trimming resistor must be fitted between pins 12 and 11. If this is 100 kΩ a trim of ± 25 % is allowed. At the mid point the multiplying factor (K_{50}) is 3700.

$$T = K_{50}C_tR_t$$

Since $T = 2$ hours, $C_tR_t = 1.946$ seconds

Reasonable values for the two components are:

> C_t 2.2 μF ± 20 % 16 V wkg tantalum
> R_t 910 kΩ ∓ 1 % metal film

Trigger

For the mode of operation required the trigger input must be held low when the power is applied. For the ZN1034 this is simply achieved by tying pin 1 to ground.

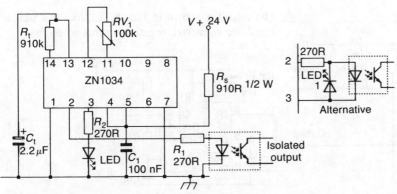

Fig. 5.29 Using the ZN1034 to give a 2-hour delay

Output circuit

The $\overline{Q}$ output (pin 2) will go low when timing is begun and will switch high at the end of the timing period. This output is connected via a suitable resistor (270 Ω) to the input LED of the opto-isolator.

The Q output, which will be high while timing is in progress, is connected by another 270 Ω current-limiting resistor to the LED indicator.

An alternative circuit arrangement, which saves one 270 Ω resistor, is to connect the two LEDs with one 270 Ω resistor between the output pins (2 and 3) as shown in the inset. Since the diodes are connected in opposite polarity only one will conduct when the timer output is low while the other conducts when the timer output is high.

EXAMPLE 4

This final monostable example looks at the way a 2240 programmable timer can be used to give a 5 minute pulse, Fig. 5.30.

Target specification

> Power supply : 9 V
> Time duration : 5 min ±2.5%

For the 2240 the basic timer equation is:

$$T = NR_t C_t$$

where N is a number between 1 and 255. If C_t is a 470 nF capacitor and R_t a 3.3 MΩ resistor, for $T = 300$ s:

$$N = 300/1.551 = 193.4$$

Here the choice of timing components has been made from standard values well within the range of those suitable for the 2240.

Since $N = 193$ as the nearest whole number O_{128}, O_{64} and O_0 must be connected together to a common pull-up resistor of 10 kΩ and back to the reset input on pin 10.

The trigger input on pin 11 has to be a positive short duration pulse. In this case it is shown buffered via an open collector TTL gate.

The time base output on pin 14 must be provided with a load resistor of 18 kΩ. A small 270 pF capacitor is used here to improve noise immunity.

The MOD input (pin 12) is shown decoupled with a 10 nF capacitor.

5.7   ASTABLES AND PULSE GENERATORS

A timer IC can be made to give continuous oscillations by suitably connecting the timing components back to the trigger input of the device. An asymmetric output often results so that additional modifications are necesary if square wave output is required. The limitations on timing components also mean that the maximum frequency is restricted. Some typical circuits are illustrated in the following examples.

1   50 KHZ PULSE GENERATOR USING A 555

Design specification

> Power supply : +5 V
> Frequency : 50 kHz ±10%
> Duty cycle : 60%

The circuit is shown in Fig. 5.31. Note that pins 6 and 2 are connected together so that when the

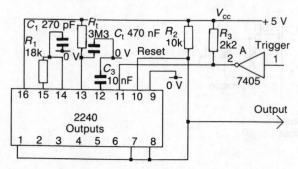

Fig. 5.30 The 2240 wired to generate a 5 minute pulse

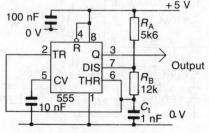

Fig. 5.31 A 50 kHz pulse generator

capacitor has discharged via R_B to $1/3$ V_{CC} the circuit is retriggered.

The output is high for time t_1:

$$t_1 = 0.7 (R_A + R_B) C_t$$

and the output is low for time t_2:

$$t_2 = 0.7 R_B C_t$$

The 'duty cycle' of a waveform is the percentage of time the output is high relative to the total periodic time.

$$\text{Duty cycle} = t_1/T$$

where $T = t_1 + t_2$ and $t_1 = 0.6T$.

Since the frequency required is 50 kHz the total time T is:

$$T = 1/f = 20 \, \mu s$$

Therefore $t_1 = 12 \, \mu s$ and $t_2 = 8 \, \mu s$.

As there is a wide tolerance on the specification of frequency the design can be realised using fixed value components. Using the formulae for t_1 and t_2 we get:

$$R_A + R_B = 17.14 \times 10^{-6}/C_t \quad (1)$$
$$\text{and } R_B = 11.43 \times 10^{-6}/C_t \quad (2)$$

Therefore if C_t is made a 1 nF $\pm 2.5\%$ polystyrene:

$$R_A \approx 5.6 \, k\Omega \ \pm 2\%$$
$$R_B \approx 12 \, k\Omega \ \pm 2\%$$

These components give a nominal 50 kHz output with a duty cycle of 61.6%.

With this sort of generator a perfect square wave is not possible but can be approximated by making R_B much greater than R_A. If a duty cycle of 50% or lower is required the timing circuit can be modified as shown in Fig. 5.32(a). Diode D_1

conducts when the capacitor C_t is charging and D_2 on discharge. The timing formulae are then:

$$t_1 \approx 0.7 R_A C_t$$
$$t_2 \approx 0.7 R_B C_t$$

Two diodes are normally needed so that temperature stability is maintained. The mark-to-space ratio can be varied without changing frequency if R_B is made a potentiometer as shown in Fig. 5.33(b). An even simpler astable using one resistor is shown in Fig. 5.32(c).

2 LAMP FLASHING CIRCUIT

A circuit is required to flash a miniature 6 V, 50 mA filament lamp for 0.25 second every 2 seconds.

Design specification

Power supply : 6 V
Frequency : 0.5 Hz $\pm 25\%$
Duty cycle : 12.5%

This circuit can use a standard 555 with the output connected in 'sink' mode allowing the output transistor inside the 555 to conduct in the low output state, Fig. 5.33. Thus the lamp will be 'on' for time t_2 and 'off' for time t_1, where:

$$t_1 = 0.7 (T_A + R_B) C_t$$
and $t_2 = 0.7 R_B C_t$
Therefore $R_A + R_B = t_1/0.7 C_t$
and $R_B = t_2/0.7 C_t$

$t_1 = 1.75$ s and $t_2 = 0.25$ s. Assume that C_t is a 4.7 μF tantalum. Then:

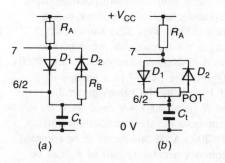

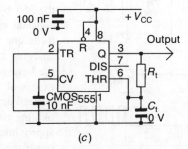

Fig. 5.32 (a) Modification to give fixed duty cycle; (b) using a pot to vary the duty cycle; (c) simple square wave generator

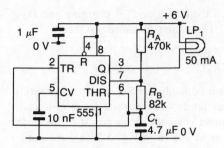

Fig. 5.33 Lamp flashing circuit

$$R_A + R_B = 532 \text{ k}\Omega$$
$$R_B = 76 \text{ k}\Omega$$

In the circuit R_B can be 82 kΩ and R_A 470 kΩ, or if necessary resistors from the E24 range can be used.

3 A PROGRAMMABLE ASTABLE USING THE 2240

The 2240 (Fig. 5.34) can be used as an astable up to frequencies of about 130 kHz. In this mode the selected counter output is not connected back to the reset input but simply connected to a 10 kΩ pull-up. The circuit will not self start and a positive trigger pulse is necessary. This can be a useful feature as it allows the generator to be externally synchronised and controlled. A positive reset pulse switches the device off. Self starting can be achieved by connecting pin 11 directly to pin 15 (regulator output).

By selecting outputs singly the generator can be programmed to give square waves at the frequency

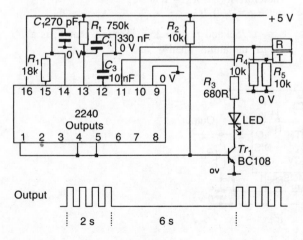

Fig. 5.34 A programmable astable

set by the external RC network divided by 2, 4, 8, 16, 32, 64 or 128. An interesting feature of this IC is that complex repeating bit patterns can also be generated by wiring a combination of the counter outputs together to the common pull-up resistor. For example, with pins 1 and 3 shorted to the output two short pulses (width of each = $1RC$) will be generated with a gap of $5RC$ between the next two pulses.

The rate at which the output repeats the pattern is set by the period of the highest counter output connected to the common output line, and the width of pulses is determined by the lowest counter output connected to this line.

The design example is for a bit pattern generator that outputs 4 pulses with a width of 0.25 s repeating every 8 s. For this the output pins 5, 4 and 1 are shorted together and connected to the output pull-up. Since each pulse has a time period of 0.25 seconds:

$$RC = 0.25$$

Select C to be 330 nF. Then

$$R = 757.6 \text{ k}\Omega \quad 750\text{k is n.p.v.}$$

A positive trigger pulse is necessary to start the oscillator and the output can be checked using an LED connected by a suitable transistor switch as shown.

5.8 OTHER APPLICATIONS OF TIMER ICs

Timer ICs can be used in a wide range of other applications, including alarm circuits, sawtooth generators, measurements, power supplies and so on. In this section a few of these possibilities will be outlined.

Sawtooth or ramp generators are possible using the 555 by replacing the timing resistor with a constant current circuit. Fig. 5.35 shows one technique using a p-n-p transistor set to give a charging current of 200 μA. Resistors R_1 and R_2 fix the base voltage of the BC477 to a voltage in excess of 2/3 V_{CC}. With the values given the voltage across R_3 is about 1.4 V, and since R_3 is 6k8 the current from the transistor's collector is approximately 200 μA. If this needs to be trimmed to set the frequency accurately part of R_3 can be made variable.

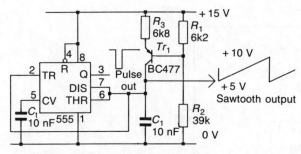

Fig. 5.35 A 4 kHz sawtooth generator

When a capacitor is charged with a constant current the voltage across it rises linearly.

$$dV = \frac{I\,dt}{C}$$

where dt is the time taken for the voltage across the capacitor to change by dV volts, for the 555 dV will be equal to $1/3\ V_{CC}$, in this case 5 V:

$$dt = 0.25\ \text{ms}$$

Since the flyback time is very fast, typically a few microseconds, the frequency of the oscillations is 4 kHz. The sawtooth waveform at C_t will be offset from zero by 5 V and will require buffering to prevent a load from degrading the linearity. Short duration negative going (V_{CC} to ground) pulses will appear at pin 3. If high values of capacitor are used a small resistor ($\approx 500\ \Omega$) should be fitted in series with pin 7.

A variation of the previous circuit uses bootstrapping (see Fig. 5.36) where, after buffering via an emitter follower, the waveform across the timing capacitor is fed back to a junction made in the timing resistor R_A. As the output rises, the mid point of R_1 and R_2 also rises, which ensures that an almost constant value of charging current is supplied to C_t. The problem with this type of circuit

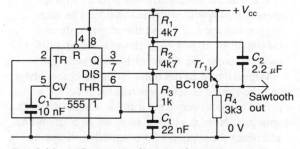

Fig. 5.36 A 'Bootstrapped' sawtooth circuit

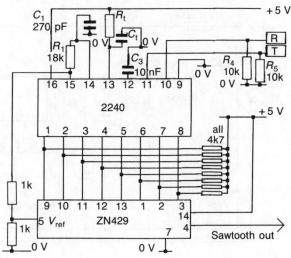

Fig. 5.37 Very low frequency sawtooth generator using the 2240 and an 8-bit DAC

is that the value of C_t can become excessively large if low frequencies are required.

The problem of generating really *low frequency sawtooth waveforms* can be tackled by using a programmable timer and a low cost DAC. This is really a mix of analog and digital methods but will yield the best performance in terms of linearity and stability.

The principle is to set the timer, a 2240 in this example (Fig. 5.37), to run at a frequency:

$$f_o = 1/(512\ R_t C_t)$$

All counter outputs are decoded using a low cost 8-bit DAC (ZN429) which has its reference connected to a portion of the regulated output from the 2240 timer. In this way a slowly varying 'ramp' is generated which has 256 steps and a maximum amplitude of 2.5 volts. The circuit is started by a positive trigger pulse to pin 11 and can be reset by a positive pulse to pin 10. Since the counter outputs on the 2240 are open collector, eight pull-up resistors are necessary.

The ZN1034 can be used to switch *loads connected in the a.c. mains*. A simple rectifier, filter and voltage-dropping circuit is necessary to supply the d.c. voltage to the timer, while its output from pin 2 or 3 can be used to switch a triac. See Fig. 5.38(*a*). Let's take an example of a 2 A resistive load connected to a 240 V, 50 Hz supply. This very simple arrangement uses no transformer,

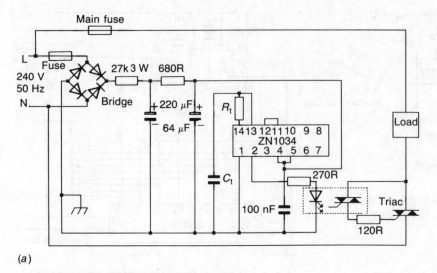

(a)

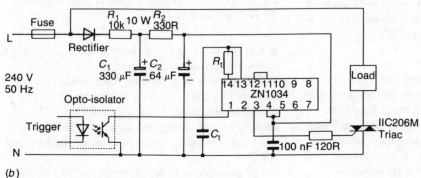

(b)

Fig. 5.38 (a) The ZN1034 used to give delayed switch on of an a.c. load; (b) Modification for half-wave rectification only

the a.c. mains supply is half-wave rectified by D_1 (Fig. 5.38(b)), smoothed and then dropped to give a low ripple d.c. voltage across the IC pins. The values of the components are calculated using the following:

V_R : 5 V (supply to the IC)

I_R : 5 mA

I_{CC} : 5 mA

I_o : 10 mA (current to fire the triac)

V_1 : set to 15 V

$$R_1 \approx \frac{(\sqrt{2} \times 240) - 15}{30} \text{ k}\Omega$$

Therefore $R_1 \approx 10.8 \text{ k}\Omega$ (10 kΩ n.p.v.)

Power rating: 6.5 W (use a 10 W rating)

$$C_1 \approx \frac{I}{f_R V_R}$$

where f_R = 50Hz and V_R is the peak-to-peak ripple voltage.

Therefore $C_1 \approx 300 \mu$F, 25 V wkg (2 V pk–pk ripple at V_1) and $R_2 \approx (15-5)/30 = 330 \Omega$ (n.p.v.)

The triac, a TIC206M, will pass an average current of 4 A and withstand 400 V. The gate trigger voltage is 2 V and the trigger current a maximum of 10 mA. A series resistor of 120 Ω is used to couple the Q output to the triac's gate.

Trigger input to the timer is via an opto-isolator and the timing is set to operate the triac for a period of 30 s every time a pulse is sent across the opto-gap. Note the use of fuses for protection and additional decoupling to prevent false triggering. In a very noisy electrical environment it may be

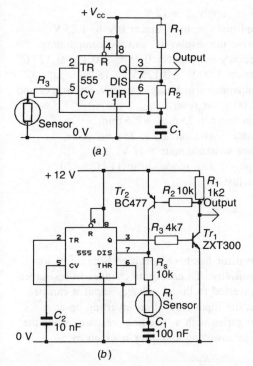

(a)

(b)

Fig. 5.39 Using the 555 in sensing applications

sensible to screen the sensitive parts of the timer circuit.

Remote sensing is often best achieved by sending an oscillating signal and varying the frequency or duty cycle of the signal according to the value of parameter being sensed. Two examples for light level or temperature sensing using transducers that vary their resistance with input quantity are shown in Fig. 5.39. In the first the sensor (an LDR or

thermistor) is connected from the control pin of a 555 to ground. As the sensor resistance varies the frequency of the astable will also change. A slightly more complicated circuit has the sensor connected in the timing position. When the output of the 555 switches high Tr_1 conducts and turns on Tr_2. The timing capacitor now charges from $1/3$ V_{CC} to $2/3$ V_{CC} with a time of:

$$t_1 = 0.7 \ (R_T + R_S) \ C_t$$

When the threshold level is exceeded the 555 output turns off Tr_1 and Tr_2 allowing C_t to discharge again by R_t and R_S.

$$t_2 = 0.7 \ (R_T + R_S) \ C_t$$

In this way a square wave, with a frequency determined by the sensor's resistance, is produced by the circuit.

$$f_0 = 1/1.4(R_T + R_S) \ C_t$$

Timer ICs, operated in the astable mode, can be connected as *power supply circuits*. The output is fed to a voltage doubler to give a negative or positive output voltage. Some degree of regulation can be provided by feeding a portion of the output back to the timer's control pin. Circuits like this, however, have poor regulation and very limited current output. A better method is to use the 555 as the oscillator and control section for a *switching regulator*. A step-down circuit is shown in Fig. 5.40. The oscillator output drives the series switch Tr_1 and after the filter a portion of the output is fed back to the base of Tr_2. If the output rises above a level set by R_7, Tr_2 switches on and resets the

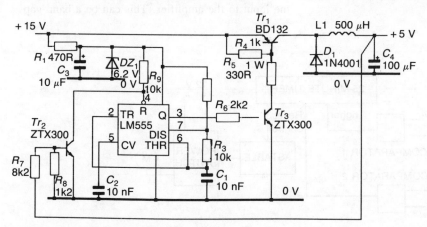

Fig. 5.40 A switching regulator using the 555 timer

oscillator. For the values given the output voltage will be approximately 5 V with a load current rating of 200 mA. Regulation is about 1% for both load and line changes.

5.9 A WORKED DESIGN PROBLEM

PROCESS CONTROLLER

An industrial plant requires an agitation process, driven by a geared 12 V, 2 A d.c. motor, to be operated 'on' and 'off' for a 25 minute period if the temperature of the mix being agitated falls below 12 °C ±1 °C. The process is to be halted if the temperature of the mix rises above 18 °C ±1 °C. A thermistor type GM472 is specified as the temperature sensor and this must be arranged in a circuit to give a linear output voltage to drive a simple 10-segment bar graph display. The 'on' and 'off' periods for agitation are nominally 10 seconds and 25 seconds.

Design specification

To assist in setting the design specification it is helpful first to draw a block diagram of the overall system (Fig. 5.41). This also enables one to see the key sub-units and to plan the overall design strategy. The block diagram consists of the temperature sensing circuit, two comparators, a long duration timer, an oscillator with its output driving the motor via a power switch, and a display driver and 10-segment display for temperature indication.

Power supply : ±12 V
Amplified output : Linear 0 V to 1.25 V to drive the display IC and the comparators
Accuracy of output : 0.25 V ±0.1 V at 12 °C input; 1.00 V ±0.125 V at 18 °C input
Comparator trip levels : 0.25 V for trigger and 1.00 V for reset
Main timer : 25 min ±2.5 min
Astable : 10 s on ±2 s, 25 s off ±2 s
Power switch output : 12 V, 2 A
Display : Dot mode, from 11 °C to 20 °C inclusive

Options

The thermistor has been specified because of its good sensitivity. To enable its changes in resistance to be converted to linear voltage output it can be placed in the input lead of an inverting op-amp circuit in series with a 'padding' resistor, since the gain of the inverting amplifier is given by:

$$A_{\mathrm{vcl}} = \frac{-R_{\mathrm{F}}}{(R_{\mathrm{T}} + R_1)}$$

where R_{T} is the thermistor's resistance, R_1 is the padding resistance and R_{F} is the feedback resistor.

Then: A_{vcl} is proportional to $\dfrac{-1}{R_{\mathrm{T}} + R_1}$.

In this way the non-linearity of the sensor's changes in resistance with temperature will be made to give an almost linear output voltage (Fig. 5.42).

A stable reference source must be set up to give the input to the amplifier. This can be a band-gap

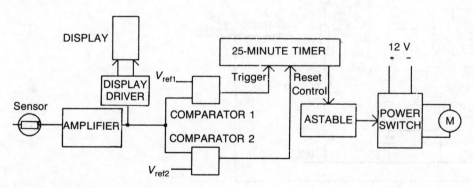

Fig. 5.41 Block diagram of system

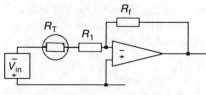

A_{vcl} proportional to $1/(R_T + R_1)$

Fig. 5.42 Outline of sensing amplifier

device or a reference diode with good temperature stability. The op-amp must exhibit low values of drift, in other words a precision type op-amp is indicated.

The two comparators could be op-amps but the saturation characteristics would need to be checked. A dual comparator would be a better choice.

The long duration timer has to be either a ZN1034 or 2240 type. But since both trigger and reset inputs are required we shall use a 2240. This also allows simple modifications to be made to timing if required on site by linking in other outputs.

The astable circuit, since the specification on timing is not tight, can be designed around a 555. This has a good output drive which will allow the power to be switched smartly to the motor using a Darlington or a powerFET.

Design calculations

(a) *Amplifier* (Fig. 5.43)
For the GM472 thermistor:

$$R_2 = R_1 e^{B(1/T_2 - 1/T_1)}$$

where R_1 is resistance at temperature T_1 (4700 Ω at 25 °C)
R_2 is resistance at temperature T_2.

(NB: temperature is in kelvin — add 273 to the °C value.)

B is the characteristic temperature constant (3390).
Using this formula a series of resistance values for the sensor can be calculated.

Temperature °C	$R_T\,\Omega$
10	8589
12	7897
14	7268
16	6698
18	6179
20	5707

The tolerance on the 25 °C value given in the specification is ±20% so some form of preset is going to be necessary to set the output.

In order to minimise non-linearity the padding resistor R_1 should be a value equal to the change in resistance over the specified temperature range. A 3.3 kΩ is suitable, and if you check this out, you will find the non-linearity is about ±15% over the 10 °C to 20 °C change.

The input to the amplifier is set to a stable value using a 5 V band-gap reference REF50Z which has a 40 ppm temperature coefficient. With its current set to 2 mA (the maximum is 5 mA):

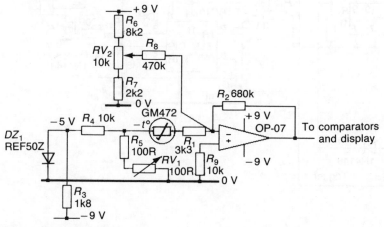

Fig. 5.43 Full amplifier circuit

$$R_3 = \frac{(V_S^- - V_Z)}{I_Z}$$

Therefore $R_3 = 2\,k\Omega$; a 1k8 is specified.

The $-5\,V$ is reduced to about $-75\,mV$ by R_4, R_5 and RV_1. RV_1 is used to set the overall output level of the circuit.

Given that $\Delta V_o = 125\,mV\,°C^{-1}$ (a value necessary to drive the bar graph display one increment) and $V_{in} = 75\,mV$, the value for R_2, the feedback resistor, can be found using:

$$\left[\frac{R_2}{R_{T2} + R_1}\right]V_{in} - \left[\frac{R_2}{R_{T1} + R_1}\right]V_{in} = \Delta V_o$$

Rearranging gives

$$V_{in}R_2\left[\frac{1}{R_{T2} + R_1} - \frac{1}{R_{T1} + R_1}\right] = \Delta V_o$$

where R_{T2} = thermistor resistance at 12 °C
and R_{T1} = thermistor resistance 10 °C

$$75R_2(8.93 \times 10^{-5} - 8.411 \times 10^{-5}) = 0.25$$

Therefore $R_2 = 642\,k\Omega$ (680k is specified).

When the temperature being sensed is 10 °C the output of the amplifier must be arranged to be zero volts. An offset adjustment circuit using a resistor connected to a portion of the positive rail will do this. To ensure that all tolerances are covered this

is made a preset using the potential divider chain R_6, RV_2 and R_7. With RV_2 in mid track the positive voltage at the input end of R_8 will be 3 V.

Therefore $R_8 = 3R_2/V_o$
where $V_o = 4.3\,V$ (temperature = 10 °C)
$R_8 \approx 475\,k\Omega$ (470k is n.p.v.)

R_9 is an op-amp temperature drift compensating resistor which should have a value exactly equal to the resistance from the inverting input to ground. In this case, since part of this resistance is the thermistor which varies, a suitable value for R_9 is about 10 kΩ.

In order to minimise drifts an op-amp with good temperature stability of V_{io} and I_{io} should be specified. An OP-07 is suitable.

(b) Design of the comparator and timer circuit (Fig. 5.44)
These parts must be considered together because the trigger and reset characteristics of the timer affect the comparator design.

The 2240, connected across the +9 V supply, has the monostable period set by R_{10} and C_1 with the overall time delay given by:

$$T = NR_{10}C_1$$

In this case $T = 1500$ seconds. To arrive at the

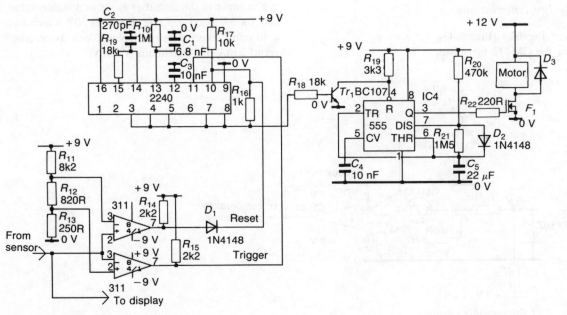

Fig. 5.44 Comparator and timing circuits

maximum values for the RC time constant imagine N is at 255 (all outputs on the 2240 used). Then:

$$R_{10}C_1 = 1500/255 = 5.88 \text{ seconds}$$

To allow for tolerance effects make RC higher than this, say 6.8 s, by using R_{10} as 1 MΩ and C_1 as 6.8 μF. Then:

$$N = 1500/6.8 = 220$$

This means that the outputs O_{128}, O_{64}, O_{16}, O_8 and O_4 must be connected together and taken back to the reset input to get the timer to give the 25 minute delay. The problem of resetting is complicated by the fact that the output of comparator 2 must also reset the timer, overriding the state of the counter outputs. The output from this point must also control the 555 astable. Careful choice of pull-up resistors and possible use of diodes is necessary to ensure that a satisfactory reset level with good noise immunity is achieved. First let's finalise the comparator section. Here the two comparators must have their reference inputs set to 0.5 V (12 °C level) and 1 V (18 °C level). The potential divider connected across the 9 V rail R_{11}, R_{12} and R_{13} is used for this. The total current through the chain is set to about 1 mA so that the values required are 8 kΩ, 750 Ω and 250 Ω respectively. The two comparators, which have open-collector outputs, require pull-up resistors to the +9 V rail. These should be not greater than 10 kΩ to ensure relatively sharp edges on the trigger and reset pulses. 2.2 kΩ resistors have been specified. The output from comparator 1, the trigger level, is connected directly to pin 11 of the 2240. Comparator 2's output, which will rise high if the 18 °C trip value is exceeded, is connected via signal diode D_1 to the junction of R_{16} and R_{17}, the reset pin of the 2240. The values of the components have to be chosen to ensure that a satisfactory reset is possible both from the counter outputs of the IC or from the comparator. When the comparator output is low D_1 is reversed so that the reset pin is at a voltage given by:

$$V_R \approx \frac{V_{CC}R_{16}}{R_{17}+R_{16}}$$

Therefore $V_R \approx 0.9$ V

This gives a noise margin on the reset of about 500 mV since the reset threshold is specified as 1.4 V. Increasing R_{17}, to, say, 15 kΩ would improve reset noise immunity but at the expense of base drive for Tr_1. This switching transistor is used to control the 555 astable and is connected from pin 4 (the 555 reset) to ground. A pull-up of 3k3 is used from pin 4 to the +9 V rail.

Tr_1 base is connected back to the command output lines of the 2240 via R_{18}. While the timer is in the monostable mode Tr_1 will therefore be off, allowing the 555 oscillator to run. At the end of the timing period, or after a reset, Tr_1 base will rise positive with its base current limited by resistors R_{17}, R_{16} and R_{18}. Since R_{17} is 3k3 the base current to fully saturate Tr_1 needs to be:

$$I_B \approx V_{CC}/10R_{19} \approx 0.3 \text{ mA}$$

R_{18} can be found using:

$$R_{18} = \frac{V_{CC}}{I_B} - (R_{16} + R_{17})$$

Therefore $R_{18} = 19$ kΩ (18 kΩ is n.p.v.)

The astable is a standard circuit with a duty cycle of 28.6% (10 seconds on, 25 seconds off) except for the fact that the time durations required are on the upper limits for the IC. However, the specification limits are not tight so a relatively high value tantalum capacitor can be used for C_5.

Diode D_2 shorts out R_{21} when C_5 is charging:

$$t_1 = 0.7R_{20}C_5$$

Since $t_1 = 10$ seconds,

$$R_{20}C_5 = 14.14 \text{ seconds}$$

Suppose we make C_5 22 μF, then R_{20} is 642 kΩ (640 kΩ is n.p.v.). On the discharge of C_5 the time delay is given by:

$$t_2 = 0.7 \, R_{21}C_5$$

For $t_2 = 25$ s and $C_5 = 22$ μF,

$$R_{21} = 1.62 \text{ MΩ (1M5 is n.p.v.)}$$

The output pin of the 555 is used to drive the switch for the 2 A motor. This switch can either be a powerFET or a Darlington. The powerFET option is given in the circuit diagram of the system in Fig. 5.44.

(c) Display circuit
A standard 10-segment bar graph LED display is an obvious choice for this part of the circuit and this is driven by a 3914 IC. This chip contains all the

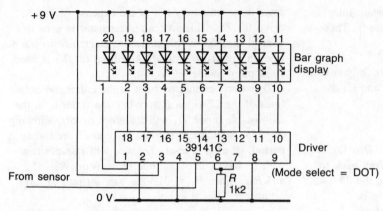

Fig. 5.45 Bar graph display

necessary comparators, a precision divider chain, a stable 1.25 V reference and LED switches. With pins 6 and 7 connected together the input range is from 0 to 1.25 volts. In other words, every 125 mV change on the input line will cause the next comparator in the chain to operate. One resistor, R_{22}, fixes the current through each LED (Fig. 5.45).

$$\text{LED current} \approx \frac{10V_{\text{ref}}}{R_{22}}$$

With $R_{22} = 1.2\,\text{k}\Omega$ each LED will have an 'on' current of 10 mA.

Pin 9 of the IC determines the mode of display. For 'dot' mode this pin is left open circuit. (Bar graph display mode: connect pin 9 to $+V_{\text{CC}}$.)

The design is now complete. Try these modifications:

1. Redesign the power switch using a Darlington transistor.
2. A ZN1034 timer IC can only be reset by momentarily switching off its d.c. supply. Change the design so that the main 25 second timer uses a ZN1034 in place of the 2240.
3. A specification change is required altering the trip levels to 11 °C ±1 °C and 16 °C ±1 °C. Outline the basic modifications necessary.
4. Add an alarm circuit which will operate if the temperature of the mix rises above 20 °C.

5.10 DESIGN EXERCISES

1. An LM311 comparator is to be used to give an LED output when the input is above a 2 V reference level. Hysteresis of 100 mV is required. Design the circuit, giving all component values.

2. The low temperature detector circuit given in Fig. 5.7 is to be modified so that the trip point is −4 °C and the output is to operate a relay to switch a 1 kW heater connected in a 240 V, 50 Hz mains supply. Redesign the circuit to do this.

3. Using a JFET or MOSFET type op-amp design a high level temperature detector circuit to the following specification:

   V_S : +12 V
   Sensor : thermistor GL23
   Temperature trip : +4 °C ±1 °C
   Output : logic level suitable for TTL or CMOS input
   Hysteresis : 100 mV

4. Redesign the circuit of Fig. 5.7 using a standard LM311 comparator. The output is to operate an LED indicator.

5. Design a window comparator to the following specification:

   V_{in} : 3 V to 6 V
   V_{LL} : 4 V ±1%

V_{UL} : 4.6 V ±1%
V_S : 10 V
V_{OUT} : TTL compatible logic level

6   What advantages would a comparator IC offer over an op-amp in the design of square wave oscillators? Using an LM311, outline the design of a 100 kHz square wave oscillator suitable for TTL output.

7   A 470 nF capacitor is connected in a timing circuit with an 820 kΩ resistor to a supply of 24 V d.c.
      Determine (*a*) the time constant, (*b*) the time taken for the voltage across the capacitor to change by 10 V after the supply is switched on.

8   A capacitor is charged with a constant current of 500 μA so that the voltage across it rises linearly from zero to 9 volts in 50 μs. What is the value of the capacitor?

9   Design a square wave generator to the following specification:

      Frequency : 750 kHz ±1 kHz
      Amplitude : TTL compatible
      Duty cycle : 50%

10   A timing circuit has to switch a relay on for 150 seconds following the momentary closure of a reed switch. Prepare *three* designs using the 2240, the ZN1034 and a 555. The tolerance on the time period is ±15% and the relay has a 110 Ω, 12 V coil.

11   One often used application for the 555 is as a missing pulse detector. Research the circuit for this and design a missing pulse detector to the following specification:

      Input frequency : 8 kHz
      Pulse width : 16 μs

12   A test rig requires an oscillator to the following specification:

      Frequency : 400 kHz ±10%
      Duty cycle : 10%
      Output : positive going 9 V pulses

Using a suitable timer IC design a circuit that can do this task.

13   A ZN1034 is to be used with a nominal 50 V d.c. supply to give a 3-hour delay before a 2 A d.c. motor connected in the supply is to be operated. The delay is to be accurate within ±2%. Prepare a design.

14   Modify the sawtooth oscillator of Fig. 5.35 to give a nominal 800 Hz output frequency.

15   Modify the switching circuit of Fig. 5.38(*b*) so that it is suitable for a 110 V, 60 Hz a.c. supply.

6 DIGITAL DESIGN

6.1 LOGIC CHARACTERISTICS

In Chapter 2 the selection of digital ICs was introduced, with a discussion on the merits of CMOS and TTL logic families. This chapter takes the techniques used in digital design a stage further and brings together some of the basic concepts of digital logic design, from the low level combination logic, sometimes called combinatorial logic, through to sequential logic (state logic) and microprocessors. A working knowledge of the basic digital gates (AND, OR, NAND, etc.) is assumed which then allows us to concentrate on putting gates together to create working systems.

Although digital circuits are often considered to be in a totally separate design environment from analog, they really represent a special case or subset of analog electronic theory. This is because digital circuits are based on the transistor or FET used as a high gain saturating amplifier, i.e. a switch. It is important not to forget this fact. For example, if a digital system is to be run successfully at high frequencies the effect of tuned circuits, lead lengths, power line decoupling and so on cannot be ignored. At really high frequencies (50 MHz up) good r.f. layout techniques become essential.

First let's consider the important characteristics of a logic device. These are:

- *Switching speed* — normally called *propagation delay time* and measured in nanoseconds. (See Fig. 6.1(*a*).)
- *Power consumption* — the amount of power in milliwatts consumed by one gate.
- *Noise margin* — the level of noise (i.e. unwanted signal) that can be tolerated on an input to a gate without causing the gate to give a false output. (See Fig. 6.1(*b*).)
- *Fan-out* — the number of inputs, for a given logic family, that can be driven from one output of the same device family.

- *Noise generation* — the switching pulse noise created on the power line by the operation of the gate changing state. (See Fig. 6.1(*c*).)

It is the trade-off between speed and power consumption that is the usual compromise and also a measure of overall performance. For example, really fast logic such as ECL will have a propagation delay of less than 1 ns for certain gates in its range but the power consumption can be as high as 60 mW. It doesn't take much maths to appreciate that using a lot of ECL would require a large power supply. 1000 ECL gates using 60 watts means a -5.2 V supply at nearly 12 A. To reduce power consumption fast logic such as ECL should be used only where it is absolutely necessary. CMOS, on the other hand, has the sort of structure (Fig. 6.2) which suggests that virtually no supply current is required, reducing the power consumption to nanowatts per gate. This is true for static conditions when the gate is not switching, but as the input changes state there is a brief instant when devices in the CMOS output stage (the n and p MOSFETS) conduct, taking a pulse of current from the supply rail. Thus as the operating frequency of a system using CMOS is increased the power consumption rises. This is typically about 1 mW MHz^{-1} per gate. Above a few megahertz there is then no apparent power supply advantage in using a single CMOS gate compared with a TTL gate. However, if one considers that probably only about one-third of the gates within a system are switching at the fastest rate at any given time, then the use of CMOS in a system design will result in considerable saving in power supply. The power supply will be smaller and simpler than the equivalent TTL version.

Choosing logic to use in a design can appear to be difficult, since there are so many versions of

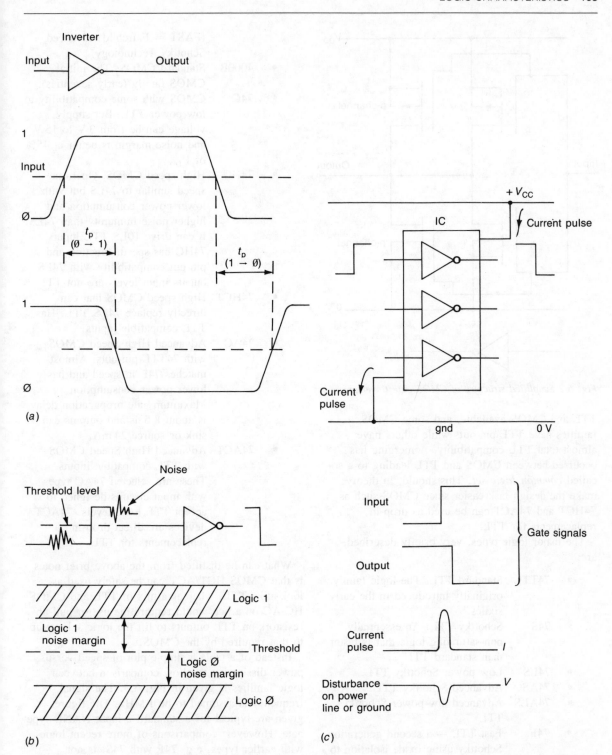

Fig. 6.1 (a) Illustration of propagation delay time — taken as the average of the two values shown; (b) Noise margin in logic; (c) Noise generation

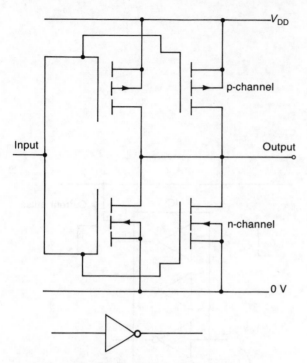

Fig. 6.2 Simplified structure of CMOS gate (invertor)

TTL and CMOS available, and some CMOS families have TTL pin-outs while others have almost total TTL compatibility. A merging has occurred between CMOS and TTL leading to a so-called *common logic set*. This should, in theory, make the design task easier since CMOS such as 74HCT and 74ACT can be used as drop-in replacements for TTL.

The major logic types, very briefly described, are:

- 74TTL   Standard TTL. The logic family originally introduced in the early sixties.
- 74S   Schottky TTL. An essentially non-saturating logic that is faster than standard TTL.
- 74LS   Low power Schottky TTL.
- 74AS   Advanced Schottky TTL.
- 74ALS   Advanced low power Schottky TTL.
- 74F   Fast TTL — a second generation Schottky using oxide-isolation to improve speed and reduce power consumption.

(FAST = Fairchild Advanced Schottky Technology)

- 4000B   Standard CMOS. The initial CMOS family (early seventies).
- 74C   CMOS with some compatibility to low power TTL. But supply voltage can be from 3 V to 15 V and noise margin is better at 45% of V_{DD}.
- 74HC   High speed CMOS. Operating speed similar to 74LS but with lower power consumption and higher noise immunity than 74LS. It can drive 10LS TTL inputs. 74HC has speed, function and pin-out compatibility with 74LS; but its input levels are not TTL.
- 74HCT   High speed CMOS that can directly replace 74LS TTL. Has TTL compatible inputs.
- 74AC   Advanced High Speed CMOS with 74TTL pin-outs. Almost matches 74F in speed and has lower power consumption. Maximum gate propagation delay is about 8.5 ns and outputs can sink or source 24 mA.
- 74ACT   Advanced High Speed CMOS with TTL compatible inputs. These are selected 74AC types with input circuits designed to accept TTL logic levels. 74ACT devices are direct drop-in replacements for TTL.

What can be distilled from the above brief notes is that CMOS HCT/ACT can be safely used as look-alike TTL, whereas a mix of TTL and CMOS HC/AC on a pcb would require the use of pull-up resistors on TTL outputs to lift the logic 1 level up to that required by the CMOS.

Instead of a table a simple plot of speed versus power dissipation to allow comparison between logic families is given in Fig. 6.3. The signal frequency is assumed to be 1 MHz. The figures given are typical for a standard 2-input NAND type gate. However, comparisons of more recent logic with earlier types, e.g. 74F with 74S, is not straightforward since the output load on the test circuit for later logic (ALS, AS, F, AC, ACT) is

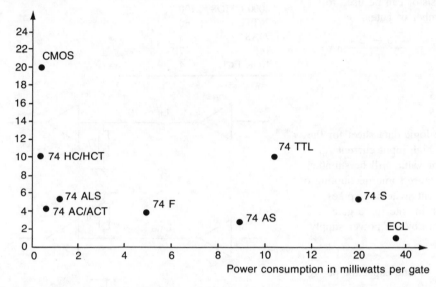

Fig. 6.3 Approximate speed and power consumption figures for standard logic

50 pF in parallel with 500 Ω, whereas most earlier logic is tested with a 15 pF in parallel with 400 Ω. The first is obviously a more stringent test.

6.2 DIGITAL DESIGN METHODS

Before moving on to discuss particular design procedures a few general points must be considered. The first is what to do with unused inputs. With CMOS no input should be left open circuit, even in unused gates. The very high input resistance of CMOS allows the input capacitance to charge up and ultimately to lift the input level into the threshold of the gate. The output circuit will then conduct and heat up the chip, which can lead to its destruction. Spare inputs on a gate should either be connected to logic 1 (i.e. the positive supply via a 1 kΩ resistor), or to logic 0 (0 V), or to another input. The method used depends on the logic function, see Fig. 6.4. Unused gates should be disabled with their inputs tied to 0.

Unused TTL gate inputs will assume the high state and could pick up noise. They should be disabled by connection to the +5 V rail via a

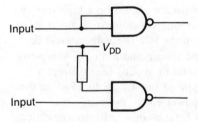

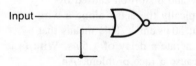

Fig. 6.4 Dealing with spare inputs

resistor (1 kΩ is typical), connected to another input, or to logic 0 depending on the logic function. Unused gates can have their inputs left unconnected. The reason for using a pull-up resistor to the +5 V supply is to prevent damage to an input should the power supply line exceed the input voltage rating. One pull-up can be used to disable several IC inputs; for example, a group of gates might need their inputs disabled. These can all be connected together via one resistor to the $+5$ V rail as long as the total current taken does not cause the voltage on the inputs to be less than 2.4 V. If each input takes 150 μA, a single 1 kΩ resistor can be used to disable the following number of gates:

$$I_T = \frac{V_{CC(min)} - V_{IH}}{R} = \frac{4.75 - 2.4}{1} \text{ mA}$$

$$= 2.35 \text{ mA}$$

Therefore, $n = \dfrac{I_T}{I} = \dfrac{2.35}{0.15} = 15$

Always check with the logic data sheet for the maximum value of logic high input current I_{IH} before assuming a resistor value will be suitable.

All digital logic ICs require some decoupling of the power supply to prevent switching spikes, generated by the logic, from entering a gate or being fed round the system by the power supply. The general rules are:

> Buffers, drivers
> Receivers, MSI chips $\Big\}$ one capacitor per IC
> TTL   one capacitor for every 2/3 ICs
> CMOS one capacitor for every 10 ICs

The decoupling capacitor should be a high quality, low inductance ceramic which must be fitted as close as possible to the IC. The value should be between 10 nF and 100 nF and a mix of values is generally most useful on a pcb. Don't forget a tantalum electrolytic of say 4.7 μF to 15 μF at the point where the power enters the pcb.

Signal paths in logic boards and interconnections should be kept as short as possible to avoid extra propagation delay and distortion caused by mismatching. Typically the delay along a wire or pcb track is about 50 ps cm^{-1}. This means that a 30 cm run can generate a delay of 1.5 ns. With fast logic this could cause a race problem. An unterminated length of wire or track will also cause signal reflection, since the logic pulse travels as a wavefront along the track and if it is not properly absorbed at the receiving end the energy is reflected. It is the rise time of the signal, not its frequency, that has to be considered, and if the track happens to be a length equal to some submulitiple of the wavelength of the rise time then resonance will occur, leading to a highly distorted signal. As a rough guide the minimum unterminated track/wire length that can be safely used is given in Table 6.1.

Table 6.1

Logic	Track length/cm
4000 CMOS	100
74TTL	30
74AS	5
74F	7.5
100K ECL	4

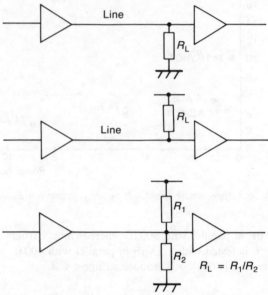

Fig. 6.5 Termination methods for logic (load termination). R_L must equal Z_0 of the line

When longer track lengths are used the termination methods shown in Fig. 6.5 should be followed.

Returning to general design procedures, the best approach to follow is similar to all other electronic design, in other words a top-down design method:

1. Start with the overall requirement in mind and write a description of this and a target specification.
2. Search for the best design approach and having listed a few possibilities choose the one most suited for the task.
3. Carry out the design using appropriate digital design tools, e.g. minimisation techniques, K-maps, state diagrams, etc.
4. Test the design using a prototype or do a simulation with a software tool. If the design meets the specification proceed to (5), otherwise return to (2).

5. Now decide on the type of logic that is required.

If the design is to be a system rather than a single circuit, try and break it up into functional blocks and then produce a flow chart showing which block should be designed first and so on. Each block should then be designed, debugged and documented before moving on to the next. But take care to define carefully the signal interconnections and timing between blocks.

The amount of detail in the design depends upon whether the system is purely combinational or sequential, with the latter requiring more checks on timing and state sequence as will be shown further on.

6.3 COMBINATIONAL LOGIC DESIGN

This is the type of logic where a specific set of input conditions must be present to give an output. For example: a switch (A) must be closed and an infrared beam to a sensor (B) broken for an alarm signal to be given. If the alarm signal (F) is to be a high state (1) then the Boolean expression for F is:

$$F = A.\bar{B}$$

The simple logic diagram for this is shown in Fig. 6.6.

The basic design procedure for combinational logic is to:

(i) generate the complete function by drawing up a truth table from the requirement;

(ii) minimise the logic function using Boolean algebra and/or Karnaugh mapping techniques;

(iii) implement the design in the most suitable logic form.

In earlier days of digital design, when fewer gate functions and less MSI ('Medium Scale Integration') chips were available, it was common practice to

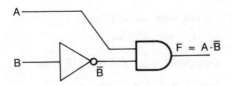

A ———

B ———

$F = A.\bar{B}$

$\bar{B}$

Fig. 6.6

Table 6.2

Inputs			Output	
C	B	A	F	
0	0	0	0	
0	0	1	0	
0	1	0	0	
0	1	1	1	Only three input
1	0	0	0	conditions result
1	0	1	1	in a logic high
1	1	0	0	output
1	1	1	1	

reduce the logic function required into an all-NAND or all-NOR gate circuit. This approach is not always advised now, since the resulting logic diagram and circuit can be difficult to follow. As long as too much redundancy does not exist, the circuit can be designed to follow the most easily understood logic expression resulting from the specification. This is even more the case when PLD (programmable logic devices) are used, since their structure is AND–OR in form and this is the Boolean expression that comes directly from the truth table. Let's consider the truth table in Table 6.2 for a logic arrangement with three inputs ABC and one output F.

The output F is high only when the following conditions are met:

A = 1 B = 1 C = 0
or A = 1 B = 0 C = 1
or A = 1 B = 1 C = 1

In Boolean algebra this becomes:

$$F = A.B.\bar{C} + A.\bar{B}.C + A.B.C$$

The AND–OR structure can be clearly seen. By using the rules of Boolean algebra (see Fig. 6.7) the expression can be simplified:

$$F = A.B.\bar{C} + A.C.(\bar{B} + B)$$

But $\bar{B} + B = 1$ and $A.C.1 = A.C$

Therefore $F = A.B.\bar{C} + A.C$
$$= A.(B.\bar{C} + C)$$

But $B.\bar{C} + C = B + C$ by the pseudo-absorption law.

Therefore $F = A.(B + C)$

This can also be expressed as:

$$F = A.B + A.C$$

Commutative law

A+B = B+A
A·B = B·A

Associative law

A+B+C = A+(B+C) = (A+B)+C
A·B·C = A·(B·C) = (A·B)·C

Distributive law

A·(B+C) = (A·B)+(A·C)
A+(B·C) = (A+B)·(A+C)

This law implies that expressions can be factorised.
e.g. (A·B)+(A·C)+(A·D) = A·(B+C+D)
(A+B)·(A+C)·(A+D) = A+(B·C·D)

AND rules

A·0 = 0
A·1 = A
A·A = A
A·Ā = 0

OR rules

A+0 = A
A+1 = 1
A+A = A
A+Ā = 1

Double NOT rule

$\overline{\overline{A}}$ = A

de Morgan's Theorem

$\overline{A+B}$ = $\overline{A}·\overline{B}$
$\overline{A·B}$ = $\overline{A}+\overline{B}$ Break line change sign

$\overline{A}·\overline{B}$ = $\overline{A+B}$
$\overline{A}+\overline{B}$ = $\overline{A·B}$ Make the line change sign

Redundancy theorem (also called the **Absorption rule**)

In a 'sum of products' Boolean expression, a product that contains *all* the factors of another product is redundant.

e.g. A+(A·B) = A

also A+Ā·B = A+B   **(pseudo-absorption rule)**

Fig. 6.7 Summary of the laws of Boolean algebra

This simplification route via Boolean algebra can be avoded by using a *Karnaugh map* or K-map. In Fig. 6.8(*b*) the three-variable K-map for the function F from the truth table is shown. The two 'couples' give the minimisation directly to:

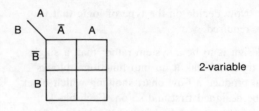

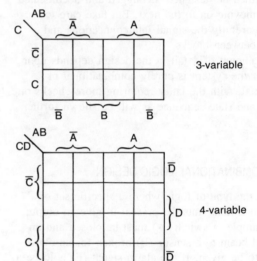

(a)

(b)

Fig. 6.8 (a) Basic grids for Karnaugh maps; (b) 3 variable map for $F = A·B·\overline{C} + A·\overline{B}·C + A·B·C$

F = A.B + A.C

This logic function can be realised in a variety of ways, Fig. 6.9.

(*a*) An OR with an AND gate:

F = A.(B + C)

(*b*) Two AND gates and one OR gate:

F = A.B + A.C

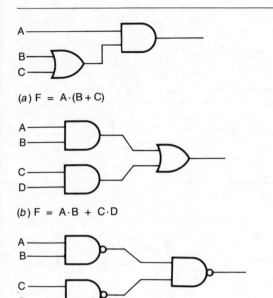

(a) F = A·(B + C)

(b) F = A·B + C·D

(c) F = $\overline{\overline{A \cdot B} \cdot \overline{A \cdot C}}$

Fig. 6.9 *Three ways of realising the circuit*

Table 6.3

D	C	B	A	O_1	O_2	O_3
0	0	0	0	0	0	0
0	0	0	1	0	1	0
0	0	1	0	0	1	0
0	0	1	1	0	1	0
0	1	0	0	0	0	0
0	1	0	1	0	1	0
0	1	1	0	1	0	0
0	1	1	1	0	0	0
1	0	0	0	0	0	1
1	0	0	1	0	0	0
1	0	1	0	1	0	1
1	0	1	1	1	0	0
1	1	0	0	0	0	1
1	1	0	1	0	0	0
1	1	1	0	1	1	1
1	1	1	1	1	0	0

(c) Three NAND gates:

$$F = \overline{\overline{A.B}.\overline{A.C}}$$

This last result is obtained by using de Morgan's theorems:

$$\overline{A + B} = \overline{A}.\overline{B}$$

$$\overline{A.B} = \overline{A} + \overline{B}$$

To obtain the NAND-only circuit, double-not both sides of the expression:

$$\overline{\overline{F}} = \overline{\overline{A.B + A.C}}$$

Therefore F = $\overline{\overline{A.B}.\overline{A.C}}$

Of the three solutions to this very simple design, (a) and (c) represent the most economical. But only the third can be realised using one IC, in this case a 7400 or 4011B Quad 21/P NAND.

Any design situation can be complicated further by an increase in the number of input variables and/or an increase in the number of outputs. Consider the truth table (Table 6.3).

Here we have a 4-input variable logic unit with three outputs. From the table:

$$O_1 = \overline{A}.B.C.\overline{D} + \overline{A}.B.\overline{C}.D + A.B.\overline{C}.D$$
$$+ \overline{A}.B.C.D + A.B.C.D$$

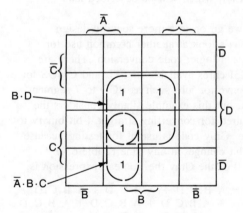

Fig. 6.10

which gives the K-map of Fig. 6.10 with the solution being:

$$O_1 = \overline{A}.B.C + B.D$$

Similarly it can be shown that:

$$O_2 = A.\overline{D}.\overline{C} + \overline{A}.B.D + A.\overline{B}.\overline{D}$$

and $O_3 = \overline{A}.D$.

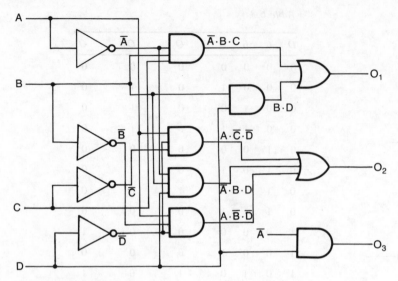

Fig. 6.11 The logic diagram

The full logic diagram can then be drawn, see Fig. 6.11. You will notice that the complement of each input variable is required and also the AND—OR structure necessary for the outputs. This could easily be implemented in a programmable logic device (PLD), which will be described later (Section 6.6).

Before we go on to a more specific design example, let's look at another common use for combinational logic: code conversion. There are several MSI chips available in TTL and CMOS for specific convertor jobs such as BCD to 7-segment and so on, but this example simply considers the logic required for converting straight 4-bit binary to Gray code. Gray code is useful for testing because only one bit changes at any time (Table 6.4).

For bit 0 of the Gray the Boolean expression is:

$$\text{bit } 0 = A.\bar{B}.\bar{C}.\bar{D} + \bar{A}.\bar{B}.\bar{C}.D + A.\bar{B}.C.\bar{D} \\ + \bar{A}.B.C.\bar{D} + A.\bar{B}.\bar{C}.D + \bar{A}.B.\bar{C}.D \\ + A.\bar{B}.C.D + \bar{A}.B.C.D$$

and the K-map of Fig. 6.12 yields the simplification:

$$\text{bit } 0 = \bar{A}.B + A.\bar{B}$$

which is the exclusive-OR of A and B.

Therefore bit 0 = A ⊕ B

Similarly we can show that:

bit 1 = B ⊕ C
bit 2 = C ⊕ D

Table 6.4

	4-bit binary				4-bit Gray			
	D	C	B	A	3	2	1	0
0	0	0	0	0	0	0	0	0
1	0	0	0	1	0	0	0	1
2	0	0	1	0	0	0	1	1
3	0	0	1	1	0	0	1	0
4	0	1	0	0	0	1	1	0
5	0	1	0	1	0	1	1	1
6	0	1	1	0	0	1	0	1
7	0	1	1	1	0	1	0	0
8	1	0	0	0	1	1	0	0
9	1	0	0	1	1	1	0	1
10	1	0	1	0	1	1	1	1
11	1	0	1	1	1	1	1	0
12	1	1	0	0	1	0	1	0
13	1	1	0	1	1	0	1	1
14	1	1	1	0	1	0	0	1
15	1	1	1	1	1	0	0	0

and bit 3 = D

The logic circuit is only three 2 I/P exclusive-OR sensor drive a pump which must be off if all three

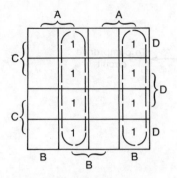

Fig. 6.12 K-map for bit 0 of the Gray code

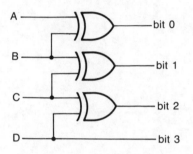

Fig. 6.13 4-bit binary-to-Gray convertor

COMBINATIONAL LOGIC DESIGN EXAMPLE 1

Three sensors with TTL digital outputs are used to sense the liquid level in a tank. The state of these sensors drives a pump which must be off if all three sensor outputs are high, but control the speed from fast, medium and slow depending on the sensor levels. The pump is to be driven using a Pulse Width Modulation (PWM) signal at about 400 Hz.

Table 6.5 shows sensor outputs and pump speed.

First let's draw a block diagram of the proposed system. See Fig. 6.14, where the outline of the

Table 6.5

C	B	A	Result
0	0	0	Pump on (fast)
0	0	1	Pump on (half speed)
0	1	0	×
0	1	1	Pump on (slow)
1	0	0	×
1	0	1	×
1	1	0	×
1	1	1	Pump off

× = invalid state — no output should result

requirement can be clearly seen. Whatever the form the oscillator takes the combinational logic is a separate block and can be designed alone.

From the truth table:

$$\text{Pump on} = \bar{A}.\bar{B}.\bar{C} + A.\bar{B}.\bar{C} + A.B.\bar{C}$$

By K-map or simplification,

$$\text{On} = A.\bar{C} + \bar{B}.\bar{C}$$

Pump on also $= \bar{C}.(A+\bar{B})$
Fast speed $= \bar{A}.\bar{B}.\bar{C}$
Half speed $= A.\bar{B}.\bar{C}$
Slow speed $= A.B.\bar{C}$

The logic diagram that initially fits these equations is shown in Fig. 6.15, which uses:

three invertors
two 2 I/P ANDs
one 2 I/P OR
three 3 I/P ANDs

This would obviously be very wasteful of ICs. Suppose we try for a NAND solution.

$$\begin{aligned}
\text{Pump on} \ &= \overline{A.\bar{C} + \bar{B}.\bar{C}} \\
&= \overline{A.C} + \overline{\bar{B}.C} \\
&= \overline{\overline{A.C}.\overline{\bar{B}.C}}
\end{aligned}$$

Fast speed $= \overline{\overline{\bar{A}.\bar{B}.\bar{C}}}$

Half speed $= \overline{\overline{A.\bar{B}.\bar{C}}}$

Slow speed $= \overline{\overline{A.B.\bar{C}}}$

It would seem that we will require six invertors, three 2 I/P NANDS and three 3 I/P NANDS (in CMOS there would be one 4049B, one 4011B and one 4023B).

The circuit using CMOS ICs is shown in Fig. 6.16. Note that one 2 I/P NAND inside the 4011B is redundant and therefore its inputs (12 and 13 in this case) must be disabled by connection to 0 V. Also the 4049B hex invertor can spring a nasty surprise unless you check its pin-out. Power for this IC is applied between pins 1 (V_{DD}) and 8 (V_{SS}), not the normal pin 16 and pin 8 as for most 16-pin ICs.

The advantage of using CMOS is that a simple oscillator can be created using feedback round either two NOR gates ($\frac{1}{2}$4001) or two NAND gates ($\frac{1}{2}$4011). The basic oscillator is shown in Fig. 6.17(a). This can be gated with a logic 1 via one gate used as a buffer and the output can also be buffered using the other spare gate to give the desired quiescent logic 0 (off state) to the pump. Another feature of CMOS is the availability of

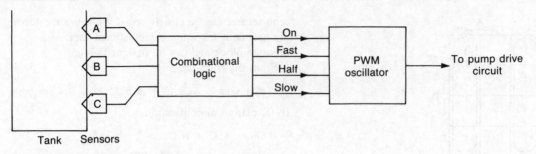

Fig. 6.14 Block diagram of system

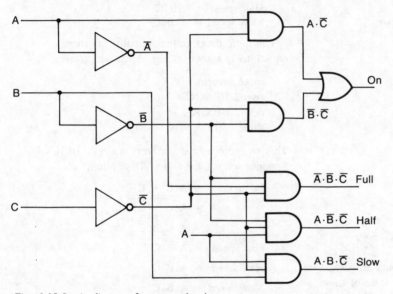

Fig. 6.15 Logic diagram for pump circuit

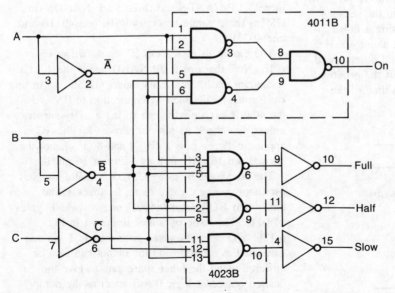

Fig. 6.16 Pump logic — second version

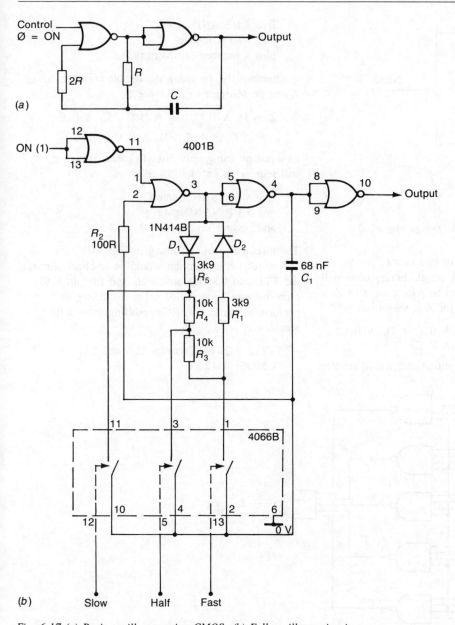

Fig. 6.17 (a) Basic oscillators using CMOS; (b) Full oscillator circuit

analog switch ICs which can be operated by logic signals. Here a 4066B Quad bilateral switch IC is used to modify the mark-to-space ratio of the oscillator by switching resistors in the charge and discharge path of the timing capacitor C_1. With the values shown the frequency is about 400 Hz with a mark-to-space ratio of 7:1 (fast), 1:1 (half speed) and 1:7 (slow). The full circuit is shown in Fig. 6.17(b).

COMBINATIONAL LOGIC DESIGN EXAMPLE 2

The digital state of five sensors has to be read one at a time over a common line at a rate of about one read every 2 milliseconds. An outline of the problem is shown in Fig. 6.18 and it can be seen that a 5-bit data multiplexer is needed. The output Z is data on D_0, D_1, D_2, D_3 or D_4 depending on the state of the control inputs ABC. Note that three

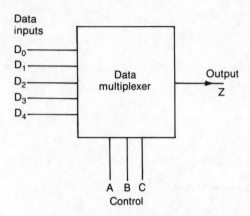

Fig. 6.18 Outline of solution to Design example 2

control inputs are needed for this task ($2^3 = 8$), with some unused states. A simple binary code will select the data line that is to be reconnected to Z.

The Boolean expression for Z is therefore:

$$Z = D_0.\bar{A}.\bar{B}.\bar{C} + D_1.A.\bar{B}.\bar{C} + D_2.\bar{A}.B.\bar{C} + D_3.A.B.\bar{C} + D_4.\bar{A}.\bar{B}.C$$

This cannot be further simplified and would require:

five 4 I/P AND gates
one 5 I/P OR gate
plus a number of invertors.

Alternatively, by using the double complement of Z and de Morgan's rule, we get:

$$Z = \overline{\overline{D_0\, \bar{A}.\bar{B}.\bar{C}} . \overline{D_1\, A.\bar{B}.\bar{C}} . \overline{D_2\, \bar{A}.B.\bar{C}} . \overline{D_3.A.B.\bar{C}} . \overline{D_4\, \bar{A}.\bar{B}.C}}$$

an equation using only NAND gates. However, it still requires a lot of ICs, i.e.

five 4 I/P NAND gates
one 5 I/P NAND gate
and several invertors.

The circuit for this is shown in Fig. 6.19.

A much better solution would be to check through the TTL and CMOs data sheets and find an MSI chip that can be modified or used directly to perform the task. Two ICs resulting from a first search are:

TTL: 74151 (also in ALS and LS)
CMOS: 4512B

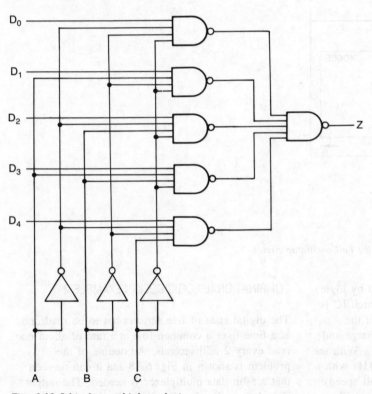

Fig. 6.19 5-bit data multiplexer logic

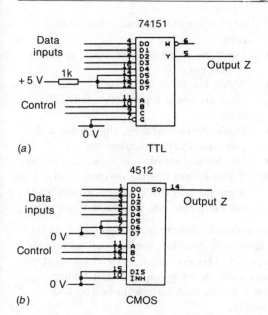

(a) TTL

(b) CMOS

Fig. 6.20 Solution to Design example 2 using (a) TTL; (b) CMOS

These are both 8-input multiplexers with some additional features such as a strobe input (G̅) to the 74151 which also has true and complement outputs (Y,W). The 4512B, on the other hand, has a tri-state output enabled by (E̅O̅) on pin 15 as well as another gate input which can be used as a strobe. In this application these inputs could be enabled by wiring them to the appropriate level, or they could be used to enhance the design, allowing, for example, a clock or strobe pulse synchronised with the 3-bit code to read the data inputs. The design solutions using either the TTL 74151 or the CMOS 4512B are shown in Fig. 6.20 and illustrate the importance of looking for an MSI chip to replace a design using many SSI devices.

6.4 SEQUENTIAL CIRCUIT DESIGN

Sequential digital circuits are circuits with state and can be classified as:

(i) *Event driven:* where the circuit elements respond directly to changes in their inputs and no clock synchronising signal is used.

(ii) *Clock driven:* a master clock generator, or state generator, controls the operation of all devices in the system.

(iii) *Pulse driven:* circuits where input signals do not overlap and where very fast response is possible.

In most sequential design it is the use of clock-driven circuits, where the operation of all units within the system is synchronised with a master clock generator, that is the standard design method. The generation of false states is minimised with this design approach.

Circuits with state are built up using the building blocks of *bistables (flip-flops)*, e.g. the R–S, clocked R–S, D and J–K types. In most cases the D and J–K bistables are preferred, since with these there can be no indeterminate states. With the J–K it's best to stick to the master–slave versions since the feedback loop is effectively disconnected when the master is isolated from the slave. In the J–K master–slave bistable the clock signal on the rising edge first isolates the master, then allows J–K inputs and the previous state to force a change of state to the master. On the clock falling edge, any J–K data is prevented from further changing the state of the master and finally the master is reconnected to the slave and the Q, Q̄ outputs can assume the new state; see Fig. 6.21.

One of the important aspects of synchronised

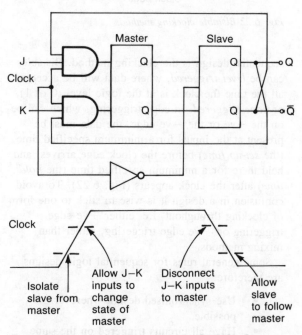

Fig. 6.21 Master–slave operation in a J–K flip-flop

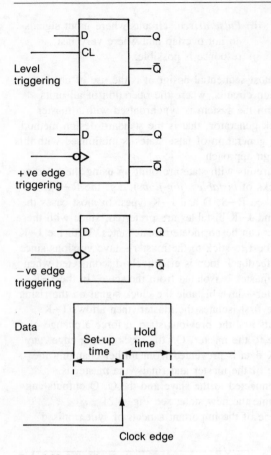

Fig. 6.22 Bistable clocking methods

sequential design is the clocking method. Bistables can be *level triggered*, where data will be accepted all the time the clock is at the logic level (0 or 1), or *edge triggered*. In edge triggering, which can be on the +ve or the −ve edge, the data must be present at the inputs for a minimum specified time (the *set-up time*) before the clock edge arrives, and held there for a minimum specified time (the *hold time*) after the clock appears (Fig. 6.22). To avoid confusion in a design it is wise to stick to one form of clocking throughout, i.e. either +ve edge triggering or −ve edge triggering, rather than mixing methods.

Some general rules for sequential logic designs are therefore:

- Use synchronised design wherever possible.
- Have all circuits triggered on the same

edge of the clock, usually the positive edge.
- Don't use more than one clock generator in the system.
- Watch out for clock 'skew' — where the clock arrives at a pcb with additional delay.
- Don't use monostables, since these will generate edges asynchronously.
- Disable any set or clear inputs to bistables.
- Try to ensure that the maximum delay time from one part of the system to another is not more than one gate delay time.

Where bistable asynchronous inputs such as $\overline{set}$ or $\overline{clear}$ have to be disabled, use one pull-up resistor for each pin. This may seem wasteful on resistors but does assist in debugging and fault finding because it allows each bistable to be checked individually.

There are several standard clock generator circuits already in existence. Standard parts such as the 4047, 74624, 74320 or even the 555 can be used as master clock circuits. In addition, Schmitt gates, invertors and NAND/NOR gates can be used to create good, clean logic clock pulse generators. A few examples of these are shown in Fig. 6.23. It's a good idea to build up a library of useful circuits such as these.

Sometimes a 2-phase non-overlapping clock is required in a design. The circuit shown in Fig. 6.24 will do this and requires only one bistable and three NOR gates. Since the NOR gates A and B require both inputs to be low simultaneously for the output to go high, the NOR gating of the clock input to the J−K (−ve edge triggered) with the Q or $\overline{Q}$ outputs will result in two non-overlapping positive-going clock signals. The frequency of the oscillator must be twice that required at the output.

Distribution of the clock round a system may need careful attention. It is obviously important to preserve the wave shape and to retain the rise and fall times. Clock signals must also be kept as clean as possible by minimising cross talk and reflections. Clock 'skew', where the clock signals become out of phase with the clock at another part of the system, can be kept to a minimum by keeping track lengths of all clock lines almost the same. If very long connections, say more than 60 cm, have to be used then a buffer or line driver and a receiver are

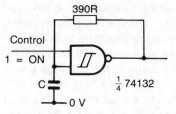

(a) Using TTL Schmitt $C \approx 200$ pF for 10 MHz

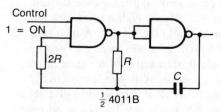

(b) Using CMOS

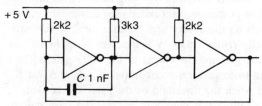

(c) Using TTL open-collector invertors with values
$f = 1$ MHz

Fig. 6.23 Simple clock generator circuits

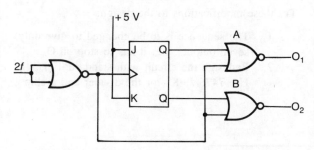

Fig. 6.24 Circuit to generate a 2-phase non-overlapping clock output

probably necessary. Don't forget that waveforms can easily be reshaped by Schmitt gates and that decoupling, careful layout and the use of a proper ground plan will all reduce clock degradation. Where level inputs have to be applied it may sometimes be necessary to synchronise these with clock and produce one output change for one clock

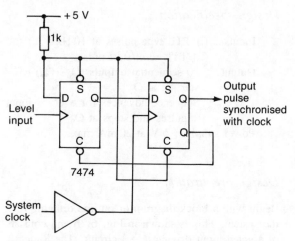

Fig. 6.25 One method for synchronising a level input to system clock

period. A circuit like the one shown in Fig. 6.25 will do this.

Sequential design requires the use of additional tools such as state diagrams and state tables. A rigorous approach should eliminate the possibility of false states being generated by the finalised sequential design. However, by careful use of MSI chips, which have been produced to be synchronous, some designs can be pieced together without recourse to elaborate state analysis. The first sequential design example that follows is like that.

SEQUENTIAL DESIGN EXAMPLE 1 – DIGITAL SEQUENCER

A sequence controller that accepts logic pulse inputs from a conditioned detector has to provide ten sequential outputs, only one of which is to be high at any one time. After switch on, or if a start input pulse is received, the unit has to output a logic high on the first output (O_0) and then advance the sequence for every three pulses accepted at its input. When the final output (O_9) is high the sequence is halted and further input pulses are locked out. The output levels do not require buffering. All inputs are TTL compatible and the maximum input rate is 10 Hz. The power supply provided is a well regulated 5 V but less than 20 mA of current is available.

Design specification

Inputs : (i) TTL type pulses at 10 Hz
          (ii) TTL reset/start pulse
Outputs : 10 sequential outputs ($O_0 \rightarrow O_9$)
          starting at O_0
          Sequence advances for every 3 input
          pulses and stops at O_9
Power supply : 5 V at 20 mA max.

Design preparation

Begin with a block diagram or outline drawing of the system. This is shown in Fig. 6.26 and consists of a gated input driving a $\div 3$ circuit. The logic output of this $\div 3$ is then used to advance a sequence generator, which is created using a 5-stage *Johnson counter*. A reset to both the counter and the $\div 3$ circuit is provided by *power-on* or the start input.

The options open for the type of logic are dictated by the restriction on available power and are:

(*a*) a standard CMOS logic (4000B series),
(*b*) low power Schottky TTL (74LS series),
(*c*) high speed CMOS (74HCT series).

Since the required speed of operation is very low the unit is best designed using standard CMOS.

Design

The divider is a standard $\div 3$ circuit using a dual J–K bistable IC type 4027. The circuit is

synchronous and advances its count on the positive edge of the clock input. The direct set inputs (active high) are disabled by connecting them to 0 V.

The sequence circuit requires a Johnson counter with ten outputs and the 4017B IC, a 5-stage circuit with ten spike-free decoded active high outputs is specified (Fig. 6.27). The *master reset* (MR) pin on this chip is connected to the direct clear inputs of the two J–K bistables to allow a power-on reset or a start/reset pulse to be applied. When the last output of the 4017B goes high it must lock out further input pulses to the divider. A high state on the input of a NOR gate will force the output to remain at logic 0 irrespective of the state of other inputs. Thus a 2-input NOR gate is required. A 4001B Quad 2I/P NOR is then used to give this gate function and also to gate the power-on reset pulse with the start input. Two of the NOR gates are used as invertors by tying their inputs together.

The power-on reset pulse uses a standard circuit based on the ability of a Schmitt input to tolerate slowly rising inputs. When power is applied C_1 is uncharged and the output of the 4093 gate will go high to force a reset condition. C_1 charges via R_1 and when the threshold of the gate is exceeded (typically 2.9 V with $V_{DD} = 5$ V) the reset pulse then returns low. Note the use of R_2 which prevents C_1 discharging via the CMOS input-gate protection diode at switch-off.

Try these modifications to the design:

1. The sequence is to be changed to give only seven outputs, i.e. it has to stop on O_6.
2. Redesign the circuit with standard TTL. Use 7476 J–Ks for the divider and a chip

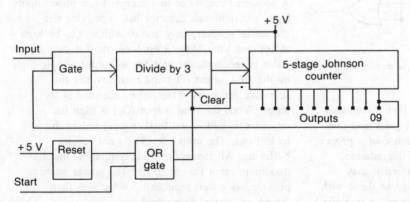

Fig. 6.26 Block diagram for sequencer

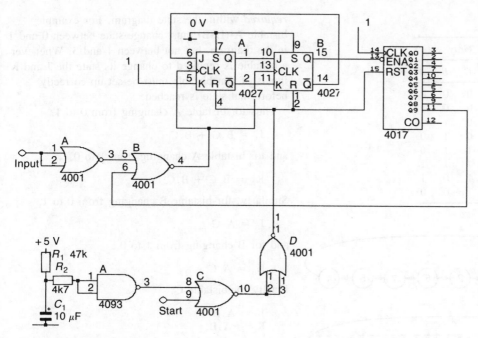

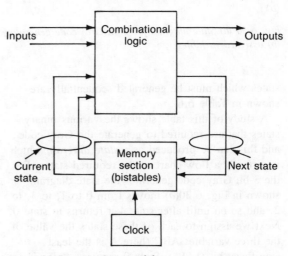

Fig. 6.29 State machine model

Fig. 6.27 Completed design

SEQUENTIAL DESIGN EXAMPLE 2 — A 4-BIT GRAY CODE GENERATOR

This requires the design of a state machine that will generate without error the cyclic 4-bit Gray code already shown on page 170, where we discussed a circuit to convert from 4-bit binary to Gray. In this case the need is for a clock-generated (i.e. synchronised), glitch-free Gray code (Fig. 6.28).

The standard model for a state machine is shown in Fig. 6.29. It consists of a number of inputs and outputs and is divided into a combinational logic section and a memory or state section. The circuit

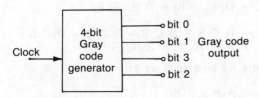

Fig. 6.28

exists in a particular state defined by the internal signals which are referred to as *state variables* or *present-state variables*. For example, with two state variables and two flip-flops there could be four different states. In a state machine each subsequent state is a consequence of both input and previous or current state. Consider the simpler example of a 3-bit Gray code state generator. The required output

Table 6.6

	Binary			Gray		
	C	B	A	C	B	A
0	0	0	0	0	0	0
1	0	0	1	0	0	1
2	0	1	0	0	1	1
3	0	1	1	0	1	0
4	1	0	0	1	1	0
5	1	0	1	1	1	1
6	1	1	0	1	0	1
7	1	1	1	1	0	0

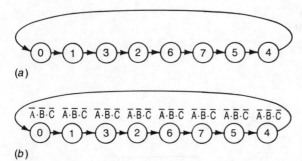

(a)

(b)

Fig. 6.30 (a) State diagram for 3-bit Gray code generator; (b) assigned variables

states which must be generated sequentially are shown in Table 6.6.

A study of this table shows the various binary states that are required to generate the Gray code and this can be produced as a *state diagram* which is virtually a flow chart of the required states. For the 3-bit Gray code generator the state diagram shown in Fig. 6.30(*a*) moves from 0 to 1, to 3, to 2, and so on until after state 4 it returns to state 0. Next we assign to each of these states the value of the three variables ABC (here A is the least significant bit (LSB)). State 0 requires $\bar{A}.\bar{B}.\bar{C}$, state 1 $A.\bar{B}.\bar{C}$, state 3 $A.B.\bar{C}$, and so on (Fig. 6.30(*b*)).

Thinking back to the general diagram of a state generator we can see that the eight states must require three bistables. Note that in this example there are no redundant or 'don't care' states, so the design is simplified. Suppose we select J—K bistables for the design; then the 'next state' signals are only necessary to change a bistable's state *if*

required within the state diagram. For example, bistable A (LSB) must change state between 0 and 1 in the diagram, but not between 1 and 3. Whenever a bistable is required to change its state the J and K inputs of that bistable must be set up correctly before that state is reached.

Thus for bistable A changing from 0 to 1,

$$J_A = \bar{B}.\bar{C} + B.C$$

and for bistable A changing from 1 to 0,

$$K_A = B.\bar{C} + \bar{B}.C.$$

Similarly, for bistable B changing from 0 to 1,

$$J_B = A.\bar{C}$$

and for B changing from 1 to 0,

$$K_B = A.C.$$

Finally for bistable C,

$$J_C = \bar{A}.B$$
$$K_C = \bar{A}.\bar{B}.$$

We now have the logic required to drive the 3-bit Gray code state generator in the right sequence. This is shown in Fig. 6.31 and uses an exclusive-NOR of B and C for the J input of bistable A, with an exclusive-OR of B and C for the K input of the same bistable. The overall circuit looks as if it requires at least three ICs. If it is necessary that the sequence always begins at state 0, then a power-up initialisation circuit connected to the asynchronous reset inputs of all four bistables is required. Note that the asynchronous set inputs would have to be disabled if the design is to work correctly.

Returning to the actual example of the 4-bit Gray code generator, the 16 states, from the previous table, are in sequence: 0, 1, 3, 2, 6, 7, 5, 4, 12, 13, 15, 14, 10, 11, 9 and 8. See Fig. 6.32.

Four bistables are required and the assigned states are as shown below.

For bistable A (transition from 0 to 1):

$$J_A = \bar{D}.\bar{C}.\bar{B} + \bar{D}.C.B + D.C.\bar{B} + D.\bar{C}.B$$
$$= \bar{D}.(C \oplus B) + D.(C \oplus B)$$

and

$$K_A = \bar{D}.\bar{C}.B + \bar{D}.C.\bar{B} + D.C.B + D.\bar{C}.\bar{B}$$
$$= B.(C \oplus D) + \bar{B}.(C \oplus D)$$

Similarly for bistable B we get:

$$\overline{J_B} = A.\overline{(C \oplus D)}$$
$$K_B = A.(C \oplus D)$$

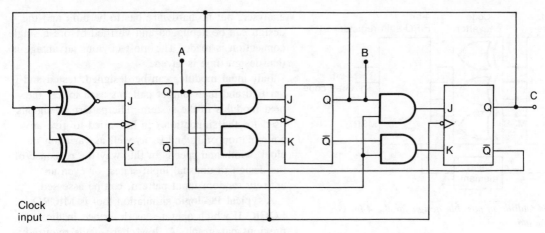

Fig. 6.31 Proposed circuit for a 3-bit Gray code generator

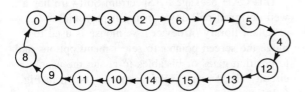

Fig. 6.32 State diagram for 4-bit Gray code generator

For bistable C we get:

$$J_C = \overline{A}.B.\overline{D}$$
$$K_B = \overline{A}.B.D$$

and for bistable D:

$$J_C = \overline{A}.\overline{B}.C$$
$$K_B = A.\overline{B}.C$$

The logic, just for bistable A (LSB), is shown in Fig. 6.32, and suggests a dual exclusive-OR and an AND−OR gate type IC. Obviously the design route chosen here will result in a well populated pcb! It is rather a cumbersome design. An alternative approach would be to use a PLD (one IC) or to look for a method using MSI devices. Using a PLD is discussed later in Section 6.6.

For the MSI design the binary-to-Gray decoder discussed in Section 6.3 will serve as a lead in to the possible solution. If we used a synchronous 4-bit binary counter, a decorder, based on the three exclusive-OR gates developed earlier, could then be used to generate the 4-bit Gray code. To make the design absolutely glitch free the decoded Gray code output could be loaded into a 4-bit PIPO register which would then be clocked at the same time as

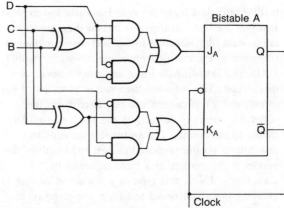

Fig. 6.33 Logic for bistable A

the counter. An outline of the proposed design is given in Fig. 6.34.

A search through the TTL data book indicates that several 4-bit binary counters are available but many of them are not synchronous and therefore cannot be used. The 74161, which is a synchronous 4-bit binary counter (+ve edge triggered), will be suitable and the 74299 PIPO 4-bit register or the 74175 can be used to hold the decoded Gray code. The suggested circuit is shown in Fig. 6.35.

6.5 LOGIC SIMULATION

Several useful CAD packages, ranging from low cost software designed to run on PCs up to very expensive systems, exist for the simulation and

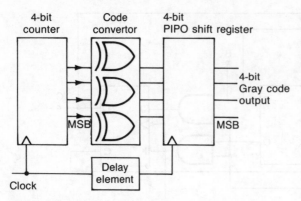

Fig. 6.34 Outline of possible design for the 4-bit Gray code generator

testing of digital logic designs. Basically the method involves the user creating his circuit diagram using component-libraries held in the software package or transporting the circuit from some other compatible CAD, and labelling all input and output nodes on this circuit. The software then makes a netlist of the circuit and a test pattern can be called from the software, normally defined by the user, to simulate inputs to the circuit. The software then runs this test pattern on the proposed design and displays the results at the outputs as a table or series of waveforms. Using this type of software is similar to carrying out a functional test on a prototype of the actual logic with a pattern generator and a logic

analyser, but no hardware has to be built and the design can be debugged and verified before a single connection is made. The most obvious advantage is that design time is saved.

Individual modules can be designed, tested and verified and their output patterns used to test the next modules in the system. The pattern of signals used for the simulation can be varied to give any combination of 1s and 0s as well as variation in clock width and speed. In this way the response of the design to unusual input states, or even an entirely random input pattern, can be assessed.

A typical PC logic simulation tool is MICRO-LOGIC II which operates as described in the previous paragraph. A flow chart of the required user actions is shown in Fig. 6.36(a).

This CAD package by Spectrum Software has a well designed pull-down menu display and an excellent library of devices. A mouse is used to move the screen pointer to select menu options and to position gates or bistables to create the user's circuit. The screen display layout is shown in Fig. 6.36(b).

Let's consider the very simple example of simulating the 4-bit binary-to-Gray convertor already discussed on page 180. Using the drawing facility of MICRO-LOGIC II, an EOR (exclusive-OR) gate package is selected from the library and placed on the screen using the mouse. The mouse is then used to place two more EOR gates on the screen (Fig. 6.37(a)). If these placements are not

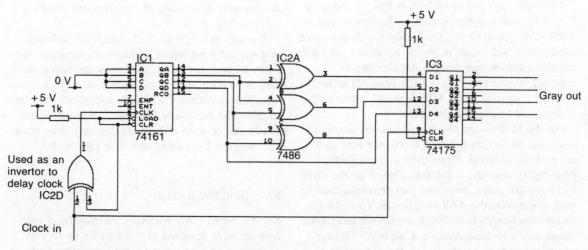

Fig. 6.35 Alternative design for the 4-bit Gray code generator

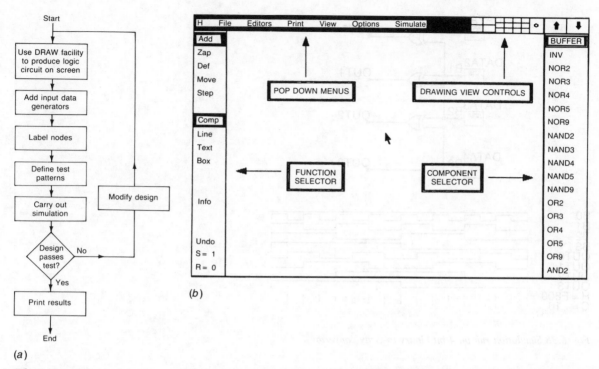

(b)

Fig. 6.36 (a) User actions for a CAD digital simulation package; (b) Screen display layout

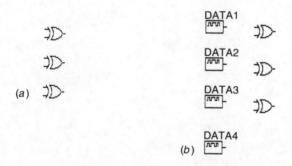

(a)

(b)

Fig. 6.37 Creating the circuit on screen

exactly as required, a MOVE facility enables a component to be repositioned on the screen. The circuit has four inputs and so four separate data generators are selected from the component library and placed appropriately on the screen (Fig. 6.37(b)).

Connecting lines and nodes are then made using the ADD and LINE commands from the menu. Finally, the nodes are labelled using the ADD and TEXT facility. In this case the input nodes are

labelled B0, B1, B2 and B3 and the outputs as OUT0 to OUT3.

The EDITOR pop-down menu can then be used to define a pattern generator required by the user. The *simulation* option can now be selected from the menu and within this portion of the software the signal patterns for the selected data generators used in the design can be set up. In this example a binary pattern is selected for the 4-bit input. The simulation is run and the input and outputs displayed on the screen. A typical hard copy of the result is shown in Fig. 6.38 where it can be seen that the 4-bit output pattern corresponds to the expected Gray code.

The design of the pump logic of Design example 1 (page 171) has also been verified by the MICRO-LOGIC II package. The NAND version of the circuit drawn using the package is shown in Fig. 6.39(a), where the nodes are labelled A, B and C for inputs, and ON (motor) FAST, HALF and SLOW for the outputs. You will recall the NAND version of this circuit was developed from the Boolean logic equation using de Morgan's rules, so it would be very appropriate to verify the design

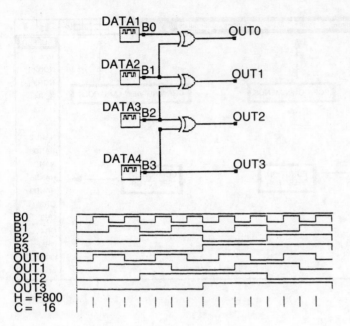

Fig. 6.38 Simulation run on 4-bit binary-to-Gray convertor

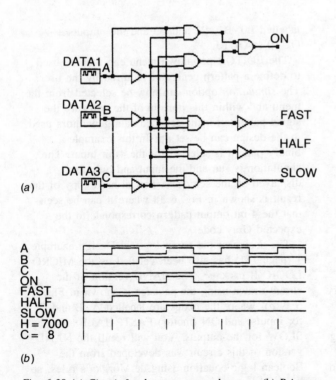

Fig. 6.39 (a) Circuit for the pump control system; (b) Printout

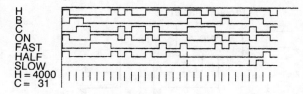

H
B
C
ON
FAST
HALF
SLOW
H = 4000
C = 31

Fig. 6.40 Running a random input pattern

work before building the prototype. The simulation uses three input data generators all set up in a binary sequence. The printout for eight clock cycles is given in Fig. 6.39(*b*) and shows the required outputs result for the various input combinations, i.e.

$$ON = \bar{A}.\bar{B}.\bar{C} + A.\bar{B}.\bar{C} + A.B.\bar{C}$$
$$FAST = \bar{A}.\bar{B}.\bar{C}$$
$$HALF = A.\bar{B}.\bar{C}$$
$$SLOW = A.B.\bar{C}$$

For all other input combinations the four outputs are at logic 0.

CAD tools such as MICRO-LOGIC II are relatively easy to learn and operate and could save many hours of hardware testing. Suppose we investigate the operation of the pump circuit further. If a random binary pattern is selected for the three input data channels, two 'glitches' show up on the HALF and SLOW outputs for a change of state in inputs ABC from $\bar{A}.\bar{B}.\bar{C}$ to $A.B.C$, i.e. all zeros to all ones, see Fig. 6.40. This is not something that might be found during a hardware test. It results because these two outputs, while C is at 0, have one gate delay less than the FAST and ON outputs.

$$HALF \ A.\bar{B}.\bar{C}$$
$$and \ SLOW \ A.B.\bar{C}$$

Thus when inputs A.B.C all change state from 0 to 1 there is a short delay while the $\bar{C}$ signal remains valid. In this design the glitches, or false outputs equal to one gate delay, would not cause a problem since the three sensors should never generate a simultaneous 0 to 1 transition, nor in fact would the short pulse generated if they did produce any output be recognised by the PWM oscillator circuit. But this test does indicate the advantages of simulation, especially if the outputs

of such a circuit are to be used as input signals to a sequential logic board. In that case the short duration false outputs could easily trigger bistables. The solution would be to add a non-inverting buffer to the A and B inputs driving the 3-input NAND gates, to equalise the delay times.

6.6 DESIGNING WITH PROGRAMMABLE LOGIC DEVICES (PLDs)

Reducing the chip count of a system improves reliability and lowers the time that has to be spent on testing. Many faults on pcbs are due to open or shorted tracks, so the more connections that can be fitted inside the ICs the better. Thus the move in design has been away from SSI devices, first to MSI and then, wherever possible, to LSI and VLSI chips. Custom designed ICs or ASICs (Application Specific Integrated Circuits) are a possible route for the medium to high volume production of digital equipment, since these original equipment manufacturers (OEMs) can afford the very high investment necessary. A less costly and faster design approach is to use PLDs. The basic principle of a PLD is to have programmable AND–OR arrays (either one or both functions programmable depending on the type of PLD) within one IC. This structure is used because the majority of logic equations required for a design are either in this form or can be converted to it, e.g. $F = A.B.C + \bar{A}.B.C + A.\bar{B}.C$, etc.

The simplest type of PLD consists of a set of buffered inputs which give the true and complement of each input, a rank of AND gates so that various combinations of the inputs can be ANDed together to give *product terms*, and then a bank of OR gates to allow selected product terms to be combined into output signals or *sum-of-products*. See Fig. 6.41.

There are basically three main types of PLD:

(*a*) PAL (programmable array logic) using a programmable AND and fixed OR structure,

(*b*) PROM (programmable read only memory) with a fixed AND and programmable OR structure,

(*c*) FPLA (field programmable logic array) with both AND and OR programmable. (Fig. 6.42.)

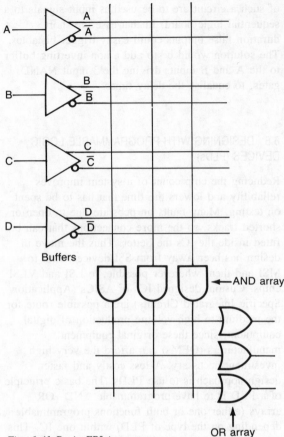

Fig. 6.41 Basic FPLA structure

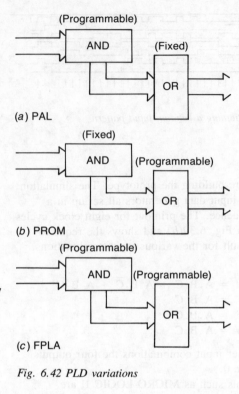

Fig. 6.42 PLD variations

Most of these industry standard PLDs are *once only* user programmable. Much more flexibility is offered with the erasable types (EPLD and EEPLD) which are:

(d) GAL (generic array logic)
(e) PEEL (programmable electrically erasable logic)

Another advantage of devices such as a GAL is that they can be used to emulate the 20-pin and 24-pin PAL devices. By using a device with erasable technology the designer is given maximum flexibility. The design doesn't have to be right first time.

PLDs use a slightly different notation to normal logic. The connection method is shown in Fig. 6.43, where a programmed, i.e. intact, cell is shown with an '×' at the intersection. An erased or open connection is shown without this '×'. The AND gate in the diagram will therefore have the

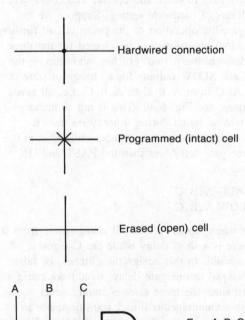

Fig. 6.43 PLD connections

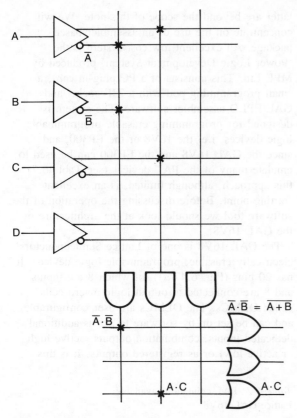

Fig. 6.44 An illustration of logic equation creation

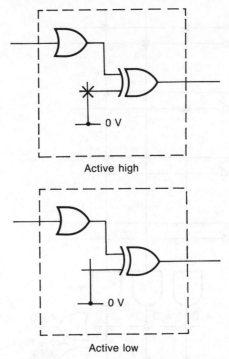

Active high

Active low

Fig. 6.45 Output cell programming

output A.B.C. Let's take this a step further and look at a typical FPLA structure (both AND and OR programmable). The next diagram, Fig. 6.44, shows a portion of an FPLA programmed to give two outputs: one a NOR function ($\overline{A+B}$) where only the connections $\overline{A}$ and $\overline{B}$ have been left intact to one AND gate and only that AND output is connected to the OR gate, and one AND function (A.C). Programming is slightly more complicated than this since the OR gates that give the sum-of-product terms can themselves be programmed to be active high or active low (Fig. 6.45). In the device this is achieved by incorporating an exclusive-OR gate on the output of each OR. If the programmable input to this exclusive-OR is left intact (i.e. connected to logic 0) the exclusive-OR acts as a non-inverting buffer (active high), whereas if the connection is 'blown' the exclusive-OR input goes to logic 1 and the gate acts as an invertor (active low). A simple example using this principle is given in Fig. 6.46, where the exclusive-OR and exclusive-

NOR of AB is developed and also the NAND output $\overline{A.B.C}$.

The design process for PLDs requires the generation of the full functional specification and the Boolean equations or state diagrams needed to implement the specification. The design should preferably then be verified by logic simulation. Only then should the device be programmed. This is obviously very important for devices such as PALs, which are once only programmed. Any mistakes in design, which could have been picked up by simulation and verification, can be rather costly.

The tools required for the design and blowing of PLDs depend on the complexity of the devices to be blown and also the range of devices that are to be covered by the one tool. The basic requirement is for software to enable the user to select the device being used (i.e. a PAL, GAL, PEEL, etc.) and which will accept Boolean equations that define what the programmed IC has to do. The software must then assemble the text file containing the user define data (Boolean equations/state diagrams) and produce a fuse map that can be 'blown' into the device. Additional hardware is necessary to translate

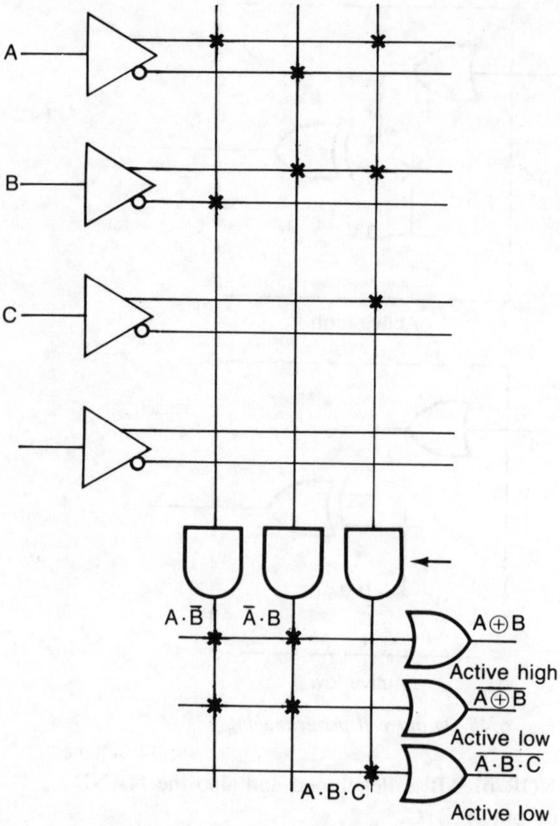

Fig. 6.46 Using the output cell programming

latter are beyond the scope of this note. We will concentrate on the use of an assembler-based package. An excellent low cost system is the 'Power Logic Development System' produced by MPE Ltd. This consists of a PC plug-in card, a small programming pod with a ZIF socket and GAL/EPLD assembler software. The system is designed for programming erasable programmable logic devices, i.e. the 16V8 or the EP300, and since the GAL 16V8 and the EP300 can be used to emulate many of the PAL devices (see Table 6.7) this approach, although limited, is an excellent starting point. Before discussing the operation of the software tool we should look at the architecture of the GAL 16V8.

The GAL 16V8 is one of Lattice Semiconductors' electrically erasable, programmable logic devices. It has 20 pins (Fig. 6.47(*a*)), of which 8 are inputs and 8 are connected to output logic macro cells called OLMCs. The OLMCs are user configurable and can be set up by software to act as additional dedicated inputs, combination outputs (active high or active low) or as registered outputs. It is this

this fuse map into signals that will enable the software to download the correct pattern to the IC. The IC will be connected to a Zero Insertion Force socket (ZIF socket) and via cable or link to the programming hardware.

Most manufacturers of PLD devices have developed software packages that can be used to program their devices (often free to the user) but the hardware programmer itself can be expensive. Typical software packages are:

AMAZE (Signetics/Mullard) ⎫
PALASM (AMD)   ⎬ Assemblers

ABEL (Data I/O)   ⎫
CUPL (Logical Devices) ⎬ Compilers

Assembler-based software requires the user to define input and output pins and the desired Boolean logic equations, whereas with the compiler packages the user has only to define the truth table or the state diagram for the proposed design. The

Table 6.7 PAL emulations available Lattice GAL 16V8

PAL type	Architecture Control Word			
	SYN	AC0	AC1(n)	XOR(n)
10H8	1	0	00	FF
10L8	1	0	00	00
10P8	1	0	00	00
12H6	1	0	81	FF
12L6	1	0	81	00
12P6	1	0	81	00
14H4	1	0	C3	FF
14L4	1	0	C3	00
14P4	1	0	C3	00
16H2	1	0	E7	FF
16L2	1	0	E7	00
16P2	1	0	E7	00
16H8	1	1	FF	FF
16R8	0	1	00	00
16RP8	0	1	00	00
16L8	1	1	FF	00
16R6	0	1	81	00
16RP6	0	1	81	00
16P8	1	1	FF	00
16R4	0	1	C3	00
16RP4	0	1	C3	00

programmability of the OLMCs that allows the 16V8 to emulate the PAL devices. The OLMC diagram Fig. 6.47(b) shows how this is achieved. The heart of the OLMC is a D-bistable which has as its input the outputs of the AND array summed by the multiple input OR gate and fed from an exclusive-OR (EX-OR) gate. It is the programming of SYN, ACO, ACI(n) and EX-OR(n) which allows the user to select five operating modes for the output macrocell (Table 6.8). These various modes are illustrated in Fig. 6.48.

The actual programming of the function for the OLMCs is done, by the software, using selected bits of an 82-bit control word in location 60. An additional feature of the GAL 16V8 is the use of a security cell in row address 61. If this is programmed no one is able to read the device. This prevents others from (a) discovering the logic design and (b) reprogramming the device.

Within the software of the MPE Power Logic Development System the user can either define the mode in which the GAL/EPLD device is to be used or define the PAL type that it is required to emulate. For example, suppose we wish to make the GAL 16V8 emulate a PAL 16L8, a combinational device only with active low outputs. The Lattice GAL architecture control word could be set up as follows:

SYN : 1
ACO : 1
ACI(n) : FF
XOR(n) : ∞

Alternatively, an initial statement in the text file can be:

Lattice
PAL 16L8
. . . . . .

Let's now look at a specific example using this development tool to set up a GAL 16V8 to carry out the task of the pump logic circuit of Fig. 6.15. In this circuit you will recall that three sensors gave TTL logic type inputs of ABC and four active high outputs called ON, FAST, HALF and SLOW. The Boolean logic equations are:

$$ON = \overline{A}.\overline{B}.\overline{C} + A.\overline{B}.\overline{C} + A.B.\overline{C}$$

which simplifies to $ON = A.\overline{C} + \overline{B}.\overline{C}$.

$$FAST = \overline{A}.\overline{B}.\overline{C}$$
$$HALF = A.\overline{B}.\overline{C}$$
$$SLOW = A.B.\overline{C}$$

Obviously this relatively simple example will only be using about one-third of the available circuitry on the 16V8, but even so it will demonstrate that the three SS1 ICs required for the circuit (see Fig. 6.16) can be replaced by one GAL IC.

Having installed the MPE Power Logic Card in a spare slot in the PC (Location 0300 Hex is normally used, but the user is allowed to change this) and the Assembler Software on the hard disk, the development tool can be put to use. The main menu is called by typing:

CD PLDs

then PLDs to run the software.

The layout of the main menu is shown in Fig. 6.49, where the Edit File has been named.

Test 1: DCF

A DCF, or Device Configuration File, will consist of three sections:

(a) device configuration,
(b) pin names,
(c) equations.

From the main menu the options can be selected, either using the mouse or the ⟨up⟩ and ⟨down⟩ keys to move the highlighted yellow marker to the required option. Alternatively the key which is shown highlighted will also select the option: e.g. for 'select device Type', simply press the key T.

The first step is to edit the file. In my case the editor used is LANCS\ASS68000\EC.EXE but other user editors are allowed, e.g. EDITORS\WS\EXE. Within the configuration option the user can set up the editor of his choice — no text editor is provided with the Power Logic Software. After selection F (edit the File) the text is entered. The text file printout is shown in Fig. 6.50. Here the device selected is a Lattice emulating a PAL 16H8 (active high outputs combinational device). Pin definition follows and then the Boolean equations that state the relationships between the outputs and the inputs. As in logic expressions:

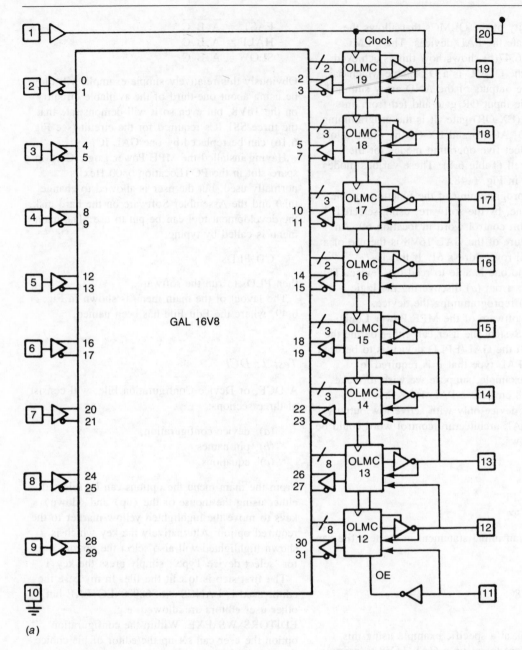

(a)

. = and
+ = or
but / = complement

Therefore ON is typed as:

ON = a./c + /b./c ;

The statement is ended with a semicolon. (NB: don't forget the spaces, otherwise the file cannot be assembled.)

Comments on each line can be added following a slash, e.g.:

pin 2 = a ;   \ input sensor A
and fast = /a./b./c. ; \ maximum output

The text file is terminated with the END statement and saved on disk. The user then returns from his text editor to the PLDS main menu. Option A, Assemble file, is then used to assemble the text file to produce the fuse pattern necesary to

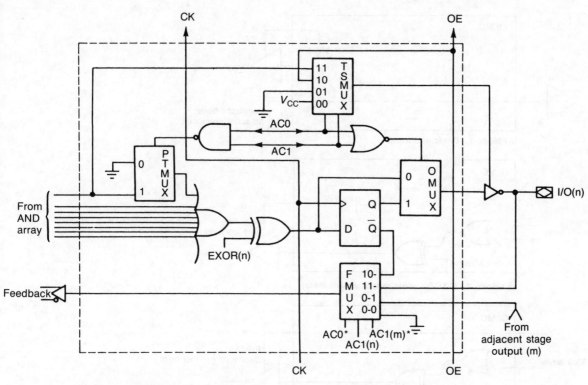

(*b*)   *$\overline{\text{SYN}}$ replaces ACO and SYN replaces AC1(m) as an input to the FMUX in OLMC(15) and OLMC(22).

Fig. 6.47 (a) Block diagram of GAL 16V8; (b) Output logic macrocell structure (Copyright © 1988 Lattice Semiconductors Corp.)

Table 6.8

Mode	SYN	AC0	AC1(n)	EX-OR(n)	Function
1	1	0	1	—	Dedicated input
2A	1	0	0	0	Combinational output (active low o/p)
2B	1	0	0	1	Combinational output (active high)
3A	1	1	1	0	Combinational output using the enable input (active low)
3B	1	1	1	1	Combinational output using enable (active high)
4A	0	1	1	0	Combinational output with clock (active low)
4B	0	1	1	1	Combinational output with clock (active high)
5A	0	1	0	0	Registered output (active low)
5B	0	1	0	1	Registered output (active high)

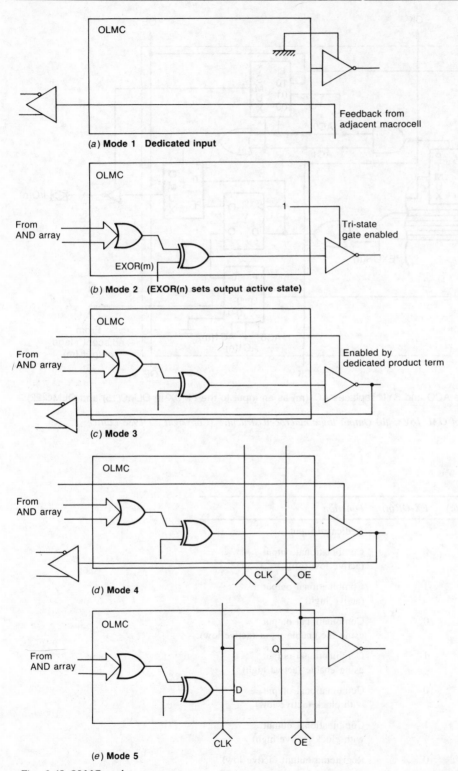

(a) **Mode 1   Dedicated input**

Feedback from adjacent macrocell

(b) **Mode 2   (EXOR(n) sets output active state)**

From AND array

EXOR(m)

1

Tri-state gate enabled

(c) **Mode 3**

From AND array

Enabled by dedicated product term

(d) **Mode 4**

From AND array

CLK   OE

(e) **Mode 5**

From AND array

D   Q

CLK   OE

Fig. 6.48 OLMC modes

```
PowerLogic Development System        v2.0
(c) MicroProcessor Engineering Ltd, 1989


Edit file        PLD.DCF
Assemble file
Edit fuse map
Program device
                      Device at top of socket
Select device
   type      GAL16V8  Family:      Lattice
Erase device         Checksum:    10F1
Blank check          Security fuse: OFF
Read device          Fam/Pinout:  3655
Verify device        Signature:   . . . . . . . .
Set security fuse    Erase cycles: 255
                                   MASTER

Device identification menu
JEDEC file menu
Configuration menu
Documentation utilities
DOS commands

Quit
```

Fig. 6.49 PLDS main menu

```
lattice
pal 16h8

pins

pin 1 = clk
pin 2 = a
pin 3 = b
pin 4 = c
pin 19 = op
pin 18 = or
pin 17 = os
pin 16 = ot

equations

op =    a./c
    + /b./c ;

or = /a./b./c ;

os = a./b./c ;

ot = a.b./c ;

end
```

Fig. 6.50 Printout for pump logic file

program the selected device. All that is required from the user is to select option P to do this.

Programming takes only a few seconds. The GAL 16V8 is then ready for use in the circuit, replacing the three CMOS ICs previously specified for the

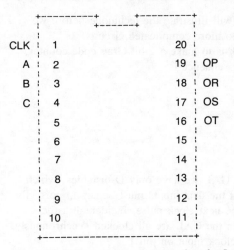

Fig. 6.51 PLD assembler device outline for Lattice GAL 16V8

pump logic. Since the GAL is CMOS, all unused inputs must be disabled by connection to 0 V or V_{CC}, whichever is more convenient.

Obviously in this rather brief note it is not possible to cover all the features of the MPE Power Logic Development System. The software is very user helpful, simple to operate, and comes with good documentation. All options are clearly explained in the manuals and are logically arranged. For example, if option U is called, the display switches to the documentation Utilities menu. This allows the user to print a fuse map and a device outline (outline for this example is shown in Fig. 6.51). Another important feature is that JEDEC* files can be produced or imported from disk to allow programming from another source.

USING A PLD FOR STATE LOGIC

Since the OLMC of a GAL (and many other PLDs) has a D-bistable, it is relatively easy to program the device to act as a state machine. In the case of the GAL 16V8 mode 5 would be selected to give registered output and the $\overline{Q}$ of the bistable is then available to be fed back to the AND array. A very simple example (very wasteful of the GAL's

---

*JEDEC is the Joint Electronic Device Engineering Council. In this case JEDEC implies a programmable logic standard format which could be used with any software which accepts this approved format.

potential) will illustrate the technique before we move on to more complicated circuits.

The task is to make a 2-bit Gray code counter. The count sequence is:

B	A
0	0
0	1
1	1
1	0

Inside the GAL we have only D-bistables, which means that the data inputs must be set up correctly prior to the next clock pulse. Incidentally, the bistables in the GAL are all clocked synchronously from the clock input on pin 1.

The method that should be used to find the required logic input for the bistables is to make up a table showing both the current and the next state of the desired sequence, i.e.

Current state		Next state	
B	A	B_n	A_n
0	0	0	1
0	1	1	1
1	1	1	0
1	0	0	0

When $A_n = 1$ we have the required input for the D input of the first bistable:

$$A_n = \bar{A}.\bar{B} + A.\bar{B} = \bar{B}.(\bar{A}+A) = \bar{B}$$

and for B_n we get

$$B_n = A.\bar{B} + A.B = A(\bar{B}+B) = A$$

The circuit for the 2-bit Gray code state generator is therefore as shown in Fig. 6.52.

To implement this in the GAL 16V8 the text file would be:

```
Lattice
Pal 16R8          \emulating a registered PAL
Pins
Pin 1 = CLK \clock input
Pin 19 = b
Pin 18 = a
Equations
a = /b;           \feedback bar Q of b to array
b = a;
end
```

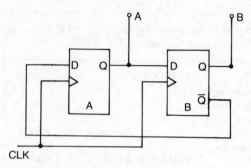

Fig. 6.52 2-bit Gray code circuit

We can extend this technique to make a 3-bit Gray code generator.

Current state			Next state		
C	B	A	C_n	B_n	A_n
0	0	0	0	0	1
0	0	1	0	1	1
0	1	1	0	1	0
0	1	0	1	1	0
1	1	0	1	1	1
1	1	1	1	0	1
1	0	1	1	0	0
1	0	0	0	0	0

For this design:

$$A_n = \bar{A}.\bar{B}.\bar{C} + A.\bar{B}.\bar{C} + \bar{A}.B.C + A.B.C$$

Using a K-map this can be simplified to

$$A_n = B.C + \bar{B}.\bar{C}$$

Similarly,

$$B_n = A.\bar{B}.\bar{C} + A.B.\bar{C} + \bar{A}.B.\bar{C} + \bar{A}.B.C$$
$$= A.\bar{C} + \bar{A}.B$$

and $C_n = \bar{A}.B.\bar{C} + \bar{A}.B.C + A.B.C + A.\bar{B}.\bar{C}$
$$= A.C + \bar{A}.B$$

(The K-maps are not shown for these simplifications; try and prove them for yourself.)

The circuit for the 3-bit Gray code state generator is given in Fig. 6.53 which can be programmed using the PDLS software and programmer. The text file is given in Fig. 6.54. Note that a Lattice GAL 16V8 is specified, with registered outputs (SYN 0) all active high (XOR(n) = FF).

Now we can consider the design of the 4-bit Gray code state generator using a GAL. You will recall that previously the design needed at least three ICs.

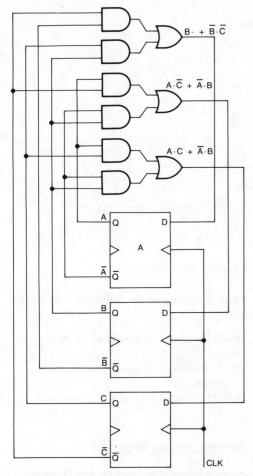

Fig. 6.53 Logic for 3-bit Gray code counter

```
    lattice
    gal 16v8              \ programmed for 3 bit gray

definitions
    hex
    syn 0                 \ registered outputs
    ac0 1                 \ outputs with feedback
    ac1(n) 00             \ registers
    xor(n) ff             \ active high outputs

pins

pin 1 = clk
pin 19 = c               \ msb out
pin 18 = b
pin 17 = a               \ lsb out

equations

a = b.c + /b./c ;        \ feedback for data a input
b = a./c + /a.b ;        \ feedback for data b input
c = a.c + /a.b ;         \ feedback for data c input

end
```
Fig. 6.54

The present state/next state table is:

Present state				Next state			
D	C	B	A	D_n	C_n	B_n	A_n
0	0	0	0	0	0	0	1
0	0	0	1	0	0	1	1
0	0	1	1	0	0	1	0
0	0	1	0	0	1	1	0
0	1	1	0	0	1	1	1
0	1	1	1	0	1	0	1
0	1	0	1	0	1	0	0
0	1	0	0	1	1	0	0
1	1	0	0	1	1	0	1
1	1	0	1	1	1	1	1
1	1	1	1	1	1	1	0
1	1	1	0	1	0	1	0
1	0	1	0	1	0	1	1
1	0	1	1	1	0	0	1
1	0	0	1	1	0	0	0
1	0	0	0	0	0	0	0

Before any simplification we get:

$$A_n = \bar{A}.\bar{B}.\bar{C}.\bar{D} + A.\bar{B}.\bar{C}.\bar{D} + \bar{A}.B.C.\bar{D}$$
$$+ A.B.C.\bar{D} + \bar{A}.\bar{B}.C.D + A.\bar{B}.C.D$$
$$+ \bar{A}.B.\bar{C}.D + A.B.\bar{C}.D$$

and

$$B_n = A.\bar{B}.\bar{C}.\bar{D} + A.B.\bar{C}.\bar{D} + \bar{A}.B.\bar{C}.\bar{D}$$
$$+ \bar{A}.B.C.\bar{D} + A.\bar{B}.C.D + A.B.C.D$$
$$+ \bar{A}.B.C.D + \bar{A}.\bar{B}.C.D$$

and

$$C_n = \bar{A}.B.\bar{C}.\bar{D} + A.B.\bar{C}.\bar{D} + A.B.\bar{C}.\bar{D}$$
$$+ A.\bar{B}.C.\bar{D} + \bar{A}.\bar{B}.C.\bar{D} + A.\bar{B}.C.D$$
$$+ A.\bar{B}.C.D + A.B.C.D$$

and finally

$$D_n = \bar{A}.B.C.\bar{D} + \bar{A}.\bar{B}.C.D + A.\bar{B}.C.D$$
$$+ A.B.\bar{C}.D + \bar{A}.B.\bar{C}.D + A.\bar{B}.\bar{C}.D$$
$$+ A.B.\bar{C}.D + A.\bar{B}.\bar{C}.D$$

The K-maps to provide the following simplifications are given in Fig. 6.55.

$$A_n = \bar{B}.\bar{C}.\bar{D} + \bar{C}.D.B + C.\bar{B}.D + B.C.\bar{D}$$
$$B_n = \bar{A}.B + A.\bar{C}.\bar{D} + A.C.D$$
$$C_n = C.\bar{D} + B.\bar{A}.\bar{D} + \bar{C}.\bar{B}.D$$
$$D_m = A.D + B.D + C.\bar{A}.\bar{B}$$

When using PLDs it is essential to obtain the minimised logic form to avoid cumbersome equations and to reduce the risk of running out of space in the device map.

The above equations are used to produce the text file (Fig. 6.56) and after assembly this is downloaded via the programmer to the GAL.

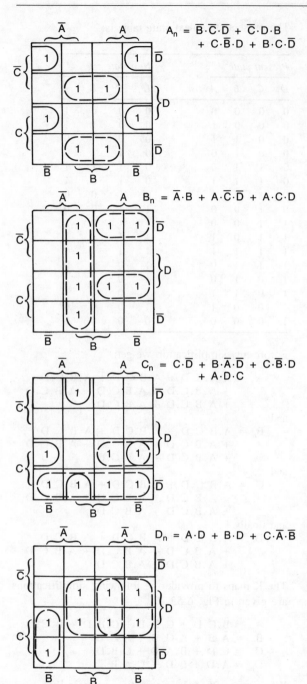

$$A_n = \overline{B} \cdot \overline{C} \cdot \overline{D} + \overline{C} \cdot D \cdot B + C \cdot \overline{B} \cdot D + B \cdot C \cdot \overline{D}$$

$$B_n = \overline{A} \cdot B + A \cdot \overline{C} \cdot \overline{D} + A \cdot C \cdot D$$

$$C_n = C \cdot \overline{D} + B \cdot \overline{A} \cdot \overline{D} + C \cdot \overline{B} \cdot D + A \cdot D \cdot C$$

$$D_n = A \cdot D + B \cdot D + C \cdot \overline{A} \cdot \overline{B}$$

Fig. 6.55 K-maps for logic equation reduction

```
lattice
gal 16v8

definitions
hex
syn 0
ac0 1
ac1(n) 00
xor(n) ff

pins
pin 1 = clk
pin 19 = d
pin 18 = c
pin 17 = b
pin 16 = a

equations

a = /b./c./d + /c.d.b + c./b.d + b.c./d ;
b = /a.b + a./c./d + a.c.d ;
c = c./d + b./a./d + c./b.d + a.d.c ;
d = a.d + b.d + c./a./b ;
end
```

Fig. 6.56 The text file

design. Further reading of the following data books is advised:

- PAL Handbook (Monolithic Memories Inc.)
- GAL Handbook (Lattice Semiconductor Corporation)
- EPLD Handbook (Altera Corporation)

6.7 MICROPROCESSORS IN DESIGN

This chapter on digital logic design would not be complete without some discussion on the use of microprocessors. However, designing with any microprocessor can seem a daunting task, since using a processor correctly requires detailed understanding of its architecture, clock and timing signals, bus structure, addressing modes, interrupt methods and instruction set. In addition, access to some form of software development support is essential. Without this it is not possible to create a program of instructions to prove that the hardware works as planned.

Initially the decision to use a microprocessor in the design has to be justified. The advantage is that the programmable nature of a microprocessor system enables it to perform a variety of complex tasks and to get it to change tasks one has only to arrange for a change in software.

The alternatives to a microprocessor for a design are to use either (*a*) Hardwired logic or (*b*) PLDs.

Obviously these examples showing the use of PLD chips and a low cost programmer and software are simple but do illustrate the potential gains in lower chip count and improved reliability for logic

The PLD represents a middle position in design in that it provides some of the flexibility afforded by the microprocessor system.

The decision to go for a microprocessor-based system is really determined by the sort of task that has to be performed. For example, a small microprocessor target board would be ideal for use within a control system reading inputs from sensors, computing errors and then outputting command words to drive external devices such as motors and heaters. This would be more difficult to achieve with ordinary hardwired logic where it would not be easy to change values of parameters within the control algorithm. The programmability of the microprocessor means it is relatively easy to input data from a keypad or switches to alter or tune the system's performance.

Following an assessment of the requirement, the first decision is: does a microprocessor-based system give the best solution? If the answer is yes, the next questions are: what type of microsystem is best and which microprocessor should be used? In other words, do we need an 8, 16 or even 32-bit dataword for the system? How complex is the program? How much memory is required? and so on.

It would not be possible or desirable to start

listing all the various microprocessors currently available nor to cover any particular one in detail, some understanding of the theory is assumed. Here we are interested in the steps necessary to get a chosen design up and running.

The basic parts that are required for a microprocessor-based system (Fig. 6.57) are:

- a CPU (the microprocessor),
- some RAM (read/write memory),
- some ROM (read only memory),
- one or two interface chips (serial and/or parallel),
- address decoding logic.

One of the surprising things about creating a breadboard of such a system is that it invariably works first time or at least after some minor adjustment.

There are, of course, several single chip microcomputers available that incorporate all these parts (sometimes more, e.g. a timer) as shown in Fig. 6.58, so that all the user has to do is connect it up correctly and download some suitable software. However, it is useful to look at the design of a small system using, say, an 8-bit CPU such as the 6502, the 6802 or the 6809, since from this it is possible to gain experience which can then be used

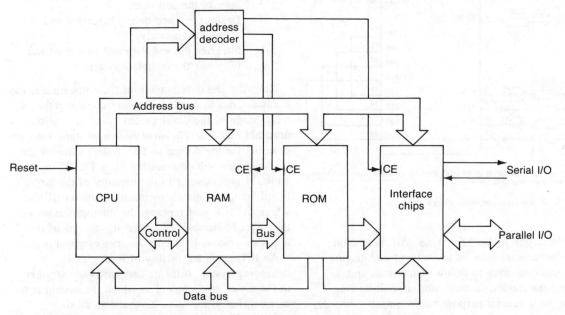

Fig. 6.57 Simplified view of a microprocessor-based system

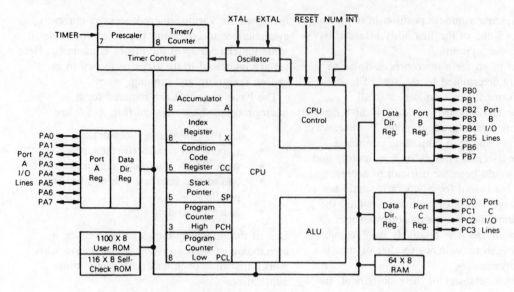

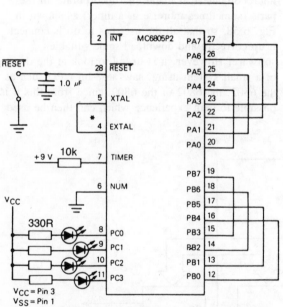

V_{CC} = Pin 3
V_{SS} = Pin 1

*This connection depends on the clock oscillator user selectable mask option.
Use crystal if that option is selected.

Fig. 6.58 A microcomputer chip

for the design of larger systems. All these 8-bit microprocessors have an uncluttered architecture and relatively easy to follow instructions and addressing modes, so they form a good starting point for a general purpose microcontroller board. The steps necessary for the design are:

1. Define the tasks that the system has to perform.
2. Draw up a specification of the system hardware, i.e.:
    (a) Data width,
    (b) Memory capacity,
    (c) Memory map,
    (d) Interface ICs,
    (e) Clock and clock speed.
3. Specify the software.
4. Design, test and debug hardware and software separately.
5. Integrate the software and hardware and fully test the complete system.

Normally the development of the software and the hardware run in parallel and only come together at a late stage of the development cycle. It is also apparent that a *development system* of some kind is essential for the design so that system software can be developed and downloaded via a PROM or EPROM programmer to the memory of the target board being designed. In-circuit emulation (ICE), where the ICE unit replaces the microprocessor on the target board and 'emulates' the actions of the target processor, is usually another essential tool.

An ICE gives the facility of testing and debugging system software and hardware *together* in the actual environment in which the system is to be used, but at the same time allows all the facilities of the development system to be employed.

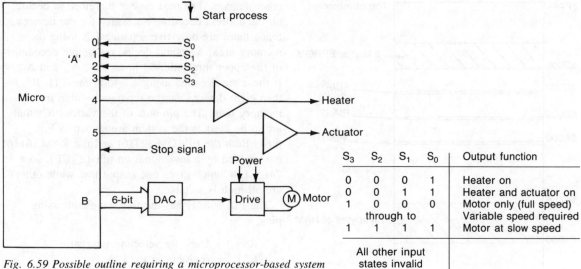

Fig. 6.59 Possible outline requiring a microprocessor-based system

S_3	S_2	S_1	S_0	Output function
0	0	0	1	Heater on
0	0	1	1	Heater and actuator on
1	0	0	0	Motor only (full speed)
	through to			Variable speed required
1	1	1	1	Motor at slow speed

All other input
states invalid

This reduces the time spent testing the board and the software, and enables faults in design to be isolated to either the software or the hardware early on and for these to be quickly corrected. However, ICE systems are relatively costly and are considered beyond the scope of this book. We shall look at design with the minimum of aids.

Suppose we require a microprocessor system that can perform a task such as the control of a small process consisting of a set of digital inputs and a motor, heater and actuator as outputs (see Fig. 6.59). The action required is that, depending on the state of the sensor inputs, which are read every 5 seconds, the output devices are set according to the table given with the diagram.

This is only an illustration of *one* task that the final target board design could perform. It does, however, point up the sort of minimal system requirements which are:

1. an 8-bit CPU,
2. a limited requirement for RAM,
3. probably no more than 2k bytes of ROM,
4. one parallel interface chip.

This could lead us to draw up the following specification:

CPU : 6809 (Motorola) (or 6502/6802/Z80 etc.)
RAM : 2k bytes 6116
EPROM : 2k bytes 2716

PIA : 6821 (Motorola)
Address decoder : One 74LS138 or similar
Clock speed : 4 MHz crystal to give 1 MHz clock

Memory allocation could be chosen as:

Memory map :   RAM at $4000
EPROM at $E000
PIA at $A000*

Obviously there are several microcomputer ICs that can perform this task, so let's assume we allow future expansion of the design to include another PIA so that a keypad can be interfaced and possibly a simple display, an ACIA communication (serial interface IC) for serial communication plus another 2k bytes of RAM.

The memory map becomes:

RAM 4k bytes from $4000 to $47FF
EPROM 2k bytes from $E000 to $E3FF
PIA (1) at $A000 to $A003
PIA (2) at $B000 to $B003
ACIA at $C000 to $C001

You can see that this leaves a lot of spare space in the available memory. An 8-bit microprocessor like the 6809 has a 16-bit address bus giving memory space $0000 up to $FFFF (64k bytes). Also, the decisions as to where to place memory

---

* A PIA requires four memory locations.

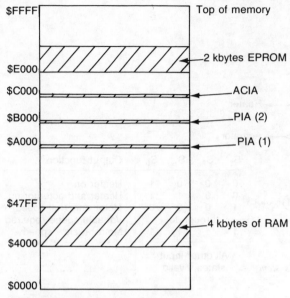

(a) Proposed memory map for system

(b) Memory map for interrupt vectors

| Memory Map for Vector Locations | | Interrupt Vector Description |
MS	LS	
FFFE	FFFF	RESET
FFFC	FFFD	NMI
FFFA	FFFB	SWI
FFF8	FFF9	IRQ
FFF6	FFF7	FIRQ
FFF4	FFF5	SWI2
FFF2	FFF3	SWI3
FFF0	FFF1	Reserved

Fig. 6.60 The memory map

and I/O ICs within the memory space are totally under the control of the designer. The RAM memory could just as well be placed at $0000 up to $07FF or from $8000 to $87FF. Similarly, the I/O chips could be moved to other base addresses. Only the EPROM has restriction placed on it, since the vectored addresses of the 6809 (see Fig. 6.60) are at the top of memory. This point will be explained later.

Because the memory space is almost empty we can allow overwrite for most of the ICs without one memory or I/O chip overlapping another's space. This means that total address decoding is not a requirement. The address decoder only has to ensure that the actual ICs used do not overlap each

other's space. The next task is therefore to decide on the address decoding necessary for the devices. Since there are only five separate ICs using the memory area, we could decide on simple decoding of the upper three address lines, A_{13}, A_{14} and A_{15}. If these are decoded using a 3-to-8 line TTL IC, then eight devices can be separated within the memory map. The pin-outs of the various ICs that are to be used in the system are shown in Fig. 6.61. Both the EPROM (2716) and the RAM (6116) are enabled by a low signal on pin 18 ($\overline{CE}$), so a 74LS 138 which gives one output low while others are all high is suitable.

The PIA (6821) has the following addressing pins:

$$\left.\begin{matrix} RS0 \\ RS1 \end{matrix}\right\} \text{ Used for selecting internal registers in the PIA}$$

and $$\left.\begin{matrix} CS0 \\ CS1 \\ \overline{CS2} \end{matrix}\right\} \text{ Address decoding pins}$$

Register select 0 and register select 1 must be connected to address lines A_0 and A_1, respectively, so that the PIA addresses are contiguous, and with simple decoding $\overline{CS2}$ could be connected to a suitable output line of the address decoder while CS0 and CS1 (both active high) can be permanently wired to V_{CC} via a 1 kΩ resistor. But as we shall see later this is not possible for the chosen addresses.

Let's consider the memory locations required for the initial design. In small systems this is relatively easy, since only minimal addressing is being used. What is required is a table showing all the address lines and the number of these necessary for each memory and I/O chip — see Table 6.9.

Here × = don't care (i.e. the address line is not decoded). With this minimal decoding the following address space and overwrite will be set up:

  (i) RAM from $4000 to $47FF
       with overwrite up to $5FFF (since A_{11} and
       A_{12} are not decoded),
  (ii) PIA 1 from $A000 to $A003
       with overwrite up to $AFFF,
  (iii) PIA 2 from $B000 to $B003
       with overwrite up to $BFFF,
  (iv) ACIA from $C000 to $C001
       with overwrite up to $CFFF,
  and finally:

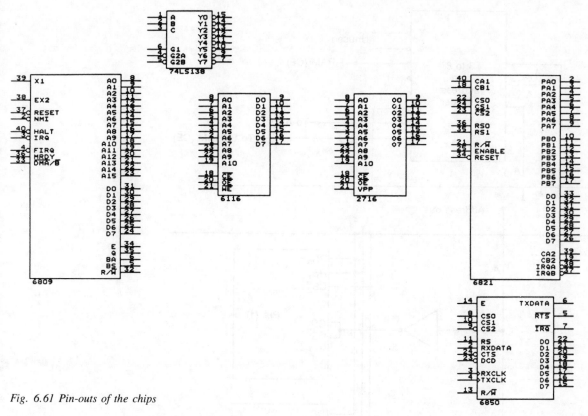

Fig. 6.61 Pin-outs of the chips

Table 6.9

A_{15}	A_{14}	A_{13}	A_{12}	A_{11}	A_{10}	A_9	A_8	A_7	A_6	A_5	A_4	A_3	A_2	A_1	Device
0	1	0	×	×	0	0	0	0	0	0	0	0	0	0	RAM
0	1	0	×	×	1	1	1	1	1	1	1	1	1	1	4k bytes
1	0	1	0	×	×	×	×	×	×	×	×	×	0	0	} PIA 1
1	0	1	0	×	×	×	×	×	×	×	×	×	1	1	
1	0	1	1	×	×	×	×	×	×	×	×	×	0	0	} PIA 2
1	0	1	1	×	×	×	×	×	×	×	×	×	1	1	
1	1	0	0	×	×	×	×	×	×	×	×	×	×	0	} ACIA
1	1	0	0	×	×	×	×	×	×	×	×	×	×	1	
1	1	1	×	×	×	0	0	0	0	0	0	0	0	0	EPROM
1	1	1	×	×	×	1	1	1	1	1	1	1	1	1	

(v) EPROM from \$E000 to \$E3FF but with overwrite to the top of memory at \$FFFF.

What becomes apparent from the table is that address line A_{12} must also be decoded in addition to A_{13}, A_{14} and A_{15} in order to fully separate the I/O chips. One solution to this is shown in Fig. 6.62, where the 3-to-8 line decoder (active low outputs)

has its Y_5 output ($A_{15}.\overline{A}_{14}.A_{13} = 101$) connected to both the PIAs and their $\overline{CS2}$ pins. In order to separate the two PIAs, address line A_{12} is also decoded so that when

$A_{12} = 0$ (addresses \$A000 to \$AFFF) PIA 1 only is enabled

but when

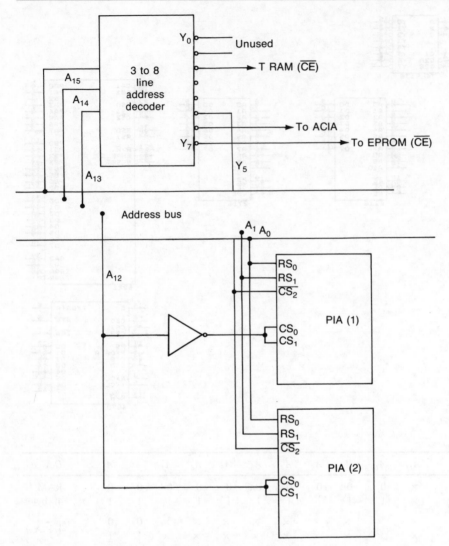

Fig. 6.62 Possible address decoding solution

$A_{12} = 1$ (addresses \$B000 to \$BFFF) only PIA 2 is enabled.

Hopefully there will be a spare invertor in the design to allow this simple decoding to be set up. Alternatively, we could relocate the PIAs to addresses such as \$6000 and \$8000 where no additional decoding of lower order address lines would be necessary. This can be shown by Table 6.10.

There are obviously several other variations that could be used. For one of these, to allow for more RAM expansion, we could locate the initial 2k of RAM at \$0000 and move the PIAs up to \$8000 and

Table 6.10

Top address lines			Initial design	Alternative
A_{15}	A_{14}	A_{13}		
0	0	0	unused	unused
0	0	1	unused	unused
0	1	0	RAM	RAM
0	1	1	unused	PIA 1
1	0	0	unused	PIA 2
1	0	1	PIA (1 & 2)	spare
1	1	0	ACIA	ACIA
1	1	1	EPROM	EPROM

74LS139

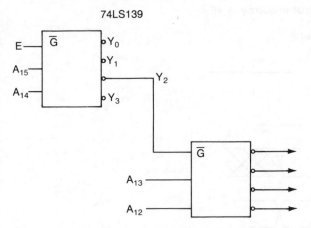

Fig. 6.63 Using address decoders to partition memory

$9000. However, let us assume that the user still wants his initial specification so that the address decoding circuit of Fig. 6.62 is the one to be used in the design.

Some 3-to-8 line decoders for bus systems are:

- 74131 which has address registers and a clock input,
- 74137 with address latches (no clock),
- 74138 simple but fast 3-to-8 line decoding (no registers),
- 74139 dual 2-to-4 line decoder (no registers).

In our example the 74138 will be used. Incidentally, these ICs can also be wired to partition memory by cascading the outputs to enable decoding of lower order addresses (see Fig. 6.63). In this circuit, using the dual 2-to-4 line decoder IC 74139, when $A_{15} A_{14} = 10$, Y_2 goes low and enables the lower 2-to-4 decoder. This allows the addresses $8000, $9000, $A000 and $B000 to be selected according to the value of A_{12} and A_{13}. This memory section has been partitioned into 4 kilobyte blocks.

The design of any microprocessor-based system requires a careful study of bus and control signal timing. It would be essential to have the data sheets of the processor being used and of the memory and I/O chips. An easy mistake would be to select a fast microprocessor and interface it to relatively slow memory chips. The typical timing diagram of the 6809 is shown in Fig. 6.64. The outputs from the 6809 that are of concern are:

E: The main timing signal that is derived

from the crystal oscillator, and is a quarter of the crystal frequency.

Q: A quadrative clock signal that leads E by a quarter cycle.

BA: Bus available (not needed in this design).

BS: Bus status, which when decoded with BA indicates the processor state (also not needed).

R/$\overline{W}$: A control signal that shows the direction of data transfer. A low state indicates that the processor is writing data onto the data bus and vice versa.

With a 4 MHz crystal the E signal will be running at 1 MHz, giving an instruction cycle time of 1 μs. From the timing diagram the available access time for memory chips is therefore approximately 690 ns. This is the difference between the R/$\overline{W}$ line going high and the minimum data set-up time required by the 6809 before the E signal returns low.

The access times of the two memory ICs are:

RAM 6116   Access time = 120 ns max,
EPROM 2716   Access time = 450 ns max,

which are well within the available time limits.

The PIA, which requires both the E and R/$\overline{W}$ control signals for correct operation, has a typical output data delay time of just 290 ns max.

To control the read/write operation of the RAM and to read the ROM, the R/$\overline{W}$ signal must be inverted from the 6809 to the $\overline{OE}$ (output enable). Note also that the $\overline{WE}$ (write enable) of the RAM is to be directly connected to the R/$\overline{W}$ pin (Fig. 6.65).

The clock circuit is internal to the 6809 and only requires the connection of a suitable crystal (4 MHz in this case) between pins 38 and 39. Two 24 pF capacitors are specified by Motorola to be connected as shown in Fig. 6.65. Since the design is not using DMA/BREQ, MRDY and HALT these pins can be connected via a suitable pull-up to V_{CC}.

The interrupt lines FIRQ (fast interrupt request) and IRQ (normal interrupt request) are connected to IRQA and IRQB of the PIA respectively. The NMI (non maskable interrupt) is also available. Since the IRQA/B of a PIA is open-drain, pull-up resistors on the interrupt lines are required. If the extra PIA is added, its IRQA and IRQB can be wired-or to the same pull-ups. This allows either PIA to interrupt the processor.

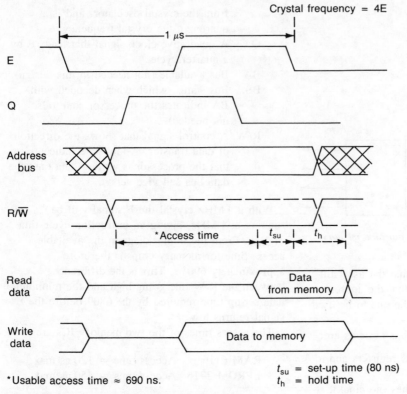

Crystal frequency = 4E

E

Q

Address bus

R/W̄

*Access time | t_{su} | t_h

Read data   Data from memory

Write data   Data to memory

t_{su} = set-up time (80 ns)
t_h = hold time

*Usable access time ≈ 690 ns.

Fig. 6.64 Simplified timing diagram for the 6809

A RESET circuit must be included, for without this the processor will not be able to start at the correct point in the program at power-up or if a reset is required. The 6809 $\overline{\text{RESET}}$ is on pin 37 and when a low level is detected on this pin the processor goes to the RESET vector location at the top of memory ($FFFE and $FFFF) and fetches the start address of the program. This start address is loaded into the 6809's program counter and program execution begins. The input circuitry on pin 37 is a Schmitt type, so it is quite possible to have a simple CR network at this point with sufficient time constant to hold $\overline{\text{RESET}}$ low for a few clock cycles to allow the crystal oscillator to stabilise. However, in the design some invertors are already required so part of a 74LS14 (Hex Schmitt invertor) is used to buffer the CR network and switch to pin 37. The CR time constant is set to approximately 2 ms by $R_1 C_1$, which also sets the input current of the 74LS14 invertor (this is typically 0.4 mA). D_1 is included to rapidly discharge C_1 when the power is switched off.

The hardware design has followed a logical path, namely:

1. Task description
2. Specification
3. Memory allocation
4. Address decoding
5. Timing and control signals
6. Clock circuitry
7. Connection of interrupt
8. Design of the RESET

The proposed hardware circuit is shown in Fig. 6.65 and this incorporates all the features already discussed. Meanwhile the software development should have been continuing alongside the hardware so that at this point a suitable proven test program could be loaded into the EPROM and the hardware checked. Bascially the software, for a minimum test run, must:

(a) Define the start address of the program and load this into the reset vector location ($FFFE and $FFFF).

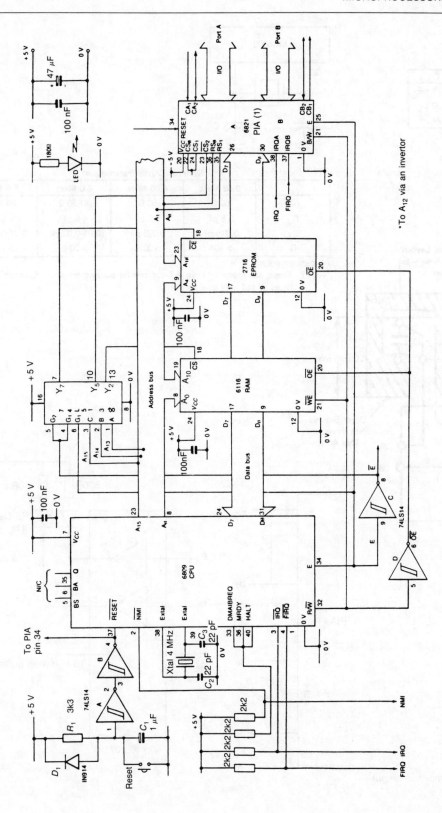

Fig. 6.65 6809 Target board (basic system)

Y1	C_{in}	C_{out}
8 MHz	18 pF	18 pF
6 MHz	20 pF	20 pF
4 MHz	24 pF	24 pF

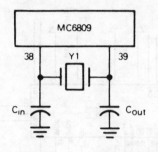

Nominal Crystal Parameters*

	3.58 MHz	4.00 MHz	6.0 MHz	8.0 MHz
RS	60 Ω	50 Ω	30-50 Ω	20-40 Ω
C_0	3.5 pF	6.5 pF	4-6 pF	4-6 pF
C_1	0.015 pF	0.025 pF	0.01-0.02 pF	0.01-0.02 pF
Q	>40K*	>30 K	>20 K	>20 K

All parameters are 10%

*NOTE: These are representative AT-cut crystal parameters only. Crystals of other types of cut may also be used.

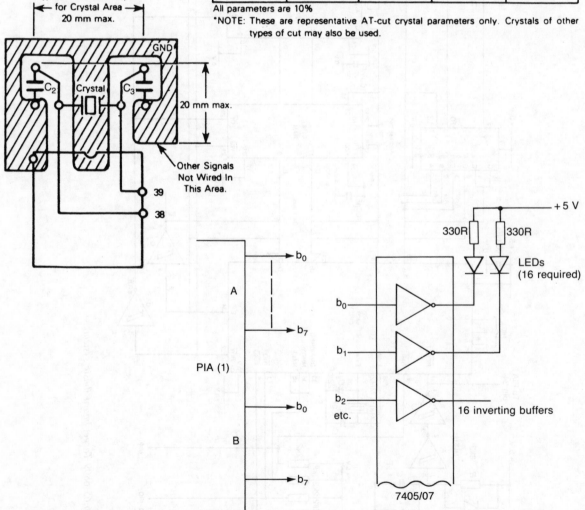

Fig. 6.66 Simple output test circuit

(b) Set the system and user stack pointers. These should be set to point to upper portions of the RAM.

(c) Define any 'interrupt' vector addresses.

(d) Initialise the PIA so that I/O conditions can be set up.

(e) Test the RAM and I/O.

The simplest test would be to make both the A and B sides of the PIA outputs and connect these via suitable buffers to LEDs. The software could then be made to output a pattern read from the RAM with a suitable delay between outputs to allow visual examination. If LEDs are not used a CRO or meter can be employed to read the outputs at the ports. (See Fig. 6.66.) Let us assume a very simple program that first writes a checkerboard pattern to 1k of the RAM and then reads this back and outputs the result to the ports. As you can see from the flow chart, Fig. 6.67, the micro system can be made to stop if this data byte read back from memory is not $55. This sort of program to test RAM and I/O can be repeated with the hex value $AA.

The program start address will be $E000, i.e. the base address of the EPROM. This address must be loaded into the RESET vector and this is done in the example software by using the FDB (form double byte) directive which appears as the last statement.

The system and user stack pointers are set to point to upper areas in RAM, in this case the system stack at the top of RAM ($43FF) and the user stack at a slightly lower address ($42FF).

The PIA type 6821 has to be set up so that both its A and B sides are outputs. The initialisation routine first clears the A side control register (bit 2 is then 0) to gain access to the Data Direction Register A. In this I/O chip the Data Register and Data Direction Register (DRA/DDRA) share one address and access is controlled by bit 2 of the CRA. The DDRA is then loaded with all 1s, which sets the A side to all outputs. The instructions are repeated for the B side of the PIA (addressses $A003 for the CRB and $A002 for the DRB/DDRB) to set its I/O lines as all outputs also. Finally, the value of bit 2 in both CRA and CRB is set to 7 so that in the program when PORTA or PORTB are called it is the data registers not the data direction registers that are used.

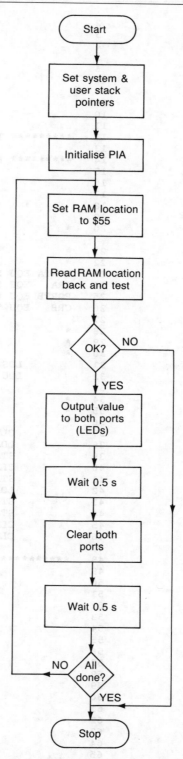

Fig. 6.67 Flow chart for part of checkerboard test

```
                        2
                        3
                        4
                        5
                        6
                        7
                        8
                        9
                       10
                       11
                       12   ********* TEST ROUTINE
                       13
                       14   ********* PROGRAM ORIGIN
                       15
                       16            DEFSEG FIRST,ABSOLUTE
                       17            SEG FIRST
=E000                  18            ORG $E000
                       19
                       20   *            **************
                       21   *            *   EQUATES   *
                       22   *            **************
=A000          PORTA   23   PORTA EQU $A000
=A001                  24   CRA   EQU $A001
=A002                  25   PORTB EQU $A002
=A003                  26   CRB   EQU $A003
                       27
                       28   *            *********************
                       29   *            * SET STACK POINTERS *
                       30   *            *********************
E000 10 CE 43FF        31         LDS #$43FF ; set system stack
E004 CE 42FF           32         LDU #$42FF ; set user stack
                       33
                       34   *            *****************
                       35   *            * INITIALISE PIA *
                       36   *            *****************
E007 7F A001           37         CLR CRA ; get access to DDRA
E00A 86 FF             38         LDA #$FF
E00C B7 A000           39         STA PORTA ; set A side as outputs
E00F 7F A003           40         CLR CRB ;
E012 B7 A002           41         STA PORTB ; set B side as outputs
E015 86 04             42         LDA #4   ;
E017 B7 A001           43         STA CRA ; allow access to portA
E01A B7 A003           44         STA CRB ; allow access to portB
E01D 7F A000           45         CLR PORTA ; all LEDS off portA
E020 7F A002           46         CLR PORTB ; all LEDS off portB
                       47
                       48   *******************************************
                       49
                       50
                       51
                       52
                       53
                       54
                       55
                       56
                       57
                       58
                       59
                       60
                       61
                       62
                       63
                       64
                       65
```

```
              66
              67
              68
              69
              70    *       *********************
              71    *       *  TEST PROGRAM   *
              72    *       *********************
E023 86 55    73           LDA #$55 ; load pattern
E025 C6 AA    74           LDB #$AA ; next pattern
E027 10 8E 4000 75         LDY #$4000 ; set pointer to RAM
E02B A7 A0    76  RAML5    STA 0,Y+ ; put pattern into RAM
E02D 10 8C 4200 77         CMPY #$4200 ; at top of RAM?
E031 26 F8    78           BNE RAML5 ; if not continue load
E033 10 8E 4000 79         LDY #$4000 ; reset pointer
E037 A6 A0    80  RAMC5    LDA 0,Y+ ; get RAM data
E039 81 55    81           CMPA #$55 ; is it correct?
E03B 26 46    82           BNE FIN  ; if not end
E03D B7 A000  83           STA PORTA ; output to portA
E040 B7 A002  84           STA PORTB ; and to portB
E043 17 003E  85           LBSR WAIT ; time delay
E046 7F A000  86           CLR PORTA ; output zeros
E049 7F A002  87           CLR PORTB ; output zeros
E04C 17 0035  88           LBSR WAIT ; time delay
E04F 10 8C 4200 89         CMPY #$4200 ; at top of RAM?
E053 26 E2    90           BNE RAMC5 ; if not continue
E055 10 8E 4000 91         LDY #$4000 ; reset pointer
E059 E7 A0    92  RAMLA    STB 0,Y+ ; put data into RAM
E05B 10 8C 4200 93         CMPY #$4200 ; at top of RAM?
E05F 26 F8    94           BNE RAMLA ; if not continue
E061 10 8E 4000 95         LDY #$4000 ; reset pointer
E065 E6 A0    96  RAMCA    LDB 0,Y+ ; read RAM
E067 C1 AA    97           CMPB #$AA ; is it correct?
E069 26 18    98           BNE FIN ; if not stop
E06B F7 A000  99           STB PORTA ; output to portA
E06E F7 A002  100          STB PORTB ; output to portB
E071 17 0010  101          LBSR WAIT ; go to delay
E074 7F A000  102          CLR PORTA ; all LEDs off
E077 7F A002  103          CLR PORTB ; all LEDs off
E07A 17 0007  104          LBSR WAIT ; go to delay
E07D 10 8C 4200 105        CMPY #$4200 ; at top of RAM?
E081 26 E2    106          BNE RAMCA
E083 3F       107  FIN     SWI
              108   *
              109   *       *********************
              110   *       *  SUBROUTINE WAIT  *
              111   *       *********************
E084 8E D000  112  WAIT    LDX #$D000 ; load multiplier
E087 12       113  LOOP    NOP
E088 30 1F    114          LEAX -1,X  ; decrement counter
E08A 26 FB    115          BNE LOOP
E08C 39       116          RTS
              117   *
              118   *
              119   *       *********************
              120   *       *  SET VECTOR LOCATION *
              121   *       *********************
=E7FE         122          ORG $E7FE
E7FE E000     123          FDB $E000
              124          END
```

Fig. 6.68

The PIA is now initialised and the main test routine can be run. This begins by loading ACCA with the hex value $55 and ACCB with the hex value $AA. The index register Y is set to point to the RAM base address $4000 and then all locations from $4000 to $41FF are set to $55 by storing the contents of ACCA indexed from Y with zero offset. When the top of the 1k block has been set, the program then outputs each RAM location via ACCA to both ports with a short delay of approximately 0.5 s between reads. If ACCA does not receive the value $55 the program stops. Otherwise the process is repeated using ACCB and the hex value $AA. The assembly language program with its assembled code is given in Fig. 6.68.

This is a very simple program that uses most of the registers in the CPU and tests the output lines. It tests, of course, only a tiny fraction of the instruction set and the variety of addressing modes, but if it runs correctly on the board there is a good probability that no faults exist. The program should start at power-up or when the reset switch is operated.

6.8 DESIGN PROBLEMS AND EXERCISES

1 Two switches are required to give an output function according to the following table:

B	A	Output
0	0	1
0	1	0
1	0	1
1	1	1

Obtain the minimised Boolean expression and design a logic circuit.

2 Three sensors P, Q and R are required from a process to give two digital outputs as follows:

R	Q	P	O_1	O_2
0	0	0	0	1
0	0	1	0	1
0	1	0	1	0
0	1	1	1	0
1	0	0	1	0
1	0	1	1	0
1	1	0	0	0
1	1	1	1	0

Design the most easily implemented logic circuit.

3 Four inputs to a logic board are required to implement the logic equation:

$$F = \bar{A}.B.C.\bar{D} + \bar{A}.B.\bar{C}.D + A.B.\bar{C}.D + A.B.C.D + A.B.C.D$$

(a) Draw the 4-variable K-map.
(b) Minimise the expression.
(c) Design a NAND-only logic circuit.

4 Design a logic circuit that will give a logic high output when the majority of its five inputs are high. What would be the best ways of implementing the circuit?

5 Convert the logic circuits of Fig. 6.69 to NAND-only.

6 (a) Determine the logic circuit for a 4-bit digital multiplexer with inputs A, B, C and D and control inputs E and F. Write a text file suitable for use with the PLD Assembler discussed in this chapter to implement this circuit. Expand the design to provide an additional enable input (active high).

(b) Design the logic circuit for a 4-bit demultiplexer.

7 Standard circuits for ÷3 and ÷5 counters are shown in Fig. 6.70.
(a) Prove that the count sequence is correct.

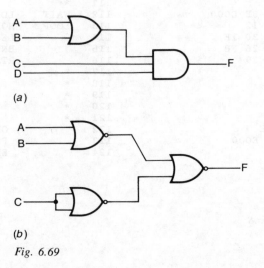

(a)

(b)

Fig. 6.69

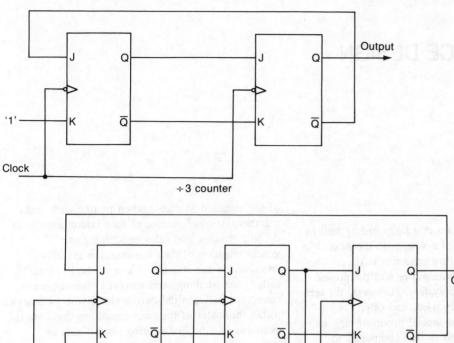

Fig. 6.70

(b) Modify the design using D-bistables.

(c) Design a synchronous ÷6 Johnson counter.

8 The circuit of a one-off address decoder is required where if one of the address lines A_{13}, A_{14} and A_{15} is high a 2-to-4 line decoder with inputs of address lines A_{11} and A_{12} to give four outputs Y_0, Y_1, Y_2 and Y_3 is enabled. Show how the design could be implemented using a GAL 16V8.

9 Modify the 6809 target system to give:
(a) RAM (2k) from address $2000,
(b) the PIA at address $3000,
(c) EPROM (2k) from address $E800 with overwrite to $FFFF.

7 INTERFACE DESIGN

7.1 DEFINITIONS

An interface is any circuit that links one system to another or one portion of a system to the next. We could say that the coupling capacitor is the 'interface' between a preamplifier and the power output stage in an audio system. However, the term 'interface' is now widely used, and often understood, to mean the special group of circuits and devices that are used to link computers to peripherals. The peripheral devices on the output side are printers, plotters, motors, DACs, other computers, etc., while on the input side signals come from scanners, sensors, switches and so on. The interface is really the 'translator' of signals from one device to another. Thus the tasks of interface circuits include:

- buffering, e.g. impedance matching or temporary data storage,
- isolation to prevent damage to either the sender or the receiver, depending on which is the more prone to damage,
- changing the number of lines; this may involve multiplexing or converting from parallel to serial,
- conversion, i.e. analog to digital or digital to analog,
- level changing, i.e. power or voltage amplification,
- timing adjustment so that the exchange of data is synchronised.

Normally, for the commonly used interface situations, such as the linking of a computer to a serial device, there will be a well defined industry standard. Some typical examples are the RS-232-C, IEEE 488 and the RS-423-A, all of which have their own sets of rules governing the way in which the interface should be made. These rules are called *protocols*. It is obviously advisable to have a copy of the standard available when putting such links together. Another feature of data interchange is to do with timing, and rules concerning the synchronization of data transmission are also contained in the standards. The method is usually called 'handshaking' and involves control signals connected between the two devices, with one device (often the faster of the two) signalling that data is available to send and waiting until it gets an acknowledging signal back from the other device to say that it is ready to receive the data, and so on.

From the foregoing paragraph it is clear that the area to be covered in interface design is very wide. This chapter can only cover some of the more standard techniques.

7.2 INTERFACING BETWEEN LOGIC

It was pointed out in Chapter 6 that there is now a lot of overlap between the different logic families, with 74HCT and 74ACT (both CMOS) being pin and level compatible with 74LS TTL. But there will still be situations where it will be necessary to link logic signals from one logic family to another, i.e. CMOS to TTL, TTL to CMOS, and ECL to TTL or CMOS. The situation is made more difficult if the power supply to one set of logic is different to the other. This is very apparent when interfacing ECL which has a -5.2 V supply. Special purpose ICs must be used.

Logic power supplies
TTL $+5$ V
ECL -5.2 V
CMOS $+3$ V up to $+18$ V

Obviously, special care is needed if signals from CMOS (4000 series) running from a supply of 10 V are to be connected into TTL or vice versa.

First let's consider the more usual case of both

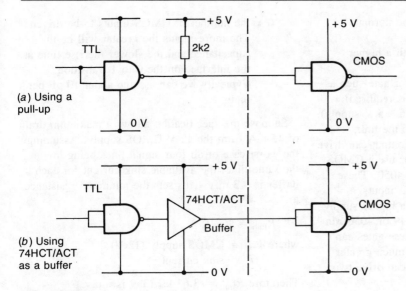

(a) Using a pull-up

(b) Using 74HCT/ACT as a buffer

TTL to CMOS

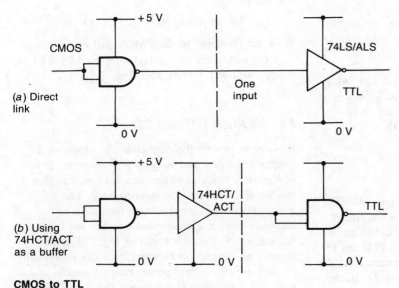

(a) Direct link

(b) Using 74HCT/ACT as a buffer

CMOS to TTL

Fig. 7.1

systems having the same power rail of 5 V. Since 74HCT/ACT are level compatible, the simplest interface between TTL and CMOS is to use an HCT or ACT buffer between the two systems. If this is not possible then a pull-up resistor on the TTL output is essential to 'lift' the logic 1 level of the TTL above the threshold of the CMOS. Figure 7.1 illustrates the possibilities. Note that for CMOS

to TTL, with both using the same +5 V supply, any CMOS gate output will drive one low power Schottky TTL (74LS/ALS) input. The general rules are:

- TTL to CMOS (both with +5 V supply): best to use 74HCT/ACT CMOS as the link, otherwise the TTL output must have a pull-up resistor (2k2 is the normal value).

- TTL to CMOS (CMOS with a higher supply voltage):
buffer with an open-collector gate such as a 7406 or 7407 (a pull-up is required).
- CMOS to TTL (both with a +5 V supply): best to use 74HCT/ACT as the link, otherwise one CMOS gate output can drive one LS/ALS TTL input. Or use a CMOS buffer such as the 4049 or 4050. These can drive two standard TTL inputs.
- CMOS to TTL (CMOS at a higher supply rail, up to 15 V): use a 4049 or 4050 run from the TTL 5 V rail. These gates can withstand an input voltage much greater than their supply and they can drive two TTL inputs.

The use of pull-ups should be restricted if you want to maintain operating speed. They slow down the rising edge of the logic waveform.

DESIGN EXAMPLE 1

A link is required between a pcb which has 74LS TTL to another board containing CMOS running at a supply of +12 V. Four logic lines are to be connected from the TTL to the CMOS.

Solution

Following the general rules we need one 74LS07 hex buffer. Each buffer in this IC has the circuit shown in Fig. 7.2(*b*). The main part of the buffer is powered from the 5 V used for the TTL and the open-collector output transistor is connected via the pull-up resistor to the 12 V CMOS supply. Each output in the IC can withstand a maximum voltage of 30 V when off in the high state and sink 30 mA in the low state. The full circuit connections are also shown in Fig. 7.2(*a*).

The value of the pull-up resistor to be specified depends on three factors:

- (*a*) the maximum current that is available from the 12 V supply,
- (*b*) the maximum sink current of the 74LS07 output (30 mA), and

(*c*) the number of CMOS inputs to be driven. The more inputs the greater will be the capacitance and the slower the rise time at the interface on the 0 to 1 transition. Typically we can assume about 10 pF per input.

Suppose the specification allows a maximum drain of 15 mA from the 12 V CMOS supply. Assuming the worst case of all four signal lines being low at the same time, the available sink current for each buffer is 3.3 mA. This sets the minimum resistance to:

$$R_{min} = V_{dd}/I_s$$

where V_{dd} = CMOS supply (12 V)
   I_s = sink current

Therefore R_{min} = 3.63 kΩ (3k9 is n.p.v.)

If the number of CMOS inputs being driven does not exceed three, the time constant formed by R_p and C_{in} is:

$$T = 3.9 \times 10^3 \times 30 \times 10^{-9} = 117 \text{ ns}$$

Since the threshold of the CMOS will be 6 V (half V_{dd}) the additional time delay introduced by the link is approximately 100 ns. (See Fig. 7.3.)

7.3 ISOLATION TECHNIQUES

In order to protect the outputs or the inputs of a system it is often necessary to provide some form of electrical isolation. The main devices that give this are the *relay* and the *opto-isolator*. The important point of any isolation method is to eliminate electrical connection between the input and output. This is illustrated in Fig. 7.4, where there is no connection between the input power rails (+ and −), the output power rails (+ and −) as well as no electrical link between the signal paths. This isolation protects the low voltage or more sensitive side of the link from being damaged by an inadvertent spike or fault on the higher voltage side.

The electromagnetic relay, still an excellent device to specify for many applications, achieves the isolation because the coil is operated by the input signal and the movement of the armature caused by the coil current is used to open or close electrical contacts which are on the output side. The electrical isolation depends on both the insulation

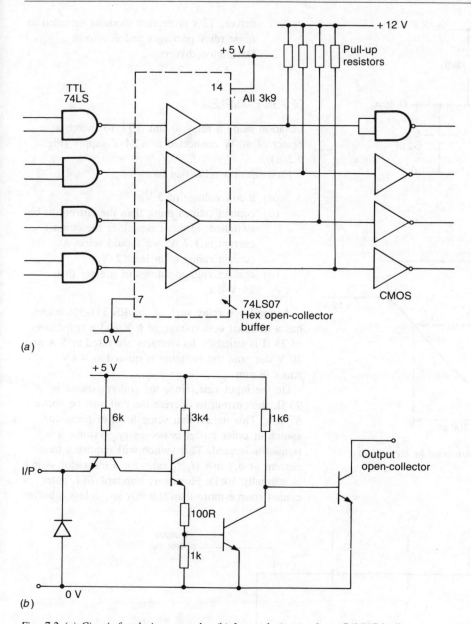

(a)

(b)

Fig. 7.2 (a) Circuit for design example; (b) Internal circuit of one 74LS07 buffer

between the contacts and the coil connections and on the insulation at the relay pins on the plug and socket. This insulation will be extremely high.

With a relay there are two points to watch out for:

    (a) Ensure that the relay coil voltage is not greater than the power rail of the signal source, otherwise there is still the danger that the coil supply can cause damage to the input driver. It is best to power the relay coil from the same supply as the driver if this is possible.

    (b) A diode must be included across the coil to prevent the back e.m.f. generated when the coil is switched off from damaging the

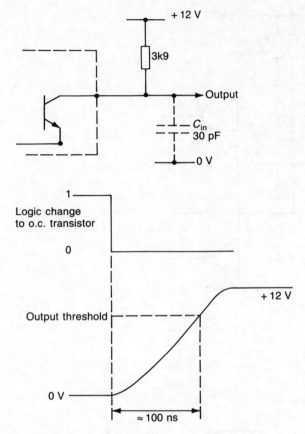

Fig. 7.3 Rise time delay introduced by the pull-up

driver. This protection diode is included in some relay packages and is also in Darlington drivers.

DESIGN EXAMPLE 2

Isolation using a relay to link TTL to switch a heater of 40 W connected to a 24 V supply (Fig. 7.5(a)).

First select a relay that has:

(a) a coil voltage of 5 V;
(b) contact ratings more than the current to be switched; in this case, since the contact current is 1.7 A, we should select a contact rating of at least 2 A;
(c) contact voltage ratings of greater than 24 V d.c.

A small pcb relay such as the RS 351-566 which has a nominal coil voltage of 6 V and a resistance of 75 Ω is suitable. Its contacts are rated at 5 A and 30 V d.c. and the isolation is quoted as 4 kV r.m.s./8 mm.

On the input side, since the coil resistance is 75 Ω, the current to operate the coil will be above 67 mA. This means that some form of transistor switch or other buffer is necessary. Assume a transistor is used. This switch will require a base current of 6.7 mA (I_c:I_b ratio for a transistor switch is normally 10:1). However, standard TTL gates cannot source more than 0.5 mA so, unless a buffer

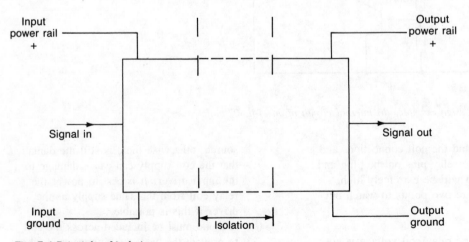

Fig. 7.4 Principle of isolation

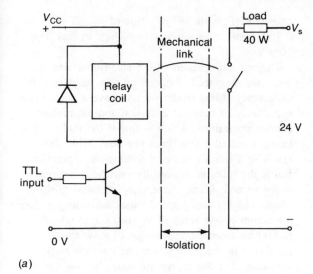

(a)

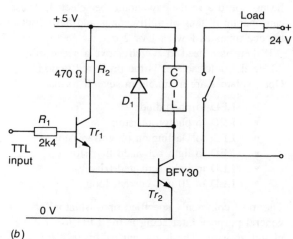

(b)

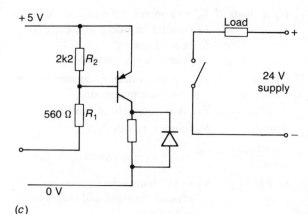

(c)

Fig. 7.5 Relay isolation

gate is to be used, an additional transistor is required. At first sight it might appear that the overall switch could be a Darlington. However, the $V_{ce(sat)}$ of a Darlington can often be more than 1 V which would restrict the coil voltage to 4 V and this is not sufficient to operate the relay fully.

One solution is shown in Fig. 7.5(b) where an additional transistor is used to buffer the TTL to the switch driving the relay. This is almost like a Darlington but in this case the collector of the first transistor is connected via a resistor to the 5 V rail. This reduces the $V_{ce(sat)}$ of the connection to probably less than 0.2 V. The additional transistor, when switched by a logic high, has to pass the 6.7 mA to the main switching transistor. The two resistor values are calculated as follows:

$$R_1 = [V_{OH} - 2V_{BE(sat)}]/I_{B1}$$

where V_{OH} is the TTL logic 1 state (2.4 V)
$V_{BE(sat)}$ is 0.7 V
I_{B1} is 0.5 mA (assuming an $I_c:I_b$ ratio of 15:1)

Therefore

$$R_1 = (2.4 - 1.2)/0.5 \text{ k}\Omega = 2.4 \text{ k}\Omega$$
$$R_2 = [V_{CC} - (V_{CE(sat)} + V_{BE(sat)})]/I_{C1}$$
$$= [5 - 0.8]/6.7 \text{ k}\Omega = 627 \text{ }\Omega$$

To prevent Tr_1 fully saturating, R_2 should be about 470 Ω. In fact, in this example the collector of Tr_1 can be directly connected to the 5 V rail since its maximum circuit power dissipation will be less than 50 mW. The resistor is in circuit to reduce the power dissipation of this transistor.

An alternative circuit arrangement is to use a p-n-p transistor as the switch, as shown in Fig. 7.5(c). If the TTL signal can be active low, only one transistor is necessary.

$$R_1 = V_{CC} - (V_{O1} + V_{BE(sat)})/I_B$$

where V_{O1} is the TTL low state (0.4 V)
  $V_{BE(sat)}$ is 0.7 V
and $I_B = 6.7$ mA (as before).

Therefore $R_1 = [5 - (0.4 + 0.7)]/6.7$ kΩ
  $= 582$ Ω (560 Ω is n.p.v.)

A final version of this relay interface uses a logic powerFET as the switch, the type of FET that has a very low gate threshold voltage ($V_{GS(th)}$) and can therefore be easily switched into conduction by a TTL logic 1 level (Fig. 7.6). An RFL1N20L(LL)

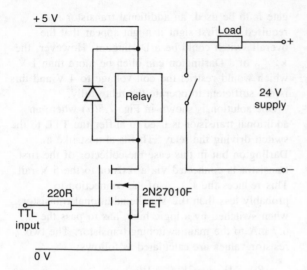

Fig. 7.6 Relay interface using a logic powerFET as a switch

or 2N27010F are suitable types. Their short-form data is as follows:

	RFL1N20L(LL)	2N27010F
$I_{d(max)}$	1 A	1.3 A
P_{tot}	8 W	1.2 W
$R_{ds(on)}$	3.65 Ω	0.35 Ω
$V_{ds(max)}$	200 V	60 V
$V_{gs(th)}$	2 V	2 V
g_m	0.8 S	1.2 S

Obviously the 2N27010F is the better device to use, although the other powerFET would also work in the circuit. Both have a low enough threshold to allow direct connection to the TTL source and will be switched fully on when the logic level is high. A low value resistor, a few hundred ohms, should be wired in series with the gate to prevent any parasitic oscillations. The 'on' resistance of the FET needs to be as low as possible so that the relay coil receives most of the voltage. The voltage across the FET in the on state is given by:

$$V_{ds(on)} = I_d \cdot R_{ds(on)}$$

where I_d is the 67 mA required by the relay coil.

For the first FET the value of this drain to source voltage is 0.24 V, which reduces the coil voltage to 4.75 V. This will still operate the relay because the minimum coil voltage is specified as 4.2 V. But the

chosen FET, with its low value of $R_{ds(on)}$ of 0.35 Ω, only causes a loss in voltage of less than 50 mV.

The main limitations of the electromechanical relay are the speed of operation and the overall life expectancy. Most modern relays have a quoted life expectancy of between a million and ten million contact operations, which is fine if the relay is just being operated a few times per hour. This should result in a year or more of trouble-free operation. But if the relay is continually switched, say once every second, it may have to be replaced fairly often. The operating speed varies according to size; a medium power relay (2 W coil) might take 50 ms to 100 ms from the application of a switch-on command to the point where the contacts stop bouncing. Smaller relays are faster but for the fastest speed a reed relay should be selected. These can operate in tens of milliseconds and have contact bounce times as low as 1 or 2 ms.

If there is a need to switch above a speed of 20 Hz the opto-isolator is the preferred option. Opto-isolators are available in several formats:

- LED to photodiode
- LED to phototransistor
- LED to Darlington phototransistor
- LED to light activated thyristor
- LED to light activated triac
- LED to 20 mA current loop

The most commonly specified opto-isolator for general purpose interfacing is the LED to phototransistor. The important parameters are:

Input diode :	V_R reverse voltage rating of the LED
	V_F forward volt drop of the LED
	I_F forward current
	P_{tot} max. diode dissipation
Output transistor :	V_{CEO} max. collector–emitter voltage of the phototransistor
	P_{tot} max. transistor dissipation
Transfer :	h_{ctr} current transfer ratio
Switching speed :	t_{on} t_{off} both for the output transistor
Isolation :	The maximum voltage allowed between the input and output connections

Typical values for a range of devices are shown in Table 7.1.

Table 7.1 Short-form data for opto-isolators

Type	MCT2E	SFH610–2	MCT277	H11A1	MCA2231
V_R	3 V	6 V	3 V	6 V	3 V
V_F	1.5 V max at 20 mA	1.25 V at 60 mA	1.5 V max at 20 mA		1.5 V max at 20 mA
I_F	60 mA max	60 mA max	60 mA max	60 mA max	60 mA max
V_{CEO}	30 V	70 V	30 V	30 V	30 V
Transfer ratio h_{ctr} (min)	20%	40% at $I_F = 10$ mA	100% at $I_F = 10$ mA	50%	500%
Speed (type)	t_{on} 3 μs t_{off} 2.7 μs (100 Ω load)	t_{on} 5 μs t_{off} 4.3 μs (75 Ω load)	t_{on} 15 μs t_{off} (100 Ω load)	t_{on} 2 μs t_{off} (100 Ω load)	t_{on} 10 μs t_{off} 100 μs (100 Ω load)
Features	Isolation voltage 2.5 kV a.c. (1 min)	4-pin device grouped according to transfer ratio 40% 63% 100% and 160%	High gain general purpose	High isolation 5.3 kV a.c. (5 s)	Photo-Darlington 5.3 kV a.c. (5 s)

DESIGN EXAMPLE 3

Isolated data link from a computer port to CMOS logic running at V_{DD} of 15 V. Maximum data rate is not greater than 10 kHz.

The solution is to use a standard opto-isolator such as the MCT2E with the proposed circuit arrangement as shown in Fig. 7.7. On the input side the LED current is set to a value of about 10 mA. Since current transfer for the MCT2E is quoted as a minimum of 20% the minimum collector current in the phototransistor will be 2 mA. The output transistor is best arranged as a common emitter saturating switch as shown, since this way it is relatively easy to ensure that the correct logic level is achieved at the output.

In this first version Tr_1 can be any small signal, general purpose n-p-n transistor. The resistor values are calculated as follows:

$$R_1 = (V_{OH} - V_{BE(sat)})/I_{B1}$$

where V_{OH} is TTL high state
$V_{BE(sat)} = 0.7$ V
and $I_{B1} = 0.1 \times I_c = 1$ mA

Therefore $R_1 = 1.7$ kΩ (1k8 is n.p.v.)

R_2 sets the required LED on current:

$$R_2 = (V_{CC} - V_F)/I_F \text{ (the } V_{CE(sat)} \text{ of the transistor is small and is ignored)}$$

where $V_{CC} = 5$ V
$I_F = 10$ mA
and $V_F = 1.5$ V

Hence $R_2 = 350$ Ω (330 or 390 are the n.p.v.s)
Since h_{ctr} is 20% minimum I_C is 2 mA. To make sure that the phototransistor at the output fully saturates:

$$R_3 = \frac{V_{DD} - V_{CE(sat)}}{I_C} \approx \frac{V_{CC}}{I_C}$$

hence

$$V_{CC} = V_{DD} = 7.5 \text{ k}\Omega$$

In order to shape the output pulse into a logic signal a CMOS Schmitt buffer is necessary.

The calculated value of R_3 can seem relatively large and is a partial determinant of the maximum rate at which data can be sent across the link. The resistor forms a time constant with the capacitance at the input of the CMOS Schmitt gate. Suppose we

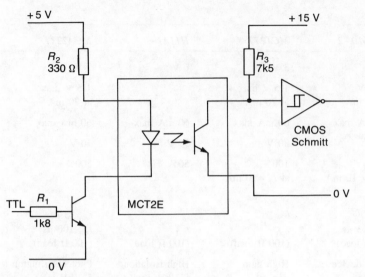

Fig. 7.7 Link from TTL compatible port to CMOS

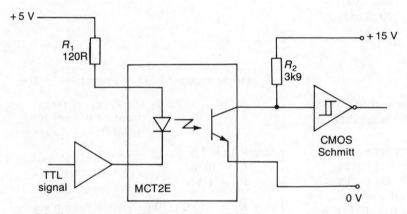

Fig. 7.8 Alternative using TTL open-collector buffer

assume an input capacitance of 50 pF (relatively high). Then the time constant is:

$$T = R_3 \cdot C_{in} = 375 \text{ ns}$$

However, the switching speed of the opto-isolator is not fast, with typical rise and fall times quoted as 2 μs, so reducing R_3 would not greatly affect the speed of the link. If the value of R_3 needs to be reduced the input current to the LED must be raised. One method is shown in Fig. 7.8, where the transistor is replaced by an open-collector TTL invertor (7406 or 7407). The diode current is set to

20 mA ($R_1 = 150 \text{ Ω}$) and the phototransistor pull-up can be reduced to 3.9 kΩ.

Opto-isolators with Darlington output transistors are very sensitive but not generally fast: typical turn-off times can be as high as 100 μs. Since these types have a minimum transfer ratio of 500% or more, the LED can be directly connected via a limiting resistor to a TTL or CMOS gate output. In the high state a standard TTL gate can source 0.4 mA, which would result in at least 2 mA in the Darlington output (Fig. 7.9).

For really fast isolated data transfer, devices such

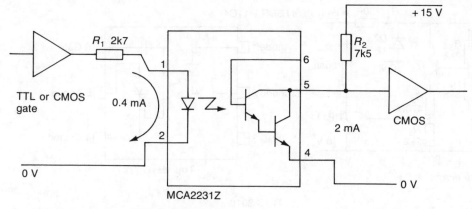

Fig. 7.9 The link made with a Darlington opto-isolator

as the 6N135 or the 6N137 should be used. The latter has a diode as the receiver, connected to a high gain linear amplifier and then to the output via a Schottky (non-saturating) transistor. A maximum data transfer rate of 10 Mbits/s is claimed.

Before turning to a.c. isolation we shall consider an opto-isolator circuit as a replacement for a relay.

DESIGN EXAMPLE 4

An isolated interface is required between a microcomputer port and a resistive load of 2 A connected in a 50 V d.c. supply.

Starting from the load end, since this will be the determining factor in the size of current required at the input to the isolator, we need a device that will switch at least 2 A of resistive load current and be capable of withstanding an off-voltage of 50 V. Using derating techniques the search should be for a switching device that can pass 3 A and withstand an off-voltage of 75 V. There are two possibilities:

(*a*) an n-p-n Darlington transistor, or
(*b*) an n-channel power MOSFET.

Consider the use of a Darlington: TIP111 is a good choice. This has the following characteristics:

V_{CEO} : 80 V
I_c : 4 A (continuous)
$V_{CE(sat)}$: 2.5 V at I_c = 2 A and I_B = 8 mA
V_{BE} : 2.5 V max

With the 2 A load connected in the collector circuit

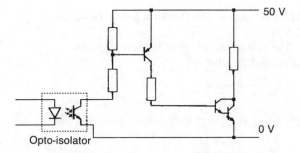

Fig. 7.10 Outline for the switch

and a switching current gain ratio taken as 100:1, the base drive required is 20 mA. Another stage of gain is going to be required between the opto-isolator output transistor and the base of the TIP111. This can be a p-n-p type such as BC212L. The outline of the circuit is shown in Fig. 7.10. The drive current required from the opto-isolator is now only 2 mA. However, a problem exists concerning the type of opto-isolator to be specified. The standard OPI-2046 is suitable but, like most other isolators, the output transistor has a limited working voltage. In this case the maximum rating is 30 V. Thus an additional supply needs to be created using a Zener diode to ensure that this is not exceeded. Assume a 12 V Zener is used as shown in Fig. 7.11; a BZX61 1.3 W rated type will be suitable. The Zener current *with the switch off* should be set to a value higher than the base drive current required by the TIP111. Therefore I_z will be set to 50 mA. The Zener dissipation is 600 mW.

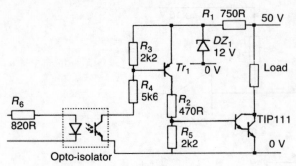

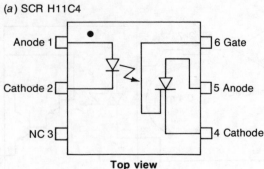

(a) SCR H11C4

Fig. 7.11 Completed switch design

$$R_1 \approx \frac{Vs - Vz}{I_z}$$

Therefore $R_1 \approx 750\ \Omega$ with a power rating of 2.5 W.

The rest of the resistors in the circuit are calculated as follows:

$$R_2 = \frac{Vz - V_{BE(2)}}{I_{B(2)}}$$

Therefore $R_2 = 470\ \Omega$

$$R_4 \approx \frac{Vz - V_{BE(1)}}{I_{B(1)}}$$

Therefore $R_4 \approx 5.6\ k\Omega$

R_3 and R_5 are included to ensure that the transistors are off when the comparator output is low. Both can be 2.2 kΩ.

Since the minimum transfer ratio of the opto-isolator is quoted as 20%, an input current to the LED of 10 mA is necessary.

Therefore

$$R_6 \approx \frac{V_H - V_F}{I_{in}}$$

where V_H = high state output from the comparator and V_F = forward drop of the LED.

Therefore $R_6 = 820\ \Omega$

Returning to the Darlington, we now need to check the maximum power dissipation and specify a heat sink should it be necessary. For the TIP111,

$$P_{tot} = I_B V_{BE} + I_C V_{CE(sat)}$$

Therefore $P_{tot} \approx 5\ W$

The maximum safe dissipation for the TIP111 in

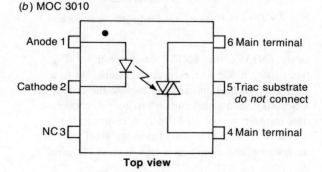

Fig. 7.12 Opto-coupled thyristors and triacs

free air at $T_{amb} = 25\ °C$ is given as 2 W. A heat sink is essential.

To maintain the case temperature to a maximum of 100 °C a heat sink with a thermal resistance of at least 15 °C W^{-1} is required.

The opto-isolated thyristor and opto-triac devices are designed for applications in interfacing logic signals to loads in a.c. supplies, typically to the 240 V or 155 V a.c. mains. Isolation is usually 4 kV r.m.s. or more (Fig. 7.12).

DESIGN EXAMPLE 5

Interfacing from a TTL logic level to switch a 5 A a.c. load with a supply of 240 V r.m.s. only on/off control is required.

The outline of the solution is shown in Fig. 7.13 where an opto-isolated triac device is selected. Available ICs for this include:

(a) the MOC 3010,
(b) the MOC 3020,

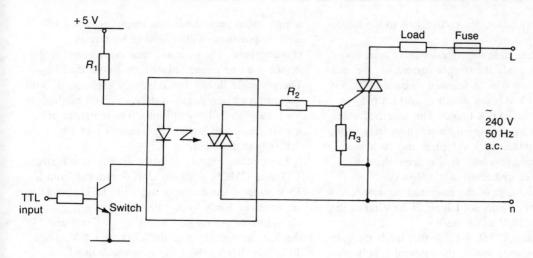

Fig. 7.13 Outline solution

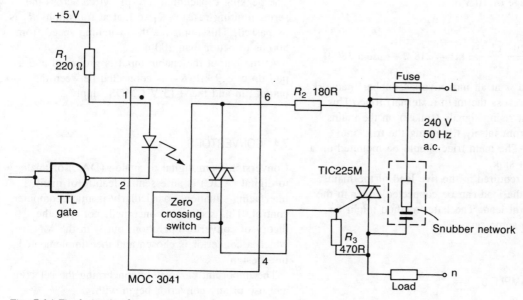

Fig. 7.14 Final circuit of a.c. power switch

(c) the MOC 3041.

All three devices have a single LED input which can be directly driven via a TTL inverting buffer. The first device has a rated output at the triac of 250 V which rules it out for mains circuits. Of the other two devices, the MOC 3020 requires a relatively large value of input current to the LED to trigger the triac. It has a quoted trigger current value of 15 mA typical, but 30 mA maximum. The off-state terminal voltage for both devices is given as 400 V. The first advantage of the MOC 3041 over the MOC 3020 is its sensitivity; its trigger current is 15 mA max. Another very important advantage lies in the fact that this IC includes a zero-crossing detector in the trigger circuit of the internal triac which has the effect of virtually eliminating any generated noise, since power to the external device can be switched on only when the a.c. mains supply is passing through zero.

In the final circuit, Fig. 7.14, the LED input current is set to 15 mA by R_1 (220 Ω) and the TTL gate is directly connected (active low to the LED cathode).

On the output side the light-sensitive triac is required to provide the trigger current for the main triac. This main triac is selected to be a TIC225M (an 8 A, 600 V device) which requires a trigger pulse of 2 V at 30 mA (max). The specified value of inhibit voltage for the light-sensitive triac in the MC3041 is quoted as 5 V typical and 20 V max. This is the voltage which results from the zero crossing switch characteristics and is the MT1−MT2 voltage of the internal triac alone, which the device will not trigger. I have taken the voltage to be 10 V in the design.

If R_3 is made 470 Ω, a value that holds the gate to MT2 impedance low in the external triac's off-state, then R_2 must allow a current of 32 mA at the trigger voltage of 10 V.

Therefore,

$$R_2 = \frac{10 - (2 + 1)}{32} \text{ k}\Omega = 218 \ \Omega - \text{use a } 180 \ \Omega$$

If the load is at all inductive a 'snubber' network is required across the main (external) triac. This prevents fast rising signals (spikes) on the mains waveform from falsely triggering the triac into conduction. The main triac should be mounted on a suitable heat sink.

A fuse is required in the live lead of the mains supply and the load can be connected either in the live or neutral lead. The latter method might be preferred in some cases.

DESIGN EXAMPLE 6

Isolating TTL logic from CMOS. In Section 7.2 methods of interfacing logic families were discussed. To give further protection in high speed logic systems, logic gate opto-isolators have been developed. These are very useful in preventing fault conditions from a higher voltage rail causing damage to sensitive logic. It also allows the ground systems of the two logic boards to be completely isolated, which prevents ground loops and ground injected noise.

A typical IC is the HCPL2200 which has an LED input and what is described as an integrated high gain photodetector. This detector, which consists of

a high speed photodiode and amplifier, has a tri-state output stage with a built-in hysteresis characteristic. The tri-state input can be used if the device is to be connected directly into a data bus. The complete device has relatively high speed, with quoted typical propagation delays of 160 ns (high to low) and 115 ns (low to high). These figures are for circuits using a peaking capacitor (see Fig. 7.15(b)) at the input.

The circuit, Fig. 7.15, is for an interface between TTL and CMOS, with the CMOS running from a 15 V supply. On the input side, the LED current is set to about 3 mA by R_1. For the device $I_{F(on)}$ should be in the range 1.6 mA up to 5 mA and V_F, the forward volt drop of the LED, is 1.5 V. The TTL gate driving the LED is in the active low (current sink) mode and can be 74TTL or 74LS. The peaking capacitor is 120 pF wired across the series limiting resistor R_1 so that at transitions R_1 is by-passed. This improves the switching speed from 500 ns to better than 200 ns.

At the output the enable input is grounded and a pull-up of 3.9 kΩ (R_2) is connected between the output pin and the +15 V CMOS supply.

7.4 CONVERTORS

Conversion from digital to analog (DAC) or analog to digital (ADC) is an essential feature of many interfacing situations, particularly in microcomputer control. This section is concerned, not with the theory of convertor operation, but with the way in which a convertor is chosen and then implemented in a design.

The important parameters concerning the selection and use of any convertor begin with:

(a) the number of bits (n) to be used, and
(b) the required speed of conversion.

The number of bits determines the overall resolution of the interface. For example, a 10-bit convertor will have 1024 levels or quantization steps, whereas a 6-bit convertor will have only 64. Now 64 different speeds for a pump may be more than sufficient for, say, flow control but might be totally inadequate for converting analog data from a temperature sensor. Suppose the temperature sensor reads from 0 °C to 500 °C and a resolution of better than ± 1 °C is required. It is fairly obvious

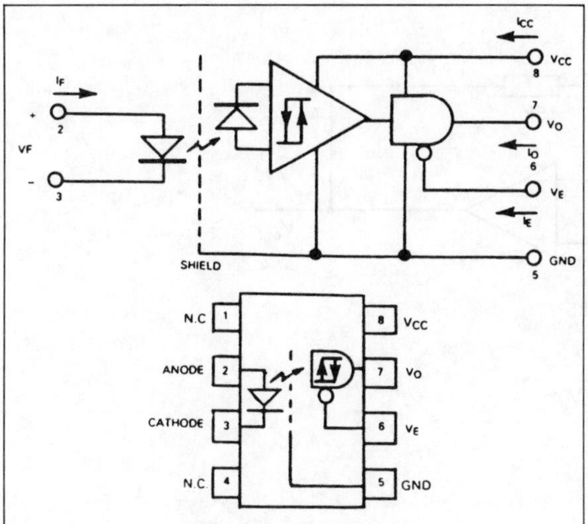

TRUTH TABLE
(Positive Logic)

Input	Enable	Output
H	H	Z
L	H	Z
H	L	H
L	L	L

(a)

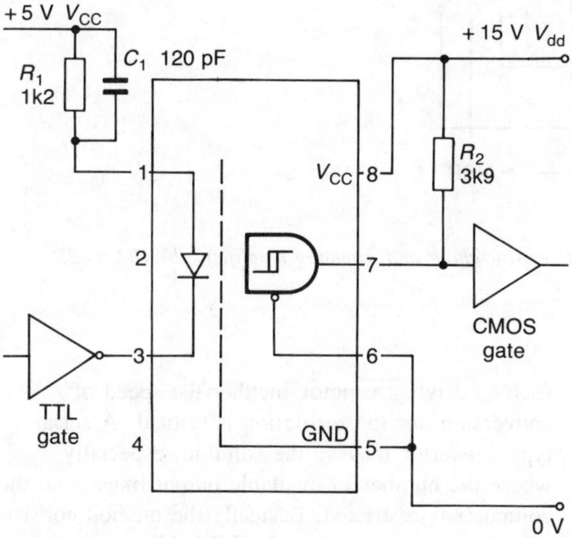

(b)

Fig. 7.15 (a) The HCPL 2200; (b) Used as an interface between TTL and CMOS

that something like nine or ten bits is going to be necessary for the conversion.

Speed in a DAC is called 'settling time'. The worst case situation, for which the settling time should be quoted, is when all the bits used in the conversion change state from 0 to 1 or vice versa. Settling time is measured from the instant the digital command forces a change in all input bits to the time the output settles to within $\pm 1\text{LSB}$. A typical value is 1 microsecond.

An ADC, however, has a finite conversion time or conversion rate. The general purpose, and therefore slower, devices have conversion times of from a few microseconds up to milliseconds and 't_c' is measured as the time between the 'start conversion' command and the time that the digital word, equivalent to the analog value being converted, is available at the output. Very fast ADCs, called *flash convertors*, have nanosecond conversion time.

Other parameters that need to be watched in convertor choice are:

- (c) linearity — deviation from a straight line characteristic,
- (d) monotonicity — every step giving an increase in output,
- (e) offset errors — zero input, not resulting in zero output,
- (f) stability with temperature drift of the offset.

All these parameter values need to be low in value.

Simple DACs can be designed with binary weighted resistors and a summing op-amp, Fig. 7.16(a), which is fine for a convertor of very restricted bit size. Above eight bits the values of resistors become unwieldy and tracking errors with temperature will cause the stability to be poor. The preferred method in most DAC chips is to use the $R-2R$ ladder, Fig. 7.16(b), which has only two values of resistor and can be extended to any number of bits. Thus a basic DAC chip consists of a set of switches, a stable reference supply and a precision $R-2R$ ladder network. Typical data for some standard DAC ICs is given in Table 7.2, but before we look in detail at using one of these standard DACs let's consider a very low cost simple serial DAC using a counter and an $R-2R$ ladder.

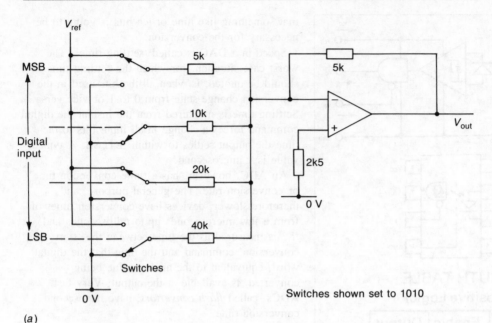

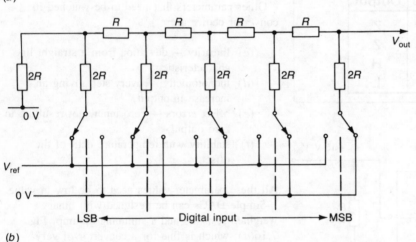

Fig. 7.16 (a) Simple 4-bit convertor using a binary weighted resistor chain and summing amplifier; (b) The R−2R ladder network: 5 bits shown with digital input of 00011

DESIGN EXAMPLE 7

A low cost 6-bit serial DAC for interfacing from a microprocessor system to devices such as motors and heaters.

The problem with most accurate digital-to-analog conversion is that the number of bits used has to be large and this means using several connections from the digital system to the convertor. In many cases,

such as driving a motor, neither the speed of conversion nor the resolution is critical. A serial type convertor may be the solution, especially where the number of available output lines from the computer is restricted. Basically the method consists of a 6-bit counter and an $R-2R$ ladder network, Fig. 7.17. The counter as shown is made up of 4013 dual D flip-flops, but other CMOS bistables or counter packages could easily be used and the

Table 7.2 DAC data (short form)

Type No.	PNA 7518P	ZN 425E	DAC 0800	AD 557JN	MC 3410F	AD 667JN	DAC 8-8JP
No. of bits	8	8	8	8	10	12	16
Linearity	$\pm\frac{1}{2}$LSB	$\pm\frac{1}{2}$LSB	$\pm 0.19\%$FS	$\pm\frac{1}{2}$LSB	$\pm\frac{1}{4}$LSB	$\pm\frac{1}{2}$LSB	$\pm 0.003\%$FS
Settling time	NQ 12 MHz B.W.	1 μs	0.1 μs	0.8 μs	250 ns	4 μs	2.5 μs
Supply	5 V at 50 mA	5 V	± 4.5 V to ± 18 V	5 V	5 V at 20 mA	± 12 V to ± 15 V	5 V and ± 15 V
Features	High speed	General purpose	Current output	Fast interfacing to bus system	Needs separate amplifier and reference	Double buffered input latch	High resolution and micro compatible

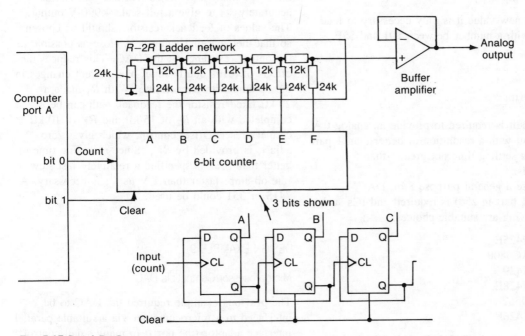

Fig. 7.17 Serial DAC

$R-2R$ ladder has 12 kΩ and 24 kΩ resistors. With CMOS the logic levels are normally fairly well defined so that conversion errors will not be large. Two input lines from the microcomputer are required:

    CLEAR — which resets all bistables and therefore gives a 0 V analog output, and

    COUNT — which is pulsed by software to increment the counter.

Since the counter is 6 bits the software must output 63 pulses to give V_{FSO}. This value will be 5 V $-$ 1LSB, i.e. about 4.92 V.

For half full scale (2.50 V) the required number of output pulses will be 32, and so on. Thus we have a serial convertor that can give motor control with 64 possible speed settings (including off). The only drawback is that more software is necessary to drive the convertor than for its equivalent parallel system. In 6809 assembly language this software could be written as two routines as follows. (Here bit 0 of port A is assumed connected to the COUNT line and bit 1 to the CLEAR.) The piece of code is to output quarter full scale to the DAC.

```
            LDA #$10, load in value
            BSR CLEAR, output clear pulse
            BSR PULSE, output pulses
    CLEAR   LDB #$02
            STB PORTA, clear line high
            CLR PORTA, end of clear pulse
            RTS
    PULSE   INC PORTA
            DEC PORTA, one count pulse
            DECA
            BNE PULSE
            RTS
```

To output a new value it is only necessary to load register A with a number between $01 and $3F.

DESIGN EXAMPLE 8

A DAC circuit is required to provide an analog 0 V to 5 V output with a resolution of better than 1 part in 200 and a settling time not greater than 5 microseconds.

In this case a general purpose 8-bit DAC (resolution 1 part in 256) is required and ICs such as the following are suitable choices:

- ZN425E
- DAC0800
- ZN429
- ZN428E
- AD557
- ZN426E

Suppose we select the ZN426E. This IC is a basic 8-bit DAC consisting of an internal reference supply, switches and a diffused $R-2R$ ladder network (Fig. 7.18). The specification figures are:

Resolution : 8 bits
Non-linearity : ± 0.5LSB
Settling time : 2 μs to 0.5LSB (all bits OFF to ON
          or vice versa)
Offset voltage V_{os} : 8 mV max
V_{os} TC : ± 5 μV $°C^{-1}$
Output resistance R_o : 10 kΩ
Supply : 5 V at 9 mA max

Reference : 1.475 V min to 2.625 V max
          ($R_S = 390$ Ω)

The internal reference supply needs a 390 Ω resistor to V_{CC} and a 1 μF decoupling capacitor from pin 6 to pin 7.

In order to increase the DAC output level to the required 5 V a non-inverting amplifier is necessary. A buffer is advisable anyway, since the output impedance of this DAC is relatively high at 10 kΩ and because the offset voltage will need to be adjusted. The voltage gain of the amplifier is nominally 2 and could be set by using two equal resistors; but since the internal reference has a tolerance of ± 75 mV part of the feedback resistor has to be made a preset so that the gain can be accurately set to give a full scale 4.990 V output. The values of feedback resistors should be chosen so that their parallel value is as close as possible to the output resistance of the DAC. This reduces the effects of drifts due to input bias current changes in the op-amp with temperature. With R_1 made a 20 kΩ fixed resistor the feedback path can be completed with an R_2 of 15 kΩ and RV_2 a 10 kΩ cermet preset. Offset control, which gives zero adjust, is provided by RV_1. Since a settling time of better than 5 μs is specified a relatively fast slew rate op-amp, faster than 1 V μs^{-1}, is necessary. A 741S or 351 could be used.

DESIGN EXAMPLE 9

Microprocessor Compatible DAC

The previous example required the DAC to be interfaced to a microcomputer via a suitable parallel interface adaptor (the port). In many small control systems it is possible to save on these PIO chips by using DACs (or ADCs) that can be directly connected into the bus system. This means that the DAC has to have an in-built data latch that can be enabled by an address signal. The ZN428 is a typical example, Fig. 7.19(*a*). The enable input allows data to be latched into the DAC only when it is low. This means that the data inputs can be directly connected to the data bus while the enable input is derived from a suitable address decoder. The principle is illustrated in Fig. 7.19(*b*) where only the top three address lines in a 6809 system

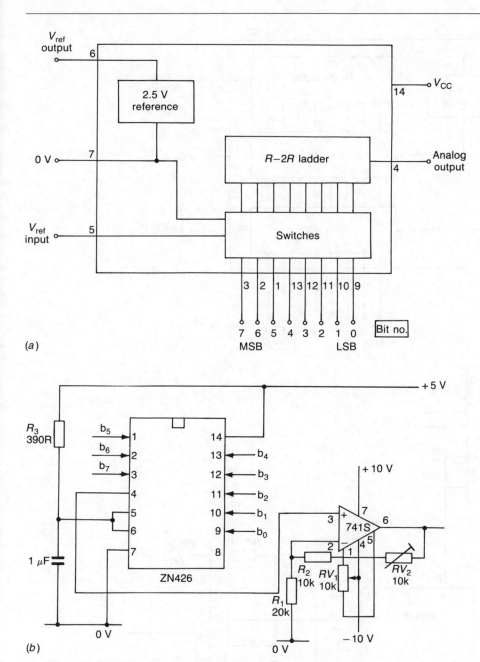

Fig. 7.18 (a) The ZN426E; (b) Using the ZN426E to give 5 V FS output

are shown decoded to give the DAC a nominal address of $6000 ($Y_5$ output from the decoder). There would be a lot of overwrite in this method, but this might not be a problem in a small digital control system. In this case, when address $6000 is called in the program the enable input to the DAC

would go low and data sent from the microprocessor would be latched into the DAC. Typical instructions would be:

```
LDA #$80
STA $6000
```

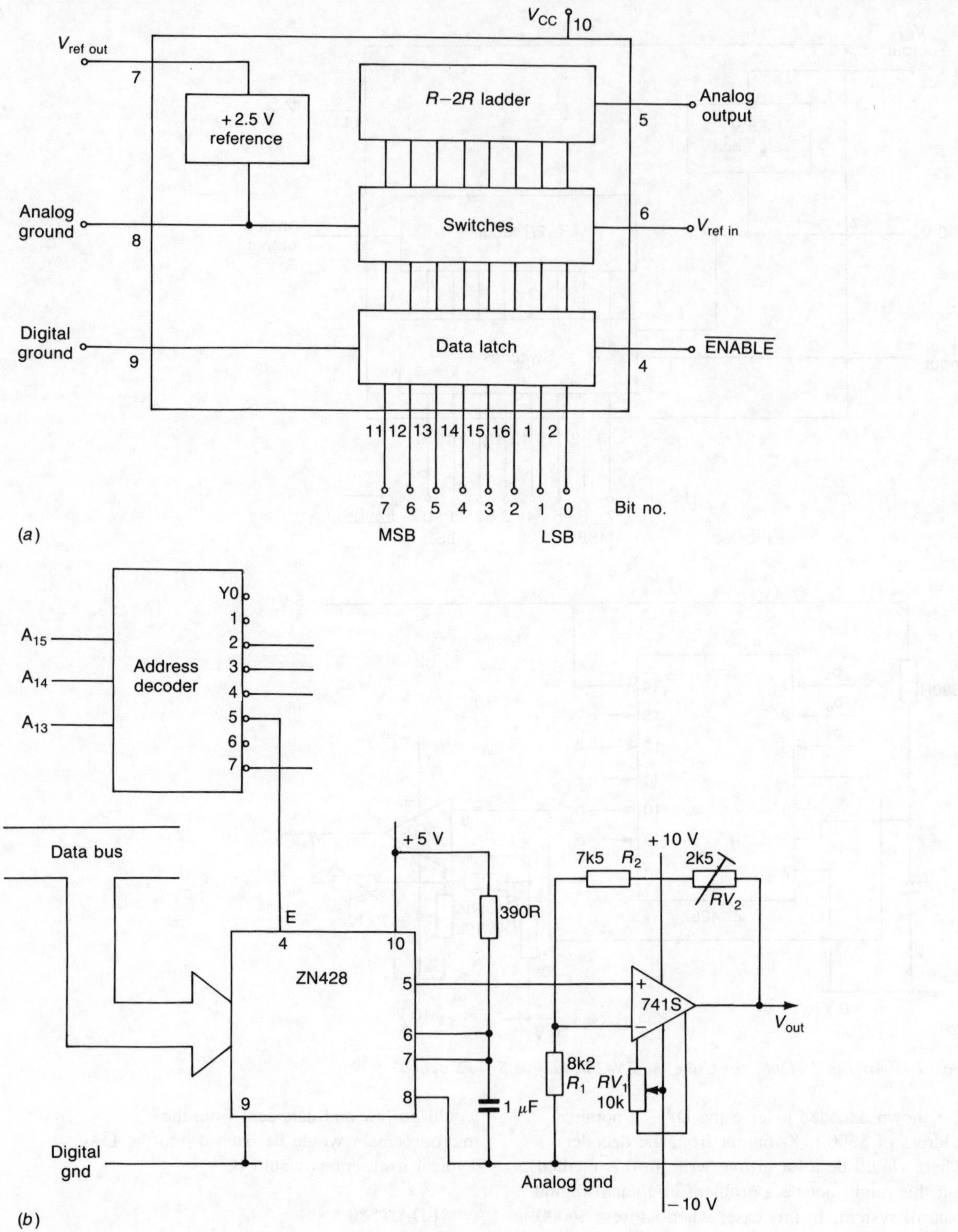

Fig. 7.19 (a) The ZN428; (b) Interfacing the DAC with a microprocessor system

These would set the DAC output to half full scale.
  The ZN428 specification is:

Resolution : 8 bits
Non-linearity : ±0.5LSB
Settling time : 1.25 μs (all bits ON to OFF or vice versa)
Offset voltage V_{os} : 5 mV max
V_{os} TC : ±6 μV °C^{-1}
Output resistance R_o : 4 kΩ
Supply : 5 V at 30 mA max
Reference : 1.550 ±75 mV (390 Ω series resistor needed)
Enable pulse width : 100 ns min
Data set-up time : 150 ns min
Data hold time : 10 ns

The data set-up time is the minimum time data must be present before the enable goes high, while the hold time is the minimum time the data must be held after the enable goes high. In a relatively slow microprocessor system (see Chapter 6) these conditions are easily met.

  As in the previous example, a non-inverting buffer amplifier with offset and gain adjust trimpots is required to give an accurate low offset output voltage. Since the ZN428's output resistance is only 4 kΩ the feedback resistors are lower in value than in the last example at 8k2 (R_1), 7.5 k (R_2) and 2k5 (RV_2). An essential feature of this DAC is the separation of the analog and digital grounds. This avoids unwanted ground interference in both systems, but particularly reduces switching spikes and digital noise appearing on the analog output.

Interfacing ADCs can be more complicated than DACs depending on the type of ADC being used. The ultrafast flash convertors with nanosecond conversion times do not usually require additional control lines as they carry out continuous conversion of the analog signal presented at the input. These ICs are still expensive since they are complex LSI chips using a large bank of fast comparators and a mass of encoding logic. Slower ADCs, such as the successive approximation type or the ramp and counter, must have 'start conversion' and 'ready' (or end of conversion) pins that allow data synchronization. Fig. 7.20 shows a typical sequence:

  (a) The computer via a control line outputs a brief 'start conversion' pulse to the ADC.

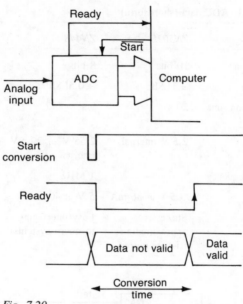

Fig. 7.20

  (b) The ADC carries out the conversion process and after a set conversion time the digital data are available. The ADC 'ready' line now goes high to signal to the microcomputer that data are valid and can be collected.

  (c) The computer collects the data.

  Some comparisons between typical industry standard ADCs can be seen from Table 7.3, which also indicates the way in which ADCs are specified.

DESIGN EXAMPLE 10

Interfacing a successive approximation ADC to a microcomputer.

  Two popular ADCs of this type are the ZN427 and the ZN448 with the specification of:

	ZN427	ZN448
Resolution:	8 bits	8 bits
Linearity:	±0.5LSB	±0.5LSB
Conversion time:	10 μs	9 μs
Reference:	1.56 ±75 mV	2.55 ±20 mV
Clock frequency:	900 kHz	1 MHz
Supply:	5 V at 40 mA	5 V at 40 mA

Apart from a tighter specification on V_{ref} and a faster conversion time, the ZN448 also has an internal clock circuit.

Table 7.3 ADC data (short form)

Type	ZN502E	ZN448	ADC-302	TSC-8703CJ	CA 3306CE
Resolution	10 bits	8 bits	8 bits	8 bits	6 bits
Linearity	± 1LSB	± 0.5LSB	$\pm \frac{1}{2}$LSB	$\pm \frac{1}{2}$LSB	± 0.5LSB
Conversion time or rate	20 s	9 s	50 MHz	1.25 ms	15MSPS
Reference	2.5 V internal	2.55 V $\pm$ 20 mV internal	internal	external current reference required	—
Clock frequency	—	1 MHz	—	—	10 MHz
Supply	± 5 V at 36 mA	5 V at 40 mA	-5.2 V at 75 mA	± 3.5 V to ± 7.5 V	3 V to 7.5 V
Features	Successive approximation tri-state output	Easy interfacing to micro systems	Video (flash) convertor	CMOS low power	Low cost flash ADC

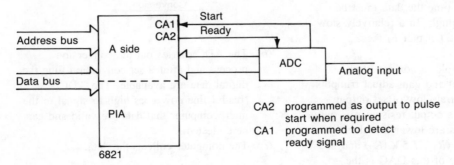

CA2 programmed as output to pulse start when required
CA1 programmed to detect ready signal

Fig. 7.21 Using a PIA with an ADC

Both types can be directly connected into a microprocessor system to give memory mapped ADC, but some care has to be taken over the timing of the address decoding since this signal must provide the 'start conversion' command. A better method is to drive the ADC from a standard PIO chip. For example, the PIA 6821 used in the 6809 microprocessor system has control lines CA1 CA2 on the A side (CB1 CB2 on B) that can be programmed to act as the handshake for the ADC, Fig. 7.21.

The ZN427 requires an external clock and a negative supply for the internal comparator. One 74132 quad Schmitt can be used to give both these features, two Schmitt gates used for a gated oscillator and the other two as an oscillator driving a diode pump circuit to provide a -3.5 V supply.

Consider the negative supply circuit first, Fig. 7.22. With C_1 as 47 nF and R_1 as 390 Ω, the oscillator runs at about 50 kHz (this varies with ICs

depending on the threshold levels). The buffer gate then drives the pump circuit. Since the maximum 'tail' current required for the ZN427 comparator is 150 μA, C_2 and C_3 need not be large value capacitors. The value of 220 nF chosen gives an output time constant of about 5.5 ms, which will ensure that only a tiny ripple voltage appears across C_3. Taking a nominal value for I_{ext} for the ZN427 pin 5 input of 65 μA (mid-point between the quoted values of 25 μA min and 150 μ max), the -3.5 V supply will be connected to pin 5 via a 56 kΩ resistor.

The self-synchronising clock circuit, formed around the other two gates in the 74132, has to be gated by the EOC signal from the ADC. When the 'start conversion' command is given EOC will go low and the clock must operate to produce nine pulses to drive the ADC through its successive approximation cycle. The 'start conversion' pulse is specified as a minimum length of 250 ns but at least

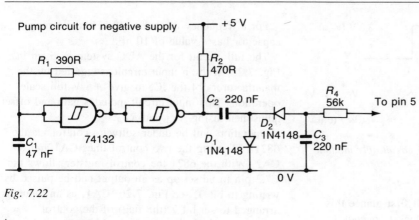

Fig. 7.22

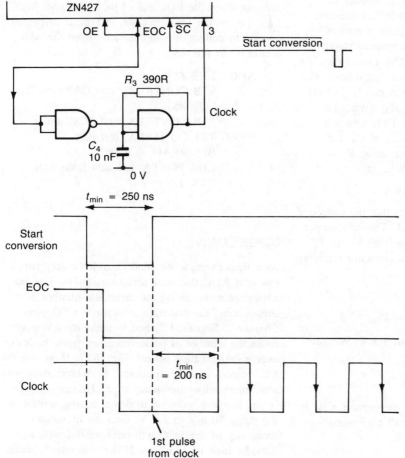

Fig. 7.23 The self-synchronising clock

200 ns shorter than the width of the first clock pulse, see Fig. 7.23. The frequency of the clock generator, and therefore the overall conversion time of the system, will depend on the width of the start conversion pulse. If this is generated by software

from a relatively slow microprocessor system the width might take up at least four instruction cycle times, i.e. 4 μs for a 1 MHz system. Let's assume this is the worst case, which means that the first clock pulse positive edge must occur no earlier than

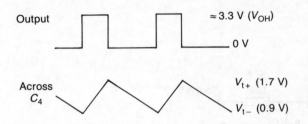

Output ≈3.3 V (V_{OH})

0 V

Across
C_4

V_{t+} (1.7 V)

V_{t-} (0.9 V)

Fig. 7.24 Waveforms in the clock circuit after the first pulse

4.2 μs from the clock start. At first glance this would appear to restrict the clock frequency to something like 110 kHz max, but in fact the first cycle of the simple Schmitt oscillator is always longer than the rest because the capacitor starts from a fully charged condition. This makes the first pulse nearly twice as long as those that follow. The basic oscillator can therefore run at nearly 240 kHz. In the circuit the timing resistor (R_3) cannot be higher than 390 Ω, otherwise the TTL gate will latch with its output low. The value of C_4, the timing capacitor, can be calculated using $R_3 = 390$ Ω as follows. For the TTL Schmitt:

$$V_t^+ = 1.7 \text{ V} \quad \text{and} \quad V_t^- = 0.9 \text{ V}$$

and it is between these two values that the capacitor charges and discharges, Fig. 7.24. The gate output will be high while C_4 is charging from V_t^- to V_t^+. Using the standard equation for a capacitor charging via a resistor:

$$V_c = V (1 - e^{-t/CR})$$

where $V_C = V_t^+ - V_t^-$ and $V = V_{OH} - V_t^-$

In this case V_{OH} is taken as about 3.3 V. We get:

$$0.8 = 2.4 (1 - e^{-t/CR})$$

Therefore $t_1 \approx 0.4CR$

When the output switches low the capacitor is discharged from V_t^+ to V_t^-. For this we use:

$$V_C = V e^{-t/CR}$$

We get:

$$0.9 = 1.7 e^{-t/CR}$$

Therefore, $t_2 \approx 0.65CR$

The periodic time $T = t_1 + t_2$.

Therefore $T = 1.05CR$

For a frequency of about 240 kHz the timing capacitor has a value of 10 nF.

The full circuit for the ADC system is given in Fig. 7.25, with an input circuit, suggested by the manufacturers of the IC, to give +5 V full scale operation. This input circuit includes gain and offset adjustment using RV_1 and RV_2.

Operation will be under software control via the 6821 PIA using the two control lines CA1 and CA2. With the 6821 the control register allows the CA2 pin to be set up as an output and be pulsed by writing to bit 3, see Fig. 7.26. CA1, as an input, is arranged to set bit 7 (the flag) of the control register when the EOC pin of the ADC goes high ($\uparrow$), i.e. on the positive edge. A typical software routine to collect one digital value from the ADC would be as follows:

```
ADC   LDB #$36
      STB CONTRLA, send CA2 low
      LDB #$3E
      STB CONTRLA, end of SC pulse
READ  TST CONTRLA, test flag
      BPL READ, is it set?
      LDA PORTA, get data from ADC
      RTS, return
```

DESIGN EXAMPLE 11

As a final example we shall consider a very simple low cost ADC that uses serial input. This has the advantage of requiring the minimum number of connections; the principle is to use a VCO (see Chapter 1, Section 1.5) and to make the computer count the number of pulses received from the VCO over a defined time period, Fig. 7.27. If we use the VCO circuit already discussed, its specification was a nominal output frequency of 3 kHz per volt of input. Suppose we wish to detect analog signals in the range 50 mV to 2.5 V; then the maximum frequency of the VCO will be 7.5 kHz, with a periodic time of 133.3 μs. If the computer is made to count over a period of 250 T, i.e. 33.33 ms, an 8-bit register will read 250_{10} for an analog input to the VCO of 2.5 V.

Note that this simple circuit will not be highly accurate but eliminates the need for additional data inputs. A flow chart for the actions necessary for one read is shown in Fig. 7.28. The VCO free runs

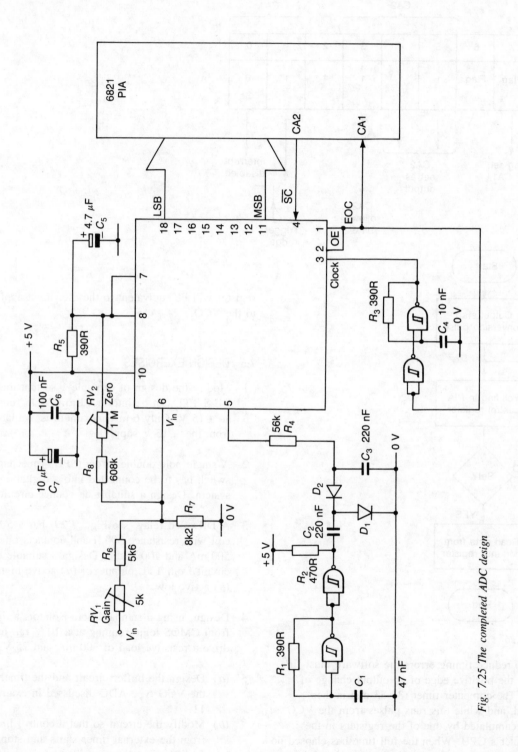

Fig. 7.25 The completed ADC design

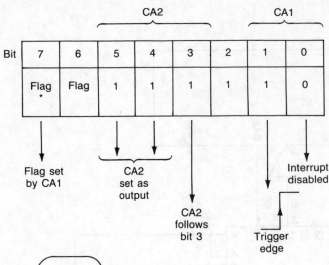

Bit	7	6	5	4	3	2	1	0
	Flag *	Flag	1	1	1	1	1	0

Flag set by CA1

CA2 set as output

CA2 follows bit 3

Interrupt disabled

Trigger edge

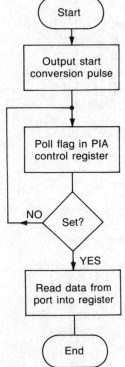

Fig. 7.26

and to reduce timing errors the software must first detect the positive edge of an output change of state. The computer timer (33.33 ms) is then started, and while this runs pulses from the VCO are accumulated by one of the registers in the computer's CPU. When the full time has elapsed no more pulses are counted and the contents of the

register will be equivalent to the d.c. input applied to the VCO.

7.5 DESIGN EXERCISES

1 Modify the design of example 1 so that the 74LS TTL can be interfaced to CMOS running at ±15 V. Only 6 mA maximum is available from the ±15 V supply.

2 A single pole double throw (SPDT) mechanical switch has to be connected into a digital system. Design a suitable de-bounce circuit.

3 A DIL reed relay (see Fig,. 7.29) has a 5 V coil with resistance 500 Ω and contacts rated at 500 mA and 100 V d.c. Design a suitable drive circuit from TTL outputs of (a) active high and (b) active low.

4 Design, using a standard opto-isolator, a link from CMOS logic running at a 10 V rail to drive a resistive load of 300 mA and 75 V.

5 (a) Design the buffer circuit and the timer for the VCO type ADC discussed in example 11.
   (b) Modify the circuit so that a control line from the external timer starts and stops the oscillator.

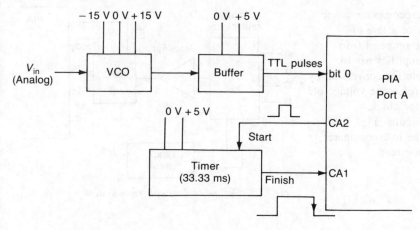

Fig. 7.27 Outline of simple serial type ADC using a VCO

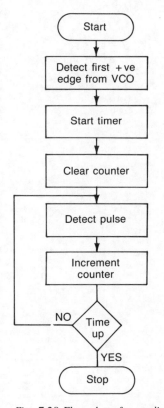

Fig. 7.28 Flow chart for reading VCO

6 Modify the circuit of example 8 so that a full scale output of 7.5 V can be obtained.

7 (a) Determine the conversion speed of the ADC in example 10.

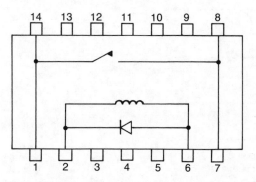

Fig. 7.29 DIL reed relay

(b) If the microprocessor cycle time is reduced to 125 ns, redesign the clock circuit so that the conversion speed can match the increase in speed.

8 A powerFET is to be used to drive a 5 A, 150 W resistive load (d.c.). Design an isolated link to allow a microcomputer line to drive the load. Detail the specification required from the powerFET.

9 If the value of $R_{DS(on)}$ for a powerFET is quoted as 0.15 Ω at 10 A, what is the power dissipation of the powerFET under static conditions? What size of heat sink will be required by the FET if:

$R_{th(J-C)} = 1.5$ °C W^{-1} and
$R_{th(c-h)} = 0.9$ °C W^{-1}
$T_{j(max)} = 110$ °C and $T_{A(max)} = 35$ °C

10 Four analog inputs to a microcomputer are to be multiplexed continuously at a rate of 0.2 Hz. Each input is in the range of 0 to 500 mV and the common amplifier has to increase these signals suitable for conversion by an 8-bit ADC which has a reference voltage of 2.55 V ± 75 mV. Design the clock, multiplexer and amplifier circuits, Fig. 7.30. Modify the design so that the microcomputer can tell which sensor is being read.

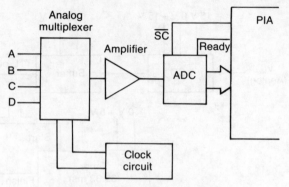

Fig. 7.30 Outline of data collection system

8 ANSWERS TO DESIGN EXERCISES

8.1 CHAPTER ONE

1 The full working circuit diagram is given in Fig. 8.1.

The frequency of the 555 astable is set to 102.4 kHz. Using $C_T = 470$ pF values of R_A and R_B are above the minimum recommended. With the 5 kΩ trimpot the frequency can be adjusted from 97 kHz to 115 kHz.

Maximum load currents for the 555 and the ZN423E are 10 mA and 40 mA respectively. With I_Z set to 10 mA the series resistor for the simple regulator is 75 Ω.

The non-inverting amplifier has a gain set to 2.4.

2 With $C_1 = 100$ nF the required charging current is:

$$I = C dV/dt = 240 \ \mu A$$

Suitable values for resistors are therefore:

R_1 6k8
R_2 33k

(These two resistors could, however, remain at their previous values with no effect on circuit performance.)

R_3 2k7
RV_1 2k

All other values remain unchanged.

3 An inverting unity gain op-amp circuit is required which should be fed directly from the output of the non-inverting amplifier. No further offset controls are necessary and suitable resistors (both equal value to give unity gain) are in the range 6k8 to 15k. Values of 10k are shown in Fig. 8.2.

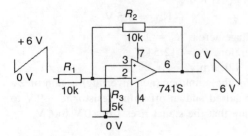

Fig. 8.2 Inverting amplifier

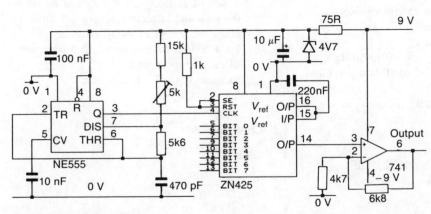

Fig. 8.1 Digital ramp generator

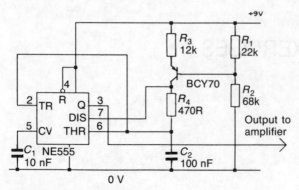

Fig. 8.3 555 ramp generator

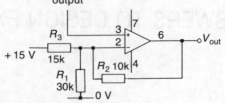

Fig. 8.4 Circuit modification

Measured gain is 41.8 (32.4 dB)
Error is $\pm 0.65\%$

4 See Fig. 8.3.

Charging current required for C_T is found using

$$I = CdV/dt$$

where $dt = 2.5\,\text{ms}$ and $dV = 3\,\text{V}$
Therefore $I = 120\,\mu\text{A}$.

Set V_B to 7 V (this allows for at least 1.5 V between collector and emitter of Tr_1 and ensures good linearity).

Set the current through R_1 and R_2 to, say, $200\,\mu\text{A}$. Therefore $R_2 = 33\,\text{k}\Omega$

$$R_1 = 10\,\text{k}\Omega$$
$$V_B = 6.9\,\text{V}$$
$$V_E = V_B + V_{BE} = 7.5\,\text{V}$$

Voltage across $R_3 = 1.5\,\text{V}$
Therefore $R_3 = 12.5\,\text{k}\Omega$
Use 12k n.p.v.

For the amplifier (non-inverting) a gain of 2 is required and an offsetting resistor to +9 V to ensure that the signal rises from 0 V to 6 V.

6 30 dB is 31.62 as a ratio.

Modify circuit as follows:
(i) Change R_1 and R_2 to 25 kΩ. This sets correct input resistance.
(ii) Change R_3 to 750 kΩ.
(iii) To set low frequency cut-off to 50 Hz change C_1 to 127 nF (220 nF is n.p.v.) and C_2 to 2.2 μF.
(iv) Op-amp must have GBP in excess of 5 MHz.

7 (a) For the oscilloscope:
Measured gain is 40 (32.04 dB)
Error is $\pm 8.5\%$
(b) For the DMM:

9 The output of the integrator has an amplitude of 5 V, set by the threshold and trigger points of the 555.

For the integrator:

$$t = C_1 \frac{dV}{I} \quad \text{where } dV = 5\,\text{V}$$

For $V_C = 1\,\text{V}$ the charging current I is fixed at $33\,\mu\text{A}$ by the input resistors. When Tr_1 is off:

$$I = \frac{V_C - 0.33V_C}{R_1 + R_2}$$

and when Tr_1 is on:

$$I = 0.33V_C/R_2$$

In both cases the current is $33\,\mu\text{A}$.
Therefore $t = 1 \times 10^{-9} \times 5/33 \times 10^{-6} = 151\,\mu\text{s}$

$$f = \frac{1}{2t} = 3.3\,\text{kHz V}^{-1}$$

10 (a) See circuit modification given in Fig. 8.4. Here a non-inverting op-amp, which has a high input impedance, is used to buffer the triangle wave from pin 6 of IC and to give a gain of 2. Resistors R_1, R_2 and R_3 set the gain and introduce the correct offset to allow the output to swing about zero.
(b) Fit a 200 kΩ trimpot from pin 5 (control) of the 555 to ground.
(c) Increase C_1 to 3.3 nF.

8.2 CHAPTER TWO

1 Since

(i) $$V_o = \frac{V_i R_2}{R_1 + R_2}$$

(ii) $R_2 = \dfrac{V_o R_1}{V_i - V_o}$ by transposition

Therefore $R_2 = 7.71\,\text{k}\Omega - 7\text{k}5$ is n.p.v. in E24 series.

Using (i), $V_o = 5.88\,\text{V}$

2 $R_1 = \dfrac{V_i - V_z}{I_z + I_L} = 357\,\Omega$

Therefore use $360\,\Omega$.

Assume output short circuit.

Therefore power dissipated by $R_1 = V_z^2 / R_1$
$$= 0.711\,\text{W}$$

A 1 watt rated resistor should be specified. The type could be (a) 1 W high stability carbon film or (b) a wirewound resistor.

3 $T_A = 4.4 R_T C_T$

Therefore $R_T = T_A / 4.4 C_T$

$$= \dfrac{166.6 \times 10^{-6}}{4.4 \times 2.2 \times 10^{-9}} = 17.2\,\text{k}\Omega$$

18k is n.p.v.

Error in $f_o = -4.33\%$

4 $\delta C = 35 \times 10^{-6} \times 2.2 \times^{-9} \times 20\,\text{F}$
$$= 1.54\,\text{pF}$$

Therefore $\delta f_o = -4\,\text{Hz}$

5   (a) Since

Reg $= \dfrac{V_{OL} - V_L}{V_{OL}} \times 100\%$

$V_{OL} = \dfrac{V_L}{1 - R/100}$

Therefore $V_{OL} = 17.6\,\text{V}$

(b) Since $VA = 6$ each secondary current can be 200 mA.

6   For the thyristor the parameters and ratings of importance are:

(a) V_{GT} the gate trigger voltage,
(b) I_{GT} the gate trigger current,
(c) I_{TSM} the peak (surge) forward current.

In the circuit the value of V_{GT} is given by:

$$V_{GT} \approx (V_{\text{trip}} - V_z) \dfrac{R_3}{R_2 + R_3}$$

where $V_{\text{trip}} = 12\,\text{V}$ and $V_z = 10\,\text{V}$ (nominal).
Therefore V_{GT} is 0.9 V.

A thyristor with a V_{GT} of less than 0.9 V is required.

I_{GT} must be a value that does not load the sensing network. Make I_{GT} one-tenth of I_{R3}

$$I_{R3} = \dfrac{(V_{\text{trip}} - V_z)}{R_2 + R_3} = 2.32\,\text{mA}$$

Therefore $I_{GT} \approx 0.23\,\text{mA}$

When the thyristor conducts the peak forward current that occurs before the fuse blows is:

$$I_{TSM} = V_{\text{unreg}}/R_1 \approx 7.5\,\text{A}$$

I_{TSM} to be not less than 7.5 A.

Both the C103YY and the C106 would appear to be suitable but the C106 with its I_{TSM} rating of 20 A would be preferred.

7   Using the fact that R_T changes from $4700\,\Omega$ at 25 °C to $1100\,\Omega$ at 70 °C the output voltage change for an input of 45 °C can be calculated. The value is 330 mV, i.e. approx. 7.25 mV °C⁻¹.

V_{in}, the voltage across R_3, is nominally $-50\,\text{mV}$.

Suppose the temperature being measured is held constant, then we must calculate how much V_{in} can change to give an error of 0.25 °C. 0.25 °C $\equiv$ 1.825 mV at the output (ΔV_o).

Therefore $\Delta V_{\text{in}} = \Delta V_o \dfrac{(R_T + R_4)}{R_f}$

$$= 0.17\,\text{mV}$$

Therefore $\Delta V_{\text{ref}} = \Delta V_{\text{in}} \dfrac{(R_3 + R_2)}{R_3}$

$$= 17.2\,\text{mV}$$

To keep errors over an ambient temperature range of 10 °C to less than 0.25 °C the reference diode must have a temperature coefficient of better than 1.72 mV °C⁻¹.

For the reference the requirements are

V_z : 5 V $\pm 5\%$
I_z : 9 mA
P_z : 45 mW
TC : better than 1.72 mV °C⁻¹

A BZX79 5.1 V Zener diode would be suitable. This has

V_z : 5.1 V $\pm 5\%$

P_z : 500 mW
TC : -0.8 mV $°C^{-1}$

For the op-amp the parameters of interest are the temperature coefficients of input offset current and input offset voltage. The drift for a 10 °C ambient charge at the input is given by:

$$\Delta V_i = \Delta T \left[\frac{dI_{io}}{dT} R_s + \frac{dV_{io}}{dT} \frac{R_f + R_5}{R_f} \right]$$

Assume a 741 is used.
Then $\Delta V_i = 10(0.5 \times 10^{-9} \times 8.2 \times 10^3$
$+ 5 \times 10^{-6} \times 108.2/100)$
$= 95.1 \mu V$
This gives an output change (ΔV_o) of:

$$\Delta V_o = \Delta V_i \frac{R_f}{R_T + R_4} \approx 1.06 \text{ mV}$$

Thus using a standard 741 results in a maximum error of 0.15 °C.

8.3 CHAPTER THREE

DESIGN EXAMPLE USING A ZENER DIODE TO PROVIDE A 10 V REFERENCE

1   $\Delta V_{z1} = 25.64$ mV
Therefore $\Delta V_{z2} = 0.57$ mV $°C^{-1}$
and $\Delta V_{ref} = 0.57 \times 1.613 = 0.9123$ mV
This is within specification.

2   Temperature coefficient of $DZ_1 =$
$+5.5$ mV $°C^{-1}$
therefore $\Delta V_{ref} = \Delta V_{z2} A_v$

$$= \frac{5.5 \times 15}{695} \times 1.613 \text{ mV } °C^{-1}$$

$$= 0.1915 \text{ mV } °C^{-1}$$

This is less than 0.002%/°C.

3   $\Delta V_o = 1.613(12 \times 10^{-12} \times 2.7 \times 10^{-3}$
$+ 0.5 \times 10^{-6} \times 1.63)$
$= 1.37 \mu V °C^{-1}$
which is negligible compared with the drift of the reference diode.

DESIGN EXERCISES

1   Efficiency $= P_o/P_{in} \times 100\%$
Therefore $P_{in} = P_o/Eff \times 100 \approx 38.6$ W
Internal power loss $= P_{in} - P_o = 11.6$ W

2   Load regulation $= \dfrac{V_{o1} - V_{o2}}{V_{o1}} \times 100$

$$= 0.64\%$$

This is not within specification.

3   Output resistance of supply $r_0 = \Delta V_o / \Delta I_L$
$= 0.024/0.6$
$= 0.04 \, \Omega$

Therefore for the changes listed

$\Delta V_o = \Delta I_L . r_o + (\text{line regulation}) \Delta V_{in}$
$+ (\Delta V_o / \Delta T) . T$
$= +(8 + 30 + 32.64)$ mV
$= +70.64$ mV

4   (a) The V_{CC} supply for TTL is 5 V ± 250 mV with an absolute maximum rating of 7 V. The trip must therefore be set between 5.25 V and 7 V — a good choice being 6 V ± 0.5 V.

(b) The regulator should be disconnected and the fuse replaced by an indicator — see Fig. 8.5.

With the load removed an external supply is connected across the voltage

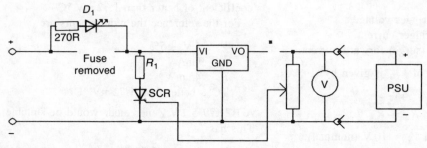

Fig. 8.5 Test circuit for the crowbar

sensing circuit and its voltage increased until the trip fires. The voltage at which this occurs can be read using a digital meter.

5 (a) $VA = 72\,\text{W}$

(b) $I_p = P_o/V_p = 300\,\text{mA}$

6 Regulation $= \dfrac{V_{OL} - V_L}{V_{OL}} \times 100\%$

Therefore $V_{OL} = \dfrac{V_{FL}}{1 - R/100} = 21.98\,\text{V}$

7 $C_{min} = \dfrac{I_{dc}\,t}{V_{R(pk-pk)}} = 13\,330\,\mu\text{F}$

Therefore make $C = 15\,000\,\mu\text{F}$

Ripple current rating to be greater than 1.5 A. Working voltage to be greater than 35 V (40 V).

8 (a) $R_S = 402\,\Omega$ therefore $390\,\Omega$ is n.p.v.
$I_{SC} = 38.46\,\text{mA}$

Therefore power dissipated by R_S is a maximum of 577 mW.
R_S should be 1 W rating.

(b) $P_{z(max)} = I_{z(max)}V_z \approx 130\,\text{mW}$

(c) (i) $\Delta V_o = \Delta I_z r_z = 375\,\text{mV}$

(ii) $\Delta V_o = \dfrac{\Delta V_{in} r_z // R_L}{R_S + r_z // R_L} = 130\,\text{mV}$

9 (a) Transformer : 15 V secondary 5 VA
Rectifiers : 4 IN5001 or suitable bridge

Smoothing capacitor : $2000\,\mu\text{F}$, 25 V,
$I_R = 0.5\,\text{A}$

(b) $R_1 \approx 820\,\Omega$
$R_2 \approx 5\text{k}6$
$\mathbf{R}_3 \approx 4\text{k}7$
$RV_1 \approx 2\text{k}2$
$R_4 \approx 3\text{k}3$
$R_5 \approx 47\text{k}$

(c) See Fig. 8.6.

$R_6 = V_{BE}/I_{sc}$
Therefore $R_6 \approx 2.7\,\Omega$

Tr_2 BC107 or similar.

(d) See Fig. 8.7.
Since $I_{sc} = 220\,\text{mA}$
$P_{tot} = 15 \times 0.22 = 3.3\,\text{W}$
$R_{th(h-a)} = 12.7\,^{\circ}\text{C}\,\text{W}^{-1}$

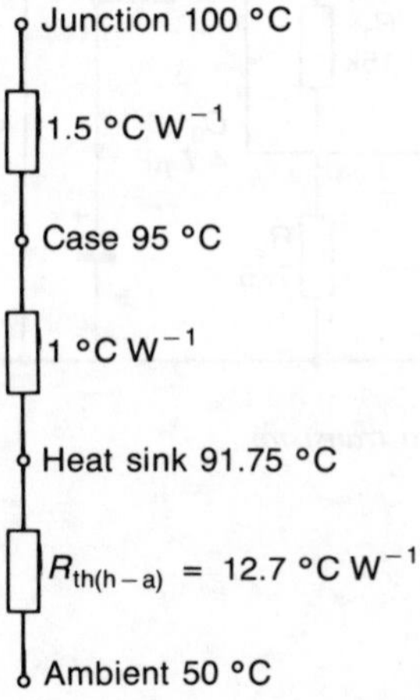

Junction 100 °C

1.5 °C W^{-1}

Case 95 °C

1 °C W^{-1}

Heat sink 91.75 °C

$R_{th(h-a)} = 12.7\,^{\circ}\text{C}\,\text{W}^{-1}$

Ambient 50 °C

Fig. 8.7 Heat sink diagram for BD135

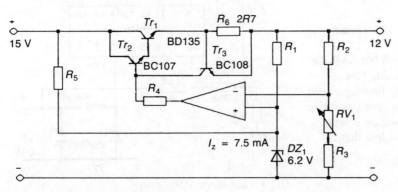

$I_z = 7.5\,\text{mA}$

Fig. 8.6 Fixed current limit added

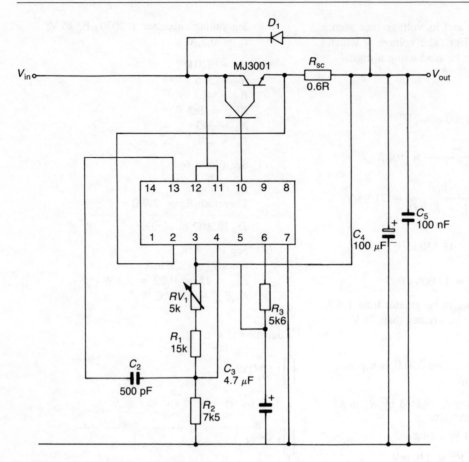

Fig. 8.8 723 with external boost transistor

10 See circuit Fig. 8.8.
For the 723

$$V_o = V_{ref}(1 + R_1/R_2)$$

where $V_{ref} = 7.15$ V.
R_2 can be 4k7.
Therefore $R_1 = 12$ kΩ, $RV_1 = 10$ k cermet preset.

A simple current limit is shown but foldback current limiting would be preferable (see Chapter 5) since with the simple limiting circuit the dissipation of the series transistor could rise to over 30 W. This would necessitate a heat sink with a thermal resistance of less than 1.5 °C W^{-1}.

11 See circuit, Fig. 8.9.

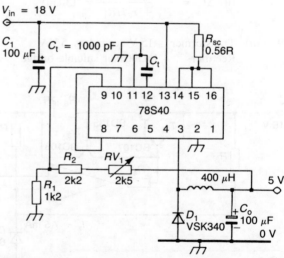

Fig. 8.9 Step-down SMPU design

$$t_{on}/t_{off} = \frac{5 + 1.25}{17 - (6.3)} = 0.58$$

Since $t_{on} + t_{off} = 59 \,\mu s$,

$$t_{on} \approx 21.7 \,\mu s$$
$$t_{off} \approx 37.3 \,\mu s$$

$C_t = 866 \,pF$, therefore use 1 nF.

$$L_{min} = \frac{17 - 6.3}{0.6} \times 21.7 \times 10^{-6} \,H$$

Therefore $L_{min} = 390 \,\mu H$

$$C_o = \frac{0.6 \times 59 \times 10^{-6}}{8 \times 0.075}$$

Therefore $C_o \approx 60 \,\mu F$

$$R_{sc} = 0.33/0.6 = 0.55 \,\Omega \ (0.56 \,\Omega \text{ is n.p.v.})$$
$$R_1 = 1k2$$
$$R_2 + RV_1 = 3R_1$$

Therefore $R_2 = 2k2$
and $RV_1 = 2k5$ cermet.

12 (a) See circuit, Fig. 8.10.
Voltage gain of non-inverting amplifier nominally 2.9.

(b) Line stability $= \dfrac{\Delta V_{Z1} r_{Z2}}{R_2 + r_{Z2}}$

where $\Delta V_{Z1} \approx \dfrac{\Delta V_{in} r_{Z1}}{R_1 + r_{Z1}}$

Thus for a 10% change in the 30 V input the change in V_{ref} is 0.54 mV.

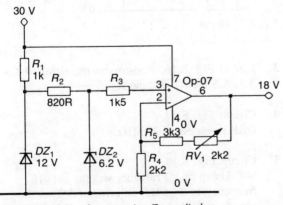

Fig. 8.10 18 V reference using Zener diodes

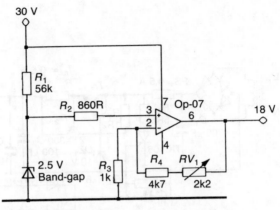

Fig. 8.11 18 V reference using a band-gap device

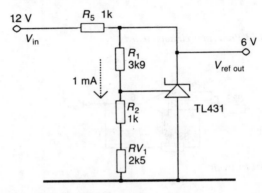

Fig. 8.12 The TL431 circuit

13 See circuit Fig. 8.11. I_{ref} set to 0.5 mA.
Change in V_{ref} for a 10% change in the 30 V input is 0.108 mV.

14 See circuit, Fig. 8.12.

$$R_S = 1 \,k\Omega$$
$$R_1 = 3k9$$
$$R_2 = 1k \text{ in series with 2k5 preset.}$$

15 0.5 A rating, anti-surge.

16 See circuit Fig. 8.13.

8.4 CHAPTER FOUR

1 $A_v = 20 \log (\text{ratio}) \,dB$

Therefore ratio $= \text{antilog} \left[\dfrac{\text{gain in dB}}{20} \right]$

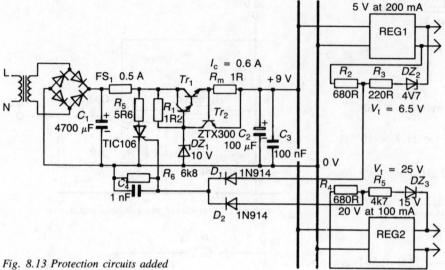

Fig. 8.13 Protection circuits added

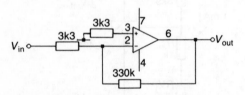

Fig. 8.14 Circuit

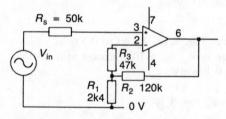

Fig. 8.15 Circuit

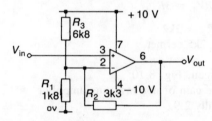

Fig. 8.16 Circuit

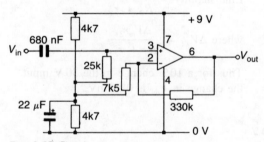

Fig. 8.17 Circuit

40 dB is equivalent to a ratio of 100.
For circuit, see Fig. 8.14.

2 Since maximum output is to be 5 V at V_{in} of 100 mV, the gain required is 50.

$$A_v = 1 + R_2/R_1$$

Make $R_2 = 120 \text{ k}\Omega$. Therefore $R_1 = 2.4 \text{ k}\Omega$.

$$R_3 = R_s - R_2//R_1 = 47 \text{ k}\Omega \text{ (n.p.v.)}$$

For circuit see Fig. 8.15.

3 Circuit Fig. 8.16. Resistors in the ratios of 1.8, 3.3, 6.6 for R_1, R_2 and R_3.

4 Circuit Fig. 8.17.
GBP in excess of 20 MHz.

5 Circuit Fig. 8.18.
NB. Using 56 kΩ resistors sets the cut-off frequency to 28.5 Hz, an error of 5% on the specified 30 Hz.

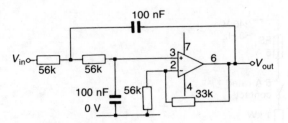

Fig. 8.18 Low-pass filter

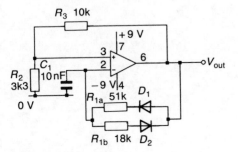

Fig. 8.19 Oscillator

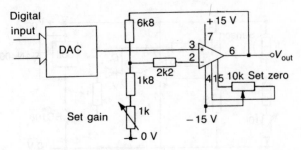

Fig. 8.20 Amplifier design

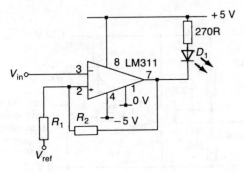

Fig. 8.21

6 340 Hz

22 Hz

7 (a) Circuit Fig. 8.19.

(b) Make part of R_2 variable.
R_2 is then a 2k2 in series with a 2k5 trimpot.

(c) Supply is now +18 V and junction of C_1 and R_2 must be made +9 V. Use two resistors, say 470 Ω each, to give this +9 V and decouple with a 22 μF capacitor.

8 (a) Use 33 nF and 47 kΩ in the frequency determining network. Other components as detailed in text.

(b) Amplifier with GBP in excess of 3 MHz.

9 Circuit Fig. 8.20.
(i) Non-inverting since this has high input resistance.
(ii) Slew rate better than 5 V μs^{-1}.
Low offset drifts with temperature.

8.5 CHAPTER FIVE

1 $R_2 = 49R_1$; suitable values are 120 k and 2k4.
Circuit Fig. 8.21.

2 At −4 °C the thermistor has a resistance of 5300 Ω.
Leaving trip point at 6 V and hysteresis at 50 mV, the simplest modification is to increase R_3 to 12 kΩ.
Output circuit Fig. 8.22.

3 Circuit Fig. 8.23.
Thermistor in 'fail-safe' position.
Use CMOS open-drain Schmitt or simple transistor switch to give high state TTL output when temperature rises above 4 °C.

4 Circuit Fig. 8.24.

5 Circuit Fig. 8.25.

6 Fast response.
Good saturation characteristics.

7 (a) TC = 385.4 ms
(b) $t = 207.73$ ms

8 $C = I dt/dV$

Therefore C is 2.78 nF.

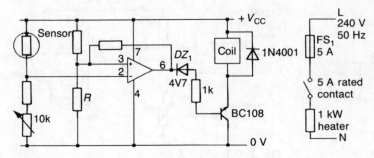

Fig. 8.22

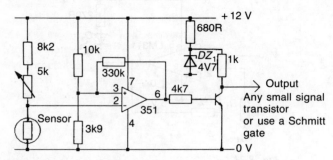

Fig. 8.23

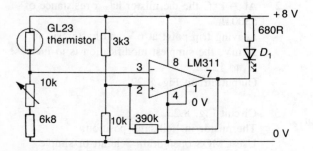

Fig. 8.24

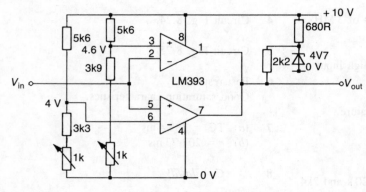

Fig. 8.25

9 A CMOS 555 timer is suitable. Use C_t at the minimum recommended value of 100 pF so that timing resistors are not excessively low.

Timing resistor R_A is 9500 Ω. Part of this must be made adjustable to meet frequency specification. Use 6k8 in series with 5 kΩ trimpot. Other timing resistor is 1 kΩ.

The duty cycle will be about 53%.

10 Relay current is 107 mA so all three designs require a buffer.

Typical circuit solutions are shown in Fig. 8.26.

12 Periodic time is 25 μs.

For 10% duty cycle the 'on' time is 2.5 μs and the 'off' time 22.5 μs. A CMOS 555 is required with duty cycle control using the two diode circuit.

With C made 220 pF the required resistor values are 16.23 kΩ (on) and 146 kΩ (off). The n.p.v.s are shown in the diagram, Fig. 8.27.

13 Time required is 10 800 seconds.

Make C_t a 2.2 μF tantalum and use a trimpot between pins 11 and 12. The timing resistor can then be 1M2 as the n.p.v.

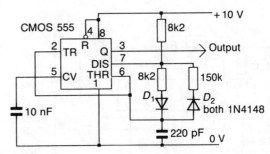

Fig. 8.27

A Darlington (TIP110) or a logic powerFET can be used as the switch drive for the motor. With the Darlington the output current from pin 2 of the ZN1034 will be approximately 15 mA. R_S should be a 2k2, 2 W rating resistor. If a powerFET is used the output current required to operate the FET will be very small. Then R_S is 5k6, 1 W rating.

The circuit is shown in Fig. 8.28.

14 Choices are either to increase the value of C_t or to reduce the current from Tr_1. For 800 Hz make C_t 47 nF or increase R_3 to 33 kΩ. (An alternative is to increase C_t to 22 nF and R_3 to 10 kΩ.)

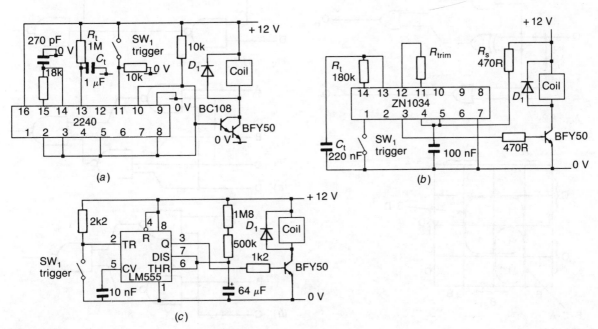

Fig. 8.26

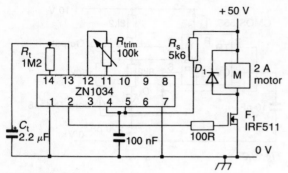

Fig. 8.28

8.6 CHAPTER SIX

1 $F = \bar{A}.\bar{B} + \bar{A}.B + A.B$
which simplifies to $F + A + B$ (one OR gate).

2 Using K-maps:

$$O_1 = R.\bar{Q} + P.R + \bar{R}.Q$$
$$= (R \oplus Q) + P.R$$
$$O_2 = \bar{Q}.\bar{R}$$

The circuit is shown in Fig. 8.29.

3 K-map in Fig. 8.30.

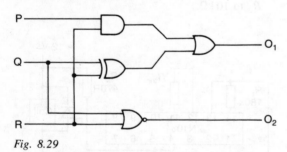

Fig. 8.29

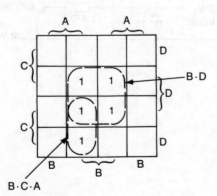

B·C·A

Fig. 8.30

4 $F = A.B.C + A.B.D + A.C.D + B.C.D$
$\qquad + A.B.E + A.C.E + B.C.E$
$\qquad + A.D.E + B.D.E + C.D.E$

Either use a PLD or by de Morgans law
convert to a NAND-only solution. This would
need ten 3-input NAND gates and one 10-input
NAND.

5 (a) $F = (A+B).C.D = A.C.D + B.C.D$
Therefore $\bar{F} = \overline{A.C.D + B.C.D}$
$\qquad\qquad = \overline{\overline{A.C.D}.\overline{B.C.D}}$

(b) $F = \overline{A + B + C}$
Therefore $F = \overline{\bar{A}.\bar{B} + \bar{C}} = \overline{(\bar{\bar{A}} + \bar{\bar{B}}).\bar{\bar{C}}}$
$\qquad\qquad = \overline{A.C + B.C}$
Therefore $F = \overline{\overline{A.C}.\overline{B.C}}$
Circuits in Fig. 8.32.

$F = B.D + \bar{A}.C.B$
Therefore $\bar{\bar{F}} = \overline{\overline{B.D + \bar{A}.C.B}} = \overline{\overline{B.D}.\overline{\bar{A}.C.B}}$
The circuit is shown in Fig. 8.31.

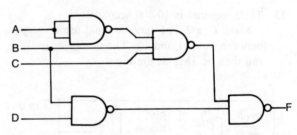

Fig. 8.31

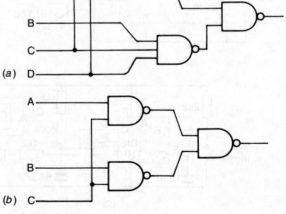

(a)

(b)

Fig. 8.32

6 (*a*) $X = A.E.F + B.E.F + C.E.F + D.E.F$

The circuit is given in Fig. 8.33(*a*), the text file in Fig. 8.33(*b*).

(*b*) $A = Z.\overline{E}.\overline{F}$; $B = Z.E.\overline{F}$; $C = Z.\overline{E}.F$; $D = Z.E.F$

Circuit in Fig. 8.34.

7 (*a*) For the $\div 3$ using D-bistables:

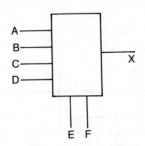

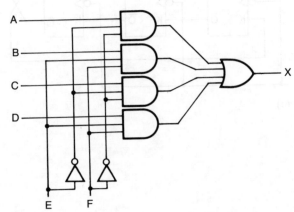

(*a*)

lattice
pal 16h8

pins
pin 2 = a
pin 3 = b
pin 4 = c
pin 5 = d
pin 6 = e
pin 7 = f
pin 19 = x

equations

x = a./e./f + b.e./f + c./e.f + d.e.f :
end

(*b*)

Fig. 8.33 (a) 4-bit multiplexer; (b) Text file

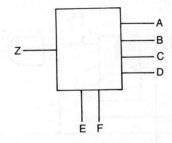

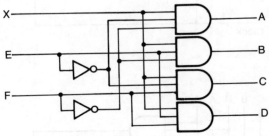

Fig. 8.34 4-bit demultiplexer

$$A_n = \overline{A}.\overline{B}; \quad B_n = A.\overline{B}$$

Circuit in Fig. 8.35(*a*)

(*b*) For the $\div 5$:

$$A_n = \overline{A}.\overline{C}$$
$$B_n = A.\overline{B}.\overline{C} + \overline{A}.B.\overline{C}$$
$$C_n = A.B.\overline{C}$$

Circuit in Fig. 8.35(*b*).

(*c*) Circuit using J–K bistables is shown in Fig. 8.35(*c*).

8 Logic circuit in Fig. 8.36(*a*).
Suggested text file in Fig. 8.36(*b*).

9 Suggested modification in Fig. 8.37.

8.7 CHAPTER SEVEN

1 Change all the pull-up resistors to $10\,\text{k}\Omega$.

2 See Fig. 8.38.

3 (*a*) See Fig. 8.39(*a*). An open-collector invertor can be specified in place of Tr_1.

(*b*) See Fig. 8.39(*b*).

4 One possible solution is shown in Fig. 8.40.

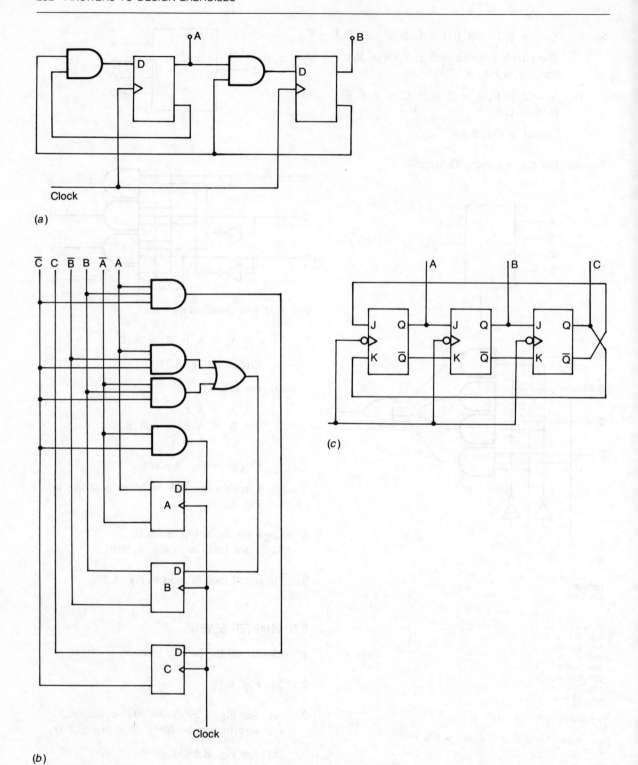

(a)

(b)

(c)

Fig. 8.35 (a) ÷3 using D-bistables; (b) ÷5 circuit; (c) ÷6 Johnson counter

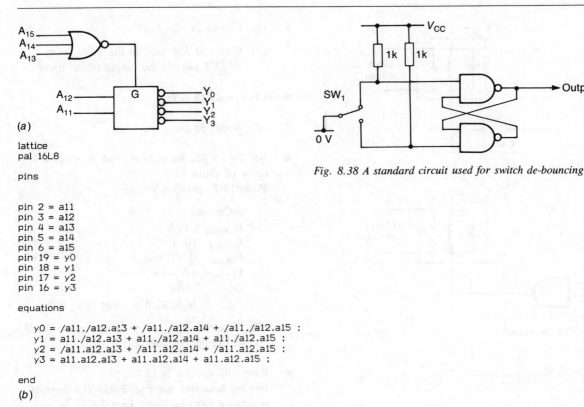

(a)

lattice
pal 16L8

pins

pin 2 = a11
pin 3 = a12
pin 4 = a13
pin 5 = a14
pin 6 = a15
pin 19 = y0
pin 18 = y1
pin 17 = y2
pin 16 = y3

equations

y0 = /a11./a12.a13 + /a11./a12.a14 + /a11./a12.a15 ;
y1 = a11./a12.a13 + a11./a12.a14 + a11./a12.a15 ;
y2 = /a11.a12.a13 + /a11.a12.a14 + /a11.a12.a15 ;
y3 = a11.a12.a13 + a11.a12.a14 + a11.a12.a15 ;

end
(b)

Fig. 8.36 (a) Address decoder circuit; (b) Text file

Fig. 8.38 A standard circuit used for switch de-bouncing

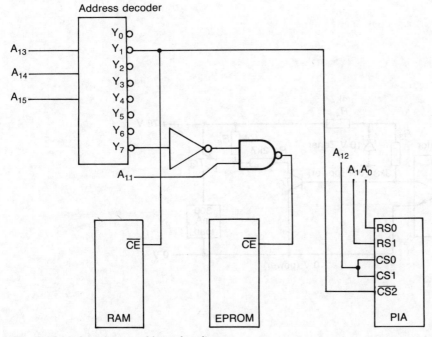

Fig. 8.37 Modification to address decoding

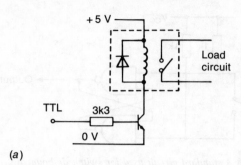

(a)

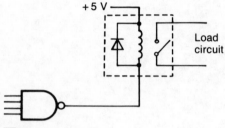

TTL
Active low output

(b)

Fig. 8.39

5 (a) Circuit in Fig. 8.41.

(b) Gate and 555 used in the VCO on its RESET pin via the output of the timer.

6 Change R_1 to 8k2.

7 (a) About 38 μs.

8 See Fig. 8.42. Ratio of R_2 and R_3 gives a V_{GS} drive of about 10 V.
PowetFET specification is:

p-Channel
$V_{DS(min)}$: 45 V
$I_{D(max)}$: 10 A
$R_{DS(on)}$: 0.5 Ω max
$V_{GS(th)}$: 4 V min
G_{fs} : 1 S min
P_{tot} : at least 12.5 W (with heat sink)

NB: If device $R_{DS(on)}$ is no greater than 0.1 Ω, P_{tot} will reduce to only 2.5 W.

9 Power dissipation is 15 W.
For the heat sink see Fig. 8.43. The thermal resistance must be lower than 2.6 °C W^{-1}.

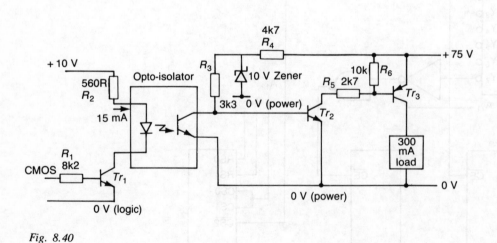

Fig. 8.40

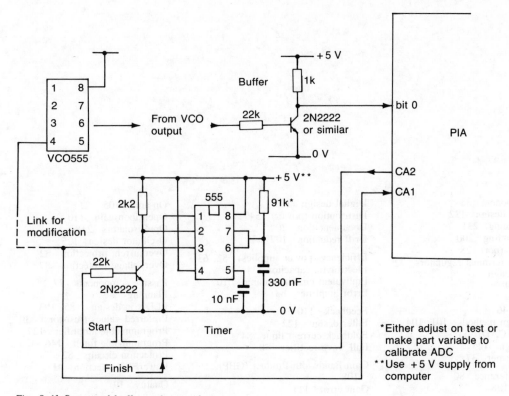

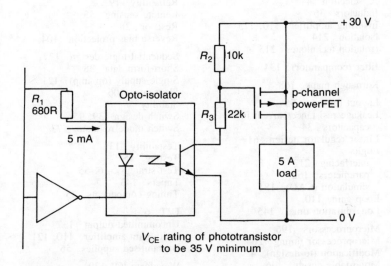

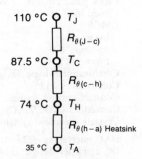

Fig. 8.41 Suggested buffer and timer design

*Either adjust on test or make part variable to calibrate ADC
**Use +5 V supply from computer

Fig. 8.42 Suggested circuit

V_{CE} rating of phototransistor to be 35 V minimum

Fig. 8.43

INDEX